Y0-BSF-596

the
Wisdom
of
Poetry

the Wisdom of Poetry

Essays in
Early English Literature
in honor of
Morton W. Bloomfield

edited by
Larry D. Benson
& Siegfried Wenzel

MEDIEVAL INSTITUTE PUBLICATIONS
Western Michigan University, Kalamazoo, Michigan—1982

Library of Congress Cataloging in Publication Data

The Wisdom of poetry.

"The publications of Morton W. Bloomfield,
1939–1981 [compiled by] George Hardon Brown": p.
Includes bibliographical references.
    1. English literature—Middle English, 1100–
1500—History and criticism—Addresses, essays,
lectures. 2. Anglo-Saxon poetry—History and
criticism—Addresses, essays, lectures. 3. Chaucer,
Geoffrey, d. 1400—Criticism and interpretation—
Addresses, essays, lectures. 4. Langland, William,
1330?–1400?—Piers the plowman—Addresses,
essays, lectures. 5. Bloomfield, Morton Wilfred,
1913–   .
I. Bloomfield, Morton Wilfred, 1913–   .
II. Benson, Larry Dean, 1929–   . III. Wenzel,
Siegfried. IV. Western Michigan Univerity.
Medieval Institute.
PR166.W5   820'.9'002   82–3577
ISBN 0-918720-15-X   AACR2
ISBN 0-918720-16-8 (pbk.)
© 1982 by the Board
of The Medieval Institute
Printed in USA

Preface

The subject chosen for the essays in this volume concerns but a part of Morton W. Bloomfield's wide range of interests, and the restriction of our attention to medieval English literature, though it is his own major subject, does not adequately reflect his contributions to the broader fields of medieval thought and literature, literary theory, and linguistics. Moreover, the essays offered here are few indeed compared to what their number would have been had space been available—volumes would have been required—to contain offerings from all the many friends, students, and admirers of Morton Bloomfield who would have wished to honor him in this manner.

The wisdom of medieval English literature, however, does seem an appropriate subject for essays intended to honor a worthy who is also wise and whose own works have so greatly illuminated this field. The subject has been broadly defined, and the essays range from Anglo-Saxon wisdom literature to the works of the great poets of the English Middle Ages. Yet, they are united by a common wish to show our warm affection for our friend. In that, our few essays are emblematic of the warm regard in which Morton Bloomfield is held throughout our profession, which, as we hope, will benefit for many years to come from his cheerful and wise presence.

The Editors

We wish to record that Professor J. A. W. Bennett (Cambridge University) was working on a contribution to the present volume at the time of his lamented death in January 1981. And, more happily, we wish to express our warm appreciation to Dr. Elise Jorgens (Western Michigan University) for her splendid editorial help in producing this book.

L.D.B.
S.W.

CAMROSE LUTHERAN COLLEGE
LIBRARY

Table of Contents

Fred C. Robinson

Understanding an Old English Wisdom Verse: Maxims II, *Lines 10ff*

The verse *soð bið swicolost* in *Maxims II*[1] has become a kind of shibboleth for Old English scholars. Those who argue that Old English poetry is subtler and more complex than its early editors have usually assumed it to be retain the manuscript reading and try to justify the arresting sense "truth is most tricky." Scholars who are wary of oversubtle literary interpretations and impatient with editorial pusillanimity before the authority of medieval scribes welcome the emendations *switolost* or *swutolost*, which allow the simpler, cheerier meaning "truth is most evident." To a certain extent, the division of opinion falls along national lines. Favoring emendation and the simpler meaning are the English scholars Sweet, Sedgefield, Whitelock, Wyatt, and Hamer, who emend to *swutolost*,[2] and the Americans Williams, Dobbie, Cassidy and Ringler, Greenfield and Evert, who emend to *switolost*.[3] Favoring the manuscript reading and the more complex sense are the Germans Brandl, Ettmüller, Grein, Kluge, and Wülcker, who retain *swicolost*, rendering it "Wahrheit ist sehr trügerisch" or something similar.[4] There are of course exceptions to the rule,[5] but the general division between German and Anglo-American readings of the passage should be noted, for Anglo-American scholars often pride themselves on their textual conservatism and their openmindedness to poetic complexity and nuance, while criticizing Germans for being incurably literal-minded and prone to needless emendation. In this case the roles are reversed, reminding us of the folly of such characterizations in the first place.

My concern here is to determine, in so far as possible, which of the two readings of the *Maxims* verse is more likely to represent the compiler's intentions and to reflect the Anglo-Saxons' conception of the nature of truth. Can a case be made for the more imaginative German reading, which allows us to retain the words the scribe transmitted to us, or is the circumstantial evidence for "truth is most evident" so compelling that we must abandon the manuscript and settle for the simpler, more hopeful conception of truth? A case can be made for either interpretation, as I shall try to show, but my preference in the end (since suspense is not part of my strategy) will be for the somber German rather than the bright Anglo-American meaning. Primarily this is because of the contextual evidence which has come to my attention and which I set out below; but I also prefer the more somber reading of this wisdom verse because it conforms better with the character of wisdom literature as it has been described by Morton Bloomfield, our undisputed authority on the subject: "Its general tone is pessimistic and worldly-wise."[6]

However blandly optimistic it may seem to some modern readers, an Old English maxim "truth is most evident" is by no means inherently implausible. The medieval proverb "veritas semper certa et perspicua est"[7] provides a Latin model, and the Anglo-Saxons themselves are known to have made observations of this order. *The Durham Proverbs* include *soþ hit sylf acypeð* (translating "veritas seipsam semper declarat" ["Truth always reveals itself"])[8] and the same maxim is quoted, apparently, in *Blickling Homily* XV ("The Story of Peter and Paul"): *Nu mæg soð hit sylf gecypan* ("Now truth can reveal itself").[9] In context, however, the quotation is ironical, for the speaker is Nero, who is expressing confidence that the spectacle he has just arranged with the delusive sorcerer Simon will reveal once for all the truth of Simon's claims and the falsity of Peter's and Paul's. In the event it is the truth of the two saints that is vindicated, of course, while Simon's tricks are exposed as frauds, and yet Nero persists in believing the sorcerer's false truth, to his ultimate doom. The tale exemplifies the extreme difficulty a man can have in discerning the truth when he is faced with alternative versions of it. Indeed, one could epitomize the plot of "The Story of Peter and Paul" in terms of Old English maxims by saying that whereas Nero thinks deludedly that *soð hit sylf gecypep* ("Truth reveals itself"), the events of the narrative show that in fact *soð bið swicolost* ("Truth is most tricky")—at least for those who do not share the Christian illumination enjoyed by Peter and Paul.

The simple meaning "truth is most evident" is possible, then, but *Blickling Homily* XV shows that Anglo-Saxons could view this cheerful interpretation of truth with a measure of irony. This should encourage a pause at least before we emend *swicolost*, and in pausing we might note that the emendation is not quite so simple a matter as some of the emenders have implied. The difference between *c* and *t* being so slight in Insular script, one might conclude that the emended form has virtually equal authority with the manuscript reading. "Why not *switolost*?" asks Blanche Colton Williams. "Palæographically this form is quite possible, *c* and *t* often being mistaken for each other."[10] Cassidy and Ringler, among others, concur: "The emendation is suggested by common sense and supported by the fact that scribal confusion of *c* and *t* is widespread."[11] The American emenders may well have been puzzled as to why Sweet and his English compatriots prefer the more complicated reconstruction *swutolost* when the minimal change to *switolost* apparently produces the same results. But there is good reason for Sweet's *swutolost*: back umlaut of *i* by *o* is to be expected when the intervening consonant is *t*, and a preceding *w* frequently caused the resulting diphthong to become *u*. Thus I find in the Healey-Venezky concordance[12] a total of 313 occurrences of the adjective *sweotol* in its various forms and derivatives, and the root is spelled *swit-* only ten times. The commonest spelling is *sweot-* (163 times), next is *swut-* (109 times), and the spellings *swyt-*, *su(u)t-*, *swot-*, *swiot-*, and *swet-* occur a total of thirty-one times. The form *switolost*, then, while not impossible, is a statistically abnormal form, and therefore a somewhat dubious emendation. Sweet's *swutolost* would be much more likely to occur in an eleventh-century manuscript like Cotton Tiberius B.i, and, indeed, in the only other occurrence of the adjective in this codex (in the poem *Menologium*, line 129), the spelling is *swutelra*.

The unemended manuscript reading *swicolost*, on the other hand, is the statistically normal spelling of that word, since back umlaut of *i* by *o* is very rare when the intervening consonant is *c*. Of a total ninety-four occurrences of *swicol* in its various forms and derivatives recorded in Healey-Venezky, ninety-three have the spelling *swic-*, while only one has *sweoc-*. (There are no spellings *suic-*, *su(u)c-*, *swuc-*, or *swyc-*.) The isolated spelling with *eo* occurs in the word *sweocolan*, which is a variant reading for *diglan* in one of the manuscripts of King Alfred's translation of *The Pastoral Care*.[13] Another such spelling (*ofersweocola*) is recorded by Alistair Campbell in his supplement to the Bosworth-Toller *Dictionary*,[14] but this is in fact a deviant and erroneous reading in one of the manuscripts of the Old English *Benedictine Rule,* and its inclusion in Campbell's *Addenda* was a mistake. *Ofersweocola* occurs in Corpus Christi College, Oxford, MS 197 where other manuscripts have *ofersprecola*.[15] Since the Latin word being translated is *linguosus*, it is obvious that *ofersprecola* is correct and the apparent hapax legomenon *ofersweocola* is in fact nothing but a careless scribe's miscopy of *ofersprecola*. *Swicol* being, then, the correct and practically invariable spelling of the adjective, we have in the manuscript reading a legitimate word. The emendation *switolost* is statistically dubious: if we are to emend at all, we must adopt Sweet's *swutolost*, and this form requires a more elaborate rationale than the mere citation of close similarity between *t* and *c* in Insular script.

If we retain the reading of the manuscript, what is to be made of the resulting maxim *soð bið swicolost*? Bosworth-Toller offers a very tentative suggestion that *swicol* might carry, in this one occurrence, the sense "occasioning offense."[16] A maxim "truth is most offensive" would not be implausible if viewed within the context of popular proverbs such as "whoso says the sooth shall be shent" or "all sooth is not to be said."[17] The latter saying, as Whiting notes, is attested in the Old English *Durham Proverbs*, no. 19: "Ne deah eall soþ asæd ne eall sar ætwiten." If one Anglo-Saxon thought truth could give offense, then clearly another could think so as well. But the evidence for *swicol* meaning "offensive" is unfortunately thin (hence Bosworth-Toller's warning queries around the conjecture). The well-attested senses of the word are in the semantic areas of delusion and deception.

Blanche Colton Williams, before deciding that emendation was unavoidable, tried briefly to make a case for "truth is treacherous" by referring to Chantepie de la Saussaye's account of how Norsemen, in order to give themselves freedom of action without violating their word of honor, used ambiguous language in phrasing their treaties:

> . . . truthfulness did not by any means preclude everything that we are accustomed to regard as deceit. If truth was only adhered to from an external and formal point of view and the feeling of personal honor thereby preserved, there was felt to be no objection against relying upon the deceit contained in an equivocal word, or a dissembling mien, by which the enemy was misled. Such shrewdness was viewed as redounding to a man's honor and glory rather than to his shame. Keeping this distinction in mind, it will be seen that the notorious faithlessness with which so many medieval writers charge the Norsemen is not at all imcompatible with their love of truth. With great subtleness and acumen, they made use, in the terms of a treaty, of ambiguous expressions: their honor thus remained unstained, their word unbroken.[18]

Among some Scandinavians, it may be added, one can find an actual aversion for the truth. Stanza 45 of the *Hávamál* tells us

> Ef þú átt annan,   þannz þú illa trúir,
>   vildu af hánom þó gott geta:
> fagrt skaltu við þann mæla,   en flátt hyggia
>   ok gialda lausung við lygi.[19]

> (If you have another [friend], whom you mistrust, and yet you want to receive good from him, you must speak fair to him and think false and pay back lying with lies.)

And Saxo Grammaticus at one point refers to himself and his people as "We who do not account lying and deceiving as wicked and despicable."[20] But the Norsemen's occasional approbation of lying or duplicitous phrasing seems not to have been shared by the Anglo-Saxons, and the maxim's adjective *swicolost*, moreover, seems to suggest a dangerous uncertainty or unreliability in truth rather than approval of skillful lying.

The most probable meaning of the maxim would seem to be that suggested above in the discussion of the Blickling Homily on Saints Peter and Paul. That is, truth is tricky, or deceptive, or perhaps elusive (cf. *swice*, "escape," and *swīcan*, "to escape") because it is difficult to recognize, the distinction between truth and falsehood being a subtle one. This idea is by no means alien to Western thought. The Book of Proverbs emphasizes the value of truth (3:3, 23:23), but it acknowledges at the same time that one may have difficulty in recognizing it: "There is a way that seemeth to a man right, and the ends thereof lead to death" (16:25). Diogenes Laertius's somber observation on truth has become proverbial in many European tongues: "We know nothing certain; for truth is hidden at the bottom of an abyss."[21] Wander records a wealth of *Sprichwörter* on the difficulty of discerning the truth: "Zwischen Wahrheit und Lüge ist ein schlüpfriger Pfad" ("Between falsehood and truth is a slippery path" p. 1763, no. 410); "Wer die Wahrheit sehen will, muss gute Augen haben" ("He who wishes to see the truth must have sharp eyes" p. 1761, no. 365); "Auch Wahrheit ist eine Lüge, zur Unzeit geredet" ("Even truth is a lie when told out of season" p. 1747, no. 4); "Wahrheiten hier sind Irrtümer dort" ("Truths here are errors there" p. 1758, no. 292); etc. The last of these, emphasizing the relativity of truth, finds an analogue in Pascal: "Chacun suive les mœurs de son pays. . . . Vérité au deçà des Pyrénées, erreur au delà" ("Each follows the customs of his country. . . . Truth on this side of the Pyrenees is error on the other side").[22] Later, Pascal adds the almost despairing observation, "La vérité est si obscurcie en ce temps, et le mensonge si établi, qu'à moins que d'aimer la vérité, on ne saurait la connaitre" ("Truth is so obscure now and lying so entrenched that unless one loved the truth one would not be able to recognize it" p.412). Such scepticism espoused within the context of religious faith was as easy for a medieval cleric as for the seventeenth-century Christian apologist. The Italian canon Tommasino dei Circhieri, in line 1126 of his German poem *Der Welsche Gast* (composed between 1215 and 1216), defends courtly literature with the observation that "wâr man mit lüge kleit"

("Truth is clothed with lies").²³ Similarly, the intense religiosity of Spinoza, derived in part from Jewish medieval philosophy, did not prevent his remarking the fine line between truth and deception.²⁴ Cynical assertions about the nature of truth can (especially in modern times) take on the tone of jesting Pilate, of course, as in the Spaniard's

> En este mundo traidor
> Nada hay verdad ni mentira;
> Todo es según el color
> Del cristal con que se mira.²⁵

(In this perfidious world there is no truth or falsehood; everything depends upon the color of the glass through which it is viewed.)

The *cristal* of the poet has little in common with the lenses of Spinoza, and yet the perception of truth articulated by the two writers is mutual, suggesting how wide and flexible is the applicability of this motif of the deceptiveness of truth.

Allusions to the deceptiveness of truth or to the successful subreption of truth by evil schemers occur in Old English documents in a variety of contexts. Two Wulfstanian tracts refer to a past era when those men were thought wisest who could most craftily transform untruth into truth: "þuhte hwilum wisast se þe wæs swicolost and se þe lytelicost cuðe leaslice hiwian unsoð to soðe...."²⁶ Elsewhere Wulfstan says that it is arch-liars instructed by Antichrist who are capable of overpowering truth with untruth: "And swa doð þa þeodlogan eac þe taliað þæt to wærscype þæt man cunne and mæge lytelice swician and mid unsoðe soð oferswiðan."²⁷ To distinguish between truth and untruth, one needs special understanding bestowed by God's grace: "And se hæfð god ingehygd þurh Godes gyfe þe ... can him gescead betweox soðe and unsoðe."²⁸ What may seem truth and wisdom to men of this world, says another homilist, is folly to God: "Ærest ealre þingen æighwylce mæn is to secene hwæt seo se soðe wisedom, oððe hwylc seo seo soðe snytere, for þan þe see wisedom þyssere wurlde is dysignysse beforen Gode."²⁹ For a more philosophical meditation on the nature of truth, one might turn to the Old English version of Augustine's *Soliloquies*, where the relationship between *soþ* and *soþfæstnes* is debated.³⁰

Truth and its simulacra were, then, a current topic among the Anglo-Saxons, who dealt with the subject in various contexts. This would seem to support the contention that the unemended maxim meaning "truth is most tricky" accurately represents one line of thought on the nature of truth in early England. What remains to be asked is whether it is possible to specify the context of the verse and thus narrow the reference of *soð bið swicolost* in *Maxims II*. Since maxims are by nature more general in their reference than specific, to raise this question may be a mistake. And yet, more than one scholar has adverted to the interconnectedness of the items in the opening section of this collection of maxims,[31] so it may be advisable, in closing this analysis, to consider at least tentatively whether *soð bið swicolost* stands in meaningful relation with juxtaposed elements in the passage. The full context of our verse is a series of superlatives:

> Winter byð cealdost,
> lencten hrimigost   (he byð lengest ceald),
> sumor sunwlitegost   (swegel byð hatost),
> hærfest hreðeadegost,   hæleðum bringeð
> geres wæstmas,   þa þe him god sendeð.
> Soð bið swicolost,   sinc byð deorost,
> gold gumena gehwam,   and gomol snoterost,
> fyrngearum frod,   se þe ær feala gebideð.
>   (lines 5–12)

(Winter is most cold, spring most frosty [it is cold for the longest time], summer most radiant with sunshine [the sun is most hot], autumn most glorious—it brings to men the fruits of the year, which God sends to them. Truth is most tricky; treasure, gold, is most precious to every man, and the old man full of years who experiences much early is the wisest.)

The superlatives are logically sequential, the cold of winter being followed by the frost of spring, the frost then being explained by the verses on the duration of cold in spring. Mention of summer is followed by the verse on the sun's heat, of autumn by verses on harvest time. The expectation is thus established that a statement of a superlative will be followed by a verse or verses mentioning a cause or consequence of that statement. This being so, we might reasonably ask whether *soð bið swicolost* is in some way related to the immediately ensuing verses about riches being the most precious of things to man.

A frequent theme in Old English moralistic writings is the corruption of truth by lucre. Ælfric, in a letter to Wulfstan, sees money as the thing that prompts men to turn lies into truth and truth into lies: "Wa ðam, ðe for sceattum forsylþ hyne silfne and awent soð to leasum and leas to soðum."³² He returns to this theme in his homilies: "man ne sceal ... for nanum sceatte þæt soðe awægan";³³ "fela manna ... nellað forwandian þæt hi ne syllon soðfæstnysse wið sceattum."³⁴ He sees the theme personified in the character of Judas: since Christ is the Truth, and Judas betrayed the Truth for money, where is the traducing of truth better exemplified than in "ðam swicelan Judan" ("the deceitful Judas")? "Se ðe soðfæstnysse beceapað wið feo, he bið Iudan gefera" ("He who sells truth for money is the comrade of Judas").³⁵ Judges who sell truth for bribes, on the other hand, will have the "swicolan deofle" ("deceitful devils") for their companions through eternity: "eall swa þa unrihtwisan deman þe ... habbað æfre to cepe heora soðfæstnysse ... þonne habbað hi on ende for heora unrihtwisnysse mid þam swicolan deofle þa ecan susle" ("Likewise the iniquitous judges who always have their truth for sale, ... will in the end experience everlasting torment with the deceitful devil because of their iniquity").³⁶ One admonition of this kind which appears in both Ælfric and in the Old English *Dicts of Cato* (in one of the Anglo-Saxon translator's expansions of his Latin exemplar) goes back ultimately to a biblical verse. The Old English version of Deut. 16:19 reads, "Ne wanda ðu for rican ne for heanum ne for nanum sceatte, for ðam medsceattas ablendað wisra manna geðancas and awendaþ rihtwisnessa word" ("Do not have regard for the powerful or for the poor or for any payment, for bribes blind the thoughts of wise men and pervert the words of righteousness").³⁷ The Old English *Dicts* follows this formulation fairly closely: "ne nym þu medsceattes, for heo ablændeð wisra manna geðancas and wændeð rihtwisra word" ("Do not accept bribes, for they blind the thoughts of wise men and pervert the words of the righteous").³⁸ Ælfric's version is looser but still strongly reminiscent of Deuteronomy: "ða sceattas ablendað swa swa us bec secgað þæra manna mod þe hi manfullice nimað and ða domas awendað to wohnysse swa" ("Bribes, as books tell us, blind the mind of men who wickedly accept them and thus pervert judgements into error").³⁹

Most of these citations are from late texts, but the antagonism between money and truth can be traced back to the earlier periods of Old English as well. The discussion of the qualities of a good judge (called "Judex") published by Liebermann includes repeated admonitions against allowing money to corrupt the truth. "Seo anfengnes medsceata on domum ys soðfæstnesse forlætnes" ("The acceptance of bribes in [making] judgements is the perdition of truth")⁴⁰ is one formulation. Another appears to be yet another version of the verse from Deuteronomy: " a medsceattas ablendað þæra wisra manna heortan and hi forcyrrað ðæra rihtwisra manna word" ("Bribes blind the hearts of wise men and pervert the words of righteous men").⁴¹ Roland Torkar has demonstrated that the entire text of "Judex" is translated from Alcuin's *De virtutibus et vitiis*, Chapter 20.⁴² The Latin originals of the two passages just quoted are as follows: "Acceptio munerum in judiciis, prævaricatio est veritatis"; "munera excæcant corda prudentium, et subvertunt corda justorum."⁴³ This idea of men's thoughts or hearts being overthrown by wealth may lie behind one of the maxims in *Beowulf*:

> Sinc eaðe mæg,
> gold on grund(e)   gumcynnes gehwone
> oferhigian,   hyde se ðe wylle!⁴⁴

(Treasure, gold in the ground, can easily delude [overpower?] any man, hide it who will).

The conjecture of some scholars that the hapax legomenon *oferhigian* is etymologically related to *hyge*⁴⁵ agrees particularly well with this reading of the verses. Another poem may contain a cryptic allusion to this motif. The laconic half-line *sinc searwade* in *The Rhyming Poem* (line 37) has been translated "treasure did treachery" by Mackie⁴⁶ and "treasure was deceitful" by Alexandra Olsen.⁴⁷ Either interpretation could be read in the context of riches distorting truth in the minds and thoughts of men.

It may be then that "truth is most tricky" because man's

inordinate love of money is constantly inducing him to make falsehoods look like truth and truth like falsehoods. Money being as beloved by men as it is, truth is most tricky. Or, as another medieval poet phrases it, "Mucho faz' el dinero, mucho es de amar" ("Money does much, it is much to be loved"). Juan Ruiz's *Libro de buen Amor* has much to say about the miraculous powers of money, and one of his stanzas sums up with wry Spanish wit the concern which we have seen to have prompted so much heavy moral denunciation from the Anglo-Saxons:

> Fazié muchos priores,   obispos ë abades
> arçobispos, dotores,   patriarcas, potestades;
> muchos clérigos necios   dávales denidades;
> fazié verdat mentiras,   e mentiras, verdades.[48]

(It made many curates, bishops and abbots, archbishops, savants, patriarchs, potentates; it gave high honors to many simpleton priests; it turned truth into lies, and lies into truths.)

That the half-line from *Maxims II* is the Anglo-Saxons' version of this sentiment that money makes truth out of lies and lies out of truth seems to me possible and even appealing, but since this interpretation depends in part upon inferences drawn from juxtaposition of ideas, I cannot claim to have proven the point beyond all doubt. What does seem to me virtually certain, however, is that the general sense of the unemended verse should be accepted, for it codifies in typical gnomic language a well-attested Anglo-Saxon attitude toward truth, an attitude that is "pessimistic and worldlywise."

R. E. Kaske

Sapientia et Fortitudo
in the Old English Judith

I

Over twenty years ago, I proposed that the most basic
theme of *Beowulf* is the heroic ideal *sapientia et fortitudo*, which
appears in a variety of ways in literature possibly contribut-
ing to or reflecting aspects of the culture that produced
Beowulf;[1] a particularly clear example is Isidore's definition of
"hero" in the *Etymologiae*: "Heroicum enim carmen dictum,
quod eo virorum fortium res et facta narrantur. Nam heroes
appellantur viri quasi aerii et caelo digni propter sapientiam
et fortitudinem" ("For a poem is called heroic because by it
are told the story and deeds of brave men. For men are called
'heroes' [*heroes*] as if to say they are 'aerial' [*aerii*] and worthy
of heaven because of wisdom and fortitude").[2] Though on
the face of it such a formula may appear too simple—not to
say simple-minded—to have much potential as a literary
theme, in the hands of at least one great poet it seems to me
to provide a fertile basis for the complication, the dramatic

development, and the relation to other major themes by which the clichés of tradition are reanimated into literature.

Whatever one may think of this interpretation of *Beowulf*, I suppose it would be generally agreed that the poet did somehow make conscious use of the ideal *sapientia et fortitudo*. Its presence in other Old English poems seems equally obvious;[3] and so far as can be judged from our extant "sources," every occurrence of the formula represents an addition by the Old English poet. In *Andreas*—a poem saturated also with references to wisdom and courage separately—Matthew is described as "modes glawne, / haligne hæle ... / beadurofne" ("the holy hero, wise of heart ... valiant in battle" 143-45); Andrew praises the steersman of the ship (Christ in disguise) by saying that he has never met a "rowend rofran, rædsnotterran, / wordes wisran" ("bolder steersman, wiser in counsel, wiser of word" 473-74); and Andrew himself is characterized at least six times by variants of the heroic ideal, as for example in a speech by the steersman, who calls him "wis hæleð ... / maga mode rof" ("wise hero ... youth bold in spirit" 624-25).[4] Though I cannot see that these references to *sapientia et fortitudo* in *Andreas* fall into the kind of symmetrical, thematically central pattern that I believe exists in *Beowulf*, they seem introduced most often in contexts where Matthew and Andrew have come into some sort of particularly close contact with God; and I suppose it is worth asking whether the exchange of similar heroic compliments between Andrew and Christ as the steersman (quoted above) may not hint at a deliberate parallel, typological or otherwise, between Andrew and Christ—resting presumably on the famous "Christum Dei virtutem et Dei sapientiam" of 1 Cor. 1:24, Gregory's designation of Christ as "Dei sapientiam et fortitudinem,"[5] and descriptions like that in the Old English *Descent into Hell*, where Christ is called "modig ... / sigefæst ond snottor" ("brave ... victorious and wise" 22-23).

In *Guðlac A*, a strongly spiritualized version of the heroic ideal is applied to Guðlac, in the remark that men "his wisdomes / hlisan healdað, þæt se halga þeow / elne geeode ..." ("cherish the glory of his wisdom, which the holy servant won by courage ..." 156-58). In *Guðlac B*, a passage announcing the arrival of Easter and describing the joyful preaching of Guðlac (1094–1133) begins with a reference to Guðlac as "rof runwita" ("bold knower of mysteries" 1095), later calls him "heard hygesnottor" ("hardy, wise in thought" 1109), and concludes,

> wæs þæs deoplic eall
> word ond wisdom,   ond þæs weres stihtung,
> mod ond mægencræft,   þe him meotud engla,
> gæsta geocend   forgiefen hæfde.
>   (1130–33)

(so profound was all the word and wisdom, and the incentive of the man, the courage and might, which the Ruler of angels, the Helper of souls, had given him.)

It is not difficult to see in this whole passage, along with the speech of Guðlac to his servant which precedes it (1060–93), a kind of thematic epitome of the poem accompanied by a brightening of outlook; and the juxtaposition of Easter with the partial revival of Guðlac may be thought to carry with it a natural analogy between Guðlac and Christ. Once again it seems possible that the heroic ideal is being used to help point up such an analogy by way of Christ's traditional associations with *sapientia et fortitudo*.

The three Old English heroic poems whose heroes are women—*Juliana*, *Elene*, and *Judith*—also clearly make some use of the ideal *sapientia et fortitudo*. A question inevitably arises, however, about the appropriateness of this ideal for female heroes, particularly in Old English literary tradition; while courage and even prowess are common enough in the heroines of Icelandic and German story, they are not usually among the more prominent features of the women portrayed in Old English.[7] I would conjecture that so far as this rather formulaic heroic ideal is concerned, Old English poets take the essential quality of the hero to be a combination of wisdom and courage/prowess and that of the heroine to be simply wisdom, with its complementary courage and prowess to be somehow obtained or enlisted from elsewhere. A pattern of this kind seems borne out particularly well in *Beowulf*. Wealhþeow, for example, is a woman of graciousness, tact, and insight, justifiably concerned about a violent future which she foresees but can do nothing to prevent

(1168-87); her only recourse is a covert appeal to the strength of Beowulf and the Geats (1215-31). Hygd is described as "wis, welþungen" ("wise, accomplished" 1927), and her name apparently carries overtones of its lexical meaning "mind *or* thought." In this respect she seems clearly contrasted with her husband Hygelac, who is presented as a king of unblemished courage and prowess, but lacking in wisdom; and his reckless death on the Frankish coast leaves her in difficulties which, as a woman, she can survive only by relying on the might of Beowulf (2369-79). The "Þryð-Offa" episode (1931-62), apparently introduced as a contrast to the situation of Hygd and Hygelac, shows us a queen given to inciting violence and lacking in womanly wisdom, who reformed after marrying a man distinguished by both the heroic virtues (1957-60).[8] A passage in the *Exeter Gnomes* (*Maxims I*) closely approximates the pattern I have been suggesting, assigning to the man prowess in battle and to the woman a series of duties climaxed and apparently summarized by the knowledge of wise counsel for them both:

> Guð sceal in eorle,
> wig geweaxan,   ond wif geþeon
> leof mid hyre leodum,   leohtmod wesan,
> rune healdan,   rumheort beon
> mearum ond maþmum,   meodorædenne
> for gesiðmægen   symle æghwær
> eodor æþelinga   ærest gegretan,
> forman fulle   to frean hond
> ricene geræcan,   ond him ræd witan
> boldagendum   bæm ætsomne.
>   (83-92)

(Battle, warfare, shall wax strong in the earl, and the woman shall thrive beloved among her people, be light-hearted, keep counsel, be liberal with horses and trea-sures, at the mead-ceremony before the band of comrades always, everywhere, greet first the protector of the nobles, quickly reach the first cups to the lord's hand, and have in mind counsel for them, the house owners, both together.)

A recognition of wisdom as the characteristic virtue of women in heroic terms, if it is credible, might derive ultimately from the attribution of prophetic powers to women in Germanic culture, first reported by Tacitus: "Inesse quin etiam [feminis] sanctum aliquid et providum putant, nec aut consilia earum aspernantur aut responsa neglegunt" ("Even more, they believe there exists in women something holy and prophetic, and they neither spurn their counsels nor ignore their opinions").[9] On the other hand, it might also be influenced by the tradition of "wise women" in the Old Testament, including for example Sara, Rebecca, Abigail, Judith, and Esther.

In the Old English poem *Juliana*, the use of the ideal *sapientia et fortitudo* seems to rest on the assumption that while Juliana does indeed possess both wisdom and courage, her courage is a virtue which is not normally to be looked for in a woman and exists only as a result of her Christian wisdom. A possible early adumbration of the theme appears in her dispute with her father, where in the introductions of two successive speeches she is characterized by the epithets "gleaw" ("wise" 131) and "unforhte" ("fearless" 147). Its major statements, however, are expressions of amazement at finding such boldness in a woman, spoken by the devil after she has laid hold of him:

> þu me ærest saga,
> hu þu gedyrstig   þurh deop gehygd
> wurde þus wigþrist   ofer eall wifa cyn. . . .
> (430–32)

(Say you to me first how you, made daring by profound thought, became so bold in fight beyond all the race of women. . . .)

Later he says that none of the patriarchs or prophets was bold enough to lay hand on him as Juliana has done, even though God gave them wisdom—clearly that of the Old Law (510–22). His final lament speaks of her boldness as "perverse" among women, apparently adding that it is a result of her wisdom:

> Ic to soþe wat
> þæt ic ær ne sið   ænig ne mette
> in woruldrice   wif þe gelic,
> þristran geþohtes   ne þweorhtimbran
> mægþa cynnes. Is on me sweotul
> þæt þu unscamge   æghwæs wurde
> on ferþe frod.
> (547–53)

(I know in truth that neither early nor late have I met in the kingdom of the world any woman like you, bolder of thought or more perverse, of the race of women. It is clear to me that you would be unconfounded by anything, in your wise spirit.)[10]

In *Elene* the ideal *sapientia et fortitudo* is withheld altogether from Elene herself and is applied instead to the Jew Judas, who, after being praised repeatedly for wisdom, is said to be "wordcræftes wis" ("wise of eloquence") and "bald on meðle" ("bold in council" 592-93; see also 594-97). That this ideal represents a limited perfection under the Old Law, however, is made clear by his later reception of Christian wisdom and prowess through the Holy Ghost:

> Him ða gleawhydig Iudas oncwæð,
> hæleð hildedeor, (him wæs halig gast
> befolen fæste, fyrhat lufu,
> weallende gewitt þurh witgan snyttro),
> ond þæt word gecwæð, wisdomes ful. . . .
>   (934-38)

(To him then answered the wise-minded Judas, the hero bold in battle [the Holy Ghost was bestowed on him strongly, a fire-hot love, a surging intelligence through prophet's wisdom], and he spoke this word, full of wisdom. . . .)[11]

The general fearlessness of Elene and the occasional warlike epithets used to describe her (e.g., "guðcwen," ["battle queen" 254, 331]) are, I suppose, a natural concomitant of her rather unusual role in the poem—a powerful queen dealing with a subject race—and of her probable typological significance as the Church.[12]

II

With this sketch of how the heroic ideal *sapientia et fortitudo* seems to operate in the other Old English heroic poems, let us now turn to our subject proper: the Old English *Judith*, whose primary source is clearly the biblical Book of Judith. In any analysis of the poem, a preliminary difficulty is of course created by the fact that its beginning does not appear in our manuscript; and since the poem as we have it corresponds only to chapters 12–16 of the Book of Judith, we are left with the initial question of whether it was originally a retelling of its entire source (like *Genesis A*), or a dramatic adaptation of one incident from it (like *Exodus*). Though I lean strongly toward the opinion of Rosemary Woolf that the whole management of the poem suggests the latter,[13] the pattern I will propose need not rest on that assumption. For example, however long the poem may originally have been, it seems evident that our present text has been constructed with great concern for various kinds of symmetry;[14] if it should indeed be merely the climax of what was once a much longer poem, such symmetries will presumably be symmetries of an episode rather than—or perhaps in addition to—those of the poem as a whole.

Outside the Old English poem, no approximation of the ideal *sapientia et fortitudo* is ever explicitly applied to Judith, either in the Vulgate Book of Judith or in any other version of the story that I know of. There does, however, seem to have been a tradition of sorts concerning the wisdom of Judith, which, along with her obvious courage in cutting off the head of Holofernes, would provide a natural enough suggestion of the two heroic virtues. Her wisdom is referred to once in the Vulgate itself, where Holofernes and his servants "mirabantur sapientiam ejus, et dicebant alter ad alterum: 'Non est talis mulier super terram . . . in sensu verborum'" ("wondered at her wisdom and said to one another, 'There is not such a woman on earth . . . in intelligence of words'" 11:18–19). In the Septuagint, she is praised for σοφία ("wisdom") and σύνεσις ("sagacity") in this same passage (Sept. 11:20–21), and also by Ozias in 8:29 (cf. Vulgate 8:28). The Old Latin version, in a passage quoted by Fulgentius, introduces Judith as "bona in aspectu, et formosa facie; prudens corde, et bona in sensu, et honesta valde" ("excellent in appearance, and beautiful of face; prudent in heart, and of sound intelligence, and surpassingly noble" 8:7). The speech of Ozias elaborates on her wisdom and prudence: "Omnia quæcunque dixisti, in bono corde locuta es, & non est qui resistat verbis tuis: quoniam non ex hodierno sapientia tua manifestata est, sed ab initio dierum tuorum scit omnis populus prudentiam tuam, & quoniam bona sunt figmenta cordis tui . . ." ("All things whatsoever that you have said you have spoken with a true heart, and there is no one who may resist your words, since your wisdom has not been discovered just today, but from the beginning of your days the entire people has known your prudence; and since the creations of your heart are good . . ." 8:28); and Judith replies, "Audite me, et faciam rem prudentem . . ." ("Hear me, and I will perform a prudent work . . ." 8:30). In 11:19 (quoted above), the words "sensu verborum" ("intelligence of words") of the Vulgate appear in the Old Latin as "sapientia sermonum" ("wisdom of speech").[15] Jerome, discussing the allowable ways of using falsehood, remarks that Judith "vicit [Holofernem] prudenti simulatione verborum" ("conquered [Holofernes] by prudent deception of words").[16] A pseudo-Augustinian sermon *De Judith* says that Judith "sollicitos populos redditura securos sua sapientia consolatur" ("about to render her fearful people secure by her wisdom, consoles them [or is consoled]"; or "about to render her fearful people secure, consoles them [or is consoled] by her wisdom").[17] Rabanus Maurus, in the dedicatory epistle to his *Expositio in librum Judith*, written in 834 and addressed to the Empress Judith, wife of Louis the Pious, compares this Judith to the biblical Judith and Esther, who

quidem ob insigne meritum virtutis, tam viris quam etiam feminis sunt . imitabiles, eo quod spiritales hostes animi vigore, et corporales consilii maturitate vicerunt. Sic et vestra nunc laudabilis prudentia, quæ jam hostes suos non parva ex parte vicerat, si in bono cœpto perseverare atque semetipsam semper meliorare contenderit, cunctos adversarios suos feliciter superabit.[18]

(indeed, because of the distinguished worth of their virtue, are to be imitated as well by men as also by women, because they vanquished spiritual enemies by strength of will and corporeal enemies by mildness of counsel. So also now your laudable prudence, which in large part has already conquered its enemies, if it will strive vigorously to persevere in the good that has been initiated, will successfully overcome all its adversaries.)

In Ælfric's metrical homily on the Book of Judith, the Assyrian watchmen "wundrodon hire wlites swiðe / *and* hire wislicra worda" ("wondered greatly at her appearance, and at her wise words" [cf. Jth. 10:14–15]).[19] *Die jüngere Judith*, a German verse paraphrase dating from the eleventh or twelfth century, refers to Judith as "Dû vrouwe vil wîse"

("The lady very wise" [cf. Jth. 10:5]) and "Jûdith dû wîse" ("Judith the wise" [cf. 10:10]); and Holofernes' watchman says to her, "dû hâst vil wîslîchen getân" ("you have acted very wisely" [cf. 10:15]).[20]

In the Old English *Judith* as we have it, the abundant references to the heroine's wisdom and courage—none of which appears in the Vulgate—form a pattern in which she originally possesses woman's proper virtue, wisdom, and is granted courage for the beheading of Holofernes by a special grace of God.[21] Before the beheading, each of the three stages of the narrative involving her is accompanied by an explicit mention of her wisdom alone. Her first seeking Holofernes is described,

> þæt wæs þy feorðan dogore
> þæs ðe Iudith hyne, gleaw on geðonce,
> ides ælfscinu, ærest gesohte.
> (12–14)

(That was on the fourth day from the time that Judith, wise in thought, the elf-lovely woman, first sought him.)

When Holofernes' retainers are commanded to bring Judith to him, they

> bearhtme stopon
> to ðam gysterne, þær hie Iudithðe
> fundon ferhðgleawe. . . .
> (39–41)

(with tumult marched to the guest-chamber, where they found Judith, wise of mind. . . .)

And she is finally brought to the couch with a third comment on her wisdom: "Hie ða on reste gebrohton / snude ða snoteran idese" ("Quickly then they brought the wise lady to the couch" 54–55). After the arrival of Holofernes, her wisdom seems dramatized in her prayer to God (83–94), and particularly in the reference to her thoughtfulness which precedes it:

> þa wæs nergendes
> þeowen þrymful, þearle gemyndig

> hu heo þone atolan   eaðost mihte
> ealdre benæman. . . .
>
> (73–76)

(Then was the glorious handmaiden of the Preserver deeply mindful, how she might most easily deprive the terrible creature of life. . . .)

Following Judith's prayer to God, the direct bestowal of courage on her is clearly stated, along with a reminder of her wisdom ("mid ræde"):

>   Hi ða se hehsta dema
> ædre mid elne onbryrde,   swa he deð anra gehwylcne
> herbuendra   þe hyne him to helpe seceð
> mid ræde ond mid rihte geleafan.   Þa wearð hyre
>   rume on mode,
> haligre hyht geniwod.
>
> (94–98)

(Then the Highest Judge inspired her immediately with courage, as He does each one of the earth-dwellers who seeks Him for help with wisdom and true faith. Then she became spacious in heart, hope was renewed in the holy one.)

This gift of courage to Judith by God, while not so explicit in the Vulgate account, is strongly implied by her repeated prayers that God may grant her courage and strength for the killing of Holofernes:

Da mihi in animo constantiam ut contemnam illum, et virtutem ut evertam illum. . . (9:14). Memento, Domine, testamenti tui, et da verbum in ore meo, et in corde meo consilium corrobora. . . (9:18). Confirma me, Domine, Deus Israel. . . (13:7). Cumque evaginasset [pugionem], apprehendit comam capitis ejus, et ait: Confirma me, Domine Deus, in hac hora (13:19).

('Give me constancy in my mind that I may despise him, and strength that I may overthrow him. . . Remember, O Lord, your covenant, and give me the word in my mouth and strengthen the resolution in my heart . . . Make me strong, Lord God of Israel . . .' And when she had drawn [the sword], she seized the hair of his head and said: 'Make me strong, Lord God, in this hour').

In the Old English poem—loaded as it is with references to the other heroic virtue, wisdom—this direct granting of courage by God seems to take on added point as a parallel to the direct granting of wisdom by God, common in Scripture and in patristic thought,[22] and illustrated strikingly in the bestowal of wisdom on Judas in *Elene* (934-38, quoted above; note also lines 958-61). We may notice in passing that in our present passage from *Judith*, the expression "wearð hyre rume on mode" (97b)—evidently meaning "she became spacious in heart," and glossed by B. J. Timmer as "she felt a great relief"[23]—seems rather to be an allusive development of the wisdom mentioned in the preceding half-line. Ambrose, commenting on Ps. 118:32, "Viam mandatorum tuorum cucurri, cum dilatasti cor meum" ("I have run the way of your commandments, when you have widened my heart"), elaborates on the celebration of wisdom in the widened heart:

Viam, inquit, *mandatorum tuorum cucurri cum dilatares cor meum*. Neque enim poterat viam currere, si cor ejus coarctaretur angustiis. Denique currentibus viam Domini ait Apostolus: *Dilatamini et vos, et nolite jugum ducere cum infidelibus* (2 Cor. 6:13-14). Et de se ait: *Os nostrum patet ad vos, o Corinthii, cor nostrum dilatatum est* (ibid. 11). Ideo et de Salomone dicitur: *Latitudo cordis ejus, sicut arena maris* (3 Reg. 4:29), et vide distantiam: via sit angustior, cor latius, ut Patris, et Filii, et Spiritus sancti sustineat mansionem; ne veniat Verbum Dei, et pulset, et videns cordis ejus angustias, dedignetur habitare. Denique sapientia in exitu canitur, in plateis autem cum fiducia agit. Plateæ latæ sunt. Non igitur in viis, sed in cordis latitudine sapientia decantatur. In hoc igitur campo interioris hominis, non in angustiis mentis currendum nobis est, ut comprehendamus.[24]

(He says, *I have run the way of your commandments, since you widened my heart*. For he would not have been able to run the way if his heart were confined by narrow straits. Accordingly the Apostle says to those running the way of the Lord, *Be you also widened, and bear not the yoke with unbelievers*. And concerning himself he says, *Our mouth is open to you, O Corinthians, our heart is widened*. Therefore also it is said of Solomon, *The wideness of his heart, as the sand of the sea*, and behold a difference: the way should be quite narrow, the heart quite wide, so that it may maintain a dwelling-place of the Father and the Son and the Holy Ghost—lest the Word of God should come and knock, and seeing the narrowness of his heart, refuse to dwell there. Accordingly wisdom is celebrated in a going forth, indeed it performs with confidence in the public squares. Squares are broad.

Wisdom, then, is praised not in the narrow ways but in the breadth of the heart. We are to run, therefore, in this plain of the inner man, not in the narrows of the mind, so that we may understand.)

Similar uses of the word *rum*, all in contexts involving wisdom or knowledge, occur in *Genesis* 519, "þe weorð on þinum breostum rum" ("For you your mind will grow spacious [wise]"); *Beowulf* 278, "Ic þæs Hroðgar mæg / þurh rumne sefan ræd gelæran" ("I can give Hroðgar counsel about this, through spacious [wise] mind"); *Elene* 1240, "ær me rumran geþeaht . . . wisdom onwreah" ("before wisdom revealed to me . . . more spacious knowledge").

During Judith's beheading of Holofernes, the climactic stroke is accompanied by a simple epithet emphasizing her newly received courage, much like the earlier ones establishing her wisdom:

> sloh ða eornoste
> ides ellenrof oðre siðe
> þone hæðenan hund. . . .
>   (108–10)

(Then the courageous woman struck the heathen dog vehemently a second time. . . .)

Holofernes' death is followed immediately by another statement of God's gift of courage to Judith, closely juxtaposed with a reference to her wisdom:

> Hæfde ða gefohten foremærne blæd
> Iudith æt guðe, swa hyre god uðe,
> swegles ealdor, þe hyre sigores onleah.
> þa seo snotere mægð snude gebrohte. . . .
>   (122–25)

(Then had Judith gained by fight, in battle, illustrious renown, as God, the Lord of Heaven, had granted her, He who bestowed on her the victory. Then the wise maiden quickly brought [Holofernes' head]. . . .)

In the account of her journey back to Bethulia which follows, she (together with her servant, who seems to reflect her perfections) is lauded repeatedly as the possessor of both heroic virtues:

Þa seo snotere mægð   snude gebrohte
þæs herewæðan   heafod swa blodig
on ðam fætelse   þe hyre foregenga,
blachleor ides,   hyra begea nest,
ðeawum geðungen,   þyder on lædde,
ond hit *þa* swa heolfrig   hyre on hond ageaf,
*hige*ðoncolre,   ham to berenne,
Iudith gingr*an* sinre.   Eodon ða gegnum þanonne
þa idesa ba   ellenþriste,
oðþæt hie becomon, collenferhðe,
eadhreðige mægð,   ut of ðam herige,
þæt hie sweotollice   geseon mihte*n*
þære wlitegan byrig   weallas blican,
Bethuliam.

(125-38)

(Then the wise maiden quickly brought the warrior's head
so bloody in the sack in which her servant, the pale-
cheeked woman excellent in virtues, had brought thither
food for them both, and Judith gave it then so gory into
the hand of her the thoughtful, her handmaid, to carry
home. They went forth directly then, both courageous
women, until they passed beyond the host, elated in spirit,
the triumphant maidens, so that they could clearly see the
walls of the fair city shining—Bethulia.)

In the latter part of the poem, what might be thought of
as Judith's three most important moments are each accompanied by an allusion to her wisdom and courage. Her arrival
at Bethulia is marked by two epithets characterizing her as
wise, and one characterizing her as brave:

Wiggend sæton,
weras wæccende   wearde heoldon
in ðam fæstenne,   swa ðam folce ær
geomormodum   Iudith bebead,
searoðoncol mægð,   þa heo on sið gewat,
ides ellenrof.   Wæs ða eft cumen
leof to leodum,   ond ða lungre het
gleawhydig wif   gumena sumne
of ðære ginnan byrig   hyre togeanes gan. . . .

(141-49)

(Warriors were sitting, wakeful men kept watch in the
stronghold, just as Judith, the wise maiden, had earlier

commanded the sorrowing people when she departed on her journey, the courageous woman. Then was the beloved one come again to her people, and then the woman wise in thought quickly commanded one of the men from the spacious stronghold to come to meet her. . . .)

Her exhortation to the people is preceded by an epithet emphasizing her wisdom and an action clearly demonstrating the results of her courage:

> þa seo gleawe het,   golde gefrætewod,
> hyre ðinenne   þancolmode
> þæs herewæðan   heafod onwriðan
> ond hyt to behðe   blodig ætywan
> þam burhleodum,   hu hyre æt beaduwe gespeow.
> (171–75)

(Then the wise one, adorned with gold, bade her attentive handmaid to uncover the head of the warrior and show it, bloody, to the city-dwellers as a sign of how she had succeeded in battle.)

And the victory over the Assyrians is followed by a passage attributing the spoils of battle to her wisdom and courage:

> eal þæt ða ðeodguman   þrymme geeodon
> cene under cumblum   on compwige
> þurh Iudithe   gleawe lare,
> mægð modigre.
> (331–34)

(. . . all that the warriors, brave beneath their banners, had won by power in battle through the wise counsel of Judith, the courageous maiden.)

Finally, at the end of the description of the spoils, there is a single last reference to the wisdom of Judith, ". . . hi þæt þære beorhtan idese / ageafon gearoþoncolre" (". . . they gave that to the bright lady, ready of wit" 340–41); the point, presumably, is that with all battles over she can return to the virtue which is her natural perfection as a woman.

Though the detection of symmetrical patterns in the

epithets of Old English poetry is admittedly a slippery business—particularly in a poem whose very degree of completeness remains unknown—it would, I think, be difficult to deny at least a broadly symmetrical arrangement in the references to wisdom and courage that I have proposed. The central action, the beheading of Holofernes, is immediately preceded by God's giving Judith courage to complement her wisdom (94–98), and is followed closely by a re-statement of this gift along with another mention of her wisdom (122–25); between these two passages, and placed symmetrically between the two strokes of the climactic beheading, is the single epithet "ides ellenrof" ("courageous woman" 109). This whole central scene is in turn framed by two thematically significant actions: Judith's pondering and prayer to God (73–94, especially 74b), which I take to dramatize her wisdom, and her return to Bethulia (125–38), with its repeated emphasis on her wisdom and courage. In the early part of the poem, before the arrival of Holofernes at his pavilion, there are three simple epithets establishing the wisdom of Judith (13, 41, 55); in the last part of the poem, after her return to Bethulia, there are three brief references to her wisdom and courage (145–48, 171–75, 333–34). The final mention of her wisdom (341) serves, I take it, as a kind of epilogue to the entire pattern. Such a design, if it can be admitted, would of course support—and in turn be supported by—the other evidences of symmetrical arrangement in the poem.[25]

This essential symmetry seems complemented by a number of lesser designs based on the ideal *sapientia et fortitudo*. For example, in the early part of the poem each of the epithets characterizing Judith as wise is matched by a reference to Holofernes as powerful. In line 11 Holofernes is called "ðam rican ðeodne" ("the mighty chief"), and in line 13 Judith is "gleaw on geðonce" ("wise in thought"); in line 41 Judith is "ferhðgleawe" ("wise of mind"), and in line 44 Holofernes is "se rica" ("the powerful one"); in line 55 Judith is "ða snoteran idese" ("the wise lady"), and in line 58 Holofernes is "burga ealdor" ("lord of cities"). This basic contrast is developed by the many other references to the might and courage of both Holofernes and the Assyrians in this entire passage (9–59), and possibly also by the description of Holofernes as "niða geblonden" ("steeped in evils"

34), seen as the opposite of patristic *sapientia*.[26] In any case, there is surely a meaningful contrast between Holofernes' drunken oblivion, epitomized in the words "swa he nyste rædda nanne / on gewitlocan" ("as if he had no sense in his mind" 68–69), and Judith's sober thoughtfulness immediately following, epitomized by "Þa wæs nergendes / þeowen þrymful, þearle gemyndig ..." ("Then was the glorious handmaiden of the Preserver deeply mindful ..." 73–74); and probably another between Judith's wise gloom in the midst of her trusting prayer to God—

> Þearle ys me nu ða
> heorte onhæted   ond hige geomor,
> swyðe mid sorgum gedrefed
>   (86–88)

(sorely now is my heart inflamed and my spirit troubled, greatly afflicted with sorrows)

—and the later godless gloom of the Assyrians outside the tent of Holofernes:[27]

> Beornas stodon
> ymbe hyra þeodnes træf   þearle gebylde,
> sweorcendferhðe.   Hi ða somod ealle
> ongunnon cohhetan,   cirman hlude
> ond gristbitian,   gode orfeorme,
> mid toðon torn þoligende.
>   (267–72)

(The men stood around their lord's tent greatly excited, sad in spirit. Then all together they began to make noises, to cry out loudly and gnash their teeth—lacking a god, enduring grief with their teeth.)

If the heroic ideal *sapientia et fortitudo* does operate in the Old English *Judith* in somewhat the way I have been proposing, what finally is its contribution to the total meaning? I would begin by suggesting that the central theme of the poem is the same as that of the biblical Book of Judith: the deliverance of the Hebrew people through the providence of God.[28] If we assume that our Old English version once covered the same ground as the biblical book, we may observe that the poem as we have it seems true enough to this theme, and speculate that the lost portion is likely to have been at least comparably close; if we assume that our text is virtually complete as it stands, we can hardly overlook the fact that it begins and ends with celebrations of Judith's and the Hebrews' dependence on God. Now the very theme of God's deliverance of the Hebrews, so familiar throughout the Old Testament, is here further highlighted by the unlikely combination of forces used to effect it: armed violence performed by the hand of a woman. The paradox is enunciated clearly in the "Canticum Judith" near the end of the Vulgate version: "Dominus autem omnipotens nocuit eum, / et tradidit eum in manus feminae, et confodit eum" ("But the almighty Lord has afflicted him, and delivered him into the hands of a woman, and pierced him" 16:7). It is also a familiar feature in later commentary and paraphrase of the story of Judith—for example in Prudentius' *Psychomachia*, where Pudicitia refers to "aspera Iudith / . . . famosum mulier referens ex hoste tropaeum / non trepidante manu uindex mea caelitus audax!"[29] ("unyielding Judith . . . though a woman, bearing back from the foe, with untrembling hand, the famous trophy [Holofernes' head]—my defender, bold by heavenly prompting!"). Instead of merely stating this important aspect of God's delivery of the Hebrews from Holofernes, the Old English poet has chosen to dramatize it by a highly original manipulation of the heroic ideal *sapientia et fortitudo*: Judith, the already wise heroine, is in a critical moment granted special courage by God for a task of unwomanly violence, thus becoming His instrument for the salvation of her people and a testimony of His continuing providence.[30]

William Alfred

the Drama
of The Wanderer

A maxim is a conclusion upon observation of
matters of fact, and merely retrospective: and an
Idea, or, if you like, a Principle carries knowledge
within itself, and is prospective.

Samuel Taylor Coleridge[1]

Like R. M. Lumiansky in his classic article on the structure
of *The Wanderer*, T. P. Dunning and A. J. Bliss see the poem
"as a dramatic monologue with the poet intervening . . . to
indicate the speaker at the main stages, as it were, of his
development."[2] But in their magisterial preface to their
edition, as in R. F. Leslie's no less impressive one to his, (and,
indeed, in most of the criticism following Lumiansky's lead) I
feel the lack of some discussion of the effects which make
the monologue the drama that it is. For it is an *agon*, a
tragedy in little. It describes, as T. A. Shippey writes of all
the elegies, "a process rather than a fixed point."[3] That

process—as interesting as the conclusion at which it arrives—enacts the struggle, moment by moment, by which
mind moves from dead experience to live understanding,
and "changes reality by changing itself."⁴ It depicts that
motion as a play does, by making use of the devices of
characterization, conflict, timing, patterned repetition and
climax to trace an arc of decisive feeling from problem
through crisis to climactic resolution. The problem which
the Wanderer wrestles with is *tristitia mundi,* the sadness of
the world. Because of our modern celebration of sadness as
the hallmark of sensitivity, we tend to overlook the gravity
with which the poem's first audience would have regarded
it, as the eighth deadly sin. Since that sadness may lead to
despair of the mercy of God, the sin against the Holy Ghost
(Mark 3:28–29) that will not be forgiven, in depicting a
struggle with it for salvation the poet attempts a dangerous
sublimity. Consideration of the skill with which he achieves
that sublimity by the use of common dramatic devices
deepens our sense of his mastery.

The character tempted towards despair is old, friendless
and a wanderer, an *ānhaga / ānhoga,* a survivor even worse off
than the last survivor in *Bēowulf* (2236-70), who at least had
the solace of his duty and treasure. That the word means
"survivor" seems evident from the contexts of the verse
uses of it (the ambiguous *Andrēas* 1350 and *Ps. Lam.* 101.8
notwithstanding): Beowulf (*Bēowulf* 2236-70) is the last survivor of Hygelac's Frankish raid. Death (*Gūthlac* B 996–99)
and the Phoenix (*Phoenix* 87, 346) are survivors by very
essence. And a shield (Riddle No. 5, 1–3) that does not
survive battle is no shield.

That the Wanderer is old and that he tastes the desola-
tion of his survival every waking and sleeping moment is
driven home to us by the massive use of frequentative
adverbs and adverbial phrases throughout the poem. But
these frequentatives serve a double function: they also
characterize the Wanderer as feeling distress at having to
give vent to his complaint. They do so by their implied
apology for his violation of the heroic reserve we know the
Anglo-Saxon felt duty-bound by such texts as *Maxims* I,
121–23 and 2 Cor. 7:10 to maintain, both as a man and as a
Christian. Who would not cry out, the frequentatives imply,
if he were tormented by such relentless memories of loss?

That his right to do so must be justified intensifies our sense of the conflict which agonizes the Wanderer.

That conflict is the driving force of the poem. It is best articulated by pinpointing those moments of stress in which maxims are brought to bear against the weight of memories. As every discussion since R. C. Boer's makes clear, the maxims fall into two categories: the *Beowulf*-poet's *worold-rǣden* (1142) and *ēcne rǣd* (1201), the way of the world and the everlasting way, or, if you prefer, King Alfred's *wīg ond wīsdom*, the lore of action and that of understanding. The strongest clue to the centrality of maxims to the structure of the poem is the Wanderer's twice naming them: first, *lārcwidum* (38), as a benefit the loss of which desolates him and second, *cwidegiedda* (55), as a benefit he seeks from his waking dream of companionship. That these compounds mean "maxims" can be strongly argued from the first sense of *cwide*, which is "sentence, saying, pointed remark." For me, combination with *lār*, "instruction," and *giedd*, "song or formal discourse," emphasizes that first sense of the word. Perhaps *cwidegiedda* may be the Old English term for such sententious songs as *Maxims* I and II. But whether that be so or not, three times in the poem, 10–17, 65–72 and 112, the Wanderer attempts to cap or caps the authority of experience with the authority of maxim. Those moments are the key to the poet's timing. As inconsolable remembrance grows in power, the tempo accelerates and the periodic momentum of the syntax of the memories rides down the inelastic ligature of the worldly maxims with their frail caveats and insufficient solace till, private pain having been subsumed in the clipped maxims formulating the human transience decreed by divine order, the conventional phrasing of the maxims expands to include the promise of grace. Or, to put it in the Wanderer's terms, his suffering mind batters against the first two sets of maxims like a bird trapped in a house against a door, until brought by the force of his feeling to understand the common lot of mortality to the full, it comes to understand the promise of immortality trumpeted in the last set, and breaks out into the peace of that understanding like a bird into the light.

The first five lines of the poem establish this technique of balancing the expression of an unbearable memory with counsel meant to silence or console:

> Oft him ānhaga   āre gebīdeð,
> Metudes miltse,
>
> (1–2a)

(A survivor often lives to experience favor, the mercy of
Providence . . ,)[5]

These first verses, rendered wistful by the qualification of
the frequentative, aspire to the certainty of maxim. The
gnomic present of the verb implies a truth, the eternity of
which is beyond the limitations of tense. But that present is
immediately counterweighed by the past of the verb of
necessity in which the first memory is couched:

> þeahþe hē mōdcearig
> geond lagulāde   longe sceolde
> hrēran mid hondum   hrīmcealde sǣ.
> wadan wræclāstas.
>
> (2b–5a)

(. . . though anxious in mind, he has had to row with his
own hands through its whole watery route a sea cold as a
deep frost, to keep on going by paths of exile.)

That rebus of dereliction is broken off by a whiplash
aposiopesis, which is a proper maxim:

> Wyrd bið ful ārǣd.
>
> (56)

(Our lot is fully decided.)

Its reference, as with all aposiopeses, is ambiguous. It can
refer to "mercy" or "paths of exile." Aposiopesis, of course,
conventionally signals a retreat from unmanageable feeling.
Another device of the poet, first employed here, serves the
same function: he has the Wanderer phrase such charged
passages in the third person. The speaker's need to distance
himself thus from emotion makes for uneasiness. The
Wanderer is wrestling with himself as well as with divine
justice.

After the poet intervenes, as if to give him space to get
hold of himself, the Wanderer resumes, speaking in the first

person. His speech from 8 to 29 repeats the pattern of 1–5 with significant variation. The futility of the maxims he concessively acknowledges knowing (again as if in rebuttal of some sense of the unmanliness of his complaint) is driven home by the noble mass of the period, flawlessly built to a muted closure, in which the enormity of his loss is first spelled out:

> Oft ic sceolde āna   ūhtna gehwylce
> mīne ceare cwīþan— Nis nū cwicra nān
> þe ic him mōdsefan   mīnne durre
> sweotule āsecgan— Ic tō sōþe wāt
> þæt biþ in eorle   indryhten þēaw
> þæt hē his ferðlocan   fæste binde,
> healde his hordcofan,   hycge swā hē wille,
> ne mæg wērigmōd   wyrde wiðstondan
> ne sē hrēo hyge   helpe gefremman,
> forðon dōmgeorne   drēorigne oft
> in hyra brēostcofan   bindað fæste,
> swā ic mōdsefan   mīnne sceolde—
> oft earmcearig,   ēðle bidæled,
> frēomægum feor— feterum sælan,
> siþþan geāra iū   goldwine mīn[n]e
> hrūsan heolstre biwrāh,   ond ic hēan þonan
> wōd wintercearig   ofer waþe[m]a gebind,
> sōhte seledrēorig   sinces bryttan,
> hwǣr ic feor oþþe nēah   findan meahte,
> þone þe in meoduhealle   minne myne wisse,
> oþþe mec frēondlēas[n]e   frēfran wolde,
> wēman mid wynnum.
>
> (8–29a)

(Often in every kind of moment before first light, I have had to give vent to my grief alone—There is now no man alive to whom I dare clearly speak my mind—I know for a fact that it is a noble virtue in a man that he lock his heart's place fast, his chest of treasure, think as he will, and a worn out mind cannot stand up to our lot and the bitter business of thinking can bring no help about, because of which men eager for a good name often bind tight in the coffer of the breast someone wounded-looking, just as I— often anxious with misery, done out of my heritage, far from noble companions—my own heart have had to rope down in bonds ever since years upon years ago I covered my golden lord in a hole in the earth, and brought low, kept on going from there, worried by winter across the waves' prison, sought, wounded-looking because of the loss of a hall, a treasure-giver, somewhere far or near I could find a man in a meadhall who might know how my mind worked, or would have been willing, friendless though I am, to console me, treat me to pleasures.)

Drēorig, which I define "wounded-looking" to evoke my deriving it from *drēor*, "blood"—the derivation from *drēosan*, yielding "with falling face, crest-fallen," attractive though it is, seems less likely in light of the other uses of the adjective—does not to my mind have *hyge* as an antecedent. *Drēorigne* is an anticipative use of the substantive adjective to refer to that half of the Wanderer's spirit that appears in the simile succeeding it, roped down in the bondage of heroic reserve. That the adjective in its two later appearances in compound—*seledrēorig* (25) and *drēorighlēor* (83)—is used in each case by the Wanderer of himself (83, "with wounded-looking face," in the distancing third person) confirms that opinion.

The fluctuation back and forth from first to third person reflects the struggle for control by the kind of syntactical periphrasis described earlier as doubling with aposiopesis to convey the onset of feelings hard to manage. And again (11–16) personal reminiscence is broken off in mid-career by attempts at sententious certainty. The amalgamation of maxims vainly enjoining reserve has a dismissive effect, rather like a serious use of the comic meiosis effected by the landslides of proverbs indulged in by Sancho Panza. The chastened tone of the closure of that period is confirmed by the system of modified maxims which follow and reinforce our trepidation at his sense of shamefacedness at the show of himself he is making:

> Wāt sē þe cunnað
> hū slīþen bið   sorg tō gefēran
> þām þe him lȳt hafað   lēofra geholena;
> warað hine wræclāst   nāles wunden gold,
> ferðloca frēorig   nālæs foldan blǣd.
> Gemon hē selesecgas   ond sincþege,
> hū hine on geoguðe   his goldwine
> wenede tō wiste;   wyn eal gedrēas.
> Forþon wāt sē þe sceal   his winedryhtnes
> lēofes lārcwidum   longe forþolian.
>   (29b–38)

(He knows who puts it to the test how vicious a companion
sorrow is to man who has few to love and confide in: the
exile's path is always at him, not twisted gold, the heart's
place gone freezing cold, not earth's plenty; he remembers
the men in the hall and getting treasure, how in youth his
golden lord feted him with feasting—All joy has fallen to
pieces—Because of that the man who has long had to do
without the maxims of the lord he loved knows.)

For me *wāt* (37), as Dunning and Bliss sagely hold, must not
be attached to what follows. What the Wanderer knows is
intended to be—and must be rendered—the ellipsis that it is.
The syntax is representative: it depicts stunned distraction.
The doggedly impersonal third person in the passage bleeds
into two parallel complex sentences that stagger us with the
burden of loss they convey:

> Þonne sorg ond slæp   somod ætgædre
> earmne ānhogan   oft gebinda&,
> þince& him on mōde   þæt hē his mondryhten
> clyppe ond cysse   ond on cnēo lecge
> honda ond hēafod   swā hē hwīlum ær
> in geārdagum   giefstōlas brēac.
> Þonne onwæcne& oft   winelēas guma,
> gesih& him biforan   fealwe wēgas,
> baþian brimfuglas   brædan feþra,
> hrēosan hrīm ond snāw   hagle gemenged.
>   (39–48)

(As often as sorrow and sleep joined together bind the
poor survivor down, in his mind, it seems to him he is
embracing and kissing his liege-lord and laying hands and
head on his knee, just as in days long past he used to enjoy
the throne of bounty. As often as the lordless man
awakens, he sees before him the yellowish waves, seafowl
bathing, stretching their feathers, frost and snow falling,
mixed through with hail.)[6]

He then drives home the force of the syllogism of images by
which he gingerly argues the inconsolability of his memory
by spelling out the agony of hallucinated longing it invokes:

> Þonne bēo& þȳ hefigran   heortan benne,
> sāre æfter swæsne.   Sorg bi& genīwad;
> þonne māga gemynd   mōd geondhweorfe&,

grēteð glīwstafum,   georne geondscēawað
secga geseldan—swimmað eft onweg
flēotendra ferð—nō þær fela bringeð
cūðra cwidegiedda.   Cearo bið genīwad
þām þe sendan sceal   swīþe geneahhe
ofer waþema gebind   wērigne sefan.
                                        (49–57)

(Then the gashes in the heart grow the graver, aching for
the man beloved, sorrow comes with fresh force; then the
mind moves through memories of kinsmen, greets them
with shows of pleasure, peers deep at the soldiers, the
comrades: they swim away again. The souls of those
floating there do not bring much in the way of recogniz-
able maxims; anxiety comes with fresh force to one who
must very often indeed send a heart worn out across the
waves' prison.)

Collected for the moment by the cogency of the evidence of
the apology for complaint, he resumes the first person:

Forþon ic geþencan ne mæg   geond þās woruld
for hwan mōdsefa   mīn ne gesweorce
þonne ic eorla līf   eal geondþence,
hū hī færlīce   flet ofgēafon,
mōdge maguþegnas.   Swā þes middangeard
ealra dōgra gehwām   drēoseð ond fealleþ.
Forþon ne mæg wearþan wīs   wer ær hē āge
wintra dæl in woruldrīce.
                                        (58–65a)

(Because of that, I cannot conceive why in this world my
mind does not black out completely when I think the
whole life of men through, how all of a sudden, they
surrendered the hall, brave men in a band though they
were, just as every kind and manner of day, this planet
sinks into dust and falls. Because of that, a man cannot
grow wise before he makes his own a mass of years in the
world's dominion.)

The Wanderer has gained sufficient control to wonder
at his mind's endurance. That control enables him to realize
that the loss sifting him to the depths of his being like the
small maelstrom in the sand of an hourglass is common to all
on earth and to the earth itself. His euphemism for death, of
frequent use in Old English verse, reminds us of the

dishonor attached to it in the Anglo-Saxon imagination: death is a surrender to which all are brought, valor notwithstanding. His attempt to deduce from the awesome insight he has just had a maxim of solace for the debility of age breaks in a hypermetrical wail of a single measure that, in turn, is bitten off by a stiff-lipped recitation of maxims enjoining discretion and restraint in anger:

> Wita sceal geþyldig;
> ne sceal nō tō hātheort ne tō hrædwyrde,
> ne tō wāc wiga ne tō wanhȳdig,
> ne tō forht, ne tō fægen, ne tō feohgīfre,
> ne nǣfre gielpes tō georn ǣr hē geare cunne.
> Beorn sceal gebīdan þonne hē bēot spriceð
> oþþæt collenferð cunne gearwe
> hwider hreþra gehygd hweorfan wille.
> (65b–72)

(A wise man must be patient, must not be too fast to take offence, or too quick with words, or too craven a fighter, or too crazily brave, or too terrified or two fawning, or too hungry for goods, and not ever too eager to boast before he knows for sure. A man must bide his time when he utters a boast, until, his spirit rising, he knows for sure where the purpose in his breast means to move.)

The insistent polysyndeton, the excited leap from adjective to adjective, the dangling clause which requires 70–72 to nail down its meaning all convey distraction struggling for control, and mark, for me, the crisis of the poem. By means of these maxims the transition is made from the way of the world to the everlasting way. Counsels of worldly prudence, they prepare the path for counsels of divine providence. By means of them, the Wanderer decides to do battle against his own sense of grievance rather than against the will of God. By means of them, he can now look openeyed at the evidences of the law of loss which foreshadow the end of the world that was so often the terrible theme of the Anglo-Saxon homilist. The third person, up to now signalling tried restraint, now signals modesty at the achievement of wisdom born of suffering:

> Ongietan sceal glēaw hæle hū gæstlic bið
> þonne eall þisse worulde wela wēste stondeð,

swā nū missenlīce   geond þisne middangeard
winde biwāune   weallas stondaþ,
hrīme bihrorene,   hrȳðge þā ederas.
Woniað þā wīnsalo,   waldend licgað
drēame bidrorene;   duguþ eal gecrong
wlonc bī wealle.   Sume wīg fornōm,
ferede in forðwege;   sumne fugel oþbær
ofer hēanne holm;   sumne sē hāra wulf
dēaðe gedǣlde;   sumne drēorighlēor
in eorðscræfe   eorl gehȳdde.
Ȳþde swā þisne eardgeard   ælda Scyppend
oþþæt burgwara   breahtma lēase
eald enta geweorc   īdlu stōdon.

                              (73–87)

(A knowing man must realize how eerie it will be when all
the riches in this world will stand going to waste, as now
here and there the whole planet through, walls stand,
wailed round by wind, heaved up by the frost—Those
things meant for shelter lashed by the sleet!—The wine-
halls are thinning out, the lords lie dead, fallen away from
the revels; all the crack troop has crumpled, proud at the
wall: some war took off, brought along the way out; one a
bird bore off above the high sea-swell; one the grey wolf
shared out with death; one a man with a wounded-looking
face hid in an earthen grave. Thus the Creator of men has
laid waste this place of their dwelling, till free of the bustle
of what were its citizens, the old works of giants stood
empty.)[7]

The poet intervenes to give us a moment to come to
terms with the millennial paradox of the destructive Creator. This paradox caps the Wanderer's catalogue of human
lots from which such occasional examples of lucky chance as
bless the verses of *The Fates of Men* and *The Gifts of Men* have
been starkly excluded:

Sē þonne þisne wealsteal   wīse geþōhte
ond þis deorce līf   dēope geondþenceð
frōd in ferðe,   feor oft gemon
wælsleahta worn   ond þās word ācwið:

                              (88–91)

(He then has wisely contemplated this stand of wall; and
mature of spirit, thinks this dark life deeply through;

detached, he often remembers many massacres, and speaks this speech.)

The famous *ubi sunt* passage fuses pain and perception in the flailing lurch of its logaoedic hypermetrical lines:

> Hwǣr cwōm mearg?   Hwǣr cwōm mago?
> Hwǣr cwōm maþþumgyfa?
> Hwǣr cwōm symbla gesetu?   Hwǣr sindon sele-
> drēamas?
>
> (92–93)

(Where has the horse got to? Where has the man-at-arms got to? Where has the treasure-giver got to? Where have the places at the feast got to? Where are the revels of the hall?)

These terrible questions are succeeded by vocative ejaculations the futility of which to evoke what they call up is wonderingly acknowledged:

> Ēalā beorht būne!   Ēalā byrnwiga!
> Ēalā þeodnes þrym!   Hū sēo þrāg gewāt,
> genāp under nihthelm   swā hēo nō wǣre.
>
> (94–96)

(O, shining cup! O, the armed soldier! O, the lord's splendor! How that time has gone, blackened under night's hood, as if it never were!)

From this point on the Wanderer speaks only once more (99) in the past. The past that narrated painful memories yields to a present that narrates a painful vision of the landscape as an emblematic *memento mori*. The passage's wry acceptance of the violence of human dreams of prowess is implied by the paradoxical phrasing of its last verses:

> Stondeð nū on lāste   lēofre duguþe
> weal wundrum hēah   wyrmlīcum fāh.
> Eorlas fornōman   asca þrýþe,
> wǣpen wælgīfru,   wyrd sēo mǣre
>
> (97–100)

(Now in the wake of the beloved crack troop stands a wall
marvelously high, bright with shapes weaving like ser-
pents. Glories of ashwood spears, weapons greedy for
corpses, that splendid lot, have taken the men away.)

That present tense of dazed understanding shades into a
future of apocalyptic prophecy:

> Ond þās stānhleoþu   stormas cnyssað;
> hrīð hrēosende   hrūs[an] bindeð,
> wintres wōma;   þonne won cymeð
> nīpeð nihtscūa   norþan onsendeð
> hrēo hæglfare   hæleþum on andan.
>
> (101-05)

(And storms are battering these stone cliffs, snow falling
locks the earth, the roar of winter. When lightless, it
comes, it will blacken completely, night's shadow, it will
send from the north rough bursts of hail in mischief
towards men.)

I take the syntactically excited reference to the storm from
the north and night's shadow to be intended as portents of
the end of the world, the effects of which, as Dunning and
Bliss remark,[8] are imagined in 73-74. As we know from OE
Genesis 28-34, the Anglo-Saxons accepted Jeremiah's assignment of the north as the seat of the devil (Jer. 1:13-14).
From images in the past and facts in the present evidencing
the destruction to come, he deduces a maxim, the dreadful
truth of which again causes the pitch to rise into a hypermetrical cry of a single measure:

> Eall is earfoðlic   eorþan rīce;
> onwendeð wyrda gesceaft   weoruld under
>   heofonum.
>
> (106-07)

(Power on earth is all full of hardship; the decree of our lot
fills with change the world under heaven.)

Hammering home his verses, in a transport of perception, he
formulates from the torments of memory maxims on the
terms of the human condition, and by that very formulation
bravely implies his acceptance of them:

Hēr biÞ feoh lǣne,   hēr biÞ frēond lǣne,
hēr biÞ mon lǣne,   hēr biÞ mǣg lǣne.
Eal Þis eorÞan gesteal   īdel weorÞeÞ.
(108–10)

(Here goods are but lent us, here friend is but lent us, here
man is but lent us, here kinsman but lent us; all this place
we stand on on earth will grow empty!)

The poet again allows us a moment for meditation,

Swā cwæÞ snottor on mōde;   gesæt him sundor
æt rūne.
(111)

(So spoke a man of discerning mind, took his place apart, in
private communion.)

When the Wanderer speaks for the last time, the
timelessness of the gnomic present sings out in lengthened
measure, in the nobly augmented metre generally reserved
for utterances of elevated pathos or simple majesty, though
hitherto twice used by him to express flash paroxysms of
sorrow. The large dignity of the rhythm elevates the
meaning it has been shaped to carry. Mortal maxims have
evolved into immortal precepts:

Til biÞ sē Þe his trēowe gehealdeÞ,   ne sceal nǣfre
his torn tō rycene,
beorn of his brēostum ācȳÞan   nemÞe hē ǣr Þā
bōte cunne;
eorl mid elne gefremman.   Wel biÞ Þām Þe him āre
sēceÞ,
frōfre tō Fæder on heofonum,   Þǣr ūs eal sēo
fæstnung stondeÞ.
(112–15)

(Good is he who keeps his faith to the end, and never must
a man make known too quickly the grievance in his breast,
unless beforehand he knows the amends and how like a
man to win them. Well is it for the man who seeks favor,
solace from the Father in the heavens, where for us, all
that is sure rests.)[9]

Having made peace with the loss of his share of the world, he now makes peace with the loss of the world itself, and accepts whatever may come with that obstinacy in a bad business, that "pervicacia in re prava quam fidem vocant," which Tacitus sardonically admired in his forbears. He has won the battle against despair by transmuting the secular virtue of fidelity into the theological virtue of Faith, and by so doing has transmuted the past of memory into the Augustinian eternal present of the promise of salvation. He has changed reality, as Shippey so tellingly perceived, by changing his mind. The poet has led him second by second through the details of feeling by which that change was effected with a sure, compassionate knowingness that rivals that with which Aeschylus in his *Agamemnon* leads Cassandra from the first incoherent dochmiacs of her recoil from her fate to the heroic iambic trimeters of her acceptance of it. His poem is a dramatic masterpiece.

Stanley B. Greenfield

of Words and Deeds: the Coastguard's Maxim Once More

One of the cruxes in *Beowulf* is the maxim that begins the coastguard's response after Beowulf has answered his query as to who these strangers are who have landed thus boldly and openly on the Danish shore:

> Æghwæþres sceal
> scearp scyldwiga   gescād witan,
> worda ond worca,   sē þe wēl þenceð.
>   (287–89)[1]

Critics have been puzzled as to how to interpret the maxim, and their differences of opinion have recently been summarized by T. A. Shippey:

one scholar decided that the words were just a pompous way for the coastguard to say *he* was a keen-witted shield-bearer; another thought they were a kind of apology; a third takes them as grudging deference ("I suppose you know what you are talking about"); naturally they have been seen as conveying involved and subtle moral lessons.[2]

The basic problem, as Shippey observes, is that the words and syntax of the maxim literally say something that seems semantically unacceptable:

Æghwæpres can mean "each" or "every", and *gescad* comes from a root meaning to divide, or separate, or decide, so there is a little semantic play in the concepts, but hardly very much. The latest published rendering (Howell D. Chickering's text and translation of 1977) has: "A keen-witted shield-bearer who thinks things out carefully must know the distinction between words and deeds, keep the difference clear." This is syntactically accurate. However, it makes no sense. Any fool can tell the difference between words and deeds, and Beowulf's deeds anyway turn out much the same as his words.[3]

We have then in the coastguard's gnomic remark a statement that, all readers would agree if they thought about it, cannot be taken literally. Most of the translations I have looked at, confronted with this situation, either do as Chickering has done, and translate literally, leaving the reader to make his or her own sense out of the passage, or they interpret to the effect that "An acute warrior . . . should be a judge of both words and deeds."[4] The translator need not (and does not) account for the interpretation. It is interesting, however, to follow the arguments of the two recent critics who seem to have given most thought to the maxim and, by different routes, come to this interpretation, though, it would seem, with differing applications of it. Obviously, I do not think either has resolved the problems posed by the maxim, nor have they explored all the possibilities of its meaning and applicaton in context. I have, I think, a more satisfactory solution to offer.

The earlier critic is Robert E. Kaske, in his now-famous essay on *sapientia et fortitudo*.[5] Kaske contends that the coastguard, in his original challenge to Beowulf, has imputed recklessness to the hero, but that Beowulf's answer removes this impression for him by its wisdom, the removal being signalled particularly by "the difficult gnomic passage with which he begins." Kaske then quotes the passage and gives a literal translation: "The keen shield-warrior who thinks well must know the difference between these two—words and deeds." He then immediately continues:

We can see here, I think, a double appeal to the *sapientia et fortitudo* ideal. The coastwarden, seeing the Geats land, had formed an impression of their audacity; he now learns from Beowulf's speech that they are wisely led, and remarks that it is best to judge by words as well as deeds—words as the means of judging *sapientia*, as deeds are the means of judging *fortitudo*. His *scearp scyldwiga . . se pe wel penceð* appears to be a further appeal to the ideal, meaning, in effect, "the hero equal to all occasions through his *fortitudo* and *sapientia*."[6]

Presumably Kaske was aware of the discrepancy between his literal translation and his interpretation, though his analysis, which I have quoted in full, does not indicate such awareness. His interpretive appeal is to the widespread Graeco-Latin-Christian topos, and such an appeal, especially for a difficult passage, is certainly reasonable, given the ambience of the poem and its cultural milieu. Kaske's *application* of the maxim, if I read him aright, is to Beowulf: the coastwarden is saying, in effect, yes, you have not only *fortitudo* but also *sapientia* (though it may be that Kaske also sees the coastwarden applying the maxim to his own discernment; he is not clear on this). But apart from the lexical-syntactic leap of equating the difference between words and deeds with "judging by words as well as deeds" and the ambiguity of application, does the interpretation fit the dramatic context? Let me postpone discussion of this matter until we have looked at the second critic's analysis.

The more recent critic is T. A. Shippey, in the monograph cited above. His interpretive appeal is to the "social and dramatic context" of the maxim. Proverbs, he says, "are not merely linguistic phenomena" but have an "extra-linguistic frame." We use formulas which may be "entirely tautologous ('Business is business') or on a literal level meaningless ('Don't cross your bridges till you come to them'), without feeling any block in communication at all." And "it is this non-verbal knowledge that we need to be able to understand the coastguard's 'gnome'."[7] Shippey goes on to demonstrate that in their speeches the coastguard and Beowulf "make signals to each other of mutual respect, taking care to adopt the appropriate roles of Official Inspector (not Personal Challenger), Modest Petitioner (rather than Officious Volunteer)." The coastguard then, he argues, has to make up his mind on the basis of Beowulf's words alone, since "the situation *has not changed*," and accordingly Shippey interprets the maxim as saying that it is

the duty of a sharp shield-warrior to decide correctly, even on inadequate evidence. "He must be able to judge *everything*, words *as well as* deeds." That is what the maxim says, and the coastguard follows it immediately by doing the right thing and letting the newcomers pass. . . . He backs his judgment to the length of allowing them to keep their weapons and offering to look after their boat.[8]

Shippey's application of the maxim, unlike Kaske's, is clearly to the coastguard himself, *not* to Beowulf, and his "social context" is that of "heroic good manners" (p. 14).

This appeal to a social context has as much to recommend it, I think, as Kaske's to the topos of *sapientia et fortitudo*; but I am still concerned by the leap from the literal meaning of the words to the interpretation both critics make, a leap which ignores the rather insistent semantic stress of separation in the word *gescad*, a semantic stress apparently conceded by both critics. I think there is a better social context in which to place the maxim, one which is reinforced by the larger context of Old English poetry and of *Beowulf* itself; and the interpretation which follows from *this* appeal is better suited both to the immediate dramatic context and to the literal meaning of the passage. I should like to approach this interpretation first by looking more closely at *Æghwæpres . . . gescad witan, / worda ond worca*, then by examining the possibilities of application of the maxim to Beowulf and the coastguard in the dramatic context, and finally by suggesting the social context to which I think appeal can best be made for solving the literal-level meaninglessness of the maxim.

The only parallel of any sort I can find to *gescad witan* with a genitive referring to two different things or concepts (like *words* and *deeds*) occurs in the Old English translation of Bede's *Historia Ecclesiastica*, Bk. II, ch. 2. The occasion is Augustine's conference with the clergy of the Britons, to urge them to adopt the practices of the Roman Church. When the British monks ask one of their leaders whether they ought to adopt these practices, he replies that if

Augustine is meek and humble when they approach him,
yes; but if he is stern and proud, no. They, in turn, ask how
they can distinguish which he is: "Be hwam magan we þises
gescad witan?" (translating the Latin *unde hoc dinoscere
ualemus?*).[9] The *þises* clearly refers back to the two attitudes,
meekness or pride, just as the *Æghwæþres* of our *Beowulf*
passage is proleptic of *worda ond worca*. This parallel, even if
not exact, would seem to offer some confirmation that the
coastguard's maxim is somehow suggesting a discrimination
between words and deeds, however literally nonsensical on the
surface that may be, rather than suggesting judgment *by both*
words and deeds.

When we turn to the dramatic context of the maxim,
what do we find? The coastguard has challenged Beowulf
and his men—and his emphasis is on *who* they are and *whence*
they have come (at the beginning and ending of his speech),
and by implication *why* they have come (an implication the
hero is not slow to perceive, as his answer shows). Beowulf
responds with the information requested, and adds

> We þurh holdne hige   hlāford þīnne,
> sunu Healfdenes   sēcean cwōmon . . . ;
> (266–67)

(With loyal heart we have come to seek your lord,
Halfdane's son . . .)

and he asks diplomatically for good advice from his inter-
locutor. He concludes his speech by saying he can *advise*
Hrothgar how to overcome his enemy:

> gyf him edwenden   æfre scolde
> bealuwa bisigu   bōt eft cuman . . .
> (280–81)

(If for him change, remedy for each of woes, is ever to
come again . . .)

It is to these last remarks, presumably, that the coastguard
at first replies. In this context it is entirely possible that his
maxim is a commentary on Beowulf's wisdom, but not in
Kaske's sense. Rather it would refer to Beowulf's sense of

discrimination *between* words (the advice he would give Hrothgar) and deeds (his recognition that the action he will advocate *might not* bring about the desired result). I confess I am greatly tempted by this reading, since it retains the literal level of meaning without any semantic leap or interpolation. But I am not sure it does justice to what follows in the coastguard's speech, since it would provide no or little connection with it:

> Ic þæt gehȳre,   þæt þis is hold weorod
> frēan Scyldinga—
>
> (290–91a)

(I hear that this is a band loyal to the lord of the Scyldings—)

which picks up Beowulf's earlier "Wē þurh holdne hige hlāford þīnne. . . ." And the coastguard's following words, "Gewītaþ forð beran / wǣpen and gewǣdu, ic ēow wīsige" ("Go forth bearing weapons and mail-coats: I will guide you"), indicate that *he* has made a discrimination and will take action in line with it. All this suggests that it is more probable that the coastguard is applying the maxim to himself first and foremost.[10] If this is so, what is the social context I alluded to earlier that would reconcile this application to the meaning of discriminating between words and deeds?

I refer to the words/promises vs. deeds topos that appears in a number of Old English poems. In *The Battle of Maldon*, for instance, we are told that Offa had warned Byrhtnoth in the assembly council "þæt þær mōdiglice manega sprǣcon / þe eft æt þearfe þolian noldon" ("that there many spoke boldly who, in turn, at need would not endure"); and Wiglaf's speech to the cowardly retainers is much to the same effect. In *The Wanderer* we have the maxim that a wise warrior does not boast until he knows he is capable of carrying out that boast; and Beowulf's taunt of Unferth, that Grendel would never have done so much damage in Heorot had Unferth's heart and strength been where his mouth was, is much to the same effect. Now, since in his answer to the coastguard's official inquiry (the dramatic context), Beowulf had modestly said he had advice for Hrothgar as to how to rid Heorot of its trouble—with the obvious implication of lending his own physical aid—and since the warden had already sized the hero up as no ordinary *seldguma* (unless appearance lies), the maxim might well be taken as meaning "the sharp shield-warrior must learn to tell the difference between 'empty' words and words which have the resolution and capability of deeds behind them." As Shippey has said, tautology and literal level meaninglessness in speech formulas in no way block communication, and the semantic leap involved in this way of understanding the maxim has the virtue of preserving the idea of discrimination between the words and the deeds.

This interpretation is not entirely new. David Wright, for one, had translated the maxim: "A good soldier who has his wits about him must know how to distinguish between promise and performance."[11] But this possibility seems largely to have been ignored by translators, as I indicated earlier, and has not, so far as I know, been argued by critics.[12] My own forthcoming poetic translation of *Beowulf* tries to capture this meaning as follows:

> Discerning
> guardians of their land must learn to judge
> empty words from words embracing deeds.

I think this is what the poet probably meant by the maxim he put into the coastguard's mouth,[13] and what his audience would have understood from its specific words and syntax in the light of the "extra-linguistic frame of social and dramatic context." It then makes good sense when the coastguard says, "I hear that this is a band loyal to the lord of the Scyldings. Go forth bearing your weapons and mail-coats: I will guide you"; he has distinguished Beowulf's words as ones "embracing deeds," and he will give the hero his requested "good counsel" by leading the Geats himself on the road to Heorot.

Roberta Frank

the Beowulf *Poet's*
Sense *of History*

I don't know how humanity stands it
with a painted paradise at the end of it
without a painted paradise at the end of it
Ezra Pound, *Canto* LXXIV

Awareness of historical change, of the pastness of a past
that itself has depth, is not instinctive to man; there is
nothing natural about a sense of history. Anthropologists
report that the lack of historical perspective is a feature of
primitive thought, and historians that its absence characterizes medieval thinking: Herod in the Wakefield Cycle
swears "by Mahoun in heaven," the medieval Alexander is a
knight, and heathen Orléans boasts a university.[1] Morton
Bloomfield has shown that a sense of history, even a
tentative, underdeveloped one, was a rare thing in fourteenth-century England, and that Chaucer's attention to
chronology and his preoccupation with cultural diversity
have affinities with aspects of the early Italian Renaissance.[2]
But what in the Anglo-Saxon period stimulated a monastic
author to stress the differences between ancient days and
his own, to paint the past as if it were something other than

the present?³ The *Beowulf* poet's reconstruction of a northern heroic age is chronologically sophisticated, rich in local color and fitting speeches. The poet avoids obvious anachronisms and presents such an internally consistent picture of Scandinavian society around A.D. 500 that his illusion of historical truth has been taken for the reality.⁴

The poet's heroic age is full of men both "emphatically pagan and exceptionally good," men who believe in a God whom they thank at every imaginable opportunity.⁵ Yet they perform all the pagan rites known to Tacitus, and are not Christian. The temporal distance between past and present, acknowledged in the opening words of the poem—"in geardagum" ("in days of yore")—is heard again when Beowulf, as yet unnamed, makes his entrance. He is the strongest of men "on þæm dæge þysses lifes" ("on that day of this life" 197, 790).⁶ The alliterating demonstratives stress the remoteness of the past, here and later when a hall-servant in Heorot looks after all the visitors' bedtime needs "swylce þy dogore heaþoliðende habban scoldon" ("such as in those days seafarers were wont to have" 1797–98). The descriptive clause distances but also glosses over, shadowing with vagueness an unknown corner of the past. The poet is so attracted by the aristocratic rituals of life in the hall, so intent on historical verisimilitude, that he imagines everything, even basic human needs, to have changed over time. His proposition that golden tapestries hanging in the hall were a wondrous sight for the partying sixth-century retainers is quickly modified in the direction of reality: "þara þe on swylc staraõ" ("for those who look upon such things" 996); even in Heorot not all beefy breakers-of-rings in their cups would have had an eye for interior design. The vividness of the past underlines, paradoxically, its distance.

The *Beowulf* poet has a strong sense of cultural diversity, as strong perhaps as Chaucer's. Three times in the "Knight's Tale" Chaucer explains the behavior of characters with the clause "as was tho the gyse"; in "The Legend of Cleopatra" he has Anthony sent out to win kingdoms and honor "as was usance"; and in "The Legend of Lucrece" he notes approvingly that Roman wives prized a good name "at thilke tyme."⁷ The Old English poet maintains a similar perspective. He praises the Geats for their ancient custom of keeping armor and weapons at their sides at all times: "They were always prepared for war, whether at home or in the field, as their lord required" (1246-50). He has Hrothgar admire their steadfastness, the dependability of men who live blameless "ealde wisan" ("in the old fashion" 1865). When the dragon's ravages begin, the poet makes the aged Beowulf fear that he has transgressed "ofer ealde riht" ("against ancient law" 2330): pagans have their own moral code, separating them from the author and us. The poet emphasizes cultural differences not only between present and past but also between coeval peoples. He depicts the Swedes and Geats as more authentically primitive, more pagan in outlook and idiom, than the Danes. When a roughhewn Beowulf arrives at the Danish court he puts himself in the hands of a skilled local who "knew the custom of the retainers" (359). Ongentheow, the grizzled king of the Swedes, threatens to pierce ("getan" 2940) captives on the gallows for the pleasure of carrion birds.[8] The Geats consult auspices (204); Beowulf, like the Scandinavian heroes of old, trusts in his own might (418, 670, 1270, 1533); the messenger imagines a raven boasting to an eagle of carnage-feasts (3024-27); and Hæthcyn's slaying of Herebeald (2435-43) imitates a fratricide in the Norse pantheon: euhemerism becomes, in the poet's hands, an aid to historical research.[9]

The poet's sense of anachronism is revealed in his characters' speeches, utterances that avoid all distinctively Christian names and terms. The actors themselves have a sense of the past and of the future. They are able to look back two generations, tracing the origins of the feud between the Geats and the Swedes (2379-96, 2472-89, 2611-19, 2379-96). They can also forecast the feuds of the next generation. There is a fine display of chronological wit when Beowulf, on the basis of a piece of information picked up at the Danish court, turns the Ingeld legend into a political prophecy, a sequence of events likely to occur in the near future (2024-69). The poet's sense of historic succession is so strong and the internal chronology of the poem so carefully worked out that his audience knows why Hrothulf and Heoroweard have to be kept in the wings a little while longer. After Beowulf's death, it is clear even to the messenger that Eadgils is not likely to sit for long on the Swedish throne without avenging his brother's murder on the new king of the Geats, son of the slayer. The poet does not make earlier Danish and Germanic heroes like Scyld, Heremod, Finn, Offa, Sigemund, Eormenric and Hama contemporaneous with the sixth-century events narrated, but sets them in a distant mirror, conveying the illusion of a many-storied long-ago. Such chronological tidiness is all the more remarkable for its appearance in a poetic vernacular that has no distinctive future tense, and whose chief adverbs of recollection and continuation—"þa" and "siððan" ("thereupon": looking forward; "at that time," "from the time that": looking back)—are almost always ambiguous.[10]

Philosophically, in order to have a sense of history at all, the *Beowulf* poet had to hold certain premises about man and his role on earth. Despite his professional concern with the timeless, he had to be engaged to some extent with the things of this world; he needed a positive attitude toward secular wisdom and some notion of natural law. Above all, he had to believe that pagan Germanic legend had intellectual value and interest for Christians. These concepts were available to twelfth-century humanists. Christian Platonists like William of Conches, Bernard Silvestris, and Alan of Lille shared an unpolemical attitude toward the pagan past and stressed the importance of earthly understanding as the base of all human knowledge.[11] But in the central theological traditions of the early medieval West and, more specifically, in the teachings of Aldhelm, Bede, and Alcuin, there is no trace of this liberal mentality.[12] No contemporary of these three concerned himself with man on earth, looking upon heathen virtues and customs with an indulgent eye, and had his vision survive. The patristic tradition that pagan story is diabolically inspired, that unbaptized pagans lie lamenting in hell, was too strong.

Purely from the perspective of the history of ideas, the *Beowulf* poet's chronological acrobatics and fascination with cultural diversity, his positive view of those who lived "while men loved the lawe of kinde," needs explanation.[13] We cannot, wielding editorial knives, remove these ideas from the text the way other late-seeming growths have been excised solely on the grounds that the poem is early.[14] "It is a dangerous principle to adopt in literary investigation that nothing we do not readily understand can be rationally explained. We must as a working principle assume that everything in a work of art is capable of explanation even at the cost of oversubtlety and even error . . . . We must not assume, unless we are finally forced to it, that the writer or composer did not know what he was doing."[15] Professor Bloomfield offered this guidance in a review of Kenneth Sisam's *The Structure of Beowulf*. Sisam contends that "great difficulties stand in the way of all explanations that make the poet a deep thinker, attempting themes and ways of conveying them that might be tried on a select body of readers in a more advanced age."[16] The fact remains, however, that the poem, for an early composition, is full of oddly advanced notions. Twenty years ago Morton Bloomfield observed that "ealde riht" ("old law" 2330) in *Beowulf* referred not to the Mosaic Code, the Old Law, but to natural law, and noted that the moral laws of the Old Testament were often equated with this natural law, "although in general this equation is later than the early Middle Ages."[17] More recently, he has seen behind Beowulf's single combat with Grendel the concept of the *iudicium Dei*, a calling upon God to decide the justice of an action: "Let wise God, the holy Lord, adjudge the glory to whichever side he thinks fit," says Beowulf (685-87); the champion will rely in the coming struggle on the judgment of God (440-41).[18] Something like the judicial duel appears to have been a feature of medieval Scandinavian society. Yet all the early evidence for trial by combat from Tacitus to Pope Nicholas I is Continental; there is no documentation for multilateral ordeal in England before the Norman Conquest. The *Beowulf* poet's use of the form and spirit of the judicial duel, whether he derived the concept from Tacitus, from the Franks, or from the Danelaw, emphasizes—like his auguries, sacrifices, and exotic cremations—the temporal and cultural distance between the pagan Scandinavian past and the England of his own day. His backward glance is both admiring and antiquarian.

Anglo-Saxon scholarship has done its best to read *Beowulf* as the seventh and eighth centuries would have. Because Aldhelm and Bede insisted that the only suitable subject for poetry was a religious one, and because secular epics and long historical poems only started to appear in the later ninth century, Margaret Goldsmith had little choice but to interpret *Beowulf* allegorically.[19] Alcuin's only known

comment on heroic literature in ecclesiastical contexts is an
orthodox denunciation of it as a heathen distraction.[20] W. F.
Bolton's new book on *Alcuin and Beowulf* discovers, pre-
dictably, that the great schoolmaster would have found
Beowulf guilty, flawed, vengeful, incapable even of pro-
tecting his people.[21] Charles Donahue attempts to account
for the existence of an eighth-century Old English poem
about noble pagans by invoking Irish views of pre-Christian
goodness, legends that tell of virtuous pagans and their
natural knowledge of God.[22] Yet the stories of Cormac and
Morand that he cites are not easy to date (that of Cormac is
surely no earlier than the last quarter of the tenth century),
and Donahue concedes that they are "later than *Beowulf* and
can be viewed only as parallel developments of that early
insular Christian humanism . . . ."[23] Patrick Wormald has
recently located a social and cultural context for the composition of heroic literature in the aristocratic climate of
early English Christianity, in the integration of monastic
and royal houses.[24] Yet the aristocratic nature of the early
English church is, if anything, more pronounced with the
passage of time, reaching a kind of culmination under the
successors of Alfred.[25] The "vast zone of silence" Wormald
observes existing between Bede and the *Beowulf* poet[26] may
be due not only to Bede's fundamentalism but also to the
centuries separating the two authors.

When in the Anglo-Saxon period did pagans become
palatable? A positive attitude toward the pagans of classical
antiquity is visible in translations of the Alfredian period.
While the real Orosius, writing in the first decades of the
fifth century, was as reluctant as Bede to say anything good
about those who lived before the Christian Era, the Old
English paraphrase of *Orosius* from around 900 contemplates
with pleasure the bravery, honorable behavior, and renown
of several early Romans, adds references to Julius Caesar's
clemency, generosity, and courage, and even suggests that
in some of their customs the Romans of the Christian Era
were worse than their pagan ancestors.[27] Unlike his source,
the Old English translator does not think in an exclusively
religious way: what matters is how rulers of the past served
God's purpose, not whether they were Christians or
pagans.[28]

Boethius' *Consolation of Philosophy,* translated by King

Alfred himself, resorted to pre-Christian human history and to pagan mythology for some fifty illustrations, finding archetypal patterns in the behavior of a Nero or a Hercules just as the *Beowulf* poet locates exemplary models in Heremod and Beowulf. In the late ninth and early tenth centuries, the *Consolation* enjoyed a considerable vogue among Carolingian commentators, at least one of whom, Remigius of Auxerre, Alfred may have used.[29] Alfred thrusts aside much of Remigius' Neoplatonic speculation along with his scientific and theological information, but is quick to insert commentary material having to do with classical myths. He occasionally gives a pagan analogy for a Christian concept, something Alcuin never managed to do.[30] Alfred's story of Orpheus teaches that a man who wishes to see the true light of God must not turn back to his old errors.[31] Boethius' tale of Jupiter overthrowing the giants who warred on heaven is shown by Alfred to reflect—*secundum fidem gentilium*—Nimrod's building of the Tower of Babel and God's subsequent division of tongues.[32] Alfred stresses the underlying truthfulness of Boethius' pagan fables. The details of Hercules' taming the Centaurs, burning the Hydra's poisonous heads, and slaying Cacus are skipped, but the myth itself is universalized into a philosophic reflection on life and on the meaning of victory and defeat: good men fight for honor in this world, to win glory and fame; for their deeds, they dwell beyond the stars in eternal bliss.[33] Circe in Alfred's paraphrase is no longer the wicked enchantress of Boethius, but a vulnerable goddess who falls violently in love with Odysseus at first sight; she turns his men into animals only after they, out of homesickness, plot to abandon their lord.[34] Alfred, like the *Beowulf* poet, looks for the moral and psychological laws of things, tries to understand and learn rather than condemn. Only once in his paraphrase does he abandon the world of classical paganism for a Germanic allusion; it is a small step, but full of significance for the future of Old English poetry. He translates Boethius' "Where now are the bones of faithful Fabricius?" as "Where now are the bones of the famous and wise goldsmith Weland?"[35]

When in the Anglo-Saxon period could a Christian author exploit pagan Germanic legend for its intellectual and moral values? Seventh- and eighth-century sources furnish evidence that English monks were overfond of harpists,

CAMROSE LUTHERAN COLLEGE
LIBRARY

secular tales, eating and drinking; but such worldly tastes
provoked the scorn and hostility of their superiors: "What
has Ingeld to do with Christ? The House is narrow, it cannot
hold both. The King of Heaven wishes to have no fellowship
with so-called kings, who are pagan and lost."[36] But by the
late ninth century, even an archbishop—Fulk of Rheims,
who recruited Remigius of Auxerre, corresponded with
King Alfred and sent Grimbald to him—could in one and the
same sentence refer to a letter of Gregory the Great on
kingship and to "Teutonic books regarding a certain King
Hermenric."[37] A century and a half later, puritanical youth
can be seen shaking its fist at reckless middle age in a letter
that one cleric of Bamberg Cathedral wrote to another
complaining of their bishop, Gunther, who spent all his time
reading of Attila and Theodoric when not composing epics
himself.[38]

The *Beowulf* poet insists on the virtue and paganism of
his characters, and is unusually explicit about their heathen
rites, describing them lovingly and at length.[39] A slender
tradition of extolling the good customs of Germanic pagans
can be traced in Roman authors, but this tradition does not
enjoy a continuous run through the medieval period. The
first known use of Tacitus' *Germania* after Cassiodorus
occurs in the mid-ninth-century *Translatio Sancti Alexandri* by
the monk Rudolf of Fulda.[40] This work, commissioned by
the aristocratic abbot of the monastery of Wildeshausen in
Saxony, opens with a description of the moral practices and
brave deeds of the early pagan ancestors of the Saxons.
Bede, monk of Wearmouth-Jarrow and historian of the
English church and people (c. 731), is reticent about the
doings of the Anglo-Saxons before their conversion and
shows no inclination to celebrate heathens or their habits.[41]
Widukind, monk of Corvey and historian of the Continental
Saxons (c. 967), does not hesitate to do so. He borrows
Rudolf of Fulda's account of pagan institutions and shapes
the heathen past of his nation into a carefully contoured
whole. He develops a single thread of historical tradition
into a complex narrative, incorporating heroic dialogue,
vivid details, and dramatic scenes, in much the same way
that the *Beowulf* poet seems to have worked.[42] Widukind saw
his efforts in recording the deeds of the Saxon leaders
(*principum nostrorum res gestae litteris . . . commendare*) as equal in

value to the service he earlier performed with his two lives
of saints. He wrote his history, he said, partly by virtue of
his monastic calling, partly as a member of *gens Saxonum*.[43]
One historical sense seems to beget another: Widukind, like
the *Beowulf* poet, learned much from classical historians,
including the art of depicting people whose behavior made
sense within the framework of their age and culture.

The *Beowulf* poet's attribution of monotheism to his
good heathens is sometimes taken as revealing his ignorance
of Germanic paganism, sometimes as a sign of his inability to
see the past as anything other than the present. Like
Widukind, he mentions pagan error, briefly and in passing
(175-88), before depicting noble pagan monotheists for some
three thousand lines. In the Alfredian *Orosius*, as in the fifth-
century original, God is shown to have always guided the
world, even in pagan times. But the paraphraser adds a few
touches of his own: the pagan Leonidas places his trust in
God; even Hannibal is heard to lament that God would not
allow him domination over Rome.[44] The *Beowulf* poet, too,
makes his heroes refer again and again to the power and
providence of a single God, and he takes Beowulf's victory as
a sign that "God has always ruled mankind, as he still does"
(700-02, 1057-58). The Danes' hymn in Heorot to a single
Almighty (90-98) expresses a Boethian wonder at seeing an
invisible God through his creation. Wiglaf's contention that
the fallen Beowulf shall for a long time "abide in the Lord's
keeping" (3109) suggests a Boethian philosophy of salvation,
of individuals ascending by reason alone to a knowledge of
one God. It was probably Remigius of Auxerre who around
900 compiled a short treatise on the gods of classical
antiquity, announcing—in the final paragraph of his prologue—that a single divine being lay behind the multiplicity
of Greek and Roman names for the gods.[45] Renewed contact
with the texts of late antiquity, especially Macrobius,
Martianus Capella, and Boethius, ended by making some
men at least think in a less narrowly religious way.[46] The
Beowulf poet allows glimpses of a *paradiso terrestre* in the distant
past—brief, transitory but glowing moments whose thrust
is to remind his hearers of all the .unfulfilled potential of
their pre-Christian heritage.

What emerges from a sufficiently intense concern for
history in any literary work is a series of projections

inevitably focused by the particular anxieties of the writer. Alfred's *Boethius* reveals that king's fascination with the psychology of the tyrant, his concern for the proper uses of power and wealth, and his insistence, against Boethius, that temporal possessions can be put to good ends.[47] The *Beowulf* poet seems especially concerned to distinguish between justifiable and unjustifiable aggression, to place the warlike activities of his pagan hero in an ethical context. Beowulf resorts to arms out of concern for the defenseless and for the common good, not exclusively out of lust for conquest, ambition, or vengefulness. He is heroic and pious, a pagan prince of peace.[48] Christianity in the early barbarian West may have thought it was being assimilated by a warrior aristocracy, but it ended up—even before the Crusades— accommodating itself to the heroic values of the nobility. The blending of the two cultures would have begun at the time of conversion, but it was an extended process. At one stage, revelry in the hall, vowing oaths of fidelity to a lord, ambushes and plundering and slaughter, all the duties and responsibilities of heroic society were seen as demonic and damnable, as in the eighth-century *Life of Guthlac* by Felix of Crowland.[49] In the Old English *Guthlac A*, the poet even sends in devils to remind the royal saint and hermit of his secular obligations, to tempt him with the hall-delights long abandoned after a warlike youth (191–99). The heroic life is the opposite of the life that leads to salvation.

The synthesis of religious and heroic idealism present in *Beowulf* was probably not available to monastic authors at an early date. In the 930s, Odo of Cluny wrote his *Life of St. Gerald of Aurillac* in order to demonstrate for his own aristocratic circle how a layman and noble lord, a man out in the world, could lead a holy existence.[50] Odo gives moral and religious dimensions to Gerald's lifelong martial career. The warrior soothes the suspicious, squelches the malicious, and puts down the violent who refuse to come to terms; he does this not for personal gain but in order to achieve peace for his society. So Beowulf restrains, one after the other, coastguard, Unferth, and Grendel, making friends of two potential foes and ridding Denmark of monsters who pay no wergild. Ottonian Saxony as portrayed by Widukind is—in the heroic cast of its values and the ferocity of its feuds— very close to the world of *Beowulf*.[51] Tenth-century monastic narratives seem, like *Beowulf*, able to find a place for heroic values—even fighting and the bonds of kinship—within a Christian framework. In Hrotsvitha's *Gongolfus* the ideals of a warrior's life are fused with the Christian goal of *caritas*, while Ruotger's *Life of Bruno*, archbishop of Cologne and brother of Otto the Great, reports with some under-statement that "priestly religion and royal determination united their strength" in him.[52] Like these works, the Old English poems that we can date to the tenth century set up no unresolvable contradictions between piety and the heroic life. *The Battle of Maldon*, composed after 991 and regarded as the finest utterance of the Anglo-Saxon heroic age (and most "Germanic" since Tacitus), contains a prayer by a warlord soon to be venerated by the monks of Ely.[53] *The Battle of Brunanburh*, from around 937, is red with blood, God's rising and setting sun, and a historical perspective reminiscent of manifest destiny. *Judith*, probably from the same century, focuses on a prayerful heroine who chops off heads with only slightly less savoir-faire than Beowulf. Between *Bede's Death Song* and *Maldon* something happened to Old English poetry, whether we call this something rebarbarization or adapting Christian models for a new and only partly literate secular aristocracy. New syntheses were becoming possible. Unlike Anglian stone crosses of the eighth century, English religious sculpture after the Danish invasions was able to draw, like *Beowulf*, on pagan myth and heroic legend.[54]

In still another area, the vision of the *Beowulf* poet seems to derive from contemporary concerns, from a need to establish in the present an ideological basis for national unity. I suggested in an earlier paper that the *Beowulf* poet's incentive for composing an epic about sixth-century Scyldings may have had something to do with the fact that, by the 890s at least, Heremod, Scyld, Healfdene, and the rest, were taken to be the common ancestors both of the Anglo-Saxon royal family and of the ninth-century Danish immigrants, the *Scaldingi*.[55] The *Beowulf* poet admires kings who, like Hrothgar, have regional overlordship of surrounding tribes and who, like Beowulf, are powerful enough to keep neighbors in check. A key political catchword—"þeodcyning" ("great" or "national king")—is prominently displayed by the poet in his opening sentence.

He depicts the Danish nation's former glory in a time when powerful kings had been able to unite the various peoples of the land, something that did not occur with any permanence in Denmark or England until the tenth century.[56] The *Beowulf* poet does his best to attach his pagan champion to as many peoples as possible—Danes, Geats, Swedes, Wulfings, and Wægmundings—as if to make him the more authentically representative of the culture and traditions of central Scandinavia: an archetypal Northman. Epics have their propagandist appeal. There is a relationship, however indirect, between Virgil's account of the majesty of Rome's legendary past, the glory of her ancient traditions, and the Augustan program to bring back a "pristine" patriotism and code of morals. Both the *Aeneid* and *Beowulf* are in some sense historical novels, mythically presented, philosophically committed, and focused on the adventures of a new hero.[57] Both poets project onto the distant past features of the society of their own day, consciously and deliberately, in order to provide a sense of continuity. Virgil's Rome is grounded in an earlier Rome; the *Beowulf* poet anchors the West Saxon *imperium* in a brilliant North Germanic antiquity. By the twelfth century, the Normans were very French; yet the more French they became, the more they stressed their Danish ancestry and the heroic deeds of their founding dynasty.[58] By the first quarter of the tenth century, the Danes in England were working hard to be more Christian and English than the English: at mid-century both archbishops of England, Oda and Oskytel, were of Danish extraction.[59] An Old English poem about northern heathens and northern heroes, opening with the mythical figure of Scyld from whom the ruling houses of both Denmark and England were descended, fits nicely with the efforts of Alfred and his successors to promote an Anglo-Danish brotherhood, to see Dane and Anglo-Saxon as equal partners in a united kingdom.

The sadness, the poignancy, the *lacrimae rerum* we associate with *Beowulf* come from the epic poet's sense of duration, of how "time condemns itself and all human endeavor and hopes."[60] Yet though Heorot is snuffed out by flames and noble pagans and their works perish, the poet does not scorn the heroic fellowship whose passing he has had to tell. There is still something left worth ambition:

"The task to be accomplished is not the conservation of the past, but the redemption of the hopes of the past."[61] The last word in the poem is uttered by sixth-century Geats who commend Beowulf as "lofgeornost" ("most intent on glory"). Lady Philosophy assured Boethius (II, pr. 7) that the praise won even by noble souls is of slight value: only a small part of a tiny earth is inhabited, and by nations differing in language, custom, and philosophy; even written eulogies fail because time veils them and their authors in obscurity. King Alfred did not entirely accept her last point. He argued that the fame of a great man can also fade through a kind of *trahison des clercs*—"þurh þa heardsælþa þara writera ðæt hi for heora slæwðe 7 for gimeleste 7 eac for recceleste forleton unwriten þara monna ðeawas 7 hiora dæda, þe on hiora dagum formæroste 7 weorðgeornuste wæron"[62] ("through the bad conduct of those writers who—in their sloth and in carelessness and also in negligence—leave unwritten the virtues and deeds of those men who in their day were most renowned and most intent on honor"). The purpose of *Beowulf*, as Morton Bloomfield has often reminded us, is heroic celebration, to present the deeds of a great man in order "to give his audience new strength and a model."[63] Those of us who were privileged to be Professor Bloomfield's students at Harvard know what such a model can be worth.

E. Talbot Donaldson

Langland and
some Scriptural Quotations

In this paper I shall discuss briefly some passages from *Piers Plowman* in which Long Will's verbal wilfulness extends to his use of sacred writing. I shall begin with several instances of his treating such writing with a playfulness that seems almost light-hearted, though in fact what he is doing is exercising wit in one of its most characteristic functions, that is, to enhance accepted truths by presenting them from a somewhat unusual angle—what's oft been thought, but ne'er quite so idiosyncratically expressed. I shall conclude with a rather different though equally surprising use of Scripture, in which Langland expropriates a text from St. Paul in order to give himself authority for putting forth a theological doctrine that totters on the border of orthodoxy.

The title of Bernard F. Huppé's pioneering article of thirty years ago, "*Petrus, id est, Christus*: Word Play in *Piers Plowman*; the B-Text,"[1] glances at the most authoritative precedent for Langland's use of word play in his handling of biblical texts. In Langland's reference to Matt. 16:18, "Et ego dico tibi, quia tu es Petrus, et super hanc petram aedificabo ecclesiam meam," he does not directly exploit Christ's word play (B 15.212,[2] quoted in Huppé's title), but he reflects it when he conflates the text with 1 Cor. 10:4, "petra autem erat Christus," in order to achieve his half-identification of Piers with Christ: Peter = rock, rock = Christ, therefore Piers = Christ, things equal to the same thing being equal to each other. Elsewhere, Langland is more playful, as in Imaginative's witty proof to the Dreamer that on Judgment Day the just man will be saved: "Saluabitur vix Iustus in die Iudicij; / Ergo saluabitur" (B 12.281-82). This is a splendid abuse of a quasi-negative to achieve a triumphant affirmation, one that St. Peter, who is being quoted (1 Pet. 4:8), might well have found surprising. That Langland was pleased with this word play is suggested not only by his retaining it in C but by his pointing to it. In the B-text, in the Dreamer's recapitulation of his recent experiences (13.19) he tells us merely that Imaginative said, "vix saluabitur [iustus]"; but in C (16.22-23) this is expanded to his telling how Imaginative said that "iustus by-fore iesu in die iudicii / Non saluabitur bote uix helpe." Here poor vix is taken firmly in hand and forced to help save the just man whom vix was syntactically threatening to damn.[3]

Langland liked to use such syntactical choplogic to exploit the potentialities of language in order to give a text an added or somewhat different meaning. One is, indeed, occasionally reminded of the transformation by the French monk Radulfus Glaber of the character Nemo so that he no longer represents a human negative but becomes a human affirmation: Nemo Deum vidit means not that no one has seen God but that a certain person named Nemo has seen God. And, since in the Middle Ages Nemo is the subject of countless generalizations and prohibitions, he has done all sorts of other marvelous and forbidden things.[4] In his discussion of beggars in connection with Piers's pardon, Langland tells us (B 7.88–89) that "The book banneþ beggerie and blameþ hem in þis manere: / Iunior fui etenim senui, & non vidi iustum derelictum nec semen eius querens panem." Now the Book surely blames begging, but does so in terms less circumlocutory[5] than this passage from Ps. 36:25, which is generally rendered: "I have been young, and now am old; yet have I not seen the righteous forsaken, nor his seed begging his bread." As it stands, this seems to say that the righteous man and and his son will not have to beg, perhaps because, to quote one of Langland's favorite texts (Ps. 33:11, cited after B 9.109 and 11.283), "Inquirentes . . . Dominum non minuentur omni bono." But the fact that the just man will not have to beg amounts to a most imprecise injunction against begging. Langland seems to have exploited the syntactical ambiguity that is potential (if latent) in the collocation *iustum derelictum* by—as it were—reversing the terms. The usual translation takes *iustum* as a substantive (adjective used as a noun) and *derelictum* as a participial adjective modifying it. Langland seems to take *derelictum* as the substantive (which it has every syntactical right to be) and *iustum* as a simple adjective modifying it: I have never seen a just derelict nor his son begging bread. All beggars are unjust derelicts, hence begging is banned. It is true that no Latin dictionary I have consulted lists a substantive use of the participle *derelictus*, and even in English the word *derelict* referring to a person is not recorded until the eighteenth century. But Langland, I think, took delight in devising a new text blaming begging, another blow at those most reprehensible of mendicants, the friars.[6]

Another twisting of syntax to effect a somewhat different meaning from that of the original text occurs in Langland's treatment of a sentence from Innocent III, which he seems to have thought scriptural in origin, for at B 18.388 he speaks of it as "Holy Writ." The sentence in Innocent is, "Ipse est iudex iustus . . . qui nullum malum praeterit impunitum, nullum bonum irremuneratum."[7] In *Piers Plowman* it occurs first when Reason is urging the king to clean up the corruption of his court (B 4.143–44) in two macaronic lines: "For *Nullum malum* þe man mette with *inpunitum* / And bad *Nullum bonum* be *irremuneratum*." If the king's confessor had written down an honest response to Reason's suggestion that he construe this in English, it might have read thus: "For a man named Mr. No-Evil met with Unpunished and told Mr. No-Good to be unrewarded"—i.e., the king should not punish those who do no evil nor reward those who do no good. This seems a program less costly for the royal treasury than Innocent's original, for the king does not have to pay a reward to any one. One might, indeed, accuse Langland of providing some excuse to those confessor-clerks who, we are told, construed the riddle for the king's profit. Still, unlike the confessors', Langland's version of the injunction is for the good of the commons in the realistic setting of the king's court in the poem, where Meed has been effecting both the punishment of the good and the exaltation of the wicked. To reverse this trend may be a modest ideal, but then, first things first.

Another instance of Langland's taking liberties with sacred texts I pointed out a number of years ago, but since it was but briefly discussed and in an obscure place,[8] I repeat it here. It concerns one of the real cruxes in the poem, near the end of Scripture's harangue to the Dreamer:

> God hoteþ heiȝe and lowe þat no man hurte ooþer,
> And seiþ "slee noȝt þat semblable is to myn owene liknesse
> But if I sende þee som tokene," and seiþ *Non mecaberis,*
> Is slee noȝt but suffre.
>
> (B 10.370–73)

Scripture, of all people, should know that *Non moechaberis* means "Thou shalt not commit adultery" and not "Thou shalt not kill." On the other hand, Scripture, of all people, would know what James wrote in his Epistle (2:9–10), a work Langland seems to have known well: "Quicumque autem totam legem servaverit, offendat autem in uno, factus est omnium reus. Qui enim dixit: Non moechaberis, dixit et: Non occides." The usual reading of the second sentence is, of course, "For he that said, Thou shalt not commit adultery, said also, Thou shalt not kill." But it is possible, if perverse, to read it as saying, "He that said, Thou shalt not commit adultery, said thereby [i.e., by those very words], Thou shalt not kill." Though a most surprising word play, it is not an illogical one in view of St. James's statement in the preceding sentence that he who offends in one point of the law is guilty in all.[9] By a strict interpretation of these words, one who commits adultery is guilty of killing, and vice versa. In the A- and B-texts the passage occurs just before the Dreamer interrupts Scripture with his ill-natured complaint (B 10.377), "This is a long lesson . . . and litel am I þe wiser," which in the A-text is the beginning of the poem's conclusion.[10] Perhaps Scripture's word play was the last straw for a Dreamer exasperated by too much riddling dogma. The whole passage disappears from the C-text: the older, graver poet yielded to numerous complaints.

Langland's biblical quotations are generally understandable in context, though at times, as John Alford has ably shown,[11] they also perform an important function in giving structure to the poem by verbal concordance. But on one occasion a quotation seems most puzzling: this is from St. Paul's account (2 Cor. 12:1-5) of his having known a man in Christ fourteen years earlier who had been caught up into paradise, where "audivit arcana verba, quae non licet homini loqui." In Langland's text the line appears in Christ's speech just before he completes the harrowing of hell:

> And my mercy shal be shewed to manye of my
> [halue]breþeren,
> For blood may suffre blood boþe hungry and acale
> Ac blood may noȝt se blood blede but hym rewe:
> *Audiui archana verba que non licet loqui.*
> (B 18.393-96; C 21.438a)

Schmidt, who follows Kane-Donaldson in many readings, does not follow us here in our adoption of *halue* in *haluebreþeren* from the C-text, but he does remark on the striking quality of the quotation: "The poet implicitly identifies himself with St Paul through the verb *Audivi*, referring here to the Apostle's [mystical vision] . . . . This is Langl.'s boldest claim for the value and validity of his own 'visions and revelations.'"[12] Langland has, of course, altered the verb from the third to the first person, probably with the sanction that the man in Christ St. Paul is talking about is generally agreed to be himself. But there seems little necessity on Langland's part (and even less on Christ's) to claim a Pauline revelation of having heard secret things which man is not permitted to utter as authority for having Christ say that he will show mercy to many of his brothers. He has already told us, some ten lines earlier, that at Judgment Day

> . . . to be merciable to man þanne my kynde it askeþ
> For we beþ breþeren of blood, ac noȝt in baptisme alle.
> Ac alle þat beþ myne hole breþeren, in blood and in
> baptisme,
> Shul noȝt be dampned to the deeþ.
> (B 18.375-78; C 21.373-76).

The point in the quotation from St. Paul must lie in the mercy that is promised to many of Christ's half-brothers, the unbaptized, as well as to the baptized. And of course in having Christ say this Langland is treading on controversial if not dangerous ground. His version of the Trojan story, which omits the Emperor's baptism by Gregory's tears, has been the focal point of much discussion of Langland's belief concerning the salvation of the righteous heathen. It has been often argued[13]—most recently and most eloquently by George Russell[14]—that Langland was acquainted with the doctrine of Uthred de Boldon, that sturdy opponent of the Friars and of Friar William Jordan whom Langland satirizes in his Banquet Scene, on the salvation of the heathen. Uthred argued that all men, pagans as well as Christian, were granted a vision of God just before they died, and if, as a result of this *clara visio*, they chose God, the unbaptized might be saved. This doctrine was officially censured under Archbishop Langham, but as Russell has persuasively argued, it appears to be specifically restated in the C-text; and while Russell believes that "there is no sign of its use in B,"[15] it seems to me that the citation from St. Paul is only explicable in the B-text as an acknowledgement on Langland's part that he subscribes to a doctrine concerning the righteous heathen as liberal as Uthred's. And it may have been Uthred's own, since Langland's ascription of his special knowledge to a Pauline vision provides a kind of parallel to the vision Uthred believed might enable those dying unbaptized to obtain salvation.

The first scholarly writing I ever read on *Piers Plowman* was Morton W. Bloomfield's article of 1939 entitled "The Present State of *Piers Plowman* Studies,"[16] and it gives me pleasure to observe in 1981 how much the vastly improved state of *Piers Plowman* studies, and of our knowledge of that crotchety, wilful, apocalyptic poet William Langland, depends on the many contributions of Morton Bloomfield, a scholar of great learning and generous heart. These textual tidbits are offered to garnish the substantial dishes at his feast.

George Kane

the Perplexities
of William Langland

There are situations for which, at their height, it is impossible to achieve durable and intelligent explanations because
the forms of thinking available at that moment are inadequate. *Piers Plowman* constitutes the response of a poet
with an organizing intelligence of a considerable order to
such a situation, that of eschatology in fourteenth-century
England. Its paradigm is the variety of appearances the poem
can present: of a statement of recourse to doctrinal re-
assurances realized in powerfully imaginative expression; or
of a succession of compulsive recurrences to the ultimate
incomprehensibility of the relation of God and man as the
age conceived this historically; or of a reaction of indignation
at men's failure to respond to divine love; or of an immense
concern about the consequences of that failure.

Those appearances are contrived. They can all be related,
but they are not all complementary. Some, indeed, imply
major anomalies and contradictions; these the poem, read as
a whole, does not resolve. Its ultimate expression of help-
lessness, the real feeling of its end, must derive from

Langland's perception of the impossibility of resolution. We cannot safely impute to him the attitudes of the Dreamer, which are in the first instance only immediate dramatic registers of that sense of impossibility. The poet may well have actually refrained from defining his own attitudes. In any event his own perplexities will necessarily have been of another order of insight than those of his creation, the hasty, headlong Dreamer. The evidence for this is the poem, whether seen as a distancing of a predicament to the last point short of dismissal or as a sustained expression of optimism, an act of faith.

Langland's experience of intense spiritual unease, far from being remarkable, was part of a *"prise de la conscience* of an entire society for which the existing forms, social, intellectual, and religious, were no longer adequate." That condition arose "from the very heart of Christendom"; its preoccupation was the state of the Church, reform the focus of attention.[1] In those particulars Langland is typical.

To judge from the texts of his poem, he conceived of himself as essentially orthodox and would likely have been appalled by the imputation to himself of heterodoxy, let alone heresy. The poem clearly and repeatedly affirms the great articles of the faith: the existence of an omnipotent, personal, trinitarian God, the immortality of the soul, the original sin of Adam, the essentially necessary benevolence of the Deity toward mankind, the redemption, the divine origin and authority of scripture. Some of its most vehement writing registers that certain of those major doctrines were being questioned: a striking instance is the coarse violence in the speech of Dame Study in Passus X.[2] In the case of lesser doctrines such as that of indulgences the text allows that doubt might arise, and even harmlessly if followed by the act of faith: "This is a leef of oure bileue, as lettred men vs techeþ: . . . And so I leue leelly, lord forbede ellis" (B 7.181, 182).

It is not possible to establish whether Langland was acquainted with Wyclif's most radical works, but many Wyclifite notions were common talk in the 70s, and Langland shows acquaintance with a fair number of them. For some he clearly has no time. He accepts the need for an episcopal hierarchy, which Wyclif questioned; he insists on the value of annual, even frequent, communion and of oral confession, which Wyclif decried; and as for the latter's finespun arguments about transubstantiation, he simply scouts these: the host contains the flesh and blood of the Child that was born to the Virgin: "Here is breed yblessed, and goddes body pervnder" (B 19.385, 17.100). In such and similar matters his text shows him as a good son of the Church in bad times.

About the badness of the times Langland was in no doubt. Some of the particulars of his anxiety are commonplaces in the history books: the always imminent plague, poor harvest and famines, the difficulties and discontents of working men, concern about the government of the realm with the prospect or fact of young Richard's succession: "*væ terræ vbi puer rex est!*" (B Prologue 196). There was also a less ponderable but very real condition of the times, the insecurity which comes from an intuition of change, of the decay of institutions, or simply from these being challenged. Hatred and envy—so the sermons ran, apparently with some accuracy—were causing men to reject the divinely appointed order. Social pressure was mounting from below. With the shortage of labor, serfs could become free tenants; shopkeepers and skilled artisans showed intense hostility to their betters; soap manufacturers bought knighthoods for themselves and their sons after them.[3] One recalls in this connection the Man of Law's accumulation of a landed estate with a view to a title, the Franklin's social aspirations, the curtain lecture in the "Wife of Bath's Tale" on how *gentilesse* has nothing to do with blood descent, a subversive way of thinking that was widely current. "The order of these various ranks in the community," which in the words of John Bromyard "ought to be like the position of the strings upon the harp," was being disarranged and the instrument no longer gave forth "a sweet melody."[4] Authority both lay and clerical was being challenged on two distinct counts.

Paradoxically the challenge, in both forms, originated in the Church and specifically in the sermons of the preaching friars expressing the perennial movement of moral reform. The most formidable challenge to the doctrine and system of social gradation or *degree* originated in the dogma that men are equal in the sight of God, which was not taught with any revolutionary intention, but to restrain those less fortunately born from the sin of envy. Bishops of excellent virtue like Brunton of Rochester preached that the rich and the poor, in their common religious privileges and many other things, "are alike and equal," not for any purpose of subversion but to apply "a powerful spiritual and moral corrective." Nevertheless, from that doctrinally unassailable position it was no great distance to Bromyard's "True glory does not depend on the origin or beginning from which anything proceeds but upon its own condition,"[5] which in modern terms means that a man's worth, in the true sense of the word, depends on the state of his soul. At this point there could appear a perplexing conflict with the originally complementary doctrine that the existing social order was divinely appointed for the assignment of responsibility in the community: "ther is degree above degree as resoun is; and skile is that men do hir devoir ther as it is due" (ParsT 763).[6] For it could not fail to strike a thinking person in later fourteenth-century England that many of the magnates of the land, both lay and clerical, were honoring their obligations of care and stewardship only poorly if at all. What was *their* "true glory," their moral worth? So preaching and teaching, designed to hold envy and unrest in check, could seem to be questioning the justice of the existing order. Our thinking person of the fourteenth century would not have had the kind of information to know that Christianity has essentially nothing to do with social orders except by historical accidents. His concern would be with the interrelation of authority, social order, and morality.

The second form of the challenge was bluntly moral: those in authority were not worthy of their authority and status. Applied to the worldly great this criticism carried a brief and simple implication: they were not just likely but almost certain to be damned. Why should those who, in Langland's words, "delit in wyn and wildefowel and wite any in defaute" (B 10.367), who relish roast wild duck and burgundy and know of anyone about who is destitute, have heaven both in their enjoyable sojourn on earth and hereafter (B 14.141)?

The consequence of the moral deficiency of such men, the sin of Dives, was limited to themselves; indeed it could be held to benefit the poor, since poverty endured in patience was conceived of as "pure spiritual helpe" (B 14.285), affording opportunity to acquire merit. Lazarus, after all, ended up in Abraham's bosom. But the immorality of the great in the clerical estate, and indeed of all worldly clergy, was another matter, for this must have a direct and calamitous effect upon the whole community of Christian souls. To be sure the episcopate contained some excellent administrators such as William Courtenay, incumbent of three successive sees, and John Thoresby of York, author of the Catechism, as well as the scholar bishops Thomas Cobham and Roger Mortival, not to mention the saintly Brunton. But it appears that they were generally thought too few to provide even the little leaven that leaveneth the whole.

Of the clergy in fourteenth-century England the common criticism was that by their evil, or at any rate their worldly living, they vitiated the effect of good doctrine, instancing the unsoundness of the presumption that knowledge of right action is necessarily accompanied by the ethical sense to put it into effect. Langland's Friar Jordan of Passus XIII exemplifies this. His definition of the Three Lives is, as far as it goes, as valid as any other in the poem, but he does not live in accordance with it: "þis goddes gloton," complains the Dreamer, "wiþ his grete chekes Haþ no pite on vs pouere; he parfourneþ yuele That he precheþ and preueþ noȝt compacience" (B 13.78–80). The self-indulgence of the clergy discredited their moral teaching; to restore its effectiveness they should exemplify it themselves: "Lyue as ye leren vs," urges the reforming voice of Reason; "we shul leue yow þe bettre" (B 5.44).

Of the criticisms of the clergy which figure in the poem, both as their shortcomings injured the laity and with respect to their own salvation, most are commonplaces of estates satire and contemporary preaching. Langland was far from the first in his time to censure the grand living of the higher clergy, the illiteracy and neglectful incompetence of parish priests, the venality of the ecclesiastical courts, the deaf ear turned by the bishops to complaints about connivance between parish priests and pardoners, the uncharity between friars and the beneficed clergy, the diversion of educated priests—sadly needed for pastoral care—to lay occupations, the decay of monasticism, intellectually with the ascendancy in theology of the friars and morally through sloth and irregular living. But this circumstance does not appear to have diminished his concern. In the last version of his poem he gives to Piers, now by his career in the B version become a wholly authoritative spokesman, a particularly violent address of accusation to bishops: "You are asleep, if such a shocking thing can be said! The wolves have broken into your sheepfolds and your watchdogs are either blind or terrified (*"canes non valentes latrare"*) while the wolves gorge themselves": *"lupus lanam cacat et grex incustodits dilaceratur eo . . .* I leue by þi lachesse þow lesest many wederes" (C 10.265, 266, 269); those lost sheep are layfolk damned through the negligence of their pastors and bishops. Here is the imputation of hireling shepherd to the successors of the apostles.

Of most ecclesiastical institutions the criticism in *Piers Plowman* is somehow qualified: for instance there are "Bysshopes yblessed" who, "if þei ben as þei sholde Legistres of boþe lawes þe lewed þerwiþ to preche, And in as muche as þei mowe amenden alle synfulle, Arn peres wiþ þe Apostles" (B 7.13–16); and the criticisms of the monastic clergy— proposals for disestablishment, Abbot of Abingdon and all— appear tempered with nostalgia: "if heuene be on þis erþe, and ese to any soule, It is in cloistre or in scole."[7] But of friars almost the only good Langland can find to say is that there was once a time when Charity wore a friar's habit, but that was many years ago in St. Francis's day: "In þat secte siþþe to selde haþ he ben knowe" (B 15.232). He saw the friars as the greatest single source of peril to the contemporary Church; each of the three versions proclaims this: "But holy chirche and hij holde bettre togidres The mooste meschief on Molde is mountynge vp faste."[8]

The details of his criticism of friars do not seem novel. Some may actually have originated in the early disputes among the Franciscans themselves, others in the thirteenth-century rivalry between friars and the monastic orders.[9] Many echo remarkably a complaint against the friars laid at a Convocation in Canterbury in 1356.[10] Langland's treatment of friars is sometimes cruel as well as severe, for instance when he elaborately supports the punning misapplication of the Pauline *"periculum est in falsis fratribus"* (B 13.70, 73). The Dreamer's failure of charity here stems from fear. For him the friars were followers of Antichrist "for he gaf hem copes"; they propagated error, "made fals sprynge and sprede" (B 20.55, 58). Their admitted brilliance as theologians made them the worst instances of discrepancy between teaching and conduct, between the principles of their foundation and their immense wealth. In them had lain the hope of Christendom for the renewal of the Church and they were disappointing it. Where other religious were at fault for sloth or the sins of the flesh, their offence of cynicism and lack of principle was against truth itself. To cap it all they were brazenly insolent. That point is worth a moment's attention. In the year 1371, when Jean de Meung's *Fals Semblant*, the archetype of wicked friars, had been current for almost a century, two Austin friars were not embarrassed to lay before Parliament a petition "asking for the disendowment of the monasteries for the common good."[11] Whether Langland knew of that event is not determinable, but he expresses a lively sense of such insolence by some of his deepest irony in B VIII when the Dreamer asks two Friars Minor "where þat dowel dwelleþ" and they reply "amonges vs he dwelleþ, and euere haþ as I hope, and euere shal herafter."[12] The Dreamer's answer is "But even the *just* man sins seven times a day!" The friars were betraying the Church—it is a friar with licence to hear confessions who, in Passus XX, contrives to delude Conscience, the moral judgment which decides between right and wrong, for a moment, gets access to Contrition and drugs him, and thus achieves what the direct assaults of Antichrist could not bring about, the fall of Unity Holy Church. It seems that Langland considered the friars' exploitation of the confessional for financial profit their worst offence, for it interrupted and corrupted man's relation with God.

Had the corruption of the clergy been Langland's only concern he would not have been exceptional; that situation undoubtedly represented itself with equal force to many of his contemporaries. What is exceptional is the penetration of his insight into its implications. In this, particularly, he appears the highly intelligent poet I have called him. The prophetic quality of his poem, which recommended it so strongly to the mid-sixteenth century, was not an accident. He sensed the indivisibility of the hard-won human concept of ethics, specifically that the religious and the lay estates— as his age described them—were functionally interlocked. Of course he would not have used that expression. His text speaks of a Christendom, which ought to be united, and of mankind as God's errant creation, not of a social structure within which a self-aware species had to learn to live with and continue to respect itself. But what he unmistakably and extensively represented in his poem was man's innate tendency to sacrifice ethical principles to material advantage—*radix malorum est cupiditas*—and the consequence as a progressive and damaging devaluation of the concept of integrity in all its aspects. One recalls the values, literal and allegorical, which Langland assigned to the word Truth.[13] The Dreamer's bitter assertion in the last version of the poem, that the situation is either self-destructive or explosive—"Lyf-holynesse and loue han ben longe hennes, And wole, til hit be wered out or operwise ychaunged" (C 6.80, 81)—has more than just local dramatic force. *Piers Plowman* is in part a consideration of available explanations for that state of affairs.

There is the elementary theodicy of the pulpit preacher: the state of the world is evil because God is punishing men for their wickedness. This theme runs through the poem in all versions. The pestilences were sent purely for our sins, says Reason; the destructive gale of 1362 was a punishment for pride (B 5.13-15); famine will come to chastise idle and recalcitrant workmen (B 6.322-24); pride has now grown so rife among all classes of men that prayer has no power to hold off the pestilence (B 10.76-80); through the sinfulness of man the physical world is running down (B 15.347 ff); the present wars and wretchednesses are the consequences of avarice (B 15.542, 543); the corruption of the clergy, runs an addition in the C version, is what has made God turn away from man and from His creation (C 18.78 ff).

But here there is a plight of logic, for a part of the wickedness of the world is the sinfulness of man. Correspondingly, out of the admonition that if we did our duty there would be endless abundance and peace (C 18.92, 93) the next question arises: why then do we fail to do so? Is God permitting this by withholding grace, as if to reject us? Moreover, why is it that the innocent are so often punished with the sinful (B 10.80; C 12.62)?

The corruption of the clergy could appear the most prominent feature of that vicious spiral of reasoning. They were failing, the most exalted conspicuously so, to perform the high function of spiritual care entrusted to them. Thus the pope in Avignon seems to simple Hawkyn to lack concern for the welfare of Christendom (B 13.244–49), and the professional theologian Friar Jordan thinks the situation of the papacy beyond remedy: not all the intelligence in the world, he says, joined to the powers of valiant men, can accomplish a peace between the pope and his enemies (B 13.173–76). An ignorant country parson mocks the papal claim to precedence over the king as protector of Christian people (B 19.442–46). Extremes of simple prejudice and cynicism typify the various attitudes of Englishmen in the second half of the fourteenth century.

Criticism of how the pope exercised his authority led necessarily to discussion of its right nature and extent, culminating in Wyclif's *De Potestate Papae*. Whether or not Langland saw that work, which appeared in 1379 or 1380, *Piers Plowman* shows acquaintance with many of its propositions, some of which go back to Ockham or to Marsilius of Padua: denial of the apostolic succession; denial of an apostolic foundation for the papal claim of legal jurisdiction; assertion of papal fallibility; the question of procedure in papal election; identification of a bad pope as Antichrist. The text of the poem does not, however, support Wyclif's extreme abolitionist views. To be sure, allegorized Grace in Passus XIX warns Piers that when Antichrist comes, "Pride shal be Pope, Prynce of holy chirche," his escort the cardinals Covetousness and Unnatural Conduct (B 19.223, 224). But the *lewed vicory*, the unlettered country parson whose criticisms of the papacy later in that passus are after Reason's plea to the pope to "haue pite on holy chirche" (B 5.50) the sharpest in the poem, prays for the reform of the pope, not the abolition of the papacy (B 19.442). As to the right of election, that lies in "loue and lettrure," in charity and erudition. "Therefore," says the Dreamer in the B version "I kan ⁊ kan nauȝt of court speke moore": "There is more to be said about this but the obligation of charity restrains me from saying it" (B Prologue 110, 111). In the C version that faintly sanctimonious line has gone. Instead Langland introduces Conscience, Moral Judgement, whom he had developed in B as one of the heroes of the poem: "Do not dispute the election," he enjoins the Dreamer, "for the sake of holy church" (C 1.138). That is unmistakably an act of faith by the poet; it also has immense prophetic implications.

Controversy engendered arguments to diminish hierarchical authority. Wyclif was presently maintaining that

"Whereas the king's power was fashioned in the image of Christ as God, that of the priest was to be compared with Christ's humanity."[14] The relationship he envisaged is evident. Nothing in *Piers Plowman* seems to reflect that remarkable argument, but the poem chimes with Wyclif and earlier thinkers in representing kings as correctors. The monastic orders are threatened: "þer shal come a kyng and confesse yow Religiouses, And bete yow, as þe bible telleþ, for brekynge of youre rule" (B 10.322, 323). Allegorized Scripture, Sacred Writing, quoting Isaiah's "*Quomodo cessavit exactor?*" (B 10.333), represents the lay estates as responsible for the good conduct of the religious orders, for checking their rapacity and lordly living. In Passus XV the tenor of a long criticism of clerical delinquency appears in these lines:

> If knyghthod and kynde wit and þe commune and
> conscience
> Togideres loue leely, leueþ it wel, ye bisshopes,
> The lordshipe of londes lese ye shul for euere.
> (B 15.553–55)

That is to say, the end of prelatical temporal power is bound to come if the knightly estate and the common people, living together in harmony, exercise their intelligence in the discernment of moral issues. It would, indeed, be a charitable act to disendow the Church, to reverse the donation of Constantine by which those who inherited the authority of Peter were poisoned. The C version is most specific here in an added passage:

> Were preest-hod more parfyt, þat is, þe pope formest
> That wiþ moneye menteyneþ men to werren vpon
> cristine, . . .
> Hus prayers with hus pacience to pees sholde brynge
> Alle londes to loue, and þat in a lytel tyme.
> (C 18.233–36)

The corruption and worldliness of the clergy at all levels, from the princes of the Church down to ignorant parson and simoniac friar, seemed calamitous. The terrible notion was actually expressed, that pastoral delinquency of any sort increased the number of souls lost to God and against the bravely confident hope expressed by misquotation in *Piers*

Plowman that *"sola fides sufficit* to saue wiþ lewed peple" (B 15.389) there was the view of some, including presently Wyclif, that a sinful priest could not efficaciously administer the sacraments. In either event the words attributed to John Chrysostom in *Piers* XV would seem to apply: *"Si sacerdocium integrum fuerit tota floret ecclesia; Si autem corruptum fuerit omnium fides marcida est"* (B 15.118). By occasioning a general falling off of piety, and by threatening the efficacy of the sacraments, especially that of penance, the sinful clergy was seen to endanger the operation of that grace which appeared to constitute the only hope of mankind burdened with Adam's sin and its own.

And there is the center of the medieval perplexity: the burden of sin. "If only," says Everyman Hawkyn, "I had died immediately I was christened, in a state of grace! It is so hard to live as a sinner; we can never escape sin" (B 14.323–25). The immensity of an evolved concept of absolute excellence contains within it the individual sense of inadequacy according to its terms. Sin had come into the world by divine forbearance; why would God have seen fit to exercise this, having foreknowledge of the consequence?

> Why wolde oure Saueour suffre swich a worm in his
>   blisse
> That biwiled þe womman and þe wye after,
> Thoruȝ which werk and wil þei wente to helle,
> And al hir seed for hir synne þe same wo suffrede?
>   (B 10.108–11)

And further, is it just for God to punish present man for Adam's old sin?

> Why sholde we þat now ben for þe werkes of Adam
> Roten and torende? Reson wolde it neuere!
>   (B 10.115–16)

In these passages at the actual center of the poem, the questions of divine benevolence and justice are openly raised by Dame Study; she dismisses them with a remarkable mixture of coarse abuse of the doubters and a deeply pious act of submission to the divine will: "Al was as he wolde," she prays,

> lorde, yworshiped be þow,
> And al worþ as þow wolt, whatso we dispute.
>
> (B 10.132–33)

The poet knew the other answers: the concept *O felix culpa*, to judge from the poetry it evoked, seems to have been satisfying to him for the way its paradox conveyed a sense of the infinitude of divine love (B 5.480 ff). And there was that intriguing notion that God had permitted man to sin because otherwise man could not have understood the meaning of joy (B 18.218–21). Both were more comforting than the bald Ockhamist assertion that God is subject to no law, but acts at his own good pleasure (B 12.216), for this seemed to put man's soul at total risk. There was little warmth, moreover, in the implication which presently follows, that God made his ways mysterious so that man might gain merit by his faith (B 10.256).

Nevertheless, from their conduct many men are to be damned: "I leue fewe ben goode" (B 10.444). Works are essential to salvation: "*qui bona egerunt ibunt in vitam eternam*" (B 7.113), and in another place, "*reddit unicuique iuxta opera sua*" (B 12.213). Yet it is because of Adam's sin that salutary works are lacking in man. The sense of divine arbitrariness extends: grace of repentance was given to one of the two thieves beside Christ on the cross; why was he in particular chosen? The Dreamer is authoritatively enjoined not to ask, for this is a mystery:

> Alle þe clerkes vnder crist ne kouþe þe skile asoille.
> *Quare placuit? quia voluit.*
>
> (B 12.214–16)

But in that case what man knows whether he is to be saved? The Dreamer is shown as concerned for his own salvation; he wonders whether his name was entered in the "legend of life" or not written there for some particular offence (B 10.380–82). The theme of election recurs. The parable of the wedding feast,

> *Multi* to a mangerie and to þe mete were sompned,
> And whan þe peple was plener comen þe porter
>   vnpynned þe yate

And plukked in *Pauci* pryueliche and leet þe remenaunt
go rome,
(B 11.112-14)

many are called but few are chosen, makes the trembling
Dreamer agonize about whether he himself might or might
not be one of the elect. Langland was evidently more than
just aware of contemporary interest in the related questions
of predestination, grace and works, divine foreknowledge
and free will.

The comfort given to the Dreamer in this anxiety is of
another scripture text with contrary implication, a significant register of Langland's awareness that in this as in other
matters scripture could be used to support opposed doctrinal
positions. Theology, says Dame Study, has vexed her a
thousand times. Indeed, once, as if to demonstrate his
insight, Langland makes Ymaginatif, the allegorized reflective faculty, outrageously misapply 1 Pet. 4.18, *"Saluabitur vix
justus in die iudicii,"* by deliberate use of a faulty syllogism (B
12.281, 282).

The attribution of bad logic to the reflective faculty
registers both a deep-seated need in the poet to believe in
the salvation of mankind, and contemporary suspicion of the
intellect, which could not proffer both rationally acceptable
and spiritually reassuring explanations of the ways of God
to man. For such failure, and for even suggesting the
implication that the bases of belief might be rationally
questionable, the intellect, which could apparently only
destroy, not reassure and make secure, was suspect. It was
their passion for knowledge which had thrust Adam and Eve
out of paradise, says the poem (B 15.62, 63), and the sinful
man would be better engaged in considering the state of his
soul than the wonders of creation: *"melius est scrutari scelera
nostra quam naturas rerum"* (B 11.231). Both patristic teaching,
in that quotation making its triumph over pagan philosophy
by the echo derogatory of Lucretius, and the hierarchy of
the later thirteenth century in its turn, had depreciated the
value of human intelligence as an instrument for attaining
spiritual truth. But the fullest expression of anti-intellectu-
alism came with Ockham and his teaching of the inacces-
sibility of God to the human intellect: God's *potentia absoluta*
lay outside revealed truth. The concept was pervasive be-

cause it gave a kind of relief to fourteenth-century perplexity. "Leue we vre disputisoun," wrote an anonymous but
considerable poet of the 1380s,

> And leue we on him þat al haþ wroȝt;
> We mowe not preue by no resoun
> Hou he was born þat vs al boȝt.[15]

That Langland did not easily commit himself to anti-
intellectualism is evidenced simply by the existence of his
poem, and more intricately by the role of personified Reason
and his close association with Conscience, the personified
ethical sense. Langland is likely to have accepted that natural
knowledge is unavailing to salvation—*"sapiencia huius mundi
stultitia est apud deum"* (B 12.138)—and that only God can have
perfect knoweldge (B 15.52, 53), but he dramatically, and I
think not inadvertently, reveals his sense of pleasure in the
possession of knowledge and the effective use of intelligence
in his unsuppressable Dreamer's exclamation, "Alle þe
sciences vnder sonne and alle þe sotile craftes I wolde I knew
and kouþe kyndely in myn herte!" (B 15.48, 49) That is of
course a sinful aspiration, as he was roundly told.[16]

Piers Plowman is made up of perplexities created in
Langland's world and time by oppositions: between perfection intellectually conceived and the imperfect actuality;
knowledge of right conduct and failure in those who possess
that knowledge to act righteously; the *imago dei* and man's
tendency to besmirch it with sin; the God of Justice and the
God of Love; divine and worldly wisdom. Heresy has been
called "the outlet of a society with no outlets." In such a
situation Langland's outlet was his poem. It embodies and is
to a large extent shaped by a number of the reactions of his
world to those perplexities.

The first reaction was one of over-compensation.
Where the poem reads like pulpit moralizing the harshness
and condemnatory tone are generated, I have no doubt, not
by self-righteous zeal but by anxiety. That Langland had no
great view of his own moral condition can be seen from the
acts of humility set in various parts of his poem. But where
the matter was one of questioned moral values—the
expression "How shal the world be served?" comes to
mind—his self-reassuring reaction seems to have been to

assert those values all the more strenuously.[17] Where Langland's anxiety seems to have been deepest, about the failure of duty in those who have care of souls, his tone is harshest and most cruel.

Another reaction was to entertain, as an explanation of the state of affairs, the apocalyptic or cyclical view of history. Apocalypticism seems to reflect a socio-psychological state, generated in both individual and group mentalities which, from a highly developed ethical sense and subconscious awareness of what can be called the processes of post-type evolution, detect the imminence of major social change, which is then interpreted in terms of the concepts and language available at the time; it is of course not limited to the Middle Ages. The late medieval expression of this mentality was the cyclical view of history which Morton Bloomfield has shown to be a principal determinant of the shape of *Piers Plowman*. An element in that view is Antichrist,[18] the arch-enemy of Passus XX, a perennial figure of eschatology who materializes out of man's subconscious manichæanism at critical phases of human history and whose coming, so the thinking goes, will precipitate an apocalyptic crisis. Him Langland represents as an amalgam of the capital sins, emblematic of their corruptive and destructive force. His standard bearer is Pride; his main agents are the friars, whom he has bought with presents; it is one of these who infiltrates and is responsible for the downfall of the citadel of right.

With the onslaught of Antichrist the Dreamer withdraws from the world and from all activities but charity. Here Langland is representing a reaction like that of the Franciscan Spirituals, who put their faith in quietism and humility, suffering and patience in the name of Christ, and in the hope for the future. Such withdrawal from the world is an element in the apocalyptic view that change "was for God, not for man to achieve. . . . The very imminence of change made it an incentive to patience, not action."[19] Their position implied an abnegation of responsibility, nostalgia for more primitive levels of experience, and the negation of growth and coherence.[20] I do not impute such a state of mind to Langland, having regard to the energy implied in his poetic activity: his poem exists, after all, by virtue of its being a major response to the world in his time. But his representation of the flight from the world seems lovingly executed. The fools whom the Dreamer imitates have not merely chosen the better part; they are heroic (B 20.61–67).

A reaction of a very different sort was towards apocatastasis or universalism, the belief that it is God's purpose, through the grace revealed in Christ, to save all men. One basis of this belief is 1 Tim. 2 where Paul writes of Christ that he "wants all men to be saved and to come to the knowledge of the truth" and that he "gave himself as a redemption for all."[21] It has a history of emergence and rejection from Origen on, and was several times condemned.[22] Its persistence as a great hope was possibly encouraged in the later Middle Ages by the concept of the absoluteness of divine will: "He did all things that he wanted: therefore he saves all,"[23] expressed very specifically in the Ockhamist teaching of the ascendancy of God's *potentia absoluta*: "Righteousness consists in what he wills, and that is wholly rational which he decrees."[24] This belief, the essential attempt to reconcile divine love and divine justice, constitutes an intensely dramatic theme of Passus XVIII where, in the dream of redemption, Christ proclaims that at the final judgment he will come as a crowned king with an angelic escort "And haue out of helle alle mennes soules" (B 18.372, 373). I do not suggest that Langland embraced the heresy, and I judge that had he done so he would have ended his poem with Passus XVIII. Christ speaks, after all, in a dream, and what he says can be read as no more than expression of a deep hope for which theology affords no warrant, *"quia in inferno nulla est redemptio."*[25] That hope brings little comfort in XIX and XX.

In Passus XVIII the scale of the drama and the stature of its protagonist make to seem trivial the confusingly various and apparently discordant evidences of the fathers and doctors—and if one dares to say it, those of scripture—from which the perplexities represented in the poem derived. But the effect is local and temporary: the perplexities survive as what informs the poem. Langland was not writing as a professional theologian but as a highly intelligent and tolerably well informed poet making poetry for his own comfort out of the thought and feeling of his time. The tension of his poetry exists largely by virtue of his reserve, the selectivity of his representation, its arrangement by series of associations. These are indices of an intellect too fine to be tranquillized by the available, simple formulations of complicated issues, but with nothing to put in their place.

It must be said that he is no defiant rebel. He is always ready to renew the act of faith. What is significant of him is the recurrence of the need for renewal. For his concern is profound; he senses unmistakably that he is living within and writing about a major crisis of ethics, the outcome of which will affect the future of his world. It is in the end Conscience, the allegorization of moral judgment, the ethical sense that can appear the supreme achievement of human evolution after the development of self-awareness, who awakens the Dreamer. But Langland has no solution and proposes none: he must simply believe that in the end all will be well because the alternative is inconceivable. This appears from the major addition to the C version in which he represents the Dreamer admitting to being an inveterate speculator, a gambler hoping with a fool's optimism, against Reason and Conscience, for the change of luck that will turn all his misspent and wasted days to advantage, for a little bit of that same divine grace which Conscience invokes for Langland's world at the end of the poem.

Anne Middleton

*Narration and the
Invention of Experience:
Episodic Form
in* Piers Plowman

Nearly everyone who has ever read *Piers Plowman* has confronted an odd formal characteristic of the poem when
someone asks "What's it about? What happens in it?" These
two very ordinary questions, considered loosely equivalent
by the common reader, will not at all elicit the same kind of
answer. A description starting from "what it's about" will be
radically different from one relating "what happens" and
may imply quite different assessments of the work's poetic
intention and success, as well as different notions of its
model or root paradigm. This is not, I submit, simply a
matter of the normal distinction one may make between
literal and allegorical meaning, between narrative and symbolic "levels" of description. There seems to be an unusually
large gap between the two: one does not easily translate into
the other, and they seem not to be describing the same
work.

Thematic descriptions ("what it's about") tend to be offered as noun phrases encompassing a global statement: it is about the salvation of man's soul, the reform of the Christian community, the problem of knowledge, the grounds for, and means of, attaining faith. Such descriptions imply that there is a perceptible order, continuity, and unity of dominant and realized artistic intentions in the poem. When they suggest a particular conception of the poetic form that sustains this global statement, it is usually a progression or quest of some sort, a broadly linear or serial shape, marked perhaps by stretches of greater or less expansion, by larger or smaller steps forward, by more or less clarity or "success." The poem's own name for its divisions seems to endorse this construction: *passus,* or step, a rarely used term designating the parts of a long composition, and suggesting here the stages of a journey.

Yet attempts to recount the whole narration of this journey as a developing succession of acts and events tend to emphasize discontinuity rather than progression. It is not quite a story, nor a collection of shorter ones. The poem is most vividly remembered, and usually explicated, in episodic units whose arrangement seems somehow reiterative rather than progressive. The nature of the relationship between episode and total poetic form is problematic: it is difficult to reconcile the single event, which often ends with a rupture or abrupt shift of ground, with a plot which is said to record a progression. Yet it seems to me that a basic pattern of action informs all the episodes. A large part of my effort here will be to describe "what happens" in the episode, to clarify what I take to be its fundamental dynamic principle. Examining its character as a unit of narrative form rather than a unit of statement or meaning may indicate some reasons for its structure and its repetition, and reveal the relation of the episode to the total form of the poem. The exercise of trying to read the poem as story rather than exposition suggests why the relation between the fictive form and philosophic content of the poem has been so elusive to critics.

Such an effort is bound to be literal-minded and largely unconcerned with the allegorical significance below, or reflected in, its surface succession of temporal appearances. To read the poem as if it were a story will seem not only to ignore but to defy "deep reading" and to reject the meanings the poet was constructing by telling that story. This impression of eccentricity and neglect of intentional meaning will only be intensified for readers of this poem in the light of what is by now a generation of very detailed and informed work on the complex traditional thought patterns and metaphoric depth of Langland's figurative levels of coherence. A variety of research and interpretation of a very high order of detail and sensitivity has changed irreversibly our notion of what kind of poetic production this is and made quite untenable the older view of *Piers* as the work of a half-educated or undisciplined, if impassioned, genius. It is not my aim in reading *Piers* as a fictive record of events, to reinstate earlier, naive views, but to try to present in another way "what happens" at the level of action in this poem and what we can see by looking at it.

Accounts of a poem which seek to place it in an historical context, showing its intellectual antecedents and affiliations by expounding its images in relation to literary or other traditions, are often paradoxically those which most isolate it from history as a specific poetic production. They give fullness not to the poem, but to our attention to it, filling our rapt gaze with meaning, giving it purpose, justifying it as a moral activity, and providing us with something of permanent cognitive value. Nevertheless, these efforts leave a sense that the poem as made is relatively empty and thin.

If we invert this paradox, we find a second one: it is at the literal, ordinary surface of the poem, the level accessible to a "naive" reading, that we find what Pierre Macherey calls "the unconscious of the work (not that of the author)."[1] By this he means what the work does not say, and what the author cannot be aware of, concerning the circumstances which induced its creation. It is, he says, a kind of "latent knowledge," emerging in the specific labor of composition itself, but not "as an extension of the explicit purpose, since it arises from a completely different principle." This "knowledge" cannot be experienced by the writer as a treasury of materials or conventions, literary or otherwise, to "work with," but constitutes what he must work "against," the given realities within which he must articulate this specific piece of work. If the meaning offered to explication is what the poet's labors cause to appear, the "latent knowledge" implicit in the work is already visible to historical examination, yet not usually noted, "because the accent has shifted, so to speak," diverting attention from what "goes without saying." It is in this undeclared but unconcealed surface "unconscious of the work," Macherey argues, that we see the poem's specific relation with history. In the events through which the poet opens his meaning, "what the poet was compelled to say in order to say what he wanted to say,"[2] we may see the conditions of its production. These appear not in a deep explication of the total design of a work, but in the perceived breaks and discontinuities of its literal surface. In his view, such historical understanding is, in the geological rather than aesthetically normative sense of the term, a reading of its faults.

Literary form is in this view an aspect of a historical language mediating between the will and the work. We need not claim that the poet was unmindful or impatient of literary form, nor that, on the contrary, his narrative discontinuities and changes of direction are really signs of his conscious mastery, begging to be translated into explicit meaning. These opposed ways of describing poetic making both tend to keep the specific finite acts involved in the process of composing the poem mysterious and closed to practical question. Langland, like other poets, is mindful of form in the only way a working artist can be, that is, as what emerges as a result of specific acts and choices in a world where many utterances and artifices already exist and are remembered and used. Form is not for him a wholly free choice, an abstract or open question, but a practical one—or more properly, a very large number of practical ones. As Macherey puts it, "The writer is not called upon to resolve the vague and empty question 'Will I be believed?' but a different and determinate question, 'What must I do to be read?'"[3] It is the surface of Langland's work, with all its fissures and new starts, both as a story and as a much-revised text, that reveals to us his implicit answers to this practical question. The fact that the work is made and revised as a narrated sequence of events, as a record of a life, shows us the conception of the literary enterprise the poet took as given, the conditions of being read as they appeared to him. What we learn by following the literal level, noticing

the nature of the appearances we are explicitly urged to see
through, is not what Langland set out to display, a conception
of truth or of Christian well-doing, but his idea of "making."

An "episode," in this discussion, denotes any described
encounter between personages or animate beings in the
poem—whether one or both speak, and whatever the character of their verbal or physical exchange—which issues in
some noted change.[4] It is basically a unit of action described
as an "event," as a change or result brought about by a
"doing." It may include mental events as well as social or
material ones, so long as they are described as acts rather
than activities. When the narrative subject's travel through
the forest issues in a challenge and battle, or when the
birdsong he hears suddenly becomes intelligible as a warning,
a narrative interval becomes an episode. Though this rough
definition would not do as a description or heuristic device if
our text were, say, *To The Lighthouse*—or any narration chiefly
conducted in free indirect discourse[5]—it does suggest the
unit of composition characteristic of many kinds of medieval
narrative. In *Piers Plowman*, there may be one episode within
the boundaries of a dream, but usually there are several.
These may be multiply interlaced, as they are most artfully
in the multi-levelled dream of the Crucifixion and Harrowing
of Hell. Episodes may be joined together by a manifest, even
"overdetermined," sense of consequence and horizontal
ideational coherence, as in the encounters with Abraham,
Spes, and the Samaritan, and these linkages may extend
across the boundaries of a single dream, as this dream leads
to the following Easter vision. Their linkages may, however,
be more loosely sequential, as in the series of dialogues in
the order prescribed by each successive informant in Dowel,
from Thought to Wit to Study to Clergy and Scripture—a
sequence then intersected by another long and more diffuse
encounter with Recklessness. In this sequence the argu-
mentative encounter seems to be a more constant and stable
unit of narration than either the speaker's identity or the
topic of discourse. The implication of this is that a certain
kind of episode, played over and over again with different
actors and initiating conditions, is a root paradigm of Langland's composition.

The evidence of revision corroborates this impression. The insertions and rearrangements in the text suggest that the integrity of the narrated event had primacy in Langland's imaginative enterprise over the fixed nature of actors, or the expository integrity of their arguments. Expository passages are dropped or inserted, expanded or reduced, and essentially reworked to produce somewhat different arguments in both stages of revision. Narrative episodes are moved whole and reassigned to other speakers and actors, but their character as events—the points at which they begin and end and the general dynamic of the exchange—is scarcely ever altered and neither greatly elaborated nor reduced. Examples are the transference of Hawkyn's confession of several sins in B to the narrative accounts of several penitents who confess their sins after Reason's sermon in C, and the insertion, whole, of the coronation and rat-parliament sequence of B into the first dream, with no alteration of the course of action. It seems as if the episode is Langland's unit of composition, the one in which ideas came to him, and the one whose basic shape and outcome he was most reluctant to alter once conceived.

This unit of poetic composition should be distinguished not only from the poet's philosophic conceptions or theological schemata, but also from his associative techniques of invention, development, and ornament. "The method of concordance," as John Alford calls it,[6] not only supplied the means of developing the figurative density of the poem, but suggested specific episodic figures and stories and supplied chains of ideational association connecting them. A good example of the associative method used to link episodes is the transition from Jesus' debate with the Jews (John 8:33–58) to the new dream of Abraham immediately following.[7] It is worth noticing, however, that the poet gives both the antecedent and consequent narratives joined by this method essentially the same shape as events. They are imagined by Langland in the episodic form most deeply characteristic of his practice in turning figurative suggestion to narrated action: they are presented as disputes.

In its most basic form, the episode in *Piers* presents a combat. Whatever the visionary scene, whatever the identity of the instructor or expositor, whatever the philosophic question that initiates the encounter, at some point the interaction becomes charged with opposition. The injection of a countervening force, rather than the logical or rhetorical limits of the discursive topic, shapes the further course of the episode and determines its often abrupt end. The prospect of revealed knowledge may initiate an action, but it is almost invariably a rivalry, and an implicit pursuit of a resolving judgment, that brings it to an end.

Sometimes the "I," the narrative subject, is chiefly an observer of this conflict, as he is in the first dream of Lady Meed, the final dream of Antichrist, and the climactic Easter dream. These episodes are all imagined in the form of judicial duels, for which the dreamer's narration is, like Book's testimony, the authenticating report of a witness. Sometimes the subject is himself one of the combatants in the scene, even when his search is nominally for understanding rather than sanction, as in much of the Dowel section. Though his pugnacious interference with the ample course of exposition draws the rebuke of his informants, his questions and efforts at memorable summary implicitly raise questions about the efficacy and use of the privileged visionary exchange he has been offered—a secondary interest within the episode which becomes primary in its development.[8] In some episodes he is by turns both spectator and actor. In the Banquet scene, he provokes a "joust" with the Doctor of Divinity while the table-talk of the company ultimately produces divergence between Clergy and Conscience; these two, allies at the beginning of the scene, soberly part ways at its end. This parting of company, by means of an asserted difference from within the group or an explicit defiance of the common effort, is a characteristic turn of events. The assertion of singularity regularly makes cooperative venture, whether teaching or plowing, into competition and forces a redefinition of the initial purpose of the exchange. The search for knowledge becomes a struggle between rival claimants over the power to wield it, to use it to command assent and determine action. The exchange terminates in an expressed, but rarely achieved, desire for an assignment of authority.

The multiple expositors of the poem are similarly handled. When more than one is present at the same time, they invariably enter into competition with each other, or are urged by their pupil into declaring their differences. The poet presents their relations to each other metaphorically in

human social roles that conventionally permit such contention—garrulous husband and scolding, censorious wife (Wit
and Study, Clergy and Scripture), gossips (the Four
Daughters), rivals for the king's favorable judgment (the
Meed episode). He avoids the range of comforting familial or
ideally amicable roles we find in dialogues of counsel or
didactic visions in the Latin tradition from Boethius through
the thirteenth century—the attentive confessor and penitent, the physician and patient, the parent and child, loyal
brothers or sisters, patient teacher and devoted pupil. Dialogue in this poem is neither nurturing nor friendly, but
pervaded by a sense of injured merit, quick to censure any
slight to the speaker's dignity or powers.

It is extraordinary how fundamental this model of the
episode is for Langland. The Easter vision presents salvation
not only as a fruition of grace, but as the issue of battle, a
triumph of law and justice.[9] The Abraham-Spes-Samaritan
sequence, while revealing a cumulative pattern of significance, is also developed to call attention to mutual incom-
patibilities or gaps among the three testimonies (e.g. C
20.25-45, 94-105). While the purpose of using this procedure in expounding ideas may be, like that of scholastic
disputation, to draw explicit discrepancies to the surface so
as to show in what senses they may all point to the same
truth,[10] its narrative effect is quite different. The prophetic
testimonies of the first two members of this triad seem
discredited by their refusal to aid the man fallen among
thieves, rather than fulfilled by the Samaritan's deed. What
did not begin as a contest becomes one retrospectively; a
device for displaying relations among qualities and entities
collapses into one inviting a judicial determination between
them. There is often a discrepancy of this kind between the
interpretable significance of the event and the affect arising
in the course of its narration, and often someone remains—
as the Dreamer does after the "jangling" over the Pardon—
to reflect on, or lament, this difference.

The prevalence of these scenes of dispute and their
tendency to end in discord and irresolution have not gone
unnoticed in the critical literature, but they have usually
been considered an aspect of "content." Some early readers
assigned this quality of irascibility and restlessness to the
poet as thinker, imagining him as an angry man or a rebel
and projecting a cause of this discontent to match the

animus. This "gap between atmosphere and argument," as Priscilla Martin puts it,[11] has been more subtly analyzed in recent years. When it has appeared in systematic examinations of the poem as a whole, the disjunction has been viewed as part of the poem's general strategy for acknowledging and illustrating the claims of what Elizabeth Kirk has called the "two kinds of knowledge" active in human conscious life, and for dramatizing both the difficulty and the necessity of their synthesis.[12] These two truths correspond roughly to the Wife of Bath's "authority" and "experience." The one is revealed and cognitive, "the knowledge that comes from intellect and tradition," the other comes from "one's own normal experience and consciousness." Though ultimately complementary, these two sorts of knowledge are "in the short run tragically incommensurable," Kirk says, and she adds that it is the distinctive achievement of *Piers Plowman* to place the struggle to resolve their incommensurability in the foreground of our attention.

This seems to me a succinct and perceptive identification of the two forces that meet explosively in scene after scene of the poem and a proper estimate of the prevalence of struggle over resolution or clear progression in the narrative action. It seems to imply, however, that the episodes of dispute simply mirror the philosophic issues in the poem's speculative and didactic program, and have no distinctive formal significance in themselves.

It is, I hope, in no way dismissive of this admirably thorough and sympathetic reading of the poem to pursue its formal rather than thematic implications. By reversing Kirk's emphasis, I want to examine just the opposite possibility: that the philosophical content is in large part a sign of a highly original literary enterprise and the formal procedures and generic commitments it requires. The central intellectual and spiritual concerns of the poem are shadowed at every point by a self-referential doubt about the cultural, moral, and spiritual standing of the poem which claims to record this effort, and about the purpose of offering the record to the world as a made object or testimony. Many of the philosophical questions examined within the poem, including several which the speaker admits are detours tangential to the main theme of the exposition, may be seen as rationalized accounts of its own fitful and highly unstable yet obsessive narrative project. What most needs explaining from this perspective is not the thinness and discontinuity of the narrative but the excessive thickness of the philosophical "content" of the poem, its surplus of unsubordinated explanatory discourse, and what becomes of that discourse at the many disruptions of the narrative surface.

One of the most often-remarked qualities of this discourse is the free-floating combative animus we have noticed, which has generally been seen as disproportionate to the specific actions that occasion it. As an attribute of Will, it is most often described, both by critics and by Will's informants, as impatience or pride. It is not, however, a distinctive trait of Will. It is also common to his instructors, who lose patience with Will's impatience and turn away the face of revelation and systematic knowledge, frequently offering instead what they believe suits his amateur's condition. It is predicated of many of the poem's actors, including Piers, both in the Hunger scene and in his encounter with the priest. Trajan and Recklessness display it in their brief and pivotal appearances, as does Christ in combat with Satan, and it is the first aspect we see of Conscience, one of the most important presences in the poem. The fluidity of this animus suggests that it is neither a positive nor a negative moral attribute or sign as such, but a kind of enabling gesture which permits a particular kind of turn in the development of an episode.

As a deeply characteristic poetic quality, this combative spirit raises some of the same questions as "the wrath of Dante" does for the reader of the *Comedy*[13] and may, I think, be similarly understood. The problem is not whether in each occurrence this aggressive energy can be explained as an ethical response, justified by the event which provoked it, but in what way this emotional energy and procedure is fundamental to the formal genesis and narrative unfolding of the poem. For Dante the emphatic assertion of self with which various actors, the honored and the condemned, inscribe themselves and their entire personal histories on the memory in a brief self-revelatory action—most often and most strikingly as an intrusion into some other process or center of attention—is the constitutive gesture of the poem. Out of such irruptions into the larger continuous venture, the pilgrimage or journey, is spun the narrative sequence in all its fullness. In this respect, the wrath of Dante is the formative energy of the *Comedy*, the principle of its narrative generation, variety, and amplitude. It is what made this particular poem, rather than the articulation of its ideas, possible.

The combative animus pervading Langland's poem is likewise fundamental to its production. Its assertion disrupts expository discourse, propelling the episode to its terminus as an action and engendering a new occasion and ground for dialogue. This explosive disruptive power acquires in this way a crucial generative function: it supplies the "horizontal" motivating force of the poem as narrative, an impetus which counters the stasis of the purely expository.[14] But it does not carry allegorical meaning of its own. This energy does not cease to be disruptive, and it is difficult to regard the fissures, breaks, and impasses its assertion creates as in themselves a desired end or goal of composition. They are not, in other words, examples of imitative form, designed moments in the reading experience which, by frustrating our desire to construct a coherent meaning as we read, implicitly assert that striving toward truth is often a frustrating enterprise. Rather, they are a kind of involuntary authorial signature left in the literary material by the act of bringing the poem into being, pointing to those ways of proceeding that differentiate this poem from any other, as its "ideas" and its mode of figurative elaboration do not. Its ideas and methods were, many of them, traditional; what Langland undertook to make with them was new.

In Macherey's terms, these gestures of opposition arising within episodes exemplify "what the author was compelled to say in order to say what he wanted to say"; the fissures they create in the narrative continuity manifest the "unconscious of the work." That work, as the poet conceived it within the range of literary languages and forms available to him, could be brought to light only in opposition, as a literary design repeatedly colliding with more securely established forms and modes for making a serious and speculative work. His project, I believe, was a serious fictive work grounded, like Dante's, in first person worldly experience as the generative principle of narration; in this respect it was, like Dante's, without literary precedent in his vernacular.

Both poets make the "I" the narrative subject, a center of "sense-making" for the poem. He does, suffers, and

interprets as well as reports its actions, simultaneously
composing and reading them as personal history, a
"horizontally motivated" narration. This individual *historia*
constitutes his own counterpart to the world's salvation
history—that universal design which he can know in the
books of philosophers and as a cosmic display revealed to
him through the intercession of his guides. His effort is thus
active and practical as well as receptive and contemplative
and effectively supplants the purely visionary as a center of
narrative interest. The splendid sight of the regularities of
the created cosmos, offered by Latin didactic vision literature
from Boethius' starry harmonies through Alanus' natural
fecundity, become the background, the landscape in which
the subject composes himself as a historical being. He is
defined by this enterprise not as contemplative man, but as
homo faber. His task in the course of the narrative is to recover
what has been lost to time and thereby to understand it,
rather than to reason himself into accepting his loss. His
labor of consciousness in making intelligible his past deeds
will empower and give integrity to his future acts, supplying
a conviction and personal authority from which he had
initially been estranged. This enterprise is the reverse of the
therapeutic process Lady Philosophy offers Boethius. She
shows the grieving and dispossessed subject that in reality
he has lost nothing of value: his alienation from his story
and worldly identity is the aim of her philosophy. That
alienation is the starting point of Dante's and Langland's
poems: in both, the direction and amplitude of the narrative
effort gradually return the subject to the full possession of
his worldly history, enabling him to know it profoundly as—
and because—he has made it. What the *Consolation* ascribes to
Fortune and defines as radically unknowable, these two
great fourteenth-century poems present as the germ of
modern autobiography, developing in the interstices of an
encyclopedic display of universal knowledge.

In the *Comedy,* the subject is repeatedly provoked into
this conscious reclamation of his own historical identity by
the thickly interposed stories of others. They appear all
around him in the final throes of their own self-making,
filling the entire poetic space with their impacted and now
intensely concentrated stories, urgently making claims for
his attention. They act as a mirror to him, giving him back
his own particularity in reflection. The mirror of world

history available to him through this privileged vision thus intensifies his own historical location. His lost Florence, his youthful songs, his past private and political passions and deeds are not disavowed as illusions but are returned to him as his own forever. His temporal acts acquire particular clarity as he assumes personal authority for them among souls whose every moment in eternity is spent in recognizing and taking upon themselves the authorship of their own life stories.

This reclamation of experiential coherence, however, is realized narratively as constant interruption, an irregular series of commanding distractions crossing the subject's path through an objective terrain which visibly maps the eternal order. By assigning the autobiographical project the structural status of an interruption, Dante's poem formally raises to conscious attention the ever-present possibility of conflict between contemplative apprehension and the active recovery and memorialization of individual experience. The possibility is contained, however, by the continuous presence of a terrain and of solicitous and loving guides, who can not only rebuke when necessary the subject's excessive absorption in the local and curious but also validate his efforts to integrate the two modes of knowledge. They support the proposition that the two parallel endeavors are ultimately complementary.

In *Piers* the subject's pursuit of a worldly sense of well-doing is presented in a discontinuous series of interpositions. Langland, however, provides no secure narrative principles of mediation and neither stable landscape nor the continuous presence of expositors whose primary commitment is to the subject's understanding as a being in historical time. In *Piers*, the subject and the expositors wage a war, in a series of largely inconclusive skirmishes, about what kind of inquiry and what kind of poem this is. Dialogue turns upon itself and becomes dispute over the absent means of mediation. The two kinds of knowledge—and the fictive models that sustain the exposition of each—are set in competition, and their parallel course becomes a sequence of mutual interferences. At that characteristic moment in episodic development when exposition becomes conflict, what is always at issue is the value, autonomy, and cultural authority of personal history as a genre, and the status of a serious fictive work centered upon it. In every episode, the narrative project encounters the limits of its literary and social authority. The subject, or other representative of what experienced suffering teaches, is shown attempting—and almost without exception failing—to justify what Dante takes as given, as his fundamental narrative premise. What is pursued in every encounter is not knowledge but power: the power to wield the text that "makes" the world *as* a world. As a mode of knowing, but perhaps even more fundamentally as the organizing center of a philosophically serious long poem in English, the status of worldly experience, and the cultural authority of what the subject "makes" of it, is on trial.

While both poets interpose the autobiographical dimension of their narratives into the gradual unfolding of an objective order of truth, it is only in Langland's poem that this procedure seems to challenge that order and its traditional literary mode. In this mode, a display of universal harmony—of the stars, of natural generation, of ideal discourse—is offered to a subject in spiritual need of a restored inner equipoise. The receiver of this privileged display is conceived primarily as a receptive mind, not as a historical actor, and it is to his contemplative gaze, not to his worldly praxis, that these ministrations are addressed. He is to be made once more into a philosophic man, a seer, as the powerful encyclopedic image imprints itself on his soul through sight. The subject is specified by the rules of the genre as ideally silent, or speaking largely to lament or disown his former blindness. These are also the specifications of the narrative subject in the chivalric romance and the *roman d'aventure*. Whether he is challenged to battle or confronted by an absorbing image, the romance actor's ideal response is an intensely focused spiritual attention, yielding an exact introspective understanding of his inner state, but no reference to past events or future possibilities that would disclose an intentional pattern in their sequence. He can read his heart, but not his history. The questions he asks are silent, and he asks them of his own soul, not of the presence confronting him. His speculations about the situations or persons he meets are casuistical, not immediately practical: all objects to him are objects of contemplation, not of use. He does not seek the "horizontal motivation" of his own actions or those of others, nor attempt to convert the potentially limitless series of his "adventures" into a composed life story, a personal record which in reflection he may "read" and incorporate into further action. The romance hero and the subjects in Latin visionary dialogues contemplate and assimilate themselves to a presented cosmic image; they do not compose a story of their quarrel with it, as finite historical beings contained by the condition of mortality.

Dante's greater success in combining the cosmic and the personal as centers of interest in a long fiction has been ascribed to a greater poetic gift generally, but it owes a great deal as well to his literary-historical situation. Dante's vernacular contained a resource for which Langland's vernacular provided no counterpart—a refined and serious subjective poetic mode which memorialized the self's experience as a formative personal history indelibly imprinted in the individual soul. This was the brief but crucial coming of age of the personal voice in the *dolce stil nuovo*. Compounded of erotic and religious sentiment, vernacular song, and liturgical verse, it made possible a poetic celebration of the discrete mortal historical self; its practice by poets at once learned and cultivated,[15] clerks of civil rather than ecclesiastical eminence, made it a culturally central and serious enterprise. This vernacular poetry—a specifically literary eloquence of the subjective—attained a stature in lay cultivation that no comparable mode was to achieve securely in England until about the death of Chaucer, though the attempt was to figure prominently in the work of every major writer in English in the latter half of the fourteenth century.

For Langland, therefore, the effort to center a serious fiction upon the experience of the self as a historical integer rather than as the locus of a spiritually receptive eye is an extremely unstable enterprise and must be constantly asserted against the more established paradigms for a long speculative fiction. In *Piers*, the subject's behavior is continually rebuked as inappropriate and indecorous, when judged by the structural rules and generic claims on the subject made by the allegorical vision. In contrast to Dante, who is repeatedly welcomed into the company of the wise and learned, Will is forever being expelled from such company for violating the rule of silence, "medlyng" with verbal formulations in an effort to convert visionary comprehension to utility in the *saeculum*.

The conflict at the heart of the episode is in effect an

attempt to substitute one genre for another, to convert a didactic or revelatory encounter to a practical and determinative one. The episode begins rather like an *avanture*: we anticipate the unfolding of "wondres" before a subject who by contemplating them will become assimilated or reconciled to them. As it proceeds, however, the explanatory discourse, the verbal counterpart to the cosmic vision, is subjected to a gradually increasing double pressure implying two rival standards of didactic adequacy, method and use.[16] The conflict is represented by two sorts of actors. One is a figure who embodies inchoate desire and an indeterminate quality of "natural knowledge" based on his personal experience in the temporal world: in "leel labor" (Piers), in the making of choices (Conscience), or bodily or mental suffering (the poor, the "minstrels of God"). For this figure, knowledge arises from and conduces to action and production: the paradigmatic form for setting forth such knowledge is personal testimonial narration. His opponent has the power to cancel or devalue that enterprise and the learning and office to redefine it with an account that exposes its systematic insufficiency. He generally possesses a superior discursive logic and a demonstrative rhetoric richly stocked with explanatory figures and comprehensive schemes for articulating gradations and distinctions. This part is usually played by a representative of a traditionally authoritative institution—the ecclesiastical court, the university—with the cumulative weight of determinative written instruments or proclamations. For him, knowledge is systematic, universal, and contemplated; general questions about its worldly utility can only be signs of pride. Some actors play both parts in different scenes, or successively in the same scene; Will is a notorious shape-shifter in this respect. What is constant is not the parties to either "side" but the mechanism of raising genre conflict as a means of redirecting the event. The problem of knowledge in the poem exerts pressure on its form when it is raised on the field of contention between two actors for whom knowledge is power.

The episode reaches its point of explosion, turning discourse to contest, not over the meaning of words, but over doing things with words. The Pardon scene is the most memorable instance. It is important to the understanding of the poem not because it is exceptional in its extreme and mysterious disruptiveness, but precisely because it is not. It presents a clear instance of the "gap between atmosphere and argument," contrasting the treatise and the experiential orders of the poem, their modes of assertion, their authority, and the contrary directions in which they develop.

Whatever the figurative significance of the violent denouement of this scene in either the B or C form, what initiates it is quite clear: the priest proposes to read and "construe" the pardon because it is patently strange that a written instrument of any kind should be in the hands of an unlettered layman. It is the relation between Piers and these letters, not what they contain, that is called into question by the priest's interference. There is no evidence whatever of hostility to Piers himself in the priest's offer to "kenne it þee on englissh," and, as I read it, there is even some respect for Piers' natural literacy and eloquence when he finds that the plowman is "lettred a litel."

> "Were þow a preest, [Piers]," quod he, "þow my3test
> preche [whan þee liked]
> As diuinour in diuinite, wiþ *Dixit insipiens* to þi teme."
> (B 7.140–41)

Piers, however, for all "Abstynence þe Abbesse's" teaching, is not a priest and has not the authority to proclaim or expound a document such as the priest takes this one to be. The priest's implicit concerns are to assure that interpretation and the public proclamation of Christian truth shall be made only by those with the literacy and learning to do it correctly, and that as a consequence the teaching of doctrine, unlike devotion and witnessing to the faith, shall remain the prerogative of a properly trained clergy. Both concerns were heard frequently as lay piety movements gained adherents in the later Middle Ages,[17] and they are consistent with other passages in the poem on the presumptions of the ignorant and the abuse and neglect of learning by those charged with spiritual guidance. With the priest's interference here, Langland re-literalizes the action and raises within the episode the question of the social authority of the poem itself as a text, as distinct from its "truth."

That the document was sent by Truth and that Piers is Truth's loyal servant are not at issue: the priest does not ask its source, but the source of Piers' literacy. He does not interpret the text itself literally—or at all: he offers no comment on the several hundred lines of Truth's biddings which up to this point have seemed to form its text, or on the two lines of the Athanasian Creed which in fact constitute the only writing on the leaf. His sole challenge is not to the meaning of the text but to its public power and performative kind, its *genre*:[18] it is not, he declares, a pardon.

Piers himself understands the event as a challenge to his authority, an insult to his role in proclaiming a document with performative or determinative powers. In response he destroys the object that called forth this interference from the sanctioned and traditional *magisterium* and proposes to dismantle his literal identity as well, renouncing his worldly "swynk" and remaking himself in the image of a penitential laborer. This change—often seen as a raising of the level of perfection to which Piers is pledged to aspire and a declaration of the primacy of the spiritual over the corporal— should not obscure some of its important literal side effects at the level of narrative. It is representative of episodic endings in the poem generally in that a gain in figurative coherence is purchased at a marked and lamented loss to narrative continuity and a loss of personal authority in a figure whose integrity we have come to trust. Here Piers' occupation is gone, finally transferred from the literal frame of activity in which he is competent to one in which he is necessarily at a disadvantage and must acknowledge it. As his role as lay laborer is re-literalized, he is exposed to challenge, not for his "natural literacy" and "leel labor" as such, but for seeming to claim that these conferred on him some kind of communal authority. What is at stake here is not experience as a mode of knowing, but the social authority and uses of such literacy. Is a poem like a falsely claimed pardon, offering the illusion of absolution? Is the layman who brings it, whose only knowledge is experiential, asserting a doctrine or teaching, or simply witnessing to the faith? Is his truth and authority of some other kind than that of the *magisterium*? This public exposure of lay experiential authority enacts an important structural transformation in the narrative.

The denouement of the Pardon scene in either version marks definitively a shift in Piers' narrative valence from present authority to absent object of desire. Never again in the poem will the hope for a principle of love and truth incarnate and visible in contemporary worldly action be free from a kind of nostalgia, a lament for a lost order of time. The prospect of grounding the narrative process of making sense of this world in the unsullied conscience of a lay workman becomes attenuated, a distant hope; Hawkyn and Actyf may be seen as a sad afterimage of a possibility from which sustained conviction has been drained. The priest's intervention has carried the day, and the poem with it. The community's continuing need for Piers will be given narrative expression from here on in the almost erotic intensity of the subject's longing for him: like a romance hero seizing a token of his lady, Will swoons at the mention of Piers' name and can only summon his strained powers of attention by focusing on the tokens the absent one has left behind.

The event offers a paradigm of the basic conflict and its outcome throughout the poem. At its end Piers has been rusticated, rendered marginal to the serious uses of literacy to move and teach others, and dismissed, resigned by his own act from the company of those entitled to wield the books and texts that "make" the world by declaring its nature. Yet he continues to exert a powerful hold on the imagination of those who remain on the field. He becomes the absent beloved, always sought and never recovered—yet engendering all the while a personal narrative of uncommon power and amplitude. After the second vision, Piers becomes Langland's Beatrice, a human image held in the memory as the Other in whom his poetic subject first discovered a personal integrity and authority given him wholly within the frame of temporal experience. The removal of Piers from the action leaves the defense of Truth's historical inscription in the individual laboring life to a deeply compromised figure, Will himself, for whom pugnacious self-justification and authentic self-knowledge are mixed in almost indeterminable proportions. In this, Will is much like those two other great contemporary autobiographers and memorializers of their worldly lives—one fictive, one actual—the Wife of Bath and Margery Kempe. Like theirs, Will's urgent and discontinuous history is a story of contention, and it exhibits by turns the rhetorical manipulativeness of the one and the theatrical sincerity of the other.

And as with these two other self-appointed confessors to the incontrovertibility of experience, combat almost always arises over his encounters with, and designs upon, "textualitie" and the rivalry this implies to those "clergial" beings traditionally empowered to wield it. The trials of Will, like those of Alice and Margery, are at bottom for questionable claims on the institution of letters.

It is for his deployment of performative texts that Will himself is brought into the poem by name as an actor in the second of the three "signature" passages in the A text (A 8.42–44); the other two record him in related and complementary gestures—bewailing his sins at the injunction of Repentance (A 5.43–44) and in the act of asking to know (A 9.61–62, 116–18). Will's relation to texts continually exposes him to challenge and generally has the result of suspending him between these two flanking postures, guilty and assertive, rightly accused and self-assured. Those passages which name the fictive speaker as the maker place their writer in an important fourteenth-century generic lineage, which we will examine in conclusion; those which allude to the subject's literacy and literary pretensions, however, expose him to the same kinds of questioning that Piers received from the priest. And as it was a gesture of interposition which brought that episode to its disturbing and unprepared-for ending, it is always some form of interposition, either by the "medlyng" subject or one of his rebuking informants, that manifests the historical character of the conflict.

The poet's term for this characteristic gesture, "medlyng," sometimes represented by its synonyms *entermete* and *interponere*, is used to describe the enterprise of "making" the poem itself. In this way the disruption of the episode becomes doubly an artistic signature. It releases the energy by which the poem not only *makes* itself, but *defends* itself, though only in what may be the last addition to the C text— the so-called "autobiographical" interlude between the first and second visions—is this defense before the authorities even provisionally successful.[19] This exception is not fortuitous: it is only here that the essentially autobiographical fictive center of the whole project declares itself fully. For Langland, the invention of experience as a literary category issues in a poetics of interposition. The self as a fictive

narrative center for the work appears as an abashed inter-
loper in a stern pantheon of serious genres and clerical
modes of discourse.

It is in exactly these terms that Ymaginatif in B presents
Will's "makings" as idleness, calling the subject to account
for his use of his years and his language. The dialogue comes
at a pivotal point between the two major movements of
Dowel. In the first of these, whose main outlines had already
been laid down by the A Vita, the subject figures largely as a
pupil to a sequence of instructors. The second, following
Ymaginatif's speech, will present Will chiefly as observer in
two episodes: as sullen guest at the Banquet of Clergy and as
witness to Hawkyn's sad catechism. Since Piers' departure at
the end of the second vision, Will seeking Dowel has passed
from the tutelage of Thought ("a muche man, lik to
myselve") to Wit ("long and lene, like to noon oþer") to
Study. She is Wit's wife and sharply rebukes her husband's
indiscriminate casting of his pearls of wisdom before a
seeker with dubious credentials for serious learning: she
excoriates a host of idle talkers—flatterers, lying minstrels,
and high-table dabblers in theological speculation—with
whom she seems to associate Will. Mollified at last by Will's
persistent effort to display "mekenesse and mylde speche,"
she refers him to her "cosyn" Clergy and his wife Scripture,
her star pupil who has now progressed beyond her teacher's
powers. This succession of tutors shows a movement away
from reflection on experience toward textual sources of
knowledge, the province of the university, the regular
orders, legal institutions and the authority of the clergy. It
seems increasingly to divide Will's quest between the natural
knowledge that issues in good works or "clergie" as the
surer means to salvation. With this dilemma A breaks off,
and B's development from here through Ymaginatif's speech
provides a particularly choppy coda to this movement. In a
passus which barely controls its own scattered topicality
(e.g., B 11.232, 318), this phase of Will's philosophic quest
ends with a reversal of the narrative perspective, turning
him from the expositions of the learned and textual to the
blandishments of earthly experience, and leaving it to
Ymaginatif to resolve these two kinds of "sight" into one
synthetic vision.

To the epistemological problem presented to him by the

expository logic of Dowel thus far—does Truth manifest
itself to "plowmen and pastours and povere commune
laborers" or to "þise kete clerkes þat konne manye bokes"?—
Ymaginatif has a satisfying resolution. What appeared "to
pastours and to poetes," to laboring men and the deeply
learned Magi, is, he answers, but one truth. Clergy and
"kynde wit," traditional learning and the experience of
creatures, are "cosyns," not opponents, "for boþe ben as
mirours to amenden (our) defautes." When he was scorned
by Scripture (*multi multa sciunt et seipsos nesciunt*), and plunged
from the high "sightes" offered by texts and philosophical
learning into all that Fortune can show of the experiential
world, his fall was but the exchange of one of the "mirours"
of knowledge for the other. The problem of integrated
vision however, is attended by another which has become a
lengthening shadow of the first. It is the question of Will's
own practice: the ethical standing and social authority of
what he "makes" of such vision. Is Will a laborer or a clerk?
On this matter, Ymaginatif offers but cold comfort: as labor,
Will's making is useless, and as teaching it is at best
superfluous.

Will has arrived at this point in Dowel by a process
which reduplicates that by which Piers was gradually removed from his earthly vocation and natural authority in
the preceding dream. Handed through a succession of
teachers, each more "textual" in authority than the last, Will
has followed Piers' course, drawn further from the field he
knows by the direct experience of his enigmatic labor to the
risk-fraught terrain of action-at-a-distance carried on by
means of authoritative written instruments. He now stands
before Ymaginatif seeming to his challenger as Piers seemed
to the priest: as one who has wrongfully appropriated
clerical authority and prerogative. And as the priest who
confronts Piers is the institutionally sanctioned mirror image
of what Piers does, possessing the pastoral authority the
plowman has by nature rather than by appointed office, so
Ymaginatif presents an authorized version of what Will as
visionary and maker aspires to do, to integrate what books
and experience can show. Will, however, conducts his enterprise outside the institutional sanctions for using this
visionary capacity either as a memorial image by which he
might reform his own life or as an instrument of explicit

teaching. There is no instituted place, Ymaginatif declares, for a serious imaginative fiction outside of penitential or didactic purposes.

As the power of making similitudes and likenesses, Ymaginatif is the tutelary genius of fiction as well as prophecy.[20] To him belongs the *body* of knowledge, the form in which mental and spiritual realities are represented so that they may be possessed by living mortals as the common knowledge which secures their worldly identities. He is the faculty that makes it possible to examine one's life as a comprehensive pattern, as the story one makes; and it is upon Ymaginatif's integrated presentation that Repentance (rather than mere reverie or remorse) may arise from retrospection and Conscience, the making of choices, may be awakened in projected action. He presides, therefore, over both autobiographical "sense-making" and the human employment of knowledge generally. By nature as well as by his place in a succession of informants, he is heir to questions about the use of this faculty, and it is these he addresses first. To his view, Will's mode of living and his craft cannot be considered separately, and both are morally dubious.[21]

Since as early in the poem as Dame Study's tirade, the status of speculative fiction in general has been doubtful, and in the passus leading to Ymaginatif's intervention, Will's efforts at the poetry of social correction also stand condemned. He is twice rebuked on slightly different grounds for his invectives,[22] before Ymaginatif appears to impugn in more sweeping terms the whole fictive enterprise, both as product and as vocation. These rebukes are concerned with two questionable characteristics of the poetry of public speculation and correction: the corrosive anger, rather than brotherly sorrow and love, which tends to inform such work (Lewte); and the presumptuous claim to a godlike perspective on the world's apparent flaws by a merely human surveyor who cannot, as their maker can, know their true purposes (Reason). Both challenges concern the negative effect of such makings on the maker himself; they subject him to soul-endangering anger and pride. They do not, however, examine the character or use of the made object or the kind of life the maker must lead in order to produce it. It is at this point that Ymaginatif enters to urge upon Will a more comprehensive view of the uses of his "sights" of the world: Will's repossessed worldly history is properly an instrument of his own reform; it gives no counsel to the world at large.

Having first appeared anonymously to rebuke Will for breaking silence with his verbal "entremetynge," Ymaginatif now, at the start of a new passus, introduces himself by name and begins a more constructive task. He contrasts his mode of action with Will's way of living: though solitary by nature, he is never idle, and he can remember—what Will has deferred or suppressed—an exact account of his finite span of life and the many opportunities Will has missed in "fyve and fourty wynter"

> . . . to [mynne] on þyn ende,
> And how fele fernyeres are faren and so fewe to come.
> (B 12.3–5)

Properly examined, the incidents of this recalled life-history might have afforded Will a number of specific inducements to a long-overdue repentance, if he would only read them: "poustees of pestilences, . . . poverte and angres." It is as part of this general persuasion toward the examined life (in which, he will claim, both book-learning and experience fall into their proper reciprocal relationship) that Ymaginatif next questions Will's preoccupation with "makynges."

> And þow medlest þee wiþ makynges and myȝtest go
>   seye þi sauter,
> And bidde for hem þat ȝueþ þee breed, for þer are
>   bokes y[n]owe
> To telle men what dowel is, dobet and dobest boþe,
> And prechours to preuen what it is of many a peire
>   freres.
> (B 12.16–19)

This is the most absolute challenge to the poetic enterprise to appear in either the A or the B texts, for it attacks both the product and the profession of "making." Both are seen as fundamentally and intrinsically idle, not simply frivolous or scurrilous in execution. Unlike Dame Study, Ymaginatif is unconcerned with particular abuses of the practice and seems to attribute to Will's enterprise the high-minded, if misguided, purpose of public didacticism. It is not the purpose, however, but the activity itself that is idle, in two related ways. It is a thief of time, the medium in which man works toward his own salvation, making an empty and unaccountable space of not-doing where a fullness of restorative action, brought about by prayer and penance, should be. It is these verbal "doings," not "makings," that inscribe one's life usefully in the book of the world's history. This interlude in one's spiritual labors, the blank space in the life-story, is doubly idle, for unlike the active life of good works or pastoral governance, it also fails to produce anything for the benefit of others. Books "to telle men what dowel is" and clerics to expound the theme are already plentiful.

The poetic enterprise Will represents is a compromised activity in its essence, not merely in the debased forms criticized earlier in the poem. It has no distinctive integrity and institutional situation of its own, and in its public and practically didactic design and intent, it lacks the authority of clerical didacticism. Nor can Will's questionable mode of life authorize him to compose a testimony uniquely worthy of serious attention. As both a layman and a modern, Will is condemned to permanent disadvantage as a maker. He is left gazing reverently at the comprehensive learning of his predecessors, unable to make in his own voice anything new of any distinctive worldly use or belonging to a distinct cultural tradition and institution. Though it may consume his life, it cannot become wisdom.

This indictment presents in a particularly accusing form a fear heard frequently in the works of the makers of the fourteenth century—and not only in England—about the status and integrity of imaginative literature as an institution. As reverent heirs, conscious of their debt to "olde bokes," clerical or classical, the major authors of vernacular fictions in this period display their own peculiar and generalized brand of the anxiety of influence. Their condition was not new: literature had been made of other literature for centuries and would continue to be. What was new was the sudden variety of new fictive ways to examine that condition within their compositions. The major vernacular authors of this period present as part of their story and argument the fabricator himself, ruminating on the traditional materials of composition and displaying himself in the process of consciously re-forming them for a new and singular occasion. This range of techniques and terms of address is part of an astonishingly open and complex new contract between the poet and his public in the sustained fictions of several fourteenth-century writers—Dante, Boccaccio, and Petrarch; Machaut, Froissart, and Deschamps; Chaucer, and Gower as well as Langland. Even this limited list, however, will immediately suggest that the literary annexation of first person experience—whether of the world or of "the literary" as material for new makings—was not undertaken by all of these writers in the same way, nor with the same degree of success, nor, what is more to our immediate purpose, with the same assurance of its legitimacy or confidence in its rhetorical strategies and ethical and social purposes. Unlike the inward gaze of an earlier age—that of the great monastic contemplatives and humanists of the twelfth century—the reflexive prospect of the fourteenth-century writer disclosed not (or not only) the image of God in man, but "myselve in a mirour"—the poet as fabricator. He did not see the essence of man, but his worldly estate, revealed in his works, in the endless accidents of production. In this view, the poet's exercise seemed prey to the same self-serving stratagems as other secular crafts. For these writers, the incorporation of first person experience as fictive material, and life-history as model, permitted a newly-enlarged testimony about man's estate. It also, however, represented a fall from a kind of literary grace, from the traditional materials and social gestures which were the heritage they shared with any possible public and which authorized their literary enterprise, into a worldly multiplicity of means and local purposes in which authorization and composition become identical, and the social authority of authorship becomes newly problematic.

Will is charged by Ymaginatif with a fundamentally compromised aspiration, not bad workmanship. Like Piers confronted by the priest, he is put on the defensive and concedes to Ymaginatif virtually all of what he claims. And yet

                                somwhat me to excuse
(I) seide, "Caton conforted his sone þat, clerk þouȝ he were,

To solacen hym som tyme; [so] I do whan I make:
Interpone tuis interdum gaudia curis.
And of holy men I her[e]," quod I, "how þei ouþerwhile
[In manye places pleyden þe parfiter to ben]."
(B 12.20-24)

Will here, as in the C counterpart to this defense, refrains from claiming clerical status explicitly for himself; yet he implies that he is ruled by an analogous sense of personal discipline in his speculative activity.[23] Furthermore, he goes on, if anyone could "telle" him "what were dowel and dobet and dobest at þe laste," he would indeed abandon his present vocation and devote himself wholly to prayer. Evidently there are not "bokes ynowe," or of the right kind, to provide the special kind of conviction, certainty, and satisfaction for which Will strives in his "werk." It is, however, as restorative "pley" and not as spiritually efficacious work that he can defend his "makynges." As Milton alludes to Cato's saw in order to justify letting "our frail thoughts dally with false surmise" (*Lycidas* 152–53), Will uses it here to characterize his making as "interposed ease." This is a quizzical and perhaps feeble defense of a poetry which makes the most strenuous demands upon maker and reader alike. Yet it also insists that the value of the search it claims to record, the quest for truth in experience, should be recognized.

Will's concession conceals an assertion: there is re-creative value, the power to give solace to the soul, in the truthful and painstaking record even of a life of "spilled tyme." Like the virtuous pagan Trajan, who had boisterously inserted himself and his remarkable story of an improbable salvation into the preceding passus ("Ye, baw for bokes!"), Will has repeatedly defied "clergie." Here, in a gesture akin to the radical folly of entrusting one's life to God's own provision, taking no thought for the morrow, Will commends himself and his story into the hands of history itself. Like Trajan's, his work will be a memorial image of his life. The pagan emperor was saved when the integrity of his actions, preserved in legend, caught the imagination and sympathy of a later age:

> . . . al the þe clergie under crist ne myȝte me cracche fro helle,

> But oonliche loue and leautee and my laweful domes.
> Gregorie wiste þis wel, and wilned to my soule
> Sauacion for sooþnesse þat he seiȝ in my werkes. . . .
>
> . . . .
>
> Wiþouten bede biddyng his boone was vnderfongen
> And I saued as ye may see, wiþouten syngynge of
> masses,
> By loue and by lernyng of my lyuynge in truþe;
> Brouȝte me from bitter peyne þer no biddyng myȝte.
>   (B 11.144–53)

Will seems here to count only on the possible benefits his making affords to assure him of a similar grace. In the much fuller "autobiographical" inquest which in C replaces this exchange about "making," the interrogation of Will by Reason and Conscience as King's officers, Will closes his defense with a similar hope: that his "tyned tyme" and "spilled speche" will at last win him "a tyme / That alle tymes of my tyme to profit shal turne" (C 6.100–01). The "lyf that ys lowable and leel to the soule," authorized by Reason and Conscience, may be the same penitential activity recommended by Ymaginatif in B. It seems, however, to be the strange vocation he has just defined for himself, the testimony of a misspent life in which the same faculties are engaged, memorializing the self for the profit of others.

It is upon a kind of communal historical memory, a continuing imaginative reciprocity between the dead and the living, the just and the pious, that Will seems to rest his faint hope for salvation. Such memory was the agent of Trajan's salvation by the prayers of St. Gregory, to whom the virtuous pagan's justice was a living example. It is such remembrance and trust in God's love of truth to "keep the commune" that Ymaginatif commends to Will before departing:

> Ne of Sortes ne of Salomon no scripture kan telle.
> Ac god is so good, I hope þat siþþe he gaf hem wittes
> To wissen us [wyes] þerwiþ þat wiss[h]en to be saued—
> And þe bettre for hir bokes to bidden we ben holden—
> That god for his grace gyue hir soules reste,

For lettred men were lewed yet ne were loore of hir
bokes.
(B 12.271-76)

This communal trust defines the ideal social and literary
institution within which Will's notion of his enterprise finds
a place. Ymaginatif grants no authoritative status to his
labors, but the recreative function Will himself assigns to it
manages at once to disavow didactic claims and to assign to
his work another kind of integrity. If Will cannot claim "to
telle men what dowel is," he can at least tell his own story of
his effort to locate it in his own time, interposing this
process into the traditional display of encyclopedic and
universal knowledge of faith and reason. Although in doing
so he repeatedly breaks the decorum of traditional "philosophic" poetry, thereby repeatedly assuring the discrediting
of his enterprise by those who define the company of the
wise (*philosophus esses si tacuisses*), it is in these disruptions that
the writer declares the most original aspect of his own poetic
project. "For þyn entremetynge here artow forsake,"
Ymaginatif has reminded him. If Langland could not defend
poetic fiction as either philosophy or doctrine, he would
insist on its power, as individual testimony of his times, to
afford a kind of solace. By showing it as interposed into the
traditional genres whose rules resisted it and whose Latinate
practitioners scorned its value, he would memorialize the
doubtful nature of his vernacular fictive project, and stamp
his own character indelibly in his work. His very equivo-
cation about his labors would become his signature.

I have called the disrupted episode Langland's poetic
signature in the sense that it is deeply characteristic of his
way of composing narration. There are, however, also
signature passages in the poem in which the writer claims
the authorship of his text by having the subject, the "I,"
identified by name as a maker. There is no need to review
these here, as two of the finest critical scholars of the poem
have done so in detail.[24] What is noteworthy about them is
the kind of attitudes and activities in which they present the
poet—what they present him *as*.
Langland's signatures typically occur at the joinings of

sections, as one venture yields to another, and, with re-markable regularity, in close association with the character-istic disruptions of the narrative: they show the "I" in the act of repeatedly transforming rather than finishing his project. With an increasing fullness in each successive revision of the text,[25] they present Will primarily in the guise of an active inquirer and writer ("here is wil wolde wite") so as to ally the two activities. Will does not, like earlier poets such as Cynewulf, name himself as penitent hoping for grace and the benefit of his readers' prayers, but declares himself a writer for whom the business of writing is *finding things out.* He identifies himself as a maker not simply of verse but of fictions, in opposition to those modes of discourse which display truth as myth.

Frank Kermode makes this distinction, which describes well the place in literary history where Langland and other fourteenth-century composers of long subjective fictions found themselves.

Myth operates within the diagrams of ritual, which presupposes total and adequate explanation of things as they are and were; it is a sequence of radically unchangeable gestures. Fictions are for finding things out, and they change as the needs of sense-making change . . . . Myths call for absolute, fictions for conditional assent. Myths make sense in terms of a lost order of time; fictions, if successful, make sense of the here and now, *hoc tempus.*[26]

The interposed effort to construct a record of personal labors as a history represents in the poem the project of making sense of the here and now.[27] It presents to the mythic order of explanation and authority the prospect of a rival which offers to supplant it.

History . . . is a fictive substitute for authority and tradition, a maker of concords between past, present and future, a provider of significance to mere chronicity. Everything is relevant if its relevance can be invented . . . . The merely successive character of events has been exorcised, the synthesizing consciousness has done its work.[28]

It is this kind of perception that Ymaginatif recommends to Will; he cannot, however, justify a practical secular poetics arising from it. The fiction of the self as a center of "sense-making" presents a competing order of coherence; and it is in this act of "sense-making" that Langland repeatedly signs his poem. He declines to make the mythic claims on belief that belong to the cosmic fictions which are his models; he asks, rather, that his work be seen as the serious labor of a fabricator, and in his signatures—located, like those of Chaucer and Gower, at some distance from the moments of high drama in the work—he commends his work to the judgment and gratitude of the community. It is they who will judge the utility of his work; its truth is coextensive with that of his life and will be judged by his maker.

Chambers points out that this kind of multiple signature, presenting the poet as seeker and fabricator, is a distinctive feature of late medieval high vernacular literature. This practice, and his self-presentation within his work, allies Langland's poem more closely with the fourteenth-century formal innovations in serious sustained fictions of court, capital, and civil society than with the specifically ecclesiastical modes of discourse, both exegetical and more broadly homiletic, which pervade its style.[29] Langland shares with his great French and Italian as well as English contemporaries a formal and ethical commitment to the uses of the "fallible first person singular" whose adventures in the looking-glass of encyclopedic knowledge and philosophic vision radically alter their "fitness to mean."

The disrupted episode in Langland's life's work reveals what Barthes terms its "morality of form," which "issues from the writer's consideration of the social use he has chosen for his form, and his commitment to his choice. . . . This choice is a matter of conscience, not efficacy; it is a way of conceiving literature, not of extending its limits."[30] Although this way of conceiving literature as subjective testimony was perhaps the major literary invention of the fourteenth century, for its first major practitioners it was as fraught with tonal insecurity and moral risks as it was for some of the lay religious, like Margery Kempe, and the new classes of legal plaintiffs[31] who also in this century in large numbers commit themselves and their lives to written testimony in search of social sanction and a sympathetic hearing for what they have done and suffered. The relation of these accounts to the literary presentation of self in the century has yet to be described; the proliferation of personal records and testimonies, accounts public and private, offer the material for a rich chapter in a history of medieval mentalities. This telling, the counting-out of the self's works and passions, must seem at its beginnings a fragile venture, since its only certain resource is not the treasure of "olde bokes" but that fierce devourer against which the edifice of myth and tradition has been built, mortal time. It is this commodity that in his last defense of his vocation and his life, Will hopes to "turn to profit." It is Langland's peculiar achievement to have composed his poem to include an accounting of his poetic project, displaying to history a painstakingly circumstantial reckoning of both its profit and its loss.

Larry D. Benson

the Occasion of
The Parliament of Fowls

The Parliament of Fowls, wrote F. N. Robinson, "is one of the most charming occasional poems in the language. But what was the occasion?"[1] Decades ago most students of Chaucer thought they knew the answer: the poem concerns the negotiations for the marriage of Richard II to Anne of Bohemia; in the gathering of birds Anne is represented by the formel eagle and her three suitors—Richard, Charles of France, and Friedrich of Meissen—by the three tercel eagles that plead for the formel's hand. That theory, first advanced by John Koch and given its final form by Samuel Moore and O. F. Emerson, was attacked by John M. Manly and even more vigorously by Edith Rickert, who argued that the historical facts disproved the theory.[2] Moreover, Manly offered what seemed to many convincing proof that the poem was written in May of 1382, after Richard and Anne were married and when "to represent her as unable to decide was not a compliment but a joke, and not a joke in the best taste."[3] Other historical explanations were proposed, by Rickert (who argued that the formel eagle was John of

Gaunt's daughter even though she did not have three suitors) and by Haldeen Braddy, who dated the poem in 1377 and argued that it concerned the proposed match between Richard and Princess Marie of France (though again there were not three suitors).[4] None of the proposed identifications seemed to fit, and critics, perhaps with some relief, turned their attention away from what J. A. W. Bennett called the "whole archipelago of supposition" on which the older theories were based;[5] most accepted Manly's argument that Valentine's Day alone was sufficient occasion for the poem, with the courtship of the eagles merely a means of presenting a *demande d'amours,* and since the early 1930s criticism of *The Parliament of Fowls* has concentrated on a close study of the poem itself, its meanings and its literary relations.[6]

Over these years an impressive body of useful criticism has been developed. Yet, strangely enough in a poem so carefully wrought as this, the unity of *The Parliament of Fowls* has been a recurring problem; the poem remains a puzzle whose parts do not quite fit.[7] The opening summary of Cicero's *Somnium Scipionis* seems to many only tangentially connected to the rest of the poem, and there is no clear thematic explanation for why there should be three suitors rather than two or only one, nor for why the formel's decision should be delayed for a year, beyond the limits of the poem. Indeed, the eagles' courtship of the formel, once considered the crux of the poem, has received relatively little attention in most recent analyses, which have had more success in explicating the temple of Venus, now frequently regarded as the central concern of the poem.[8] Such studies have been invaluable; yet one is left with the feeling that the critic does not have "the thyng that he wolde," that something is missing. As Muscatine wrote, "One may guess that here, as with *The Book of the Duchess,* the 'occasional' status of the poem has helped the poet to hold his materials together."[9]

One can only guess in such matters, since certainty is impossible. Yet it seems to me that Koch, Moore, and Emerson made a very good guess indeed, that *The Parliament of Fowls* was written in 1380 on the occasion of the beginning of the negotiations that ultimately led to the marriage of Richard and Anne. An awareness of the poem's occasion can help us to understand why Chaucer began his poem with a summary of Scipio's dream, and it also solves what otherwise seem difficult problems in the scene in which the eagles plead their cases. The objections raised by Manly and Rickert to the earlier theory seemed very persuasive when they were first advanced, but as fresh examination of the evidence will show, they were based on facts that were either incomplete or erroneous.

I

The summary of the *Somnium Scipionis* with which Chaucer begins his poem has raised many problems for its critics. Few today would agree with R. K. Root's dismissal of the summary as "an unfortunate bit of introductory machinery," since the thematic relevance of much of the summary to the rest of the poem has been well explicated.[10] Many readers nevertheless detect here a tone that seems at odds with the rest of the poem. Wolfgang Clemen, in his fine study of *The Parliament*, carefully and sympathetically examined the passage and concluded:

Even a close study of Chaucer's version of the *Somnium Scipionis* cannot begin to answer the question why this sort of general view of the world should be placed at the beginning of a poem dealing with love. For it reflects, in an acute form, the medieval Christian-ascetic contempt for the world, there is no room in this conception either for love or for the appreciation of the beauty of the world as God's handiwork. The world is "ful of torment," life is "but a maner deth," and the whole of man's endeavor is fixed solely upon the next world. The only means, moreover, that can open the way to heaven, "commune profit," has little to do with the opening question about love.[11]

Likewise, Derek Brewer, who recognizes the important thematic relations of the account of the dream to the rest of the poem, finds in it a statement "of a point of view that was often dominant in the medieval view of life—the need to despise the world, and seek only heaven."[12] The stanzas on Scipio's dream thus seem to present, in its most extreme form, what Morton Bloomfield has called "the gloomy Chaucer."[13] Yet, as Bloomfield reminds us, Chaucer is not as gloomy as he is sometimes thought to be.

Certainly Chaucer's summary of the *Somnium Scipionis* is less gloomy in the *Parliament* itself than it often seems in criticism of this poem. Cicero's work is indeed suffused with asceticism (Neoplatonic rather than Christian, of course), and Macrobius in his commentary, with which the *Somnium* seems always to have circulated in the Middle Ages, stresses an ascetic scorn for this world even more than does Cicero.[14] For readers who knew Cicero's *Somnium* and Macrobius' commentary, Chaucer's summary would serve as a powerful allusion to this ascetic contempt for the world, and though the rejection of the world is touched upon but briefly, this might well have been enough to conjure up the whole idea of *contemptus mundi*. Yet, there must have been few in Chaucer's audience who actually knew these works at first hand. Chaucer himself apparently had never read them until he wrote *The Parliament*; he mentions Scipio's dream in all his major works up to the time of the *Parliament*, but each time he repeats his mistaken belief, inherited from Guillaume de Lorris, that Scipio was a "kyng."[15] For Guillaume, for the younger Chaucer, and, I suspect, for the great majority in Chaucer's audience, Macrobius was only a name, that of a celebrated authority on dreams rather than an exponent of asceticism.[16]

Those few who did know the *Somnium Scipionis* at first hand would probably have been struck not by the presence in Chaucer's account of an exhortation to despise the world but by its absence. Cicero writes:

Then Africanus continued: "I see that you are still looking at the region and home of men; if it seems (as it is) small to you, fix your gaze always on those heavenly things and despise those that are human."[17]

(pp. 135–36)

Africanus goes on at length about the folly of seeking earthly glory. Chaucer omits all that and changes Cicero's admonition to despise the world to a milder injunction not to delight in it:

> Then bad he hym, syn erthe was so lyte,
> And ful of torment and of harde grace,
> That he ne shulde hym in the world delyte.
> (64–66)

Chaucer's attitude may have been even milder than it seems in the lines just quoted. The MSS vary considerably in their readings for line 65, which Brewer in his edition prints as "And disseyuable & ful of harde grace." Brewer offers good support for this reading, which Robinson believed was possibly what Chaucer intended.[18] However, even if "ful of torment" is the correct reading, Chaucer's "ne shulde hym in the world delyte" is a good deal less harsh than Cicero's "despise those things that are human."

Likewise, Chaucer's condemnation of "likerous folk" seems much milder, perhaps because much less detailed, than Cicero's:

For the souls of those who have given themselves up to the pleasures of the body, and have become as it were slaves of the body, and who at the instigation of desires subservient to pleasure have broken the laws of gods and men, when they have left their bodies fly around the world itself and do not return to this place until after many ages of torment.

(p. 137)

Chaucer translates this as:

But brekers of the lawe, soth to seyne,
And likerous folk, after that they ben dede,
Shul whirle aboute th'erthe alwey in peyne,
Tyl many a world be passed, out of drede,
And then, foryeven al hir wikked dede,
Than shul they come into this blysful place,
To which to comen God the sende his grace.

(78–84)

Chaucer generalizes Cicero's specific condemnation of those who have violated the laws for sensual pleasure to the comparatively vague "brekers of the lawe," whom he seems to distinguish from "likerous folk," as if there were two classes of sinners. Moreover, Chaucer, who explicitly christianizes his pagan source only in this passage, does so by emphasizing not the asceticism but the ultimate forgiveness of the sinners—the effect of grace and of the love of God that underlies the harmony of the spheres and the whole created universe.

This emphasis on forgiveness is somewhat surprising in view of the resemblance of this passage to one of the most striking scenes in Dante's *Inferno*, that in Canto V, in which Dante encounters Paolo, Francesca, and their fellow sinners whirled about in eternal torment by the winds of Hell. Chaucer very probably noted the resemblance between the punishment of lechery in the *Somnium* and that in the *Inferno*; Dante's work was on his mind, since he quoted from it (2.1–3) in the very next stanza. Whether he was thinking of Dante or not, the notable fact is that Dante put his lechers in Hell, doomed forever; Chaucer chooses to assign them to a kind of Purgatory. Even lechery, one of the foulest sins from the standpoint of Christian asceticism (or of Chaucer's own Parson, for that matter), is ultimately forgiven in this more benign view of the divine plan.[19]

However, the most unascetic characteristic of Scipio's dream is Cicero's own emphasis on active involvement in this world; far from despising and withdrawing from it, one must work in it for the "commune profit" (*rem publicam*). This phrase is more appropriate to politics than to asceticism. It was frequently used as a parliamentary term in the fourteenth century (and is echoed in the "commune spede" used during the parliament of birds), and Chaucer elsewhere uses it in political contexts.[20] Macrobius was bothered by Cicero's emphasis on the necessity to engage in political activity for the good of the commonwealth, which, Macrobius notes, seems contrary to Neoplatonist doctrine and which he therefore goes to great lengths to reconcile with the need to despise this world.[21]

In Chaucer's compressed summary, the political emphasis is even more marked than in Cicero, since the condensation gives this path to heaven so much prominence. It is the principal subject of the second of the seven stanzas devoted to the *Somnium*:

> Thanne telleth it that, from a sterry place
> How Affrycan hath hym Cartage shewed,
> And warnede hym beforn of all his grace,
> And seyde hym what man, lered other lewed,
> That lovede commune profit, wel ithewed,
> He shulde into a blysful place wende,
> Ther as joye is that last withouten ende.
> (43–49)

"Commune profit" is again the subject of the sixth stanza.

Here Chaucer is adapting a long passage in the *Somnium* which reads in part:

Since, therefore, it is clear that what is self moved is eternal, who is there who will deny this to be the nature of souls? . . . If the soul is unique in that it moves itself, it has certainly not been born and is eternal.

Use it therefore for the best things. The noblest tasks concern the well being of your country: a soul busy and occupied in such matters will speed the more swiftly to this resting place, its home; and this flight will be the more swift if the soul, while still shut up in the body, will rise above it and in contemplation of what is beyond, detach itself as much as possible from the body.

(p. 137)

Chaucer omits the ascetic injunction to rise above the body in contemplation and stresses the purely political concern:

> Thanne prayede hym Scipion to telle hym al
> The wey to come into that hevene blisse.
> And he seyde, "Know thyself first immortal,
> And loke ay besyly thow werche and wysse
> To commune profit, and thow shalt not mysse
> To comen swiftly to that place deere
> That ful of blysse is and of soules cleere."
> (71–77)

The advice to work for and direct, show the way ("wysse"), to "commune profit" makes the *Somnium Scipionis* sound like a "mirror for princes." Indeed, that is what it is; Africanus' instruction of the young Scipio is to prepare him for the day when "it will be you alone on whom the safety of the state will depend." Macrobius certainly did not read the *Somnium* as mirror for princes, but it is not surprising that Chaucer did, since elsewhere in his work he seems to regard Cicero not as an ascetic philosopher but as a great rhetorician and as a purveyor of practical advice.[22]

The emphasis that Chaucer gives to the political aspects of Cicero's dream would seem out of place in a poem about love—unless, of course, the subject is the love of young King Richard. Like Scipio, Richard was destined to assume the highest office, and when he attained his majority, he would have the responsibility to "werche and wysse to commune profit." In choosing to begin his poem with a summary of the

Somnium Scipionis, Chaucer was probably influenced at least in part by the desire to provide precedent and authority for the dream as a literary device, and the dream of Scipio was the most authoritative nonbiblical dream he could have selected. But he must also have wanted to use the "book read before the dream" in the same way he used that device in *The Book of the Duchess,* as a means of introducing, if only indirectly, the major concern of the poem. In the *Book of the Duchess* the story of Seys and Alcyoune introduces the problem of bereavement and its consequences; in *The Parliament of Fowls* the *Somnium Scipionis* is a kind of miniature "mirror for princes" that introduces the theme of common profit and thus provides a tactful exhortation to Richard to "werche and wysse" the good of the commonwealth.[23]

The young king can serve the commonwealth most directly and immediately by marrying and begetting an heir. Indeed, "commune profit" is served by any marriage. Bennett notes that Thomas Aquinas, who uses the example of the birds as an argument that monogamy is in accord with nature, regards marriage as an institution that serves "ad bonum naturae" and that therefore should be governed by laws for the "common good."[24] Chaucer may not have known Aquinas directly, but he seems to echo Thomas' definition of the conditions necessary for marriage (*amor, amicitia, dilectio*) and of the proper purpose of marriage in the *House of Fame,* when Dido accuses Aeneas of wanting not one but three women:

> As thus: of oon he wolde have fame
> In magnyfyinge of hys name;
> Another for frendshippe, seyth he;
> And yet ther shal the thridde be
> That shal be take for delyt,
> Loo, or for synguler profit.
>
> (305–10)

The faithless Aeneas is capable of *amicitia* ("frendshippe") and *dilectio* ("delyt"), but *amor* is beyond him; instead, he selfishly seeks magnification of his own name and , like the "likerous folk" in the *Parliament,* he seeks his own "synguler profit" rather than the "commune profit" for which marriage was instituted.

The "commune profit" is, however, much more obviously and directly of concern in a royal marriage. Richard, of course, was still only a boy, and he probably had little to say about whether he would serve the commonwealth by marriage or who his wife would be. However, the fiction of royal marriages was that which we see in the case of Walter in the "Clerk's Tale." The participants marry of their own free will, and when a ruler like Walter or Richard marries, he does so for the good of the state. In the letter that Richard (or, most likely, his secretary) wrote in May 1381, empowering his ambassadors to sign the final agreement for the wedding with Anne, that fiction is fully exploited.[25] The letter opens with an account of how Richard pondered the fact that the happiness and stability of a realm depends on the ruler's progeny, "ex matrimonio legitimo derivata," so that the realm will pass into the hands of legitimate heirs rather than strangers. Now, his childhood having passed and the years of puberty having arrived, "We began carefully to consider these things" and, when "we directed our attention to the Lady Anne, the distinguished sister of the illustrious prince, our brother, Lord Wenzel . . . she was pleasing to us" because of her moral excellence.

The treaty that this letter empowered Richard's ambassadors to sign makes a specific connection between the phrase that Chaucer translated as "commune profit" (*rem publicam*) and the king's marriage, and it draws a contrast between the *rem publicam* and *privatis commodis*, a phrase that would translate very well into Chaucer's English as "synguler profit." It begins, in the paragraph immediately following the salutation:

The practice of righteous rulers and the custom of just princes have always been to place the common good of their subjects before any private advantage (*privatis commodis*) whatsoever, and by this means to strengthen the commonwealth (*rem publicam munire*). . . .[26]

The treaty goes on to the proposed alliance between England and the Empire and then to the marriage itself, emphasizing that Anne has all the freedom of choice that Nature allows the formel ("de eius spontanea voluntate") and depicting

Richard, busily concerned with the good of the commonwealth ("inter gloriosas republicae curas"), likewise freely
agreeing to the marriage.

Chaucer's summary of the dream of Scipio is, thus, far
from a mere "unfortunate piece of introductory machinery,"
and it has more to do with the main concern of the poem
than critics who have analyzed the work in isolation from its
occasion have generally recognized. It provides the authority
acquired by the dream vision; it provides a contrast between
those "likerous folk," some of whom we will meet later in
Venus' temple, and those who harmoniously follow the law
of Nature, thus defining the two types of love that are
emblemized by the inscription over the gate of the garden of
love; most important, it tactfully urges the young king to
follow the path of political virtue, *rem publicam munire*, and at
the same time establishes the framework within which a
royal marriage must be considered.

II.

The next part of the poem, the beginning of the dream
itself and the description of Venus' temple, has been very
well served by critics. Thematically it is the center of the
poem. Nature, as we later learn, has implanted desire in all
her creatures ("As I prike yow with pleasaunce"—perhaps
Thomas' *dilectio*—[389]) and therefore all must serve Venus
or Cupid (652). If one is to follow the dictates of Nature, the
vicar of the Almighty Lord (379), and thus work for the
common good, one must pass through Venus' temple. The
summary of Scipio's dream has tactfully defined the young
king's duty to work for the "commune profit." He must now
be shown what love is, both good and evil, if he is to avoid
the fate of those "likerous folk" and serve the commonwealth in the manner expected of a king. The didactic
element here is very indirect; there are no exhortations of
the sort we have in the summary of the *Somnium*. The
general thematic concerns are more important than their
specific application to the problem of Richard's marriage,
and the critical explications of this part of the poem apart
from that application that have appeared in recent years
have been valuable indeed.

What follows next, however, the actual parliament of

the birds with the pleadings of the three eagles, has proven
very difficult for critics. Some, as I have noted, simply ignore
it, and others concentrate on the arguments among the
lower birds without bothering with the eagles. Those critics
who have paid much attention to the eagles have tended to
see them as objects of satire or sources of disharmony,
despite the fact that Nature herself clearly approves of
them.[27] Most critics content themselves with Manly's explanation that the eagles' pleas constitute a *demande d'amours*,
though most recognize the difficulties here and none offers
a very satisfactory explanation of how such a *demande* fits
with the main themes of the poem.

The main difficulty with the assumption that Chaucer is
presenting a *demande d'amours* is that the passage makes such a
poor *demande*. A "question of love" must present a real
problem, something for the audience to ponder and debate.[28]
A good example of a *demande* appears at the end of Part I of
the "Knight's Tale":

> Yow loveres axe I now this questioun:
> Who hath the worse, Arcite or Palamoun?
> That oon may seen his lady day by day,
> But in prison he moot dwelle alway;
> The oother wher hym list may ride or go,
> But seen his lady shal he nevere mo.
> Now demeth as yow liste, ye that kan.
> (1347–53)

The situations of Arcite and Palamoun are equal but different, exactly balanced, and the question of who has the
worse could afford hours of learned debate for the courtly
ladies and gentlemen "that kan" the aristocratic craft of love.

The three eagles present no such problem since they are
by no means equal. The "royal tercel" who speaks first—
"The wyse and worthi, secre, trewe as stel" (395)—has a
command of the elegant idiom of courtly poetry (now
becoming an essential attainment for the aristocracy)[29] that
the second eagle, "of lower kynde," does not even attempt.
This royal contender is also clearly superior to the third
speaker, somewhat more eloquent than the second eagle but
merely the "thridde tercel," since there is only one royal
eagle at the gathering. The ranking of the eagles is ap-

parently emblemized by the length of their speeches—two stanzas for the second eagle of "lower kynde," three for the third tercel, but four for the "royal tercel."

As the tercelet says, there is no problem about which the formel should choose:

> Me wolde thynke how that the worthieste
> Of knyghthod, and lengest had used it,
> Most of estat, of blod the gentilleste,
> Were sittyngest for hire, if that hir leste;
> And of these thre she wot hireself, I trowe,
> Which that he be, for it is light to knowe.
> (548–53)

It is so easy to know that even the foolish goose recognizes the superiority of the royal tercel. So far as the goose is concerned, the problem is not which the formel should choose but the effect of her choice on the royal tercel:

> My wit is sharp, I love no taryinge;
> I seye I rede hym, though he were my brother,
> But she wol love hym, lat hym love another!
> (565–67)

This sets off the raucous debate, not on the merits of courtly love, as the term is most often understood, but on the question of faithfulness in love, "true love" in fourteenth century terms, as opposed to mere lechery. The problem of which tercel loves the formel best is lost in the clamour, appearing again only indirectly in the cuckoo's exasperated "Lat eche of hem be soleyn al here lyve!" (607).

The debating birds, of course, miss the point. The decision is not left to them, nor to the audience, as in a *demande d'amours*, but to the formel eagle. Before the eagles speak, Nature sets forth her rule of free choice, "that she agre to his eleccioun" (409). At the end of the parliament, when Nature has reasserted her authority—"'Now pees,' quod Nature, 'I comaunde heer!'" (617)—she reemphasizes the formel's freedom to choose as she will (626–27), though this vicar of God Himself leaves no doubt about which choice the formel should make:

> But as for conseyl for to chese a make,
> If I were Resoun, certes, thanne wolde I

> Conseyle yow the royal tercel take,
> As seyde the tercelet ful skylfully,
> As for the gentilleste and most worthi,
> Which I have wrought so wel to my plesaunce,
> That to yow hit oughte to been a suffisaunce.
> (631–37)

The formel, however, asks for

> Respit for to avise me,
> And after that to have my choys al fre.
> . . . .
> I wol nat serve Venus ne Cupide,
> Forsothe as yit, by no manere weye.
> (648–49, 652–53)

The formel is not choosing between virginity and marriage, for she does not, like Emelye in the "Knight's Tale," prefer to follow Diana. She is simply not ready now—"as yit"—to make her choice. Why she delays is not explained, though it appears that the formel, who blushed so deeply at the royal tercel's declaration of his love (perhaps a favorable sign for him since she does not react in any way to the other speeches [442–48]) and who now speaks with "dredful voys," is motivated by maidenly timidity and a becoming sense of modesty.

Our attention is thus directed not at which eagle the formel should choose nor which loves her best but solely to the question of whether the formel will make the obviously correct choice or whether she will defy the dictates of Nature and Reason and choose one of her obviously less worthy suitors.The "animated social discussion" that Manly rightly said should follow a *demande d'amours* in this case will focus not on any fine point in the doctrine of love but entirely on whether the formel will make the right decision. It seems improbable that she should fail to choose the royal tercel, but even Chaucer cannot be sure. We are left in suspense until next Valentine's Day. The poem ends with the song of the birds which, Bennett observes, has the tone of an epithalamion, and Chaucer awakes, left only with the hope that he will "mete som thyng for to fare / The bet" (698–99), perhaps another dream in which the formel will give her answer.

All this is puzzling if we consider the poem on purely internal terms. The formel's delay of making her choice has little to do with what has gone before, and it has no clear precedent in the literary tradition. The *demande d'amours* leaves the problem to the audience, but, as we have seen, we are not presented with a question of love. The literary debate, as it appears in works such as *The Owl and the Nightingale*, ordinarily ends without a decision, but the *Parliament* has only a superficial resemblance to this genre; insofar as there is a debate, it is among the lower orders of birds rather than the three eagles. Nor do any of these literary traditions explain why three suitors should appear; among the lower orders of birds we can detect differing attitudes toward love, but the three eagles share a single attitude, though they express it with varying degrees of success. The invocation of folkloric themes—the "Contending Suitors"[30]—does not help, and no thematic analysis has yet offered a good explanation of why Chaucer chose to present three suitors instead of two or even one, since one would have been sufficient to set off the dispute among the birds that follows.

As was the case with the Dream of Scipio, the assumption that *The Parliament of Fowls* is concerned with the negotiations for the marriage of Richard II and Anne of Bohemia in the year 1380 seems to me the best explanation for those features of this final scene that prove so puzzling when the poem is considered apart from this occasion.

Briefly, the situation was this.[31] Efforts to obtain a bride for young King Richard had been continuing since 1377 when Chaucer himself took part in the negotiations that were intended to lead to the marriage of Richard and Princess Marie of France. The princess, however, died in the following year, and attention turned to Milan, where the question of Richard's marriage to Caterina, daughter of Bernabò Visconti, lord of Milan, apparently came up on Chaucer's second Italian journey. Bernabò offered the hand of his daughter and an enormous dowry, and in the summer of 1379 an embassy was sent to Milan with full power to sign the marriage contract. It seemed, for the second time, that a marriage was about to be arranged.

However, the Great Schism now occurred, with France supporting Pope Clement in Avignon and England supporting Pope Urban in Rome. The new Holy Roman Emperor, Wenzel, who had just succeeded his father, also supported Pope Urban, and the Roman court saw an opportunity to drive a wedge between France and the Empire, close allies up to this point. On the urging of Cardinal Pileo da Prato, the architect and executor of this policy, the English ambassadors broke off negotiations with Bernabò Visconti and went directly to Germany, where they began discussions with Wenzel about the marriage of his sister Anne to Richard. The House of Luxembourg, whose offer of Anne to Richard in 1377 had been brusquely refused, was now of great strategic importance both to England, which could deprive France of an ancient ally, and to Rome, since a union between England and the Empire would effectively surround Clementist France with Urbanist powers. Meanwhile, there was growing impatience in England. Froissart reports that there was much talk of the king's marriage at this time, and, though John of Gaunt proposed his own daughter as a suitable bride for the king, the people insisted that a foreign princess be found, and emissaries were sent to seek the hand of Anne of Bohemia.[32]

Those emissaries left in June 1380. The negotiations they were empowered to conclude had already been started by the ambassadors who had originally gone to Milan but then journeyed to see Wenzel, but it was clear that the process would be a long one. The emperor was in a position to drive a hard bargain. Charles V had tried to prevent the match by offering his own daughter to Richard, but that offer was refused, and so Charles, having failed to gain Richard as a son-in-law, proposed his own son, the future Charles VI, as a suitable match for Anne. Moreover, Anne already had another suitor, Friedrich of Meissen, to whom she had been betrothed since 1373. Wenzel could choose whom he wished of the three. When he finally agreed that Richard should have Anne, he did not even have to offer a dowry; instead, to the great scandal of the chroniclers, Richard had to pay him 20,000 florins, plus a loan of 60,000 more.[33]

In short, in 1380 Anne had three suitors who fit the roles of the three eagles very well and among whom, according to the fiction of royal marriages, she had her free choice ("ad ejusdem spontanea voluntate"): the "royal tercel,"

King Richard II; the "thridde tercel," the future Charles VI of France, who was not royal because his country's crown was claimed by Richard and who was unable to boast of "long servyse" since he had entered the competition only after Richard's embassy had begun negotiations; and Friedrich of Meissen, "of lower kynde" because he was only a princeling and neither heir nor claimant to a kingdom. This second eagle is clearly inferior to the other two, epecially the royal tercel, but he nevertheless has a claim, if only on the basis of seniority:

> And if she shulde have loved for long lovynge,
> To me ful-longe hadde be the guerdonynge.
> (454–55)

Looking on with growing impatience were the English people, perhaps slightly exasperated that the long process of finding a wife for their young king was now beginning again—for the third time. More sophisticated observers, such as Chaucer, must have found the whole business slightly amusing. The protagonists were, after all, little more than children, though it is true that Richard, at thirteen, was the eldest and thus the one who had "longest used" knighthood (549). Chaucer, however, did not allow his amusement to reflect in any way on the young king. What satire there is in the birds' parliament is directed at the lower orders, impatient to get matters settled and not quite able to comprehend the more refined feelings of their betters.

The poem, I assume, was written in 1380, before—perhaps for the occasion of—the departure of the embassy that set out in June of that year with full power to conclude a marriage agreement with Wenzel. This is why the formel does not make her decision; though Richard's first offer had been tendered some time before by the embassy that detoured to Germany from Milan—hence perhaps Chaucer's specifying that his dream of St. Valentine's Day happened some time before he wrote, "not yore agon" (17–18)—it was well known that with two other candidates in the field an early answer could not be expected (Chaucer's prediction that there would be an answer on next Valentine's Day was almost exactly right; Wenzel agreed to the match in February of 1381). The narrator must therefore continue reading, hoping to learn what eludes him throughout the poem. Part of that must surely have been what most of the court wanted to learn at this time, that the long search for a suitable wife for the young king had finally come to an end.

III

The theory presented above was once taken as fact. Today, so far as I know, no one believes it but me. Two principal, apparently insurmountable, objections led to the general rejection of this theory. The first, advanced by Manly and developed by Rickert, was that the historical circumstances were not as I have described them. Richard II, Rickert argued, was Anne's only suitor, and neither Charles of France nor Friedrich of Meissen was a candidate for Anne's hand at the time negotiations were in progress for her marriage to King Richard.

Rickert disposed of Friedrich of Meissen on what seemed good grounds. The only proof that Emerson, the most recent advocate of the theory, had advanced for Friedrich's role as a suitor was the fact that he was engaged to Anne in 1373; Emerson found no further mention of the engagement until 1397, when Friedrich seized two towns that had been pledged to him as compensation if the marriage did not take place. Moreover, as Rickert wrote:

According to Pelzel, as Professor Emerson admits, the engagement was arbitrarily broken by Anne's relatives about 1377. . . . We do not know the authority for Pelzel's statement, but . . . until Pelzel is discredited by substantial evidence to the contrary, his statement, based upon sources to which we have not access, must outweigh an unsupported assumption that a contract, of which . . . we know nothing after 1373, continued to exist until Anne's marriage to Richard.[34]

That seemed to settle the matter.

However, though F. M. Pelzel, Wenzel's late eighteenth-century biographer, does play down the importance of Anne's engagement to Friedrich, perhaps because he does not want to imply that Wenzel was guilty of a breach of faith, he does not clearly state that the betrothal was arbitrarily broken off in 1377.[35] Friedrich's earlier eighteenth-century biographer is less reticent. Johann Gottlob Horn, in his *Lebens- und Helden-Geschichte des Glorwürdigsten Fürsten und Herren, Herrn Friedrichs des Streitbaren*, provides contemporary documentation for the fact that the betrothal was by no means cancelled in 1377 but was rather reconfirmed in that year by fresh pledges (perhaps by way of reassuring Friedrich der Strenge, our Friedrich's father, after the failure of the attempt to interest England in Anne).[36] The chroniclers whom Horn cites, one of whom, Johann Tylich, was present when the betrothal was made, tell us that the agreement was in full force until Anne's betrothal to Richard and that the betrothal to Friedrich was broken only after the deaths of Anne's father, the Emperor Karl, in 1378 and of Friedrich's father in 1381.[37] Tylich writes:

Wenzel, king of the Romans, Sigismund, king of Hungary, and Johann, Duke of Poland, brothers and sons of the deceased Emperor Karl, gave their sister, betrothed to the son of Margrave Friedrich, in marriage to the king of England, boldly violating the promises and agreements of the Emperor, which afterwards was the cause of ruin, depredation, and bitter enmity between the king of Bohemia and the margrave of Meissen.[38]

There can be little doubt that Friedrich and his supporters regarded the betrothal as in full force, and it seems most likely that this would have been known to the English embassy—indeed, it would have been in Wenzel's interest to make it known, since the English were eager for the match and the more difficulties Wenzel could raise the better his prospects of avoiding payment of a dowry and picking up 20,000 florins instead.

Rickert also rejected the idea that Charles of France was a suitor for Anne's hand, though here Emerson had offered a good deal of contemporary evidence—from Adam of Usk, who knew Cardinal Pileo da Prato and thus could have learned a good deal about the situation, from Froissart, and from the Cardinal of Viviers, who in May or June of 1380 wrote from Avignon about the high hopes there entertained for the union between Anne and Charles.[39] The "wily Valois," Charles V, was evidently pressing Wenzel for such a match, since the ambassadors whom the Emperor sent to

Paris in July of 1380 were specifically instructed to avoid the topic of marriage.[40] Whatever this may indicate about Wenzel's intentions, it shows that he expected the French to raise the topic, and it indicates that in May or June of 1380, when the English embassy was preparing to travel to Wenzel's court for the final negotiations, Charles of France was indeed a candidate with whom Richard's representatives had to reckon.

Rickert's arguments carried great weight. F. N. Robinson considered them telling evidence against the theory that the poem was written for the negotiations for the marriage of Richard and Anne,[41] and they have convinced many other scholars that the theory has no basis in historical fact. However, the documents show clearly that Richard, Charles of France, and Friedrich of Meissen were all candidates for Anne's hand in May of 1380.

The second and more serious objection to the theory that the *The Parliament of Fowls* concerns the negotiations for the marriage of Richard and Anne was raised by J. M. Manly and seemed to refute it completely. Manly, taking the reference to Venus in line 117 as an astronomical allusion, calculated that the poem could have been composed only in the year 1374, 1382, or 1390, since only in those years, he said, was Venus in that position. Rejecting 1374 as too early and 1390 as too late, he decided the poem must have been composed in 1382, well after the problem of Richard's marriage had been happily concluded by his wedding with Anne. That seemed to rule out 1380, and that date was even more firmly rejected by Haldeen Braddy, who consulted one of the most distinguished astronomers of the day, Harlow Shapley, and reported that only in the years 1374, 1377, and 1382 was Venus "visible *to a viewer in the latitude of London*" (Braddy's italics).[42] That seems to dispose of the theory I have proposed (or rather revived), which depends on the assumption that the poem was composed in 1380.

The passage on which Manly's and Braddy's calculations were based bristles with difficulties:

> Cytherea! thow blysful lady swete,
> That with thy fyrbrond dauntest whom the lest,
> And madest me this sweven for to mete,
> Be thow myn helpe in this, for thow mayst best!

As wisly as I sey the north-north-west,
Whan I began my sweven for to write,
So yif me myght to ryme and ek t'endyte!
(113-19)

The first problem is whether an astronomical reference is intended. Kemp Malone thought not; he ingeniously suggested that Cytherea was Chaucer's mistress: "My guess is that Chaucer was specifying the location of some lady who had come to visit him in his room. If he was facing south when he wrote, a lady looking over his shoulder would be north-northwest."[43] My calculations show that if she had been exactly north-northwest (N 22½° W) she would have been nuzzling his ear. This may explain Derek Brewer's note on line 113: "With this line the verse takes on a more vigorous note."[44]

If we reject Malone's theory—as I fear we must, delightful as it is—yet other problems remain. Is Chaucer referring to Venus' actual position, or is his north-northwest metaphorical, like Shakespeare's, meaning something like "in an unpropitious position"?[45] If Chaucer is referring to Venus' actual position, why does he put her so much farther north than she ever gets? "To a Londoner, Venus at her northmost goes only two degrees beyond northwest, which is some twenty degrees short of north-northwest, a considerable arc."[46] Could it be that Chaucer did not actually write "north-north-west"? Mahmoud Manzaloui argues plausibly that he did not: the MSS show "*northewest* in one manuscript tradition and *north nor west* in another, though *north north west* is the generally accepted reading . . . . For north-east and south-east in the *Astrolabe* (II, 31, 2-3) Chaucer makes use of the terms *north the est* and *south the est*; thus *north the west* or, by apocopation, *northewest* could be a straightforward description of the most northerly evening position of the planet."[47]

If Chaucer did write "north-north-west" what did he understand it to mean? Was he, as has been suggested, using a compass direction, unaware of the deviation due to the difference between magnetic and true north?[48] Or, as has been more recently suggested, was he referring to a sector of his astrolabe, which would have put Venus somewhat closer to her true position than the direction north-

northwest usually indicates?[49] Yet other possibilities have been proposed and other questions have been raised.[50]

However, those critics who accept Manly's and Braddy's arguments on the dating accept their assumption that Chaucer was referring to the planet Venus at her most northerly position. In 1970 Hamilton M. Smyser re-examined Manly's astronomical calculations for the first time since Haldeen Braddy had done so in the early 1930s. Manly had used a nineteenth-century Ephemeris, and the positions he calculated were necessarily extrapolations. Smyser found Manly's calculations a "very curious and unsatisfactory performance," and he therefore made his own calculation: "A more modern Ephemeris—I am using Bryant Tuckerman's of 1964—shows Venus at her most northerly on or about 18 May 1380, a more plausible date, it seems to me, than 1382."[51] Smyser did not comment on Braddy's point that, wherever Venus may have been in the sky, in 1380 she would not have been visible to an observer in the latitude of London. Perhaps he was less fortunate in his neighbors than I, who by happy chance live next door to Dr. Alan Lazarus of the Massachusetts Institute of Technology. He very generously looked into this problem for me—using ephemerides, a computer, and even his daughter's globe to devise a way of explaining the phenomenon in language that even I could understand. He does so in the appended note, which shows that Venus was clearly visible in the northwestern skies of London in 1380.

Chaucer's reference to Cytherea can thus no longer be regarded as proof that the poem could not have been written in 1380. If Manly, Braddy, and others were correct in assuming an astronomical reference—"a big if," Smyser warned—1380 is as strong a possibility as 1382. If, on the other hand, no such reference is intended, Manly's and Braddy's arguments are irrelevant. In either case, there remains no objection to dating the poem in May, 1380, which, as Smyser wrote, is more plausible than 1382.[52]

Late May of 1380 was a time when the proposed marriage of Richard and Anne must have been the principal topic of conversation in courtly and diplomatic circles. Michael de la Pole and John de Burley, who had begun the negotiations with Wenzel, had just returned to London with a first-hand account of how the affair was proceeding, and an embassy, led by Simon de Burley and Bernard van Zetles, was preparing to leave (they left on June 18), empowered—if Richard's suit should prevail over those of Charles of France and Friedrich of Meissen—to contract the marriage.[53] It is pleasant to speculate that *The Parliament of Fowls* was written for some gathering to bid good speed to the ambassadors.

We can only speculate about such matters and, lacking any direct contemporary testimony, the theory I have presented can not be proven. Yet it fits the facts, both historical and poetical. It explains why Chaucer chose to begin with a summary of the Dream of Scipio, why there are three eagle-suitors, and why the formel does not render, as yet, her decision. By explaining the occasion that "helped the poet to hold his materials together," it may even help us to a better understanding of the ways in which Chaucer used the occasion of a royal courtship for a wise, richly humorous and humane meditation on matters that far transcend that particular event.

Alan J. Lazarus

Venus in the "north-north-west"? (Chaucer's Parliament of Fowls, *117)*

I have been asked to determine whether to an observer in London Venus would have been visible in the northwest only in 1374, 1377, and 1382 or whether she would also have appeared there in some of the intervening years. There are two factors that determine where Venus would be seen by an observer in London: 1) the position of Venus in her orbit around the sun relative to the position of Earth in its orbit; and 2) the angle between Venus and the sun as viewed from Earth.

Figure 1 shows the orbits of Venus and Earth around the sun. The position of Earth at three-month intervals is indicated; the position of Venus varies from year to year, since her orbital period is not the same as Earth's. The axis about which Earth spins and its North Pole are also indicated. The axis is tilted 23½° away from being perpendicular to the

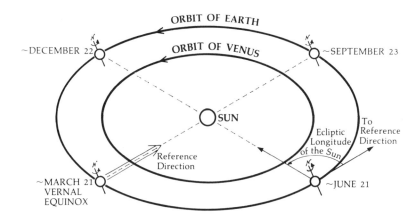

FIGURE 1

plane of Earth's orbit and points in a fixed direction as Earth
moves around its orbit. From Figure 1 it is possible to see
that the tilt of the axis is responsible for the well-known fact
that an observer on Earth sees the sun and Venus in the
northern sky in the summer (when the North Pole is tilted
toward the sun) and in the southern sky in the winter (when
the North Pole is away from the sun). Thus, in summer they
will rise in the northeast and set in the northwest, exactly
the condition we seek.

To be more quantitative, we must introduce an astron-
omer's way of describing the position of an object in the
ecliptic plane (the plane of motion of nearly all the planets).
We use the angle between a line from Earth to the object and
another line that points toward a fixed reference direction in
space. This angle is called the "ecliptic longitude" of the
object; the fixed reference direction that is used is the
direction of the sun as viewed from Earth at the time of the
Vernal Equinox (approximately March 21 on our calendar).
That direction is shown in Figure 1. As an example, also
shown is the ecliptic longitude of the sun on June 21. It is
approximately 90° on that date. The North Pole of the
Earth's spin axis is towards the sun and the sun will set in its
most northwesterly position.

Figure 2 shows Venus at a time when *her* ecliptic

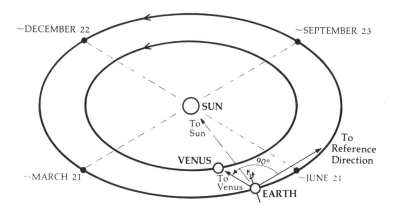

FIGURE 2

longitude is 90°. (The date illustrated is a bit before June 21; other positions are possible depending on the relative position of Venus and Earth.) The consequence of the facts shown in these illustrations is that, since the direction of Earth's spin axis is fixed, knowing the ecliptic longitude of an object tells us how far the axis is tilted toward that object and thus how far toward the northwest it sets. The exact path across the sky can be calculated by using the ecliptic longitude and the latitude of the observing position.

The left side of Figure 3 shows the direction of Venus when she sets and when she is 10° above the horizon as viewed from London. Both are plotted versus Venus' ecliptic longitude. The graph indeed shows that Venus sets most toward the northwest when her ecliptic longitude is 90°. Note that she does not quite reach the direction we would call northwest and certainly not our modern north-northwest. Therefore, we shall assume that an ecliptic longitude for Venus within the range from 60° to 120° would cause an observer in London to say that Venus could be seen in the "north-of-west."

We are not quite finished, however, because too much light from the sun would make Venus hard to see. Therefore, the second condition for seeing Venus is that her ecliptic longitude must differ from that of the sun by, say,

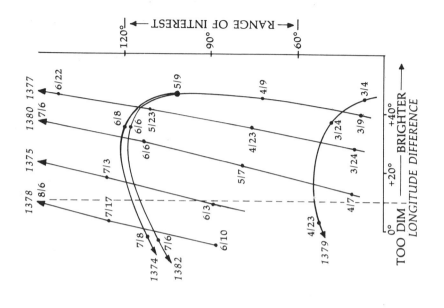

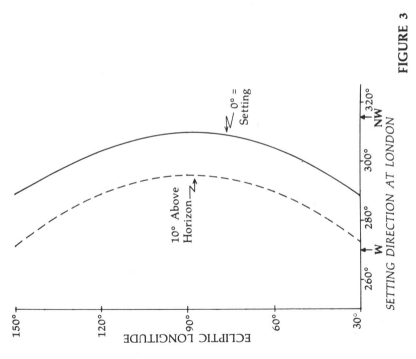

FIGURE 3

more than 10°. Also note that Venus' ecliptic longitude must be *greater* than that of the sun, so that Venus can be seen in the setting portion of its path, i.e., in the west, as the evening star, near sunset. Figure 2 illustrates just such a relationship; as the earth turns, an observer would lose sight of the sun and still be able to see Venus.

Now consider specific years: plotted on the right side of Figure 3 are curves for several years that show the ecliptic longitude of Venus and the difference between the ecliptic longitudes of Venus and the sun. The curve for each year is annotated to indicate the dates associated with points on the curve. The ecliptic longitude difference is a good measure of Venus' brightness (though not perfect, because Venus is closer to the earth and appears larger for a given longitude difference after the longitude difference has passed its maximum value). The longitude data are taken from the tables by William D. Stahlman (*Solar and Planetary Longitudes for Years −2000 to +2000*, prepared by Stahlman and Owen Gingerich [Madison, Wis., 1963]). Years which could correspond to Chaucer's reference to Venus' being visible in the "north-north-west" are 1374, 1377, 1380, and 1382; 1375 and 1379 are less likely, because Venus would not be very bright. The most likely time of observation is the late spring (see the dates indicated on the curves and Figure 2). In 1376 and 1381 Venus was visible only as the morning star. Note that the period of Venus is such that the earth and Venus are in nearly the same position relative to one another every eight years, so that the curves of Figure 3 can be extrapolated to years not shown (1383 would be nearly the same as 1375, etc.).

Venus was most bright and in the northwest in 1374, 1377, and 1382, which may account for the idea that she was only visible in those years (probably based on a misunderstanding of what the astronomers said). Venus was also clearly visible in the northwest in 1380, and perhaps in 1375 and 1379.

Donald R. Howard

the Philosophies
in Chaucer's Troilus

In 1960 I went to Italy for a year of research, armed with a
Fulbright fellowship and a letter of introduction to a staff
member of the Vatican Library, Jeanne Bignami-Odier, a
learned Frenchwoman married to an Italian surgeon. When I
asked someone to point her out, she seemed a formidable
presence, grave and obviously very busy, and I put off
introducing myself. But within a few weeks I needed help in
my research and timorously approached her as she was
making a foray on a shelf of reference works, file cards and
pencil in hand: "Signora Bignami?"

"Sí," she acknowledged, impassive.

I offered in limping Italian an explanation of my existence—I
was from *l'università di Ohio State*, I came with a letter of
introduction from my senior colleague, Morton Bloomfield, I
was doing research on "contempt of the world" . . . Her face
seemed to melt into an expression of Gallic delight, ecstatic
and tender—"*Ah, il Bloomfield!*" (her fluent Italian had a
strong French accent), "*molto intelligente, un uomo molto profondo,
molto* (squinting her eyes) *fi-lo-so-fi-co.*"

From that moment we were friends, and I had bountiful help from her and many kindnesses. But what exactly did she mean when she called our mutual friend a philosophical man? She was, after all, speaking Italian, though quite possibly thinking in French, and while I agreed with the characterization, she may have been speaking from a frame of reference alien to my own. I think she meant "philosophical" not in its everyday Italian sense, "calm," nor in its strict sense, "adept in the disciplines of philosophical discourse," but in its etymological sense: a philosophical man would be one filled with the love of wisdom, one who takes pleasure in ideas, who seeks out the significance of things— one who *thinks.*

For such a man *Troilus and Criseyde* could well be a philosophical poem, and not long before then, in 1957, Bloomfield had characterized the *Troilus* that way in his essay "Distance and Predestination in 'Troilus and Criseyde'."[1] That essay influenced my understanding of the poem more than I knew; what follows is an attempt to explore and extend that influence.

1

Chaucer's *Troilus* was always thought to *contain* philosophy to the extent that passages drawn from Boethius were recognized as philosophical, but until our century those passages seem not to have been taken very seriously. William Godwin, writing in 1803, cited Troilus's speech on predestination in Book IV (he thought it came from Bishop Bradwardine's *De Causa Dei*) as an example of Chaucer's prolixity, "offensive to true taste."[2] In 1894 Skeat in his edition, though identifying the passages from Boethius correctly, made nothing of them. And early twentieth-century critics—Root, Kittredge, Tatlock—viewed the *Troilus* as a realistic and dramatic work: they didn't deny that it had ideas and a moral, but none would have thought to call Chaucer "philosophical."

Yet Chaucer's contemporaries did so. "O Socratès plains de philosophie, / Seneque en meurs . . ." began Deschamps in the gushy balade he sent to Chaucer just about the time he was completing the *Troilus.* And at about the same time Thomas Usk had the Goddess of Love in his *Testament of Love* call Chaucer "myne owne trewe seruaunt the noble philosophical poete in Englissh." Moreover, neither seems to have had the translation of Boethius in mind. Deschamps, the refrain of whose balade is the often-quoted "Grant translateur, noble Geoffrey Chaucier," mentions rather the translation of the *Roman de la Rose,* and Usk mentions the *Troilus:* "in the boke of Troylus," his Goddess says, "the answere to thy questyon mayste thou lerne." The "question" is whether, if everything exists because God knows it, God is not the author of bad works, so it is suggestive that Usk felt the answer could be imagined available in the *Troilus.* Chaucer's friend Thomas Hoccleve, writing a few years after the poet's death, just before the passage in his *Regimen of Princes* where he offers the famous portrait of Chaucer to put us "in remembraunce / Of his persone," declared with extravagance that Chaucer was "hier in philosophie / To Aristotle"—and he must have had the *Troilus* in mind, for he went on to echo *Troilus* 5.1791–92: "but thow / The steppes of Virgile in poesie / Thow filwedist."

This feeling for "philosophy" in the *Troilus* seems not to have outlasted the generation of Chaucer's contemporaries, despite the passages from Boethius. Yet those passages could not be regarded as "additions" until it was agreed that there was a basic source for them to be additions *to,* and it was not until late in the nineteenth century that Boccaccio's *Filostrato* was known as that source. Lydgate possibly knew it, for he reported in his muddled way that in youth Chaucer made a translation of a book "in Lumbard tunge" called "Trophe" and named it "Troilus and Cresseide."[3] Dryden in 1700 said it was amplified as well as beautified from "a Lombard Author." Tyrwhitt in his edition of 1775 identified the *Filostrato* as the source, but his discovery, if it was his, was then rejected or ignored for a hundred years; Godwin, in 1803, referred to a "version made by Boccaccio of the same story, probably from the same author." In the 1840s Ralph Waldo Emerson was declaring with Bostonian confidence that the *Troilus* was adapted from a work by Lollius of Urbino. Chaucer's actual debt to *Il Filostrato* was partly demonstrated in 1867 and illustrated fully in a parallel-text edition in 1875, but even then—such is life in academe—savants went on arguing about the proportions of Chaucer's debt to Boccaccio, Benoit, or Guido.[4] Skeat counted up lines and emphasized that "Chaucer's debt to Boccaccio amounts to *less than* one-third of the whole poem."[5] Still, by the turn of the century one could see the influence of *Il Filostrato* in

parallel columns and see that the parallel passages consti-
tuted the fabric of the plot; Kittredge, in 1915, admonished,
"Let us not minimize Chaucer's indebtedness to Boccaccio. It
is very great, in gross and in detail. Without the Filostrato,
the Troilus would never have existed."[6] (Curiously enough,
once this debt was regarded as a certainty, Chaucer's debt to
the *Decameron*, which had always been taken for granted,
came under doubt. It was the subject of a tediously skeptical
book by Cummings published in 1916.[7])

In 1932 C. S. Lewis began his essay "What Chaucer
Really Did to 'Il Filostrato' "[8] with a reference to the parallel-
text edition done half a century before, as if remembering a
time when the influence had been a matter of debate. But by
then one could refer quite casually—as Lewis did—to *Il
Filostrato* as the "original" of the *Troilus*. Lewis was concerned
to show what Chaucer added to this original, and of such
additions he held that the medieval doctrines and psychology
of love were the most important. Along with historical
background and rhetorical embellishment, he saw the
"*doctryne* and sentence" in the poem as "insertions" made by
Chaucer in a process of medievalizing his original—among
those insertions such passages as Troilus's speech on
predestination, quotations from ancient authors, exempla,
proverbs and *sententiae*. At the time Lewis was writing, the
ending of the poem, by convention called the "epilog," had
been viewed as a retreat from the Renaissance back into the
Middle Ages, even as a craven addition denying all that had
gone before, but Lewis characterized it as a palinode: the
Troilus was a poem of courtly love, and courtly love was a
"truancy" from Christianity which had to be retracted in the
end.[9]

For many readers of the poem Lewis's endearing
metaphor for this palinode—of a bell clanging and children,
"suddenly hushed and grave, and a little frightened,"
trooping back to their master—is still valid, and why should
it not be? Lewis's reading of the poem, fundamentally a
religious one, was based on the historical thesis that in the
late Middle Ages there were "truancies" from Christianity
into the pseudo-paganism of "courtly love" or into the
reading of pagan authors. It now seems to be the consensus
that the phenomenon we call courtly love did exist,
whatever we choose to call it, but that it was a more complex
and less bold truancy than Lewis thought. For example, he

thought that adultery was a distinguishing trait of courtly love and that Andreas Cappellanus's treatise—one source of this idea—was completely serious; now we see that medieval love was often associated with marriage and that Andreas's treatise was probably a joke. With such adjustments it is still possible to accept Lewis's notion of the truancy and the palinode as the most sensible religious interpretation of the poem, though of course there have been others.[10]

Such an interpretation frankly acknowledges a disjunction between the middle of the poem and its end, and accounts for that disjunction by positing a religious act on the author's or narrator's part, an act of repentance and of faith. In religion, disjunction and contradiction create no difficulties and need no explanations; they are often desirable. In philosophy, reasons are sought. As Lewis must have been writing his essay, a philosophical interpretation of the *Troilus* by Howard Patch appeared.[11] Pointing to passages Chaucer added to his original, passages about the Goddess Fortune and the renunciation of earthly loves, and ignoring the fact that Troilus is a pagan, Patch argued that the God of the poem is a rational, not an arbitrary deity: when Troilus gives himself up to Love he makes a wrong choice and at the end of the poem learns that he has suffered the consequences. The "epilog" was thus made logically consistent with the body of the poem: "It is an aspect of Chaucer's greatness and his breadth that he can enter as heartily into the love affair as into the vision of the limitation of earthly things and the supreme value of lasting idealism." Such an interpretation finds the middle of the poem in the service of the end because both together illustrate a system of philosophical ideas—the ideas, to be sure, of what is called Christian philosophy. Many readings of *Troilus and Criseyde* during the last fifty years—too many, perhaps—have explored various aspects of this Christian philosophy, which seems to underlie the poem and explain the "epilog."[12] Whether or not the poem is a philosophical poem, we have succeeded in "philosophizing" it.

2

But Morton Bloomfield's article of 1957 showed how philosophy in the *Troilus* is actually embodied in the experience of the poem. The article pointed to the way the narrator, playing the role of historian, constantly reminds us of his own distance and powerlessness. It is normally taken for granted that a historian has no power over the events he describes, yet Chaucer states and restates the obvious— about distances of time and space, about "aesthetic distance" (the narrator's aloofness from the events he reports), and about the religious gulf between the characters' paganism and the narrator's Christianity. Bloomfield argued that this emphasis on distance "is the artistic correlative to the concept of predestination." The narrator's knowledge of the events through historical hindsight gives the reader a feeling about those events comparable to God's knowledge of all events as in a timeless present:

So long as the future is not known to the participants in action, they can act as if they were free. But once a position of distance from the action is taken, then all can be seen as inevitable. . . . It is just this knowledge that Chaucer the commentator-historian gives us as he reconstructs the past. Hence we are forced into an awareness of the inevitablilty of the tragedy. . . . As God with His complete knowledge of future contingents sees the world laid out before Him all in the twinkling of an eye, so, in the case of history, with a guide, we share in small measure a similar experience.[13]

In the most recent of many reprintings of this article, Bloomfield, in an "Afterword," characterized it as "an early example of formalistic 'New Criticism'" applied to a medieval work.[14] In fact it was one of the earliest examples of what has come to be called "reader response" or "affective" criticism, and is a good example of the way such criticism grew out of formalism.

While Bloomfield took the Boethian philosophy in the poem out of the realms of dialogue and "epilog" and located it in the reader's experience of the poem, he also took it away from the narrator, so to speak, and located it in Chaucer's personal convictions. He conjectured that Chaucer, like Shakespeare, was a predestinarian in that he agreed with Bishop Bradwardine, who "thundered against the libertarians and voluntarists because they depreciated God at the expense of His creatures and elevated man almost to the level of his Creator."[15] The poem, he argued, makes us experience the gulf between paganism and Christianity by making us experience first the similarity between the two religions. Troilus, as a pagan, is seen by us as caught hopelessly in what must be "the end of pagan or purely natural religion," blind necessity. Chaucer "makes his chief character awake to the fact of predestination towards the end of the story and at the conclusion has his character join, as it were, us and Chaucer the character—in space instead of time—in seeing his own story through the perspective of distance." But Troilus's famous speech on predestination, true for him, is but a half-truth for the Christian author and reader, and so another kind of distance is initiated: for Troilus and for Criseyde "there is no final but merely a temporary solution—the consolation of philosophy—from which only the betrayed lover can benefit. . . . When, in the pagan temple, he finally becomes aware of destiny, he is making an attempt to look at his own fate as Chaucer the commentator all along has been looking at it." The hero and the narrator move toward each other, the inner and outer stories begin to join; Troilus from the eighth sphere sees all in perspective and so momentarily shares Chaucer's sense of distance, as Chaucer the poetical creator shares a sense of distance with the perfect sense of distance that is God's. But then suddenly at the end this triplicity is dispersed. The true knowledge of the Christian revelation is beyond Troilus's grasp, as the Creator's perfect knowledge is beyond the grasp of His creatures. Finally Chaucer the narrator, turning from the chasm that has opened between him and his pagan hero, "escapes into the contemplation of the mysteries of the Passion and of the Trinity, the supreme paradox of all truth."[16]

This was the first and remains the best treatment of the way the poem's philosophical content *matters* in its effect upon the reader. It showed how the Christian philosophy and its pagan antecedents, which a formalist might extrapolate from the language of the poem, were part of that more fundamental or existential dynamic that exists between the author's and his readers' thoughts and feelings. Much that has been written about the poem since was foreseen here.[17] I read it at an impressionable time, before I had taught the *Troilus* or written anything about it. And of course the author was then my colleague, and I could discuss it with him. I began to build in my mind a notion of a pagan world depicted in the poem with perhaps astonishing verisimilitude, a world of behavior and ideas at once comprehensible and strange to the fourteenth-century reader. Some of the philosophy in the poem was part of this historical world. Certainly Troilus's speech on predestination seemed so pagan because it omitted what Boethius went on to explain, how the freedom of the will is consistent with divine providence's governance of the universe. And we see Troilus *struggle* with the idea: some "clerkes olde" say there is destiny, some say there is free will, "That I noot whose opinion I may holde" (4.973), he begins, and he ends praying to Jove. It is rather the same with Criseyde's briefer excursion into philosophy in 3.813–36, drawn from Boethius II, pr. 4, where she concludes that there is no true happiness in this world: she gropes towards this conclusion rather pathetically as one might who, having lived in a mad pagan world, had naively supposed there *was* happiness. The Christian reader says to himself, "Of *course* there is no true happiness in this mutable world compared to the eternal bliss revealed to *us*." This knee-jerk reaction of the Christian reader is presupposed in the poem and is part of what makes the ancient pagan world depicted in it seem interesting and exciting, and sometimes rather shocking. And it is what makes it distant. What you and I have been thinking all along is acted out for us at the end by the narrator. We see the error in the pagan philosophy because we are who we are, Christians living in the Age of Grace. Chaucer makes the narrator rehearse this circumstance by letting us see that the narrator is who *he* is, a role—"Chaucer as character," Bloomfield called him—being played by Chaucer himself.[18]

3

Looking at the poem this way, we find a false philosophy, part of the picture of Troy, and a true philosophy, part of the depiction of the narrator; and of the two, the false one is more interesting because more strange. C. S. Lewis had shown how Chaucer introduced historical matter as he "medievalized" his original, along with rhetoric, philosophy, and courtly love. Bloomfield remarked in passing that Chaucer, though he consistently represents his characters as pagans, "may violate our historic sense by making the lovers act according to the medieval courtly love code"; I came to believe that he did this on purpose.[19] In attempting to depict the religion of the ancient world it seemed natural to show the Trojans worshipping Venus and Cupid and following that medieval species of pseudo-paganism that we call "courtly love." For that matter, Chaucer depicted their religion, after the fashion of the courtly "religion of love," by applying to it Christian terms and concepts. I still believe that the medieval reader, schooled in anachronism, would have been little troubled by this procedure and probably would have imagined this *was* how pagans behaved; I suspect Boccaccio imagined the same. Chaucer, more interested in the "historial" setting than Boccaccio, was more aware that "in sundry landes sundry been usages," that "eech contree hath his lawes," and I still believe that he chose the anachronism of medieval love in ancient Troy not just to dress up Troy but *to comment on medieval love*. But what he really wanted to comment on was the philosophy that lay behind it—as we would say, its value-system.

So I came to believe that Chaucer represented the false philosophy of the ancients, which lay behind the "paganism" of medieval love conventions, *in the person of Pandarus*.[20] C. S. Lewis had argued that much of Pandarus's discourse was "doctryne" added to Chaucer's original for its inherent interest: Chaucer's audience would have experienced Pandarus as a learned man whose ideas they enjoyed and were edified by, but they would have seen the funny side of his sententiousness even while they admired much of what he said. I agreed. Where I disagreed was in believing that behind Pandarus's discourse lies *a consistent philosophical position*. If "courtly love" is in the poem as part of the pagan background, Pandarus's philosophy is in the poem as the intellectual basis of courtly love. We know that Chaucer read helter-skelter a number of classical authors and that he read *florilegia* and books like the *Polychronicon* that quoted ancient writers. From Boethius, too, he could have formed some notion of what Epicureans or Stoics or Neoplatonists had believed. So he had available to him the stuff of an imagined pagan philosophy. And what he did was to concoct one and attribute it to Pandarus.

"But how can this be," I hear the reader objecting, "when Pandarus is little better than a bawd?" There is no reason a bawd shouldn't have a philosophy, especially when we are to see that it is a false philosophy; but that is not my answer. We do Pandarus wrong if we impute to him the mind of a bawd or worse and then assume that for that reason all his discourse is platitude and hypocrisy. Pandarus has come to be much reviled in recent years: from one side we hear that he is a tempter, a corrupter of youth, from another that he is a devil or priest of Satan; we even hear from a lunatic fringe that he seduces or rapes his own niece on the morning after her first night with Troilus; and from other sides we hear pimp, voyeur, pervert. But it was not always so.[21] Assuming a man with a philosophy may live by it, we can find in Pandarus's philosophy much to explain his behavior, even his character. If we go back to the older, more generous, and more charitable view of him and begin by supposing that, whatever his faults, he may be at heart a worthy gentleman, we can at least ask what philosophy— "philosophy of life," as we might call it—provides him with his motives.

For Pandarus *is* a worthy gentleman—"a Trojan nobleman," Kittredge wrote, "next in rank, it appears, to princes of the blood and on intimate terms with the whole royal family. He is the head of a powerful clan, which he offers to rally to Troilus' assistance in preventing the exchange of Cressida for Antenor."[22] We even learn that he spent the day of Criseyde's departure in counsel with King Priam and so "it lay not in his libertee / Nowhere to goon" (5.285–86). This counsellor to princes, one must assume, is possessed of those virtues which in Chaucer's time would have been thought to qualify him for such a role: learning, wisdom, dignity, intelligence, and a command of rhetoric. And all these he has; his rank, his mental powers, and his verbal skills are uncontested. He is a keen observer of people and shrewd in judging their motives; in this he sometimes approaches cynicism—for example, he understands perfectly well that his niece is not immune to fleshly desire, and he says so with world-weary humor:

> "Was never man or woman yet begete
> That was unapt to sufferen love's heete—
> Celestial, or elles love of kinde."
> Forthy some grace I hope in her to finde.
>
> And for to speke of her in special,
> Her beautee to bethinken and her youthe,

It sit her not to been celestial
As yet. . .

(1.977–84)

His worldly wisdom is based not alone on good instincts or experience or intelligence, but on learning. He often mentions books and reading and is able to quote "auctors" in support of his points; his "proverbs" are more often book-learning than folklore, for the medievals were very respectful of proverbs, regarding them not the way we do, as "old saws," but as the inherited sayings of the "olde wise." Moreover, Pandarus can weave these bookish references into complex analogies (as in 1.624–72) that reveal a capacity for abstract thinking.

Such a man of rank, intellect, and learning might be expected to have a philosophy or at least a body of philosophical notions. These might well be the going ideas of his time, but he would hold them reflectively, understand them, and see their relationships and implications. Call it an ideology or a value-system, if you prefer; I do not mean to depict him as a systematic philosopher. But what he believes can be described as a philosophical position whose chief points are Temporality, Skepticism, Pragmaticism, and Humanism.

Pandarus seems to believe in an ever-flowing river of successive events rather like the "Heraclitean flux" of ancient thought. All that exists, exists in time. True, he refers to God and the devil, but most such references are oaths or colloquialisms like "God wot" or "God help me so"; he refers to pagan gods too in oaths or rhetorical flights: "O cruel God, O despitouse Marte! / O furies three of hell—on you I crye!" (2.435–36). We may say that he does not *dis*believe the gods of his nation: he *says* that he himself serves Venus (2.234), and he has Troilus pray to the God of Love (1.932). Twice he uses the phrase "God so wis be my salvacioun" (2.381, 563) and once, facetiously to Troilus, "God have thy soul" (2.1638), but obviously these do not mean he knows revealed Christian truth; they are references to the God of Love, if we may judge from his prayer (3.185) "Immortal God . . . that maist not dien / —Cupid I meen." What Pandarus does believe in is *creatures*, and he seems to acknowledge a god who created them, for he refers to a "God that us hath wrought" (2.577) and a "Lord that formed eest and west" (2.1053). But the only other power he seems to attribute to this god is the power to end life: the last words we hear from him are "And fro this world almighty God I praye / Deliver her soon. I can no more saye" (5.1742–43). I find no passage in which he indicates a belief in a divine wisdom or providence or in a power of evil or darkness. The power that he believes governs creatures is Fortune, goddess of mutability, just the right goddess to oversee a Heraclitean flux. Fortune with her wheel presides over a cycle or rhythm in human events, but it is not a process—it doesn't move towards progress or decline but is only change.

If you were to ask Pandarus how he knows all this, I believe he would answer, "I cannot say I *know* anything. It seems reasonable and squares with what we see every day. If you look at a river you see that it is always changing, and we may observe many analogies—the winds blow away, fire turns to ash and ash to dirt, flowers bloom and wither and bloom again or die. And we may hear in proverbs or read in books this same opinion." If you were to preach to him of God, or the Platonic Ideas, he would reply courteously that they are indeed possible but cannot be observed before our eyes as flux can be observed. If you explained about an act of faith in God, from which we may then deduce that all is part of a universal plan, and therefore that all is for the best, he would reply, "But we can see all the time that all is *not* for the best. What is wretched may improve, but what is joyous hangs only by a wire. We *know* nothing except that everything is uncertain." If then in exasperation you asked him whether he denied the very existence of knowledge, he would answer that knowledge is relative: "We know things by contraries. We cannot know gladness unless we have known sorrow, or know white without black, or shame without worthiness. Each, set beside the other, has more meaning because of the other. 'Of two contraries is oo lore'" (1.637–45). He is a skeptic, possibly like the skeptics of the ancient world, but in spirit close to the skepticism that we find sometimes in Chaucer himself as a matter of temperament, in some nominalist philosophers of Chaucer's time, and later (but without the accompanying fideism) in

Montaigne. His doctrine of contraries, however, may set him apart from skeptics such as these; to the extent that he thinks knowledge depends on binary oppositions, he is perhaps closer to a structuralist.

If you asked someone who holds such opinions "How, then, should we lead our lives?" you would get an answer in two parts. Pandarus is a pragmatist: since all things are always changing, he believes we should follow the dictates of the moment. On the one side he would say, therefore, that we should grasp any opportunity for pleasure when it presents itself and never trust the morrow. Chaucer seems to have him echo the Horatian *carpe diem* when he tells Criseyde she has found "good aventure" and should "Cacch it anon, lest aventure slacke" (2.291). Similarly his advice that one should love while young, drawn from Ovid via *Il Filostrato*, sounds like the "Horatian" sentiment dear to Renaissance poets:

> Think eek how elde wasteth every houre
> In eech of you a partie of beautee;
> And therefore, ere that age thee devoure,
> Go love, for, old, there will no wight of thee.
> (2.393–96)

This is not "hedonism" in the popular (and earlier) sense, for he believes those pleasures will only last a little while and that we should resign ourselves when they desert us. In this he comes close to what Epicurus in fact believed, that pleasure is the end of life but is attained through rational control. He is not a passive opportunist, he is an activist: we must seize opportunity, and if opportunity fails us or trouble befalls us we should "seeken boote." He is against day-dreaming or intellectualizing or procrastinating. He tells Criseyde that if a house is on fire you don't stop to ask how the candle fell in the straw (3.855–59). He is against self-pity and self absorption: he tells Troilus "Swich is delite of fooles, to beweepe / Hir woe, but seeken boote they ne keepe" (1.762–63).

That is one side of it, a sort of muscular hedonism; the other side is pessimistic. To take overmuch pleasure in one's happiness creates the possibility of a great disappointment when we lose that happiness, as we surely will. Pandarus warns Troilus of this when Troilus is at the height of his bliss:

> For of Fortune's sharp adversitee
> The worste kind of infortune is this:
> A man to han been in prosperitee,
> And it rememberen when it passed is.
> Th'art wise enough, forthy do not amiss;
> Be not too rakel, though thou sitte warme,
> For if thou be, certain, it will thee harme.
>
> Thou art at eese, and hold thee well thereinne.
> For also sure as red is every fir,
> As greet a craft is keepe well as winne.
> Bridle alway well thy speech and thy desir,
> For worldly joy halt not but by a wir.
> That preveth well—it brest alday so ofte—
> Forthy need is to worken with it softe.
>   (3.1625–38)

This is as much as to say, be prepared for the worst. Since "Alle thing hath time," everything that has its time will pass. And the right attitude is therefore one of balance between extremes, of moderation, of avoiding excess. Such an attitude is like the classical idea of the Golden Mean, and indeed Pandarus says,

> . . . bothe two been vices—
> Mistrusten all, or elles alle leve.
> But well I wot, the meen of it no vice is.
>   (1.687–89)

To the extent that this moderation is a remedy against Fortune, a way of steeling oneself against the worst, it is in the popular sense "stoical." And no doubt Roman stoicism lay behind the Boethian presentation of Fortune, which Chaucer knew, as it lay also behind *"contemptus mundi."*[23]

I am aware that this "philosophy," which I have described in the traditional sequence—metaphysics, epistemology, ethics—is a crazy-quilt of classical ideas: Heraclitean flux, skepticism, hedonism, Horatian *carpe diem*, stoic resignation. Probably no ancient Greek or Roman ever held such a combination of ancient ideas. Yet it is rather much the impression of ancient thought that an avid medieval reader might have had from a *florilegium* of the sayings of ancient philosophers, or from an eclectic work of philosophy such as the *Consolation*. It captures the spirit of the ancient (as opposed to the Christian) world-view with surprising insight. And our word for that classical world-view is humanism. Pandarus is above all a humanist. He believes fundamentally in *creatures* and sees those creatures arrayed in a hierarchy with humanity in the position of honor; he refers disparagingly to "bestiality" (1.735) and speaks of "so noble a creature / As is a man" (5.384–85). He is unaware of the hierarchies of angels or the heavenly host or the Supreme Being of the Christian revelation, as he is unaware of the God and the law of the Old Dispensation. Living in the Age of Nature, he holds that man is the measure.

And here we come to the thorniest aspect of his thinking. For it does appear that he believes the end justifies the means, believes that we can say what we please to get what we want and let our sayings be declared "inoperative" when they no longer serve us. This at least is how he behaves, and I find nothing in what he says about behavior that goes against the principle. Whether he would follow such a principle in politics, as he does in private ethics, we do not know. We do know that he lies to get Troilus and Criseyde together, that he advises Troilus to find another lover after Criseyde has left. And we know he contradicts himself. He tells Troilus that since he has had his desire fully he should be satisfied (4.393–99), and this contradicts his earlier statement to Troilus that the worst misfortune is to have been in prosperity and remember it when it is passed (3.1625–28); Troilus himself points out the contradiction in 4.481–83. Still, skeptical Pandarus would be the first to disparage a foolish consistency; or perhaps consistency can be found in his implicit suggestion that Troilus *forget* past prosperity. At all events it would be unjust to take his inconsistencies as evidence of duplicity. We are in a pagan world where love is central to the cult of Venus and Cupid, where fleeting pleasure is a legitimate end, and where marriage is not even a consideration.[24] Pandarus believes that a love between his niece and his friend would be a desirable end, and he bends the truth and plumps up his rhetoric to attain that end. This is "Machiavellian" enough, but then Machiavelli, properly understood, was thinking along solidly classical—in this case Aristotelian—lines. That Pandarus changes his estimate of Criseyde must not be raised as an objection, because he changes it only after *she* has changed.

The question to be raised about Pandarus's manipulative conduct is whether his pursuit of an end knows no ethical restraints. He never says so, any more than he *says* the end justifies the means. But judging from his behavior, the answer is that his restraints are —anachronistically—the standard restraints of honor and "gentilesse" cherished by medieval chivalry. Thus before he proceeds to the grand finale of his plan, he feels uneasiness that in his role as friend and go-between he has overstepped a bound, and he exacts Troilus's word that his intentions are honorable (3.239–343). Here Chaucer's imagined ancient humanism coincides with medieval courtly values—appropriately enough, since Pandarus's ancient paganism in effect *is* medieval "courtly love."

We are meant to see all along that this pagan "philosophy" is in error. But we must not confuse its philosophical errors with Pandarus's personal or psychological errors in following it. Of such personal errors I find two.

Pandarus makes one error of judgment: he misjudges the intensity of Troilus's emotion and the tenacity of his idealism. Throughout the poem we observe a gulf in the two men's understanding of each other. Of this gulf I will offer a small, overlooked example. In Book II when Pandarus advises Troilus what kind of love letter to write, he tells him "Be-blot it with thy teeres eek a lite" (1027)—the notion, out of Ovid, is that a love-letter conveys its message more strongly when stained with the writer's tears. Troilus writes his letter, reads it over, and in sealing it makes a splendid gesture, so natural for him that no one ever notices it, and it is exactly the opposite of Pandarus's "be-blotting." One can imagine Pandarus, like a figure in a Restoration comedy, providing the tears from a wet towel, but not Troilus. Troilus does have tears on his face as he writes, but with them he wets the seal ring before imprinting the wax:

> And with his salte teeres gan he bathe
> The ruby in his signet, and it sette

> Upon the wax deliverlich and rathe.
> (2.1086–88)

Chaucer lets us know that this spontaneous, private, and sentimental gesture, done in total earnest, not to impress the lady, is followed by the agile, quick gesture of a prince accustomed to sealing documents. (Later, in 5.1335–37, his letter *is* defaced with tears.) So it is when Pandarus warns Troilus about acting honorably: he suspects or fears a cynicism of which Troilus is incapable. So, too, after the couple's first night he reminds Troilus that such bliss cannot be expected to last, that "As greet a craft is keepe well as winne" (3.1634). But Troilus does not understand what Pandarus is getting at—he thinks that if he behaves well nothing can go wrong: "I hope . . . that I shall so me bere / That in my guilt there shall nothing be lorn." He misses the point about Fortune and adds with a touch of ineradicable lust "I had it never half so hot as now." Pandarus lets it pass. When Fortune does change, Pandarus advises him to forget; when Troilus points out his inconsistency, he suggests elopement, but Troilus explains why this will compromise her honor. Pandarus knows there is no other alternative: if they do not elope, she must go and Troilus must resign himself. But of this Troilus is temperamentally incapable.

Pandarus's other personal error is a failure of self-knowledge. There is a reason in his private emotional life that explains why he puts such emotion into promoting the love affair. He is himself unhappy in love. He has been in love with a certain lady for a long time, but without success. His plan for his niece and Troilus is a vicarious way of attaining for others what he cannot have for himself—and not any the less generous for that. But he gets carried away. Answering Troilus's question—how can he help someone else if he can't help himself—he answers pell-mell with a tour de force of proverbs and analogies and arguments almost two hundred lines long (1.624–819), a very funny passage, which, however, betrays the enormous force of his emotion. We do not understand, and he probably does not understand himself, why he has failed in love. We know that he can make a joke of it—we see him set the table on a roar at Criseyde's house. But we also see him—once—collapse into despair, at the beginning of Book II. When is that? It is on the very day when after a night of tossing and turning he wakes to remember that this was the day he must set upon his "greet emprise." And we see the thought cheer him. The passage is Chaucer's invention, clearly intended to reveal Pandarus's vicarious motivation. A "neurotic" manifestation it may be, but perhaps not more so than Troilus's single-mindedness or than Criseyde's constitutional timidity. After that, as long as the love affair is going well, Pandarus is genuinely happy and his offices are not any the less those of true friendship. But when all is lost, Pandarus does not put the energy into consoling Troilus that he had put into persuading him to reveal the lady's name and "seeken boote." He has lost his vicarious motive, and we are aware that something has gone out of him. He can only say he hates Criseyde and wishes her dead.

This turnabout at the end may mean his philosophy has failed him, but not necessarily. His emotional outburst against Criseyde might be his pragmatic way of dealing with his frustration. "Alle thing hath time"—he can change his mind tomorrow. Of such a "defense mechanism," if we can call it that, Troilus is quite incapable, and this renders him more vulnerable to disappointment. Perhaps Pandarus has collapsed in failure. But perhaps hating Criseyde, or saying so, is a way to keep his balance. While Troilus, despairing, seeks revenge and death, Pandarus may find another "outlet."

Chaucer set out to create in Pandarus a figure from the ancient world who lives by an imagined pagan philosophy, but he created unawares and by coincidence a very modern man. Pandarus's "philosophy," distilled from classical thought, is inimical to Christianity exactly as the classicism of Renaissance and post-Renaissance humanism was to be: over and over the humanists could *play* at *carpe diem*, but in the end they always had to troop back to their master admitting that the real lesson of this world's mutability was *contemptus mundi*. And if Pandarus's "pagan" style of thinking provides him with glib "defenses," if he can hate Criseyde today and forget her tomorrow, is he not very like us, or many of us, in an individualistic post-Freudian age, for whom success in life is a matter of maintaining mental health and personal autonomy even at others' expense? Perhaps this similarity to ourselves explains why he has come to be so hated.

4

The Christian or "Boethian" philosophy in the poem, shared by the narrator and his audience, is what seems to discredit this picture of ancient thought; it has been endlessly discussed, and in many such discussions it is called *contemptus mundi*.[25] When I went to the Vatican Library with my letter from Morton Bloomfield, my project was to search for unpublished works on contempt of the world. That had been the subject of my doctoral dissertation, which I conceived of as a study in the history of ideas, and I arrived in Italy with the opinion that "contempt of the world" was a philosophical idea, part of a complex of ideas which comprised the dominant ideology of the later Middle Ages; that it was in its historical provenance ascetical and monastic; and that in literary expression it came to have, during the twelfth century, a new and unaccustomed violence of rhetorical flourish, a particularity that often veered towards satire and betrayed a concern for the world. It was my thesis that this shift in style occurred because *contemptus mundi* was the dark underside of the renaissance of the twelfth century, the pessimistic and ascetical polarity of a new secularism and optimism, and as much a feature of Renaissance humanism as of medieval thought. My notion was to write a vast historical tome about this "idea."

But I never wrote it, and not solely because I was putting into practice the spirit of my topic. My notions of it faltered. I expected to uncover a small handful of manuscript works on the subject; instead I found hundreds. I began to see that "contempt of the world" was a set topic that everyone wrote about, and from a historical distance everyone seemed to say much the same things; yet from the point of view of the writers, each was saying something new or saying it in a new way. While I was studying *contemptus mundi* as a phase of literary expression, the learned Belgian historian, Robert Bultot, was studying it as a phase of Christian doctrine.[26] Of course "contempt" can be seen and justified in the light of doctrine, yet I had begun to doubt that it was in fact a doctrine in theology or in philosophy. I was no longer sure it was even an idea: or if it was, I suspected it was such an idea as A. O. Lovejoy had called "metaphysical pathos," an idea whose force resided in a shared feeling and whose use was as an outlet for emotions.

As my files grew, contempt of the world came to seem more like a secular than, strictly speaking, a religious theme, and I began to doubt that it could properly be called "ascetical" or that it had ever been monastic. I was almost afrighted by the temerity of these thoughts, yet one day in the Vatican Library I received an unexpected confirmation. Signora Bignami came scurrying up to me with a conspiratorial air and said, "*Senta, cognosce Dom Jean Leclerq?*" Yes, of course, I knew he was the great scholar of monastic spirituality. "Well, he is here for two weeks—*La faccio presentare.*" When I was introduced, he asked me in his charming way, with genuine interest, what I was working on. But while I was screwing up my courage to try some of my radical thoughts on him, he surprised me: "Ah, *contemptus mundi,* a very interesting tradition, very important. Now, you see, this is not monastic. . . ."

Reading the end of Chaucer's *Troilus* from the viewpoint of this partly abandoned project,[27] I am never certain that *contemptus mundi* is really there. The distance established at the end, with Troilus looking down from the eighth sphere and the narrator removed to the present and lost in the contemplation of the Christian mysteries, *seems* like contempt of the world. And of course we are told that Troilus "fully gan despise / This wrecched world" (5.1816-17); "Swich fin hath false worlde's brottlenesse" (1832), we are told, and "thinketh all nis but a faire / This world" (1840-41). The traditional categories of worldly vanity and corruption are named—earthly love, worldly possessions and power, even the books of "olde clerkes' speeche / In poetry" (1854-55). But in works on contempt of the world, the objects of contempt are rarely dealt with in such generalities; they are described in minute and particular detail of such a kind as to make them *seem* despicable and ugly, though one often senses ambivalence in the writers, as if they are struggling with a covert fascination.

In Chaucer's ending this ambivalence is more remarkable because we feel *regret*. The things of this world in the *Troilus* have not been presented in the *contemptus mundi* manner as slime or worm's meat or dung and corruption; they were beautiful, enthralling things, like "flowers faire," that lasted only a short time and ended in disappointment. If the ending of the *Troilus* calls into play the medieval sensibility attached to contempt of the world, it rivets attention on the themes of vanity and mutability, plays upon medieval ambivalence about the world. And if this is philosophy, it is not "Boethian" in its philosophical implication. Where Boethius argued explicitly that all is for the best, writings on contempt of the world, though they imply this, argue that all we experience in earthly life is for the worst—is corrupted, disappointing, vain. And they include learning and philosophy among worldly vanities. "There is hardly anything so cheap and easy," wrote Pope Innocent III in his *De Miseria Humane Conditionis*, the classic of the genre, "that a man can understand it fully and clearly, unless perhaps he knows for sure that *nothing* is known for sure" (1.12). Because philosophizing had in it the possibility of tempting one to the sin of curiosity or leading one into heresy, it was at best a handmaiden to those truths known through revelation or through a direct religious or mystical experience with the divine intelligence. From this point of view the most important event in the history of late medieval philosophy occurred on the Feast day of St. Nicholas, 1273, when the greatest philosopher of the age, St. Thomas Aquinas, experienced a mystical vision while saying mass, after which he never wrote or dictated another word. "All that I have written," he is reported to have said, "seems to me like so much straw compared to what I have seen and what has been revealed to me."[28]

Such a renunciation is not a palinode; no "truancy" is involved, no retraction is forthcoming. It is an awareness that everything struggled over with logic or language, in however vast a philosophical or literary edifice, is as nothing compared with what may be given direct by God in the smallest instant. If at the end of the *Troilus* such a view of worldly vanities is expressed, that view named philosophy itself among those vanities. The Christian philosophy of the poem must in the end take its place alongside Criseyde's beauty, Troilus's love, Pandarus's "doctrine," the pagans' rites and their gods and their books of poetry. The effect is like the ending of *Everyman*: each human good that supports man in life deserts him as he nears death, but some desert him sooner than others.

Something like this happens in the last stanzas of the *Troilus*, and the Christian philosophy is the last feature to be renounced. Having drawn his moral about Troilus's end and the false world's brittleness, Chaucer makes the reality of the work disperse before our eyes, as if to deconstruct or deconstitute the reality he has labored to sustain. First he renounces the loves of this world, for the world is like a fair and passes like a flower, and the love of Christ alone will not betray us in the end. Then, he renounces literature, renounces the literary traditions of which the poem is a part: his poem of earthly and "courtly" love is pagans' rites and worldly appetites and "the form of olde clerkes' speech / In poetry." Finally he unmasks himself, renounces that self-presentation he has adopted, and in so doing makes the "narrator"—the Christian narrator with his Christian philosophy—disappear. When he has said "Go, litel book," we have already begun to be aware that the historian-narrator with his "olde book" and his enthusiasm and curiosity for the ancient world it describes is only a role played by our author, who would kiss the steps of the pagan great and worry over the diversity of our tongue; and now we are made aware that this author destroying his mask is in fact the historical Geoffrey Chaucer, friend of John Gower and Ralph Strode.

In the "dedication," with its request that Gower and Strode "correct" him where there is need, is an ultimate, or possibly penultimate irony. "Moral Gower" would no doubt be in a position to correct Chaucer in literary errors, as Strode would in philosophical ones. But it happens that by 1386 Chaucer and Gower had already begun to part company, though politely and as friends; Gower was still writing medieval complaint with its explicitly moral intent while Chaucer, back from the last of his Italian journeys, had found something new in literature, the *novelle* of Italian writers (of which it may be he thought *Il Filostrato* an example)—stories told for their own interest, with only implicit moral import.[29] We cannot say Gower disapproved of the *Troilus*, but neither did he approve of it; a great deal of minute detail about a love affair in a pagan world has led up to this final moral statement, and one can imagine Gower feeling that there was too much detail, that it was too real, too interesting, too lacking in expressed morality. Very likely some such feeling was still in Chaucer's mind when some fifteen years later he named the *Troilus* among his "enditings of worldly vanitees." Nevertheless, there is a kind of assertiveness, almost of defiance, in the dedication: if Gower were to correct the *Troilus* as Gower would have wanted to, the poem would have had to be different in the most fundamental respects from what it is at this moment when it is within a stanza of being complete.

It is the same with "philosophical Strode." The request that he correct the poem is assertive too, assuming this is the Ralph Strode who disputed Wyclif's necessitarian beliefs. We seem to glimpse in the "dedication" a picture of a circle of English intellectuals who knew each other and had friendly disagreements with each other. And Strode, an opponent of necessitarian ideas, would have found much to "correct" in the *Troilus*.[30] Not that Troilus and Criseyde do not have free will in a technical sense; they make choices they could have avoided and adopt attitudes they could have altered—they have free will as Boethius defined it, in the moral sphere. But in the moral sphere neither makes virtue of necessity by patience: the choices they make are not informed by reason or by revealed truth but are conditioned by their ruling passions, by their characters. Troilus is in bondage to his own romantic and idealistic temperament, Criseyde to her constitutional hesitancy and timidity. Confronted by circumstances over which they have no control, they have little capacity for the true consolation of philosophy, resignation to a benevolent world-order. Their resignation is a *pagan* resignation, to stark Fate. Criseyde concludes that there is no happiness, Troilus that there is no freedom; she, among the Greeks, becomes hardened and callous, and he, left in Troy, becomes vengeful, self-destructive, despairing. Strode might have suspected, as I do myself and as Morton Bloomfield did in "Distance and Predestination," that Chaucer was at heart a determinist and took this picture of human action out of control as a picture of the way things really are: people are only free in their thoughts and most are barely that. Strode might have wanted to "correct" this picture by adding reminders that the way things are is not the way they have to be, that man is capable of rational control and rational choices in adversity. And Chaucer might have agreed that this is so *in theory* even for pagan man living by a pagan philosophy. But his answer to Strode or Gower might have been that to include these moralizing reminders would have spoiled the story or altered its kind.

"Vouchensauf, ther need is, to correcte, / Of your

benignitees and zeeles goode" sounds very courteous and humble, like a modesty topos, but it is an equivocal utterance. *Where* would there be any such need in a work that makes the Christian philosophy that would correct it everywhere implicit? *Benignity* and *zeal* were new words in Chaucer's time if we may judge from the citations in the OED, and it is interesting that the earliest recorded instance of *zeal*, in Wyclif, uses the word in a negative sense, glossing it "envy"—whence Chaucer is at pains to qualify it as "zeeles goode." Moral Gower and philosophical Strode, each with his benignity and his good zeal, deserved to be acknowledged here because each was a potential threat. Both may have had something to add of explicit morality and philosophy that Chaucer preferred for artistic reasons to keep tacit. So it is probably ironic that he does not wait for an answer: he escapes—"escapes into the contemplation of the mysteries of the Passion and of the Trinity," Bloomfield wrote—and thus puts himself beyond the reach of philosophical discourse.

This last escape into pure religiosity has its pagan counterpart in Troilus's last moment of objective laughter, the moment when he "dampned all our work that followeth so / The blinde lust." Embarking on an unknown future after death, Troilus adopts an attitude *like* contempt of the world but by no means the same. Nevertheless, most readers see his attitude sympathetically as a moment of understanding and release from pain, so much so that some have thought him saved. We are pleased to think, though it is not a Christian thought, that the dead can laugh at life. In this glimpse of Troilus in death, which Chaucer had via Boccaccio's *Teseida* from Lucan and Dante, and which is a genuine insight into the spirit of paganism, he allowed to pagan religion the same respectful interest he had allowed to pagan philosophies. And Chaucer's final escape into religion does share with Troilus's final moment a resignation to the inscrutable forces that wield our lives.

If Chaucer escapes the philosophical issues by a flight into religion, are we to suppose that the Christian philosophy in the poem has somehow failed to discredit the pagan philosophy? Are we to imagine that Troilus's last moment before Mercury leads his soul away is somehow, in religious terms, comparable to the contemplation of the Christian mysteries? These are not fashionable questions, and if they are asked they are answered "no" by reflex action. But the facts, if we are prepared to face them, admit no easy answers. The imagined pagan philosophy, handmaiden to the imagined pagan religion, is at the heart of the story. The love affair, as a rite of Venus, is its center. Troilus's pagan soul journey is its end. Perhaps all the artistic effort Chaucer lavished on such a story was only to make a straw man for a homily. But does it not square better with the facts to say that paganism, as explored in *Troilus and Criseyde*, seemed to Chaucer, and must seem to us, something alluring, a system with recoverable values? This is an opinion not at all palatable to the "historical criticism" of our time, which has worked hard to make the *Troilus* a unilaterally Christian poem. But I have history on my side. In Chaucer's day ancient paganism had just begun to capture the imagination of intellectuals and artists, and the *Troilus* is a product of that incipient humanism. During the centuries that followed, the study of pagan thought and myth, in spite of the tedious efforts to allegorize them, brought to Christian Europe a taste of that elemental common sense and love of wisdom that belonged to pagan Greece. Not that Chaucer, like the other humanists, did not remain secure in the mysteries of the faith; but to imagine him and them merely clicking their tongues in that security over the errors of the ancients flies in the face of history. At the heart of the "philosophy" in Chaucer's *Troilus* is the impulse which was to revolutionize, was already beginning to revolutionize, western thought— the impulse, which we call classicism, to recapture the values of pre-Christian times.

Robert Worth Frank, Jr.

Miracles of the Virgin, Medieval Anti-Semitism, and the "Prioress's Tale"

In attempting to come to terms with Chaucer's "Prioress's Tale," scholars find its anti-Semitism one of the most troublesome features. Pathos, for the teller at least, suffuses the story of the little chorister who in devotion to the Virgin learns by rote the "Alma Redemptoris" and sings it daily as he walks to and from school through the Jewish ghetto of an Asian city. There is a quivering tenderness for the martyred child, and a vibrant sympathy for the bereaved mother. But the Jews, who are protected by the lord of that country "for foule usure and lucre of vileynye" (*PrT* 1681),[1] are portrayed as heartless villains and, in turn, are treated heartlessly. Guilty of cruelly murdering the innocent child, they are themselves cruelly tortured and put to a shameful death. Why, one must ask, would Chaucer choose an anti-Semitic tale? There had been no Jews in England since they were driven from the kingdom in 1290. The choice seems gratuitous and perverse. Critics therefore tend to see the tale as a comment on the teller, the Prioress, evidence of her shallow sentimentality, and evidence of an ironic or even hostile portraiture by Chaucer.[2]

The question "why," however, is, alas, historically naïve, or so I hope to show in pursuing a larger issue here. It is naïve because anyone who reads at all extensively in the genre to which Chaucer's tale belongs, the miracles of the Virgin, soon becomes aware of the persistent presence of anti-Semitism. So far as I know, this fact has not been commented upon at any length. Beverly Boyd observes of the miracles that "their anti-Semitism is the heritage of centuries of bigotry and persecution throughout the world."[3] And Bernhard Blumenkranz has investigated a variety of miracle stories as an area of religious polemic,[4] but his study is not directed specifically at miracles of the Virgin. Investigation reveals precise and particular reasons for their anti-Semitism.

The history of the genre should be sketched first. The devotional narrative form we call miracles of the Virgin is a product of the late Middle Ages. For centuries there had been isolated tales of miracles attributed to the Virgin's intervention. "Theophilus" is one. Another is the "Jew of Bourges," told in the late sixth century by Evagrius Scholasticus and by Gregory of Tours, who told five other Marian stories as well.[5] Stories of miracles performed by the Virgin also arose at various shrines—Fécamp, Soissons, Laon—stories generally of miraculous cures at a particular shrine, not dissimilar to hundreds of other stories associated with shrines all over Europe. As a distinct form, however, the miracles of the Virgin are identified by R. W. Southern as "collections of stories which had an independent literary existence"; they possessed a general rather than a local interest and were not in fact influenced by local shrine miracles. These collections "took Europe by storm in the twelfth and thirteenth centuries, reached their fullest extension in the fourteenth and fifteenth centuries, and survived as a living literature here and there till the seventeenth century."[6]

Southern's phrase "collections of stories" possesses a special force. Though scattered miracles of the Virgin appeared in gatherings of stories like Jacques de Vitry's *Exempla* or of miracles like Caesar von Heisterbach's *Dialogus*

Miraculorum, the usual form of publication and circulation was in a collection clearly identifiable as miracles of the Virgin. One must read through several of these collections and at least the table of contents of many more to get a sense of the form to which the "Prioress's Tale" belongs.[7] What emerges very clearly is that anti-Semitic tales are a commonplace in the genre, a standard, constituent element. There are by my count eighteen miracles in which Jewish characters appear. It is a rare collection of any size that does not have several such tales, and some of them are among the miracles most frequently narrated. At a rough estimate they comprise 7½ percent of the common stock of miracles, and they are told again and again and again.[8]

To the insistent question why anti-Semitic tales are so pervasive a presence in the collections there are several answers. They may be classified as, first, historical and cultural; second, legendary and "biographical"; and, third, doctrinal.

The historical answer is, of course, the sharp rise of anti-Semitism in the high Middle Ages. After some centuries of relatively peaceful coexistence by Jewish and Christian communities in Western Europe,[9] anti-Semitism began to spread and intensify in the late eleventh and early twelfth centuries. Though the phenomenon is not completely understood, a complex of causes seems involved in this development. Both economic and political reasons for the change may be identified. In the Carolingian period the movement and exchange of goods had so ebbed that Western Europe became essentially a rural economy. During this period Jewish merchants provided almost the sole trading tie with the outside world and between distant communities within Western Europe.[10] This situation altered with the end of the barbarian invasions, the opening of the Mediterranean to Europe once more, and the rapid economic growth in the West beginning with the eleventh century. As trade became safer, more widespread, and more profitable, the Jews were systematically rooted out as competitors. Where they enjoyed a strongly entrenched position, they could be singled out to be taxed or their wealth could be confiscated. As "alien" competitors they aroused hostile feeling, so anti-Semitism served an economic purpose. Their role as usurers in a period when usury was forbidden but capital was becoming more essential was another factor in the rise of antagonism to the Jew.[11]

The political situation of Jews in Western Europe also changed at about the same time. Though their religion already isolated them in some degree, the Crusades isolated them still further from their Christian neighbors. This was the first time the Jews were excluded from participating in war against a foreign enemy.[12] Moreover, the Crusades were costly, and the Jews were taxed with special severity to support them. The wars themselves directly inflamed anti-Semitic feelings: since they were wars against nonbelievers, the Saracens, they encouraged hostility against nonbelievers everywhere. It is estimated that in a few days, in Germany, during the First Crusade, 12,000 Jews were massacred. In the Second Crusade (1147–49), a Cistercian monk named Raoul stirred up mass pogroms against the Jews until he was suppressed by St. Bernard.[13]

Papal legislation in the late twelfth and early thirteenth centuries drove a yet deeper wedge between Jews and Christians in Western Europe. Threatened by the widespread Albigensian heresy in the south of France, the Church in the Lateran Council of 1179 revived and re-enacted the long dormant anti-Jewish legislation of the early Church. It prohibited employment of Christians by Jews in any role and prohibited Christians from lodging among infidels, "thus laying the foundation of the later Ghetto system."[14] The Fourth Lateran Council in 1215, in the third of four legislative actions concerning Jews, ordered that they be distinguished from Christians by dress or sign ("Ut Judaei discernantur a Christianis in habitibus"), an action which led ultimately to the infamous Badge of Shame. Jacob R. Marcus observes that "the expulsions of the Jews from Western Europe in the course of the next three centuries were the direct result of this social isolation which Innocent put into effect."[15]

The history of the several hundred years following is one of persecution and banishment. They were expelled from England in 1290. During the Black Death in 1348–49 they were accused in Germany of having brought on the plague by poisoning the wells and were slaughtered indiscriminately. During Chaucer's lifetime, after ten years of controversy in Paris over charges that they had persuaded a

Jewish convert to renounce Christianity, Jews were expelled from northern France by Charles VI in 1394.[16]

Certain intellectual developments in the twelfth and thirteenth centuries are part of this historical explanation. After six centuries, the West was awakening from its intellectual torpor. R. W. Southern suggests that the renewal of fundamental inquiry into intellectual issues led to a new awareness of the Jew: here in their midst was a distinct and alien society which positively rejected the Christian faith on historical and intellectual grounds. Recognition of this fact gave the West a shock of alarm.[17] St. Anselm wrote his *Cur Deus Homo*, one of the first expressions of the new spirit of theological inquiry, in part to answer the Jewish unbeliever.[18] Intellectual debate with Jewish thinkers continued for at least the next century and a half before being discouraged and discontinued.[19] Some of this controversy, as we shall see, related specifically to the role of the Virgin Mary.

Certain cultural developments of the period were influential as well. Late medieval art, in which the new interest in the human Christ appears, powerfully reinforced feelings of hostility toward the Jews. In the art of this period the Jew is presented almost invariably as a hateful creature, set off from his fellow men by costume and by the caricature of the hooked nose.[20] (Indeed, the caricature of the Jew in nineteenth- and twentieth-century anti-Semitism, including Nazi anti-Semitism, goes directly back to the representations of the Jew in Western medieval art.) In late medieval art the vices, and heretics of all kinds, were often represented as Jews.[21] Synagoga was commonly represented as a blinded woman with a broken lance opposed to Ecclesia, the True Church.[22] As the portrayal of Christ's suffering in the Passion developed in detail and in intensity, the Jew emerged more and more vividly as a cruel persecutor and tormentor.[23] This was also true of the popular meditations that focused on the life of Christ and particularly on the Passion, and it was true of the dramatization of the Passion in the mystery plays.

Even more to our purpose is the fact that the age perceived a very specific antagonism between the Jews and the Virgin. One aspect of this antagonism, legendary in origin, can be called biographical. It derives from the apoc-

ryphal narrative usually called the *Transitus* which exists
with many variants in Greek, Latin, Syriac, Coptic, Arabic,
and Ethiopic versions. The original probably dates from the
fifth century and was attributed to St. John the Evangelist.
The *Transitus* tells of the events surrounding Mary's death
and burial and of the coming of angels at Christ's bidding to
take her body from the tomb and place it under the Tree of
Life in Paradise, where it is reunited with her soul. During
the procession to the tomb, the Jews of the city attack the
cortege. The chief priest or prince, who tries to touch her
bier, has his hands cut off—in some later versions his hand
withers and sticks to the bier—and all his companions are
blinded. This miraculous event converts all the Jews, who
are then healed.[24]

This attack by the Jews became part of the story of
Mary's life. Jacobus de Voragine incorporated it in his
account of the Assumption of the Virgin for the feast of that
name on August 15 in the *Legenda Aurea*. It is found in the
Rhythmical Life of the Virgin (first half of the thirteenth
century),[25] and, in England, in such works as the *Blickling
Homily*, the thirteenth-century *Assumption of Our Lady*, the
Cursor Mundi, and the *South English Legendary*.[26] Collections of
miracles of the Virgin sometimes include events from her
biography, and the account of the Assumption may include
the attack on her bier.[27] It is frequently a scene in dramatized versions of the Assumption, as in the one such drama
that has survived in English, in the *Ludus Coventriae*.[28] The
incident is often represented in art, sometimes as a scene
with the hand shown grotesquely adhering to the coffin of
the Virgin. Thus to Mary's sufferings during the Flight to
Egypt and during the Passion is added, in the *Transitus*, a
direct attack on her body, an overt act of hostility. The Jews,
it was believed, regarded her as an enemy.

There is antagonism between Mary and the Jews at the
doctrinal level as well. Jewish thinkers rejected the Incarnation as an affront to the dignity and majesty of God. In
Anselm's *Cur Deus Homo*, Boso says, "Infidels ridiculing our
simplicity charge upon us that we do injustice and dishonor
to God when we affirm that he descended to the womb of a
virgin, that he was born of a woman, that he grew on the
nourishment of milk and the food of men. . . ."[29] The
*Disputatio contra Judaeum, Leonem nomine, de Adventu Christi Filii
Dei,* by Odo, bishop of Cambrai, reporting, presumably, a

dispute with a Jew at Senlis in 1106, represents him as saying,

There is something we laugh at you about and for which we consider you crazy. You say God endured being enclosed in maternal bowels in the obscene prison of a fetid womb for nine months, and then came forth in the tenth month through a shameful passage (a matter which does not admit being considered without great embarrassment), disgracing God.[30]

Mary, we should also remember, is the confuser of heretics, and this again brings her into direct opposition to the Jewish people. In the responsoria for the third nocturn of the Feast of the Purification are the lines, "Rejoice, Mary, virgin, you who believed the words of the Archangel Gabriel, you alone have slain all heresies; while a virgin, you gave birth to God and man, and after giving birth you remained an inviolate virgin." The versus, a few lines later, reads, "Let the unhappy Jew blush, who says that Christ is born from the seed of Joseph." (In some versions of the miracle on which the "Prioress's Tale" is based, the offensive line sung by the child is "Erubescat Judaeus infelix.")[31]

If we now look at the miracles of the Virgin in which Jewish figures appear, we can see one or more of these historical and cultural, "biographical," and doctrinal sources of hostility shaping particular legends. The historical and cultural hostility may be said, of course, to be operative in all of them in a diffuse but pervasive fashion. The hostility is to be seen more specifically at work, however, in two miracles where the Jew is not a necessary figure but is introduced more or less arbitrarily in some versions to fill a hostile role. The popular image of the Jew as magician allied with the devil may on occasion influence the choice,[32] but the motivation for the choice is hostile: it evokes hostile comment and invites a hostile reaction. In the popular story of Theophilus, the intermediary between Theophilus and the devil is often a Jew, as in Sidney Sussex Cambridge MS 95, where he is described as "a most wicked Hebrew soaked in all kinds of wickedness, who had already drowned many faithless men in the chasm of perdition."[33] In the miracle of the knight who refused to deny the Virgin, the intermediary again may be a Jew.[34]

The controversy over the role and power of the Virgin

and sometimes specifically over the Incarnation is the central issue in the miracle of the blind man whose sight is restored.[35] In other tales it may be referred to in passing, as in the version of "The Chorister" in Trinity College Cambridge MS O.9.38: the boy enters the street where the Jews dwell, "who speak against the fecundity of the Virgin Mary and deny that the son of God was made flesh in the womb of a virgin."[36]

Although many of the anti-Semitic miracles end in the conversion of Jews, they may end in the slaying of the offending Jews or of the entire Jewish population of a city. There are, however, several miracles whose special purpose is conversion. In these Mary, the confuser of heretics, triumphs over the disbelief of a stubborn and literal-minded people (to use the language of the time). Three of them concern Jewish women who are converted by the intercession of the Virgin: the Jewish girl, called Katherine by the Virgin, who becomes a nun;[37] the Jewish woman who, falling from a great height, calls on the Virgin for help and is miraculously saved;[38] and the Jewish woman near death in childbirth who hears a voice from heaven urging her to call on the Virgin for aid, and having done so, gives birth painlessly and is subsequently baptized along with her child.[39] (Abuse and threats from other Jews usually acompany these conversions.) "The Jew of London" concerns a Jew who, while journeying, is converted after the Virgin reveals to him the pains of hell.[40] "The Lily in the Wine Pot" tells of a Jew who resists conversion but finally says he will accept the Christian faith if a lily (the Virgin's flower, of course) grows in a nearby wine pot; it does.[41] Finally, one miracle deals with false conversion: the Virgin reveals that a Jew who claims he has accepted Christianity has lied.[42] A concern for conversion is never far away. "How the industry of Mary labors to convert her people!" someone added to William of Malmesbury's manuscript just before the story of the Jew of Bourges.[43]

Though conversion, when not a major issue, could always be a welcome consequence, at the heart of the greater number of anti-Semitic miracles is a personal hostility, a hatred of Mary by the Jews, and, simultaneously, the power of Mary to triumph over their hostility. This takes a variety of forms: a Jew blaspheming against Mary is killed with a blow of a fist;[44] an image of Mary is abused (as in "Constantinople," where the image is thrown into a privy and defiled[45]), or it appears miraculously on the wall of a church dedicated to her, a building which the Jews of the city have claimed was their synagogue.[46] Assaults by Jews on the image of Christ are found among the miracles of the Virgin, in part, presumably, because of her role as Christ's mother: in one popular miracle a Jew wounds or deliberately injures an image of the Christ child in the Virgin's arms, whereupon blood flows from the wound;[47] in "Toledo," which is associated with the Feast of the Assumption, the Virgin's voice is heard complaining that the Jews are torturing her son again, and they are discovered reenacting the crucifixion on a wax image;[48] in "Beirut," the image of Christ on a crucifix is re-crucified by Jews.[49] This last is in no sense a miracle of the Virgin; yet it is sometimes found in collections of Mary legends.

This personal hostility toward Mary may be directed against her most ardent worshipers (and miracles involving persons specially or solely devoted to her bulk large in the collections). It is not surprising, therefore, that one of the most widespread of the anti-Semitic miracles tells of the Jews torturing or killing a devotee of the Virgin. This is the tale of the chorister that the Prioress tells.[50]

Finally, two popular miracles reveal the power of Mary in the presence of her enemies. One is the story of the Christian merchant whose only security for a loan from a Jewish merchant is a promise to repay made before an image of the Virgin and child. Though the merchant is repaid (by means themselves miraculous), he denies he has received the money; but when he is taken before the image of Mary, a voice reveals where the money is hidden.[51] The other is "Bourges," one of the oldest and most effective of the miracles. A Jewish boy who tags along with his Christian playmates when they go to mass, receives communion with them. Enraged when he discovers what has happened, the father, a glassblower, hurls the child into his furnace. The child is miraculously preserved, however, and is rescued unharmed by the Christians responding to his mother's frantic cries. He explains that the lovely lady with the child in her arms, whom he had admired in the church, had come to protect him with her cloak. Child and mother are converted; the father is thrown into the furnace and consumed.[52]

These, then, are the anti-Semitic miracles. Anyone in the late Middle Ages who wished to translate a miracle of the Virgin from Latin into the vernacular or to compose a version of his own would know the form from his reading of one or more of the collections and would find nothing unusual in their presence among the legends. They were a familiar and expected component of these collections. It would be as natural to choose one of these for treatment as any other. Indeed, these tales might be particularly attractive because of their dramatic and emotional possibilities. The anti-Semitic miracles usually involve a dramatic human conflict, something often missing or only diffusely present in other legends. In many miracles the drama arises not from a human conflict but from a tension between the expected normal consequences of actions that usually bring disgrace, disaster, death, or eternal damnation and the miraculous and welcome frustration of those normal consequences by virtue of the Virgin's special mercy and power. The anti-Semitic miracles, however, provide a human enemy and usually present a conflict with the enemy, either between Jew and Christian or between Jew and Mary. The possibilities for dramatic treatment are greatly enhanced.

A potentiality for emotional heightening is also inherent in these particular miracles. Jewish figures in the late Middle Ages offer a ready target for a spate of abuse and a consequent intensification of feeling. We can see this in rather crude form in an outburst near the end of a version of "The Chorister" in the early fifteenth-century collection in Sidney Sussex Cambridge MS 95:

O slimy stubbornness of Jewish faithlessness! They blaspheme the name of Christ, and when they cannot harm Christ they do harm to the members of Christ. It does not soften them, but renders them more stubborn, that they see so clearly fulfilled the predictions of the prophets on the coming of Christ and the abolishing of their own rituals. For they do not attend to the life-giving spirit but only to the surface meaning of the letter, which killeth. O people favored by the devil only! . . . It does not move them that everywhere they see themselves to be the scandal of mankind and the rejected of men.[53]

If our late medieval writer desired the more focused emotional impact of pathos, the figure of the Jew in a miracle was again most useful. He is the merciless villain of pathetic narrative, Bill Sykes, Simon Legree. As the human biography of Christ became more popular in art, meditations, drama, and lyric, it exploited increasingly the pathetic in the Nativity, the massacre of the Innocents, the Flight to Egypt, and above all, of course, the Passion. In the Passion especially the Jews are shown as heartless, jeering, inhuman torturers and murderers. The miracles of the Virgin not infrequently also develop pathetic situations or work for a pathetic response, and here again the Jew is available. Those that offer the richest possibilities for pathos are, in my judgment, "The Jew of Bourges," "The Chorister," and "Bread Offered to the Christ Child." There is no villain in the last, but there is in the other two, and he is a Jew.

I believe the answer to Chaucer's choice lies before us. It is naïve to underestimate how "alive" the Jew remained in England after the expulsion of 1290. He was alive in art, in the meditation, in the liturgy, and in drama, lyric, and the miracles. Though Chaucer and his countrymen had probably seen few if any Jews in their lifetime and had never lived near a Jewish community, they were familiar with the Jew at the devotional and imaginative level—or rather with a construct of the Jew created and validated by their culture, the Jew in a most distorted and hateful form.

It is naïve, too, to wonder at his choice of the miracle of the chorister or to see something in the choice that points accusingly at the teller. If we see him condemning the teller, the Prioress, then we must also see him as condemning the form itself, and beyond that as condemning a most powerful complex of beliefs, attitudes, and feelings universally shared in his age. There was, in fact, nothing extraordinary in his telling an anti-Semitic miracle; if he was interested in literary effectiveness and especially if he was interested in the pathetic mode, he could hardly find one more suited to his purposes than "The Jew of Bourges" or "The Chorister."[54] He chose "The Chorister." In his version the Jews are not converted; the guilty ones are tortured and killed. This is at least more humane than the indiscriminate slaughter of Jews we find in some versions. He may have found his ending in his source. If his source, however, did end with conversion all round, it is to the point to observe that conversion was not his theme; mass conversion would certainly have diverted attention from the final scene with the little clergeon and would thus have undercut the emotional impact of the ending. For an emotionally intense effect, the choices Chaucer made were the right ones.

If the choice saddens us today, it does so for the happy reason that we are somewhat more humanitarian in our sympathies than were the late Middle Ages—or for the unhappy reason that we think we are.[55] Historical knowledge in this instance should be used neither to condemn Chaucer nor to transform him into a premature civil libertarian—that way smugness lies—but to understand him.[56] We too are limited and imperfect in our sympathies, and we have far to go. Ideally, historical and cultural understanding should help us on that journey.

Stephen A. Barney

Chaucer's Lists

quicquid agunt homines, votum timor ira voluptas
gaudia discursus, nostri farrago libelli est.

Juvenal, *Sat.* 1.85-86

At worst, when a writer halts his narrative to make a list of
things, he merely desperately pads. In Chapter Eight of *Peri
Bathous* Pope satirically commends "a laudable *Prolixity;*
presenting the Whole and every Side at once of the Image to
view," and he defines *"Amplification* to be making the most of
a *Thought;* it is the spinning Wheel of *Bathos. . . ."*[1] No
technique more crudely amplifies than listing, naming the
trees one by one when a reference to the forest would do.
The writer slips the engine of his story into neutral, and
spins out, in Pope's metaphor, verbiage. Yet Chaucer's work
abounds in lists which yield much of that "God's plenty"
Dryden observed. Charles Muscatine has briefly addressed
Chaucer's "predilection for making lists of things" as the
expression of his sententiousness, his "lay encyclopedism"
symptomatic of the secularization of learning in the Middle
Ages, his fondness for the "enumerative, processional,
paratactic."[2]

Assuming that an accomplished writer will turn to good use any device he adopts, I will examine Chaucer's lists with an eye to their effect. Of the many ways literary lists can be studied (what objects the poet lists, what syntactic and marking techniques he uses in composing lists, how he orders his objects, whence he derives his particulars, and so forth), I have chosen first to make some effort at definition, second to survey the general sources of Chaucer's lists, and finally to look at a few of his works in which lists are especially prominent.

We distinguish between a story or narrative and a list embedded in the story. A list is extruded from some principle and it intrudes into the story. Hence lists resemble other intruders in stories: digressive matter like parables, inset narratives, prolonged descriptions, homilies and other extended comment, interlaced material from a conjoined story, songs, letters, scientific explanations, apostrophes, historical excursions, complaints, anything that breaks the narrative thread to spin another. A story wholly made of a list would be a special case. A list potentially can react with the narrative that encloses it just as its kindred intruders can. As an intruder, alien to a society's values, can threaten or refresh it with new perspectives on things, as the Canon and his Yeoman burst in late and strangely influence the Canterbury pilgrims, so a list can undermine or leaven the movement of a story.

A story is impossible, a list very difficult to define. If we say, following Aristotle, that a story recounts or tells a continuous action, then a list disrupts that continuity to linger, pointlessly from the pragmatic point of view, on some element which the story had merely used in its course. Chaucer and his tale-tellers often emphasize the apparently pointless, digressive character of lists with a show of impatience and the need to get on with it.[3] The story, moving like a river, wants to tell the knight's progress through the forest; the list, a dam, points out the species of trees. But our terms *recount* and *tell*, numbering terms, already suggest a difficulty: does not a story, like a list, merely enumerate the sub-actions of the continuous action? Is not a chivalric romance, for instance, merely a string of themes—the Damsel Imprisoned, the Siege Perilous, the Gentle Tourney—interchangeable parts listed or, in the variation, interlaced?

Four notions may help us to distinguish listing from narration, the first rough, the other three more refined but liable to exception. Aristotle speaks of a narrative action as having a certain magnitude. So a list will have a certain magnitude, which must be judged relative to the whole discourse of which it is part. We speak of a shopping list as a set of words on the refrigerator door, and it strains our language to speak of the refrigerator as a list of cool foods supporting a sub-action of shopping. Normally the knight does not ride to give us a list of trees, but the list of trees expatiates on the knight's ride. A list is smaller than a story.

Further, a list is adjectival, "thrown at" or modifying, by specifying, the kind of thing listed. In terms of Latin grammar we can say lists function as the genitive ("class," "family") case, sometimes called the adjective case.[4] Hence lists are distinct from stories, which consist of actors acting, things functioning as nouns and verbs. Descriptions, then, often take the form of lists. As sentences require no adjectives, narratives require no lists; they are expendable, pendent material like tropes or authorial comments.

I will call the object, the "what," which a list explicates in detail (Chaucer's terms for giving a list are *reherce* and, less frequently, *undo*)[5] its *principle*: the list "buckler, helmet, greaves, gauntlets, byrnie" specifies, "undoes," the principle "armor." Usually the ingredients of a list are more specific and concrete than the general and abstract principle on which the list depends. The converse—the list "a source of nutrient, a red globe, a baleful fruit, the worm's delight" for the principle "apple"—would have an effect of periphrastic riddling, usually comic, as in *Troilus* 2.904–05: "The dayes honour, and the hevenes yë, / The nyghtes foo—al this clepe I the sonne. . . ." Lists give details (things "cut off") of principles; they tend to be rather synecdochic than periphrastic; they enumerate the species of genera. A list without a principle would seem bewildering if not pointless—we need to know what is being listed—whereas to find the principle of a story (its genre? its summary plot? its main action?) seems unnecessary, a critical rather than an ontological activity. A list is adjectival and, what amounts to the same thing, principled; a story is nominal and verbal and, on the face of it, unprincipled.

A third way to distinguish lists from stories derives from some notions about order which I have got at second hand—by way of Paul G. Kuntz—from Thomas Aquinas and Whitehead.[6] Order, at least one important kind of order, requires that more than one thing be ordered (aliorelativity); it requires a common term or principle among the related things by which they may be related, for instance that A and B are both letters (connexity); it requires a fixed relation in time or magnitude or some other category such that, for instance, if A is later than or larger than B, the reverse cannot be true (asymmetry); it requires fixed sequences of these asymmetric relations, such that if A is larger than B, and B larger than C, then A is larger than C (transitivity).

The sequence "Anelida, Arcite" (in a list of two we prefer the syndetic form "Anelida and Arcite") differs from the sequence "Anelida loves, Anelida complains" (the lively plot of the extant fragment of Chaucer's *Anelida and Arcita*) in transitivity, which involves asymmetry. Only the latter sequence involves relations which cannot sensibly be reversed, here relations of cause and time (she complains because and after she loves), the relations that seem natural to narrative.

In *Aspects of the Novel* Forster speaks of the crude minimum connectives of stories, the "and then." Lists are better connected but less transitive than stories.[7] Lists require sharp aliorelativity and connexity, but may be symmetrical and intransitive. That is, lists must present a number of things (repetitions are not lists) which are related, and the things may be of equivalent status. Hence an ordered list, such as a rising climax (*gradatio*) or its opposite, a sinking catacosmesis ("For God, for Country, and for Yale"),[8] passes beyond the minimum requirements of listing into ornament. Yet sometimes a list seems to imply transitivity. Finding "Antigone, Blaunche, Canacee, Dorigen, Emelie," we next expect "Flexippe," not "Gerland." Chaucer can turn such expectations to witty effect, levelling the items listed, disordering the list in a surprising way. Part of the Friar's attack on summoners is this fine polysyndeton: "A theef, and eek a somnour, and a baude" (*FrT* 1354). The listlike symmetry enforced by the sequence deflates the vocation of summoning, just as Pope's "Puffs, Powders, Patches, Bibles, Billet-doux" defines the value of Holy Writ in the moving toyshop of Belinda's heart.[9]

Lists, then, are smaller than stories, adjectival and principled, and symmetrical and intransitive. A fourth effort at definition I take from ideas developed by Roman Jakobson, who makes a fundamental syntactic and poetic division between the two figures of speech, metonymy and metaphor, or the two syntactic modes, the syntagmatic and the paradigmatic.[10] These hard terms have, here anyway, simple senses. A metonymic or syntagmatic mode of discourse progresses by associating adjacent things, especially things in temporal and causal sequence, like the syntax of a sentence. Our writing-influenced image of metonymy or syntagm is the horizontal row. The statement "Nebuchadnezzar ruled and then he ate grass" is syntagmatic; to refer to Nebuchadnezzar in his glory as the Grasseater is metonymy (here proleptic metonymy). Metaphoric or paradigmatic discourse associates things non-temporally, quasi-spatially. Our image is the vertical row (*cata-logue*: "downward word"). "Nebuchadnezzar was pompous, partial, proud, and powerful" is paradigmatic; calling him the Ox is metaphor. *Grasseater* implies an action, *Ox* implies a state of being; metonymies are sequential, metaphors substitutional; metonymies regularly specify the thing by what it is or does, metaphors by what it is not. A paradigm is a set of equivalent variants all of which may be attributed to a thing. When two such sets are interlinked, and one item is chosen, the figure is metaphor: the strength, pride, ferocity, greed, and grass-eating of the elephant, lion, boar, hyena, and ox are linked with those same attributes of the tyrant, and *ox* is selected and substituted.

From the point of view of figurative discourse, a list is obviously paradigmatic and tends toward metaphor, whereas a story is syntagmatic and tends toward metonymy. In *Ulysses*, Stephen Dedalus defined a pier as a disappointed bridge; we may speak of a metaphor as a disappointed list. Stories are sequential orders, in which each element is fixed in the sequence, and a minimum number of elements must be expressed in order to make sense. Lists are substitutional arrays, in which neither the order nor the number of elements can be determined.[11] Paradoxically, the numberlessness of a list makes it an apt vehicle for enumeration, and its random sequence makes it apt for a display of formal order. Poets describe gardens in lists. A list offers a plenty, as if to say, "Here in its multitude is the 'what' I speak of: you choose, and you arrange."

C. S. Lewis observes that medieval and Renaissance poets enjoy giving "solid instruction" in their fiction, and that "the simplest form in which this tendency expresses itself is mere catalogue," the purest mode of the medieval "realising" (not penetrative or transforming) imagination.[12] Any poet of extensive work will compile lists. Here I take for granted what would be hard to demonstrate quantitatively, but what I think is obvious, that medieval poets generally, and Chaucer especially, were list-makers. Chaucer leans toward the adjectival, the intransitive, the paradigmatic; he endites by lists, fills with lists, progresses and retards by lists; he loads every rift with listed lore. He wants to come up close to the object and peruse it in detail, give it a presence before us, and he moves with a leisurely, deliberate pace. I give Chaucer the honorable title Pinakographos.[13]

Chaucer surely learned most about poetic listing from *The Romance of the Rose*, but because that poem itself exploits lists with sophisticated belatedness, we should go further back for the sources of Chaucer's lists. I have found it useful, as long as we recognize that they are usually interwoven, to separate seven strands of tradition which lie behind Chaucer's lists: wisdom literature, oral poetry, rhetoric, satire, encyclopedic literature, moral and homiletic literature, and technological literature, especially scientific writing.

I begin with the tradition of wisdom, the subject of this festival collection of essays and the special study of its honorand, Professor Bloomfield.[14] In Chaucer the tradition finds full expression in his marked sententiousness and proverbialism, his strings of "auctoritees" and exempla.[15] Wisdom often comes in collections, after the examples of Hesiod and the Bible. Manuscript collections of gnomes and proverbs are extant from the Old English period; collections of exempla and sentences, fostered by preachers' needs and developed in increasingly elaborate encyclopedic forms, abound in the high Middle Ages.[16] A number of poetic forms, reaching back into late antiquity and beyond, merely compile and organize tidbits of wisdom, among them centos, number rhymes, chain speeches, riddles, gnomic poems, *Reihenbildungen*, priamels.[17]

Plenty of individual bits of wisdom flavor Chaucer's work, but most striking are his many lists of wisdom lore. The big talkers among his characters—the Wife of Bath, Dame Prudence, the Pardoner, the Manciple, Chauntecleer and Pertelote, Pandarus and the rest—fill out their discourses with serial wisdom. Their sources of wisdom lie in both experience (mothers and other folk) and authority (books). The Wife of Bath claims she learned some tricks from her mother (*WBProl* 583), but most of her lore was from Jankyn's book; the boy in the "Pardoner's Tale" got his wisdom about death from his mother (684); the Manciple's dame handed down to him her wisdom about keeping well the tongue in absurdly multiplied precepts that contradict the counsel they espouse, rehearsed in the ancient sapiential form of sentences beginning "My son. . . ."[18]

Conscious that bunches of wisdom can overwhelm the listener, Chaucer sometimes has his speakers fairly threaten a list. The Monk has a hundred exemplary tragedies in his cell (*MkProl* 1972). Pluto warns Proserpine he can tell ten hundred thousand tales "notable" of women's "untrouthe and brotilnesse" (*MerchT* 2240–41). The Pardoner boasts that he would preach "an hundred false japes moore" (*PardProl* 394). The narrator could reckon a thousand more "ensamples" in Venus's oratory (*KnT* 1953–54). Pandarus, wishing for once "t'abregge / Diffusion of speche," refrains from giving "a thousand olde stories" about women lost through boasting (*TC* 3.295–98). Especially terrifying in its calm understatement is the pilgrim narrator's threat before he delivers "Melibee" that he will "telle somwhat moore / Of proverbes than ye han herd bifoore" (*Thop* 955–56). In the midst of what may be the arch-series of exempla (outside of the prose works), Dorigen says she could tell "mo than a thousand stories" of women's suicides, but "What sholde I mo ensamples heerof sayn" (*FrankT* 1412, 1419)—she goes on to say mo ensamples.

Dorigen's list has been criticized for its ineptitude, or reckoned to be a deliberate *"reductio ad absurdum* of the use of exempla."[19] It can represent for us the kinds of things that can go wrong with a list: the listed elements may not properly specify the general principle adduced; the principle of the list may seem to shift as the list is extruded; the conclusion drawn from the list (if any) may be irrelevant to its context; the very production of the list in the circumstances may seem pedantic, incongruously reflective, rhetorically self-conscious, absurdly pompous, crudely self-serving, or otherwise inappropriate to the speaker or the situation; the list may go on too long for its worth; it may wildly jumble discordant materials. Various of Chaucer's lists exhibit all of these errors. A classic problem of Chaucer criticism has been to judge whether a given silly or pompous or protracted or misdirected list is deliberate art or Chaucerian pedagogic zeal gone awry, but I think readers agree that most odd lists in Chaucer serve a humorous or characterizing purpose. We find evidence for Chaucer's intentions in many places, where the contexts of overwrought listings are obviously burlesque ("Sir Thopas," the "Canon's Yeoman's Tale," the "Merchant's Tale"), or where characters respond to threatened lists with entreaties. "Thi proverbes may me nought availle. . . . Lat be thyne olde ensaumples, I the preye," says Troilus. The Wife laments that Jankyn "knew of mo proverbes" about bad women "than in this world ther growen gras or herbes," and Chaucer as usual lets her list a few. January, having already endured hearing "of mariage manye ensamples olde," blasts Justinus: "Straw for thy Senek, and for thy proverbes!"[20] In fact Justinus's counsel, although it does cite Senek, is remarkably proverb-free for speeches of this kind; it is mainly based on Justinus's own experience with a wife. January's own thought amounts to a farrago of half-digested wisdom regurgitated to nourish his desire.

"Shal it be conseil?" asks one of the malicious fools in the "Pardoner's Tale." The taking of counsel (or more often merely the offering of it) regularly proceeds by setting arrays of authorities, lists of wisdom, one against another (or more often setting forth only one side of an argument). Chaucer loves the topic. We find Theseus (*KnT* 1748–1825), Melibee, Chauntecleer (*NPT* 3171), and King Arthour (*WBT* 894–97) actually changing their minds, at least partly under the influence of female counsel; "wommenes conseils" are not always, only *"ofte* colde" (*NPT* 3256). "Avisement" must be reckoned a principal theme of *Troilus*. Two of Chaucer's poems, the "Monk's Tale" and *The Legend of Good Women*, consist wholly of exemplary lists, explicitly directed toward thematic ends (falls of Fortune, good women) like gobs of counsel. The list of good (or bad, or suicidal) women is the most frequent type of exemplary list in Chaucer; I think each of these lists contains some comically inappropriate example.[21]

Chaucer handles his wisdom lists as he handles "auctoritee" in general, with a critical attitude. To explore the reasons for his skepticism about wisdom would require a separate study, but I can suggest one reason, which arises from the nature of the bit of wisdom, the single proverb, maxim, gnome, adage, apophthegm, sentence, mashal, paradigm. A proverb promises generality; it implies that the wisdom stored in it will apply to all relevant cases. Hence for each human situation we might expect the tradition to yield us a single sentence, a unique proverb. But, as Chaucer's bountiful lists of wisdom illustrate, wisdom comes to us in contradictory heaps, little more rationalized and categorized than raw experience itself. Lists may be small, adjectival, symmetrical, intransitive, and paradigmatic, but they make no claim to be logical. They specify some principle, but they do not prove it; they say nothing about necessary relations. Furthermore they are liable to slip somewhat away from their principle, as it were in the heat of the moment, as Chauntecleer, amid his examples of prophetic dreams, concludes, irrelevantly, that murder will out (NPT 3050-57), or as the narrator of The Book of the Duchess slips Samson into a list of damned suicides-for-love (BD 738-39). The multiplicity of wisdom betrays it.

Chaucer loves to represent the process of thought, and in nearly every case some flaw in thinking emerges. Chaucer's thinkers proceed by casting multiple images and notions before their minds' eyes, as January reflects on his marriage "inwith his thoght" like a man who sets a mirror in the marketplace (MerchT 1577), or as Troilus makes "a mirour of his mynde," reflecting on Criseyde (TC 1.365). Such thoughts are "impressiouns." The jumbled pastiches of wisdom represent the mind confused and overburdened with the weight of unrationalized lore. The counter to wisdom is logic, with its drive toward unity and universal purity, but we should notice that Chaucer's only sustained representation (outside of close translation) of a character thinking logically, Troilus's monologue on freedom and necessity (TC 4.958-1078), is likewise defective. His thought strains desperately, and it fails, less because the logic is bad than because it is, as we know from Boethius, incomplete. Human thought altogether will fail, but wisdom-thought, if we may call it that, most often ends in comical folly. Logic will not rest content with multiplicity; hence the numerousness of wisdom-lore, whose sign in Chaucer is the list, undermines its efficacy. A man learned only in wisdom can be cunning, even practically efficient, but not true.

The wisdom tradition itself came down to Chaucer largely collected, and he imitates a common form. As if to replicate its own cumulative tendency in small, wisdom is often presented in a form Curtius calls the "numerical apothegm," which briefly enumerates the features of something after the method of Prov. 30:18: "Three things are hard to me, and the fourth I am utterly ignorant of."[22] Chaucer has several examples. The gifts of old men: "Foure gleedes han we . . . Avauntyng, liyng, anger, coveitise"; nuisances: "Thre thynges dryuen a man out of his hous,— that is to seyn, smoke, droppyng of reyn, and wikked wyves."[23] Of similar form, but without mentioning the number, is the Wife's enumeration of the gifts of women: "Deceite, wepyng, spynnyng God hath yive / To wommen kyndely."[24] Slightly expanding this form, and putting the principle of the list at its end instead of its beginning, Chaucer has the Wife quote Jankyn's pleasantry:

> Whoso that buyldeth his hous al of salwes,
> And priketh his blynde hors over the falwes,
> And suffreth his wyf to go seken halwes,
> Is worthy to been hanged on the galwes!
> (WBProl 655–58)

This has the common touch of wisdom, the homely details, the biting wit, the cynicism, the claim of universality, the weary combination of shrewdness and fatalism: "they'll do it every time." Its topic—wives—is Chaucer's favorite topic of wisdom, and although it derives from a male, Chaucer has it spoken by a female, Chaucer's preferred sex for the purveyance of wisdom.[25] It is Chaucer's only example of a priamel, a form which by definition combines wisdom and listing. To its meter (oddly irregular, as if to emphasize that this poem-within-a-poem is not the Wife's own style) and its typical three-plus-one enumeration Chaucer adds a rare feature which makes its conclusion seem inevitable, quadruple rhyme. This string *must* lead to the gallows. Forgotten wisdom forgoes its nature because wisdom is nothing if it is not handed down. Jankyn's priamel is made to be remembered.[26]

> The byldere ok, and ek the hardy asshe;
> The piler elm, the coffre unto carayne;
> The boxtre pipere, holm to whippes lashe;
> The saylynge fyr; the cipresse, deth to playne;
> The shetere ew; the asp for shaftes pleyne;
> The olyve of pes, and eke the dronke vyne;
> The victor palm, the laurer to devyne.
>   (PF 176–82)

This stanza, famous for continuing a venerable tradition of lists of trees, a tradition that weaves through high Western art poetry from Virgil and Ovid to Guillaume de Lorris and Boccaccio and on to Spenser and Keats, hardly resembles an oral composition.[27] The names come too thickly, and the epithets, in themselves a sign of oral epic, have the opposite effect here, because they are not traditional—some are even surprising, especially as, imitating continental rhetorical devices, they strain English grammar. Yet because the *Parliament*'s tree-list draws attention to itself, in a poem full of lists, and points to great epic forebears, and because it is in fact memorable, it may be located in the tradition of oral poetry, adjacent to that of wisdom literature.

On the face of it, lists would seem an inappropriate adjunct to oral composition, which leans heavily on the poet's mnemonic powers. Syntagmatic narrative, whose every cause implies, and helps to recall, some later effect, would be the natural form of oral poetry. The paradigms of lists, in which each element is equivalent to the others (symmetrical), require such feats of memory that they seem incompatible with oral production. Yet Homer had his catalogue of the Achaian forces.[28] Early epic, as Plato observed (*Rep.* 10), retained encyclopedic knowledge of the arts of life and of the history and genealogies of the nation. Much of this lore had to be stored in paradigmatic form. Eric A. Havelock argues that the form of Homeric epic in fact follows from its obligation to preserve what the society found necessary to know; its prime function was not celebratory or ornamental but retentive and mnemonic.[29] He hypothesizes that "the tale itself is designed as a kind of convenience,"[30] and observes that Hesiod, more writerly than Homer, practically omits even this convenience. We would say that Homer converts the paradigmatic (lists of names, procedures, and so forth) to the syntagmatic (stories of national achievement) in order to preserve it. The methods and forms of remembering developed by oral poets were naturally retained in later ages, even though the burden of remembering was relieved by writing. Further, the art of public speaking still required a capacity to remember, and study of this art kept alive the science of mnemonics.

Following some passages in Dante, Chaucer in *The House of Fame* oddly invokes, along with Venus and the Muses, his own mind:

> O Thought, that wrot al that I mette,
> And in the tresorye hyt shette
> Of my brayn, now shal men se
> Yf any vertu in the be,
> To tellen al my drem aryght.[31]

Thought wrote the dream and shut it in the treasury of Geffrey's brain; now Geffrey calls on Thought to open the treasury. The metaphor of the store of poetic material as a treasury, a thesaurus, is ancient, and implies the paradigmatic nature of the material: one can select anything from the jumble of objects in the treasure room.[32] Chaucer's dream poems, loosed by their dreamy form from the restraints of syntagmatic narrative, are especially full of lists, and approach in their abrupt transitions and dislocations the symmetrical intransitivity of lists. The order of events is aesthetically satisfying in *The Book of the Duchess*, *The Parliament of Fowls*, and *The House of Fame*, but the order is not determined as it would be in a causally connected story like the "Miller's Tale."

Many of Chaucer's lists formally derive from oral, mnemonic sources, and display the techniques, now vestigial, once necessary for a culture without writing, or for an art (public speaking) which forbade written assistance. The thesaurus of memory, once the prime force of tradition and civilization, had in a writing culture taken on the value of copious display.[33] The lists that muster forth the contents of the treasury present those characteristics which Plato criticized as the limitations of mere opinion, *doxa* (as opposed to knowledge, *episteme*), and which Havelock finds characteristic of oral memory: the elements of the list are "happenings" (*gignomena*), they are plural (*polla*), and they are "visibles" (*horata*).[34] Each of these traits enables the elements of a catalogue to be remembered. The epithets of the list of trees provide the "happening" quality which associates the list with ancient epic: *builder* oak, *sailing* fir. We have noticed the plurality of the wisdom-lists, a plurality of which Chaucer was skeptical. And Chaucer's lists regularly involve things visible: the listed things act before us, or they have a set place in a seen locale.[35] These three characteristics are the keys that unlock the treasury of memory.

Let me illustrate these characteristics further with lists from Chaucer that seem to revert to oral poetics. In each illustration I find the characteristic—happening, plurality, visibility—in a poetically redundant form: Chaucer renders the lists of happenings in an especially active, moving style; he recounts emphatically plural lists in repetitive or distributive phrasing; he displays visible lists with emphasis on the act of beholding.

Both of Chaucer's imitations of the English alliterative tradition describe rapidly moving scenes of action, namely battles. Here are a few lines from "The Legend of Cleopatra," the less familiar passage:

> Up goth the trompe, and for to shoute and shete,
> And peynen hem to sette on with the sunne.
> With grysely soun out goth the grete gonne,
> And heterly they hurtelen al atones,
> And from the top doun come the grete stones.[36]

It is hard, here and when I read this passage before students, to stop quoting. Aside from the obvious virtuoso alliteration, we hear the native four-stress line beating behind the iambic pentameter. Perhaps less obvious, each line is nearly independent syntactically, although the passage I have quoted is not the best example of this: Robinson punctuates each of the fifteen lines of the passage in "Knight's Tale" with a semi-colon or period at line's end. The passages amount to lists of actions (a type treated more fully below) whose stave-accented phrase rhythms supplement the end-stopped line rhythms, producing a jogtrot that is hard to stop—the lines are counter-periodic. These are active lists of actions, lists of happenings which happen—rhythmically—to us. As lists of actions they form a borderline between the syntagmatic and the paradigmatic—they are half story, half list.

Rhythm itself is a borderline phenomenon. Rhythm decidedly involves, it even constitutes, the sense of before and after, the transitivity which defines the syntagmatic; yet because the lifts and sinkings which make rhythm are interchangeable, rhythm is likewise symmetrical and paradigmatic. A poundingly rhythmic list imitates the hurtling action it describes, and its superfluous beat, laid over the "normal" beat of Chaucer's verse, aids the memory. Everyone knows how mnemonic verses seem to generate themselves autonomously "once you get started," and how poundingly rhythmic the most memorable are: "Matthew, Mark, Luke, and John / Bless the bed that I lie on."[37] Rhythm can work, for paradigms, the way causal sequence works for syntagms, jogging the mind.

Plato's second critique of opinion—that it is plural, merely *polla*, has not the singleness of knowledge—is likewise taken by Havelock as a characteristic of oral epic.[38] Since lists are by definition plural, no more need be said. Some kinds of plurality, however, draw attention to themselves as such. One kind is what might be called a "distributive list," which signals with grammatical markers the parceling out of a principle. The principle usually so distributed in Chaucer is judgment: divers folk are wont to say divers things about a topic. The markers are either a repeated *some* ("Somme seyden thus, somme seyde . . . Somme helden with hym . . . Somme with . . . somme with . . . Somme seyde") or direct reference to diversity ("Diverse folk diversely they demed").[39] Such lists imply endless multiplicity, and a lack of reason for unity. Chaucer marks a second kind of plural list with, paradoxically, a single word or phrase repeated, in the ornamental figure anaphora. The repetition of the one oddly signals the many. Extended examples are the sixteen lines in a row, all beginning with *Of* (and most containing two or more further *of*s), detailing the subjects of the tidings in the house of rumor ("Of werres, of pes, of mariages . . ."*HF* 1961-76); and the list of birds in *The Parliament of Fowls*, in which twenty-five out of twenty-eight consecutive lines begin with *The* (337-64). Deservedly the best-known example is the *Swich fyn* anaphora at the end of the *Troilus* (5.1828-32), a terrific "summation scheme" which draws the plurality of the poem to a unified "fyn."[40] Anaphora can, as here, point the listed *polla* toward one principle. These tidings, these birds, these ends are after all the same. The distributive list and the anaphoric list emphasize plurality, but from opposed points of view. The former makes many one, and the latter makes one many.

Finally—and here Plato and the medieval mnemotechnicians concur—opinion consists of things visible. Again, Chaucer can emphasize the visualness of the "visibles" (*horata*) in his lists. Examples lead us to the "art poetry" side of Chaucer, those developments of classical tradition, brought to Chaucer by the continental poets, which resemble poetic forms we think of as proper to the Renaissance: triumphs, pageants, mirrors, theaters, iconic set-pieces of various kinds—the poems of "display." A Greek word for "display" is *epideixis*, whose root is the same as the root of *index*, a Latin word for "list": lists *show* the visibles.[41] When a poet lists, he often makes as if to display for the reader the things listed, rather than merely naming the principle. His ocular proof, his species of trees, helps to bring the forest alive, to give it that *enargeia*, that vivifying force which Renaissance rhetoricians looked for in descriptive poetry.[42]

Descriptions of marriages and funerals seem to evoke lists, as attendants to the sacrament heap up like logs on a pyre. In *The Complaint unto Pity*, the narrator enumerates the "vertues" that decorate and—through personification—are attendant upon Pity's hearse:

> Aboute hir herse there stoden lustely,
> Withouten any woo, as thoughte me,
> Bounte parfyt, wel armed and richely,
> And fresshe Beaute, Lust, and Jolyte,
> Assured Maner, Youthe, and Honeste,
> Wisdom, Estaat, Drede, and Governaunce,
> Confedred both by bonde and alliaunce.
> (36-42)

They are "confedred" in their defense of the hearse, their

presence real enough to deter the narrator from presenting his inscription or "bille" of complaint to Pity.[43] These same virtues are invoked again in the bill—itself a visible icon from the past, a made document brought forward into the poem—and the list of allegorical figures thus vivifies the two objects in the poem: the hearse and the bill.

When a poet represents for us another artist's work he often seems to mean intensely, to figure in small his own principal themes, or to introduce important doctrine which may enrich his story. To *see* art within a poem has special force. Examples spring to mind from all the major poets; perhaps the carved history of the Trojan war in the first book of the *Aeneid* is the greatest. The introduced art often teems with significant imagery. The art represented must allow for the intricate depiction of abundant emblems and figures—such iconic art, usually plastic, as tapestries, wall-engravings, and whole architectural spaces like palaces, temples, oratories.

These, of course, are the locales of many of Chaucer's lists: the oratories of the deities in the "Knight's Tale," with their lists of traits, attributes, effects, attendants, and examples;[44] the temples of Venus in *The House of Fame* and *The Parliament of Fowls*, with, in the former, the story of Aeneas given in the form of a list, and surrounding the latter in personified attributes, the effects, and the examples of love; and the chamber of the dreamer in *The Book of the Duchess*, perhaps among Chaucer's first efforts in the genre, with its glass depicting the story of Troy (its heroes' names listed) and its walls painted with "al the Romaunce of the Rose" (334). *The House of Fame* is a study in pinakography. It is stuffed with lists, its niches and pillars loaded with figures, who are themselves rhythm-makers, poets, historians, craftsmen of lists and the rememberers and memorials of lists. All these places work epideictically: they display the knowledge they mean to convey, just as a personification displays its meaning to the eye.

Such iconographic displays, whose purest form would be an idol (a visible) surrounded by attendant *putti*, carefully labeled, should remind us of the "places" used in mnemo-technics.[45] Like a list, a place or an architectural structure has no necessary sequence of seeing: we may go from roof to ground or ground to roof, or our eyes may (as Chaucer's seem to, as ours probably do in fact) dart about at their own sweet will. A story's setting, in its disordered, paradigmatic form, runs counter to its plot. We are to imagine that the setting of a story persists in time, from before the action of the story up to the present. Settings are often in a state of ruin, as old things and memorials often are, and they bear the traces of what is primordial and indescribable in syntagmatic narrative.

But "visible lists" can also run current with the poet's experience, presenting rather than representing. These lists usually take, in Chaucer, the form of guided tours, sometimes signaled by the narrator's persistent reference to his beholding. In *The House of Fame* we move with the narrator as he studies the "table of bras" which tells and shows the story of Aeneas, and the story, summarized so rapidly for the most part that it amounts to a list of actions (with a great retardation as he comes to Dido), moves forward with constant reference to the narrator's seeing: "First sawgh I . . . And I saugh next . . . Ther saugh I graven eke," and so forth over a dozen times (151–467), with a couple of *Lo*s thrown in (388, 398) as the narrator digresses into more lists of exempla. Chaucer transforms epic narrative into museum-tour; he is only a little less persistently guiding as he conducts us through the oratories in the "Knight's Tale."

The more interesting kind of presented, visible list derives from the Old French genre *voie*, which developed out of ancient models: the Bible, Virgil, the *Shepherd of Hermas*, the *Consolation of Philosophy*, and the many apocryphal visions of hell and the otherworld. The *voie*, the "way," presents a seer or dreamer guided through an otherworldly or allegorized landscape by an authoritative figure.[46] Old French preserves several satiric *voies* of hell and paradise, but of course the greatest *voie* is *The Divine Comedy*. Chaucer's dream visions derive in part from this genre. The dreamer's guides or psychopomps are no figures of angelic power, but variously comic figures appropriate to the dreamer: the whelp in *The Book of the Duchess* (only vestigially a *voie*), the eagle in *The House of Fame*, and (not comic himself, but comic in having to grab the dreamer and shove him into the garden) Scipio in *The Parliament of Fowls*. Only in *The House of Fame* do we have the fully developed *voie*, and even there many of the pedantic eagle's efforts to guide and list the aerial phenomena are frustrated by his unwilling pilgrim. A *voie*, in which the seer moves from object to object, is the reverse of such forms as procession, parade, or triumph—forms richly developed in the Renaissance—in which objects move past the seer, but the effect and content can be nearly the same.[47] In such forms the entire plot is the serial seeing. When the seer enters the other world, what he sees becomes encyclopedic as he seems to enter the storehouse of memory itself. List-making and story-telling become one.

The seer in a *voie*, as he walks and lists with his eyes, is a pilgrim. The "General Prologue" to *The Canterbury Tales*, an important variation on the *voie*, lists in series the pilgrims themselves. The series displays the symmetry of lists, yet it is haunted by a tantalizing ghost of order which makes us want to determine what ranking its sequence implies. The usual phrase introducing each pilgrim is *was ther* or *ther was*, and something about the intimacy and vividness of the portraits almost makes those *thers* epideictic rather than merely expletive. The narrator tells us about them "so as it semed me," and we have the sense that we walk along with him through a portrait gallery brought strangely to life.[48]

Another version of a *voie* comes near the end of *Troilus* (5.526–616) when Troilus rides about Troy and, in his grief, recalls earlier moments of happiness when he sees the places where Criseyde had been, making of them shrines (553) like the oratories of the "Knight's Tale." It is a fine, poignant example of the link between seeing and remembering, in which the whole town becomes a theater of memory, the sequence of locales summoning up the list of events in their loving. The storehouse of Troilus's mind duplicates the storehouse of great Troy. This duplication of mind and memory-theater is typical of *voies*: what Dante sees happens within him. Troilus's ride can sum up for us the kind of list which derives from oral epic. It lists "happenings": the figure literally moves by the places, where events (the quiet events proper to this un-martial poem), her dancing, laughing, playing, love-talking, singing took place. It lists "the many": at the outset of the ride he views her palace, and utters an anaphoric apostrophe to it ("O paleys desolat . . . O hous . . . O paleys . . . O thow lanterne . . . O paleys . . . O paleis . . . O ryng . . . O cause of wo") which lingers on its multiple associations, and as he rides to many places he thinks how Cupid has so harrassed him "on every side" that "Men myght a book make of it, like a storie." Troilus becomes *Troilus* as the multiple experience of his past thickens into

memory, and he imagines himself "to waxen lesse" (618). It
lists "visibles": the whole space of the town orients itself
according to his love ("to the yonder hill I gan hire gyde, . . .
ther . . . yond . . . hider . . . here" 610–16) and he says of her
palace, the most prominent theater of his recollection, "Wel
oughtestow to falle"—the town may as well become a
memory-ruin now (as it will!), and merely collapse into
storage as its story is done.[49] "The grete tounes se we wane
and wende" (KnT 3025).

That Chaucer consciously exploited the art of rhetoric,
the third source of his lists that we shall examine, hardly
needs arguing, even to the dullest reader of the "Nun's
Priest's Tale."[50] We have the same kind of evidence of his
critical attitude toward the rhetorical tradition as we have of
his critique of sententiousness: burlesque. The attitude
especially emerges when a character speaks in "terms," as
when Harry Bailly addresses certain learned pilgrims,
adopting, in his lists, his idea of their jargon. To the Man of
Law:

> Ye been submytted, thurgh youre free assent,
> To stonden in this cas at my juggement.
> Acquiteth yow now of youre biheeste;
> Thanne have ye do youre devoir atte leeste.
> (MLT 35–38)

At the end of the same tale the Shipman, or whoever is
speaking in this textually difficult passage, claims he will
avoid "termes queinte of lawe" when he tells his tale (1189).
Harry waxes medical in response to the "Physician's Tale":

> I pray to God so save thy gentil cors,
> And eek thyne urynals and thy jurdones,
> Thyn ypocras, and eek thy galiones,
> And every boyste ful of thy letuarie. . . .
> . . . .
> Seyde I nat wel? I kan nat speke in terme. . . .
> (PardT 304–11)

The Franklin claims he "kan no termes of astrologye" just
before launching into a display of such terms (1266–91); the
Canon's Yeoman repeatedly criticizes the jargon of his
elvysshe craft—"we semen wonder wise, / Oure termes

been so clergial and so queynte" (751-52)—as he pours out
its terms.

Each learned craft has its special terms, and Harry and
the pilgrim narrator reveal their awareness of the abuse of
jargon. Listing jargon inevitably draws attention to it and
mocks it. To mock jargon is to be conscious that language
can draw away from specific referents and act with its own
power on its auditors, as rhetoric. So Harry attempts to
forestall the Clerk, whose college education threatens
ponderous rhetoric:

> Telle us some murie thyng of aventures.
> Youre termes, youre colours, and youre figures,
> Keepe hem in stoor . . . .
> (ClT 15-17)

Harry wants story (aventures), not lists, syntagms and not
paradigms, and he briskly lists what he does not want. Lists,
by isolating and overextending jargon, expose and explode
it. Rhetoric is the jargon of jargons, and to demolish the art
itself is to come, indirectly, at the truth. The pomp of
"professional" rhetoric reveals character while it obscures
the art professed.[51]

If a bourgeois gentleman speaks prose all his life, poets
surely speak rhetoric all the while. Here let us examine, with
something of Harry's skeptical eye, only those lists in
Chaucer which especially make us conscious of their rhetorical background, lists which we sense would not have taken
the form they do had there been no tradition of rhetorical
precept. Such are a number of kinds we have already
examined: the relentless anaphoras, the catalogues of trees
and birds replete with classicizing epithets, the plump
strings of sentences and exempla, the heaps of personifications and crowded theaters of memory, the prolonged lists
set into an *occupatio* or *praeteritio*, all kinds of congregations of
things treated by the rhetoricians.[52]

The masters of the art gave most of their instruction by
way of translation and definition of the hard Greek terms
handed down to them. Of these terms a number signify
"list": most purely *congeries* (*synathroismus*) "list"; also *congregatio*
or *gregatio* (*anacephalaiosis*), *accumulatio*, *frequentatio*, *recapitulatio*,
acervus (*sorites*), *enumeratio*, all of which mean "gathering,   \

heaping, summing up, enumeration." The two repeated justifications for the use of lists in oratory are, first, that if one dart in the list fails to hit the opponent, another may, and second, that a summary list (*frequentatio*) of the main topics of an argument, brought together at the end, will aid the memory and overwhelm the adversary.[53] These skimpy reasons merely indicate that the rhetoricians did not choose to examine the uses of lists in general; they are more interested in pointing out special forms and uses.

Amplification, which the rhetoricians encourage, amounts to the retardation of an argument (for us, a narrative) by various means. We would call it the supplanting of the syntagmatic by the paradigmatic. A principal method of amplification is simply to describe an object as it swims into a speaker's ken, and a description regularly takes the form of a list. Chaucer lists what he will list "acordaunt to resoun" in the "General Prologue": the "condicioun," the "which," the "degree," and the "array" of the pilgrims.[54] Yet the portraits display persistent disorder, exploiting the list's property of symmetry which allows for those striking juxtapositions, that incongruous abundance which (when compared with the rhetorically correct portraits at the beginning of *The Romance of the Rose*) makes the "Prologue" seem a "flight to reality."[55]

I suppose Chaucer follows only Dante among the major poets in the number of his descriptions of people, most of which involve a list of traits. Rather than plunge in here, I will single out two kinds of descriptive lists which Chaucer often uses as representative of two tendencies—toward the active and doing, and toward the state of being. The first kind we meet in the Reeve's portrait in the "General Prologue":

> His lordes sheep, his neet, his dayerye,
> His swyn, his hors, his stoor, and his pultrye
> Was hoolly in this Reves governynge. . . .
> (597–99)

Chaucer lists the subjects under the Reeve's professional competence. Obviously lists like these could be extended indefinitely, and only Chaucer's tact keeps them in bounds and manages to make them delightful when we come across them. In the case of the Reeve, it is as if Chaucer were saying he could not go on for too long about this man's character—most reeves have no character at all!—and he had already used up, in the portrait of the Yeoman, a description based wholly on "array," and in the Cook's portrait he had listed the actions that the Cook could do ("rooste, and sethe, and broille, and frye" 383); now he would experiment with how long he could hold our attention merely with the objects that surround a person.

The Reeve seems to reply with his description of "deynous Symkyn" the miller: "Pipen he koude and fisshe, and nettes beete, / And turne coppes, and wel wrastle and sheete. . . ." (*RvT* 3927–28). Such lists revere the things of this world, and I can divine no harm in them. I must quote part of a list of trades intruded, unsanctioned by the source, in the alliterative *Destruction of Troy*:

> Goldsmythes, Glouers, Girdillers noble;
> Sadlers, souters, Semsteris fyn;
> Tailours, Telers, Turners of vesselles;
> Wrightes, websters, walkers of cloth;
> Armurers, Arowsmythis with Axes of werre;

and on for ten more lines.[56] We can safely say these passages add nothing to the narrative. Rather than tell us anything new about reeves, cooks, millers, a town's tradesmen, they merely tell the business over. In part they make up that screen of generality (we should hope all cooks can broil and fry) against which the silhouetted particulars (the mormal on this Cook's shin) get their force; they bring into this Canterbury world the great world in its small activity.[57] A final example gives the inevitable Chaucerian twist. The Wife of Bath says nowadays we find friars

> Blessynge halles, chambres, kichenes, boures,
> Citees, burghes, castels, hye toures,
> Thropes, bernes, shipnes, dayeryes—
> This maketh that ther ben no fayeryes.
>   (WBT 869–72)

The competence of friars extends beyond even that of Reeves; friars fill space like a catalogue. The spiritual content of the "Blessynge" pulls away from the vast corporality of the places they bless, just as, in the Wife's view, the friars diffuse their calling in their material multiplication and drive the spirits out. A list, a charming apostrophe, may invoke divinity, but it may also exorcise it in the banality and distastefulness of unredeemed plenitude.

As these lists wander about the periphery of character, naming the circumstances and doings of people, another set of lists attempts to name directly the central principles of character. After the Nun's Priest describes Chauntecleer, dwelling on his cocky and regal array (or as Richardson's Pamela would put it, on his *person*), he turns sharply in describing Pertelote—perhaps because she is "wonder lyk to hym, as of colours" and no more can be said about her array—and says: "Curteys she was, discreet, and debonaire, / And compaignable. . ." (*NPT* 2871-72). I call this a "virtues list," a favorite form in Chaucer. When "vice lists" are included, I have come across some three dozen examples.[58] They are oddly as little revealing about "character," what is predictable about a person's thoughts and actions, as the competence lists, because the terms are too abstract. Pertelote is doubtless courteous and discreet, but these may not be the qualities we would cite first. Obviously the list contributes to the general burlesque of courtly romance in the tale, and graciously accepts the birds' pretensions. But it draws our attention as well to a difficulty in reading Chaucer, especially the *Troilus*: how far can we qualify or redefine such virtues lists in the light of the syntagmatic narrative? Can a narrator's assessment of abstract qualities be wrong? Few would deny that the Knight "loved chivalrie, / Trouthe and honour, fredom and curteisie" (*GP* 45-46), and clearly the friar's assertion—"we mendynantz, we sely freres, / Been wedded to poverte and continence, / To charite, humblesse, and abstinence . . ." and so on (*SumT* 1906-10)—is a bold-faced, self-serving lie. But the very late assessment of Criseyde, in the familiar set-piece descriptions borrowed from Joseph of Exeter, forces us to read the virtues carefully, and to sift out the ranges of meaning in order to find out what we already know: "She sobre was, ek symple, and wys withal. . ." (*TC* 5.820).

Martin Price notices in Dryden a level of diction which, not too concrete and not too abstract, points at once to "the physical action and the moral influence."[59] My sense is that

Chaucer tends to split where Dryden joins, to give us both the too concrete and the too abstract when he describes a person, and to let us fuse an idea of character by juxtaposition. The Knight loves trouthe, and he was in Alisaundre, Lettow, Tramyssene, and the rest, and we are to decide what kind of man he is. We may compare the extreme case of this split in Icelandic sagas, where a terse virtues list often introduces a character, and where his subsequent actions, told even more sparely and without the moral guidance of the narrator, fulfill surprisingly and harshly the vaguest hint of vice in the virtues list. If we hear that a man is wealthy, generous toward his neighbors, wise in council, and somewhat high-handed with his brothers, we can be sure, once we are used to the style, that his high-handedness will be the principal motive of the tale. No expertise in reading Chaucer, however, could help us unfold the first virtues list ascribed to Criseyde:

> And ek the pure wise of hire mevynge
> Shewed wel that men might in hire gesse
> Honour, estat, and wommanly noblesse.
> (TC 1.285–87)

This is all true, yet it leaves room for a wide range of moral behavior; it is respectful toward a woman who may prove less than respectable; we can only guess from the pure wise of her moving—at the very least she causes a great line.

A paradigmatic form, rather than a set of contents, is the compact, rushing *frequentatio*. Curtius calls the extreme form "verse-filling asyndeton," in which no conjunctions relieve the string of words ("Rocks, Caves, Lakes, Fens, Bogs, Dens, and shades of death" *Paradise Lost* 2.621). Adding polysyndetic examples, which may have the same effect ("And swims or sinks, or wades, or creeps, or flies" *PL* 2.950), I call these lists "one-liners."

As in Milton, or Pope, or the Roman satirists whom Curtius quotes, these lists often suggest a chaotic busy-ness and wild disarray. Paradoxically, whereas lists normally seem to retard the flow of a story, these speed it up. The pace of delivery so outstrips the pace of the listener's ability to ingest the contents that the terms seem to fly by. Leisurely examples ("With floures white, blewe, yelwe, and rede" *PF* 186) go with ease only when the set of things listed is easy; more common are examples which, straining the listener, seem strained: "Who rubbeth now, who froteth now his lippes / With dust, with sond, with straw, with clooth, with chippes" (*MillT* 3747-48). The double verb and quintuple wipers—the form resembles *vers rapportés*—outwardly signify the inward wiping of Alison's image from Absolon's heart.[60] He doesn't love her any more, "for he was heeled of his maladie" (3757), and the violence of the healing calls for violent activity, comically done on Absolon's lips. This panoply of the material imagination suits the climax of farce, where slight details are developed and multiplied merely because we want to linger at the scene. As Absolon and the verse speed up, we and the story slow down. We welcome the dam across the stream.

To conclude this survey of the sources of Chaucer's lists, let us examine four more one-liners, chosen from many examples because they point toward four kinds of rhetoric, four worlds of style.

> Thise cookes, how they stampe, and streyne, and grynde. . . .[61]
> (PardT 538)

> She moorneth, waketh, wayleth, fasteth, pleyneth. . . .
> (FrankT 819)

> That hot, cold, hevy, lyght, moyst, and dreye. . . .
> (PF 380)

> Poudres diverse, asshes, donge, pisse, and cley. . . .
> (CYT 807)

The first has the Bible-thumping energy of the homiletic style; the second the chaotic iteration characteristic of satire; the third, the cool comprehensiveness and plenitude of the cosmological and encyclopedic; the fourth the desperately materialistic and diffuse slogging of technological or scientific literature. Together they comprise the remaining strands of tradition behind Chaucer's lists. These four sources may roughly be treated in pairs: encyclopedism with science, moral and homiletic literature with satire. But we will note special connections outside these pairings, especially of the other three with satire.

Chaucer's scientific attainments are celebrated. Doubtless because of its Aristotelian base—from our point of view
a science of partly rationalized taxonomy—much of
medieval science amounted to lists and arrays of facts
ordered by principles of genus and species. If the sign of
modern science is the terse mathematical *formula* (the purest
syntagm), the sign of medieval science is the wildly prolix
table—of numbers (for fixing events in the calendar), of
correspondences (of star to hour, of property to element to
season, of bodily organ to metal to zodiacal sign), of things
and their properties, genera and species. Tables go horizontally and vertically, as if they were syntagmatic and
paradigmatic, but because their horizontal rows repeat the
pattern of the top line, the rows are likewise paradigmatic: a
table is rank and file, crossed paradigms, a list of lists.

Hence, because science came to him largely in lists,
Chaucer regularly represents it in lists: the taxonomies of
trees and birds in *The Parliament of Fowls*, Arcite's two maladies
(hereos and trauma) in the "Knight's Tale," the types of
dreams in *The House of Fame*, the parades of astronomical
terms listed by the Franklin who claims he "kan no termes of
astrologye" (1273–90). The baggage of science, its terms and
tools and materials, absorb more attention than the effective
findings of science. Our distinction between technology and
applied science, represented by the handbook of chemistry
with all its tables, and pure science, represented by elegant
articles in the journals, could not have been much felt in the
Middle Ages. Although Pertelote's list of laxative herbs acts
as a witty counterpart, a womanly, folksy, domestic, experiential alternative, to Chauntecleer's bookish, authoritative
science of dreams, nevertheless it is she who presents—if
oversimplified—the "higher" science of humors. Both sci-
entists could claim, in the light of events, that they were
right.

Even so, Chaucer at times regards the trappings of
science with a critical attitude which, perhaps deceptively,
looks modern.[62] The spray of symptoms in the "Knight's
Tale" seems less than tactful in context; the lists in the
"Miller's Tale," *The House of Fame*, the "Nun's Priest's Tale,"
are comic; in the "Franklin's Tale," the magician's baggage
and the listed illusions he works are tainted, "supersticious
cursedness" (1272); the enormous lists of apparatus, terms,
and materials in the "Canon's Yeoman's Tale" are positively

demonic, as the Yeoman tells us again and again: "I have yow toold ynowe / To reyse a feend" (860-61). The list is a foul charm, a "Double, double, toil and and trouble." We have seen Jankyn's mnemonic priamel; in contrast, here is the Canon's Yeoman's mnemonic effort, "as ofte I herde my lord hem nevene," to name the "bodyes sevene":

> Sol gold is, and Luna silver we threpe,
> Mars iren, Mercurie quyksilver we clepe,
> Saturnus leed, and Juppiter is tyn,
> And Venus coper, by my fader kyn!
>   (826-29)

The meter jerks too roughly to aid the memory, and the padding rhymes scarcely contribute. The Yeoman delivers the lines, and the preceding lines about "the foure spirites," rather plumply, "by ordre" as he says—in contrast to his first list of things "unto oure craft apertenyng" which he "by order . . . nat reherce kan"—but his orderly list, which at least manages to get planets and metals together, still fails to find rhythm, and it sadly breaks like the alchemist's pot. Chaucer's scientific lists normally display the incompetence or irrelevance of science, or at best—as in the "Franklin's Tale"—its carefully circumscribed efficiency.

Behind the more technical sciences of medicine, alchemy, physiognomy, and astrology are the philosophical sciences we gather under the name cosmology: the general sciences of creation, generation, procreation, emanation, which define God's relation to the universe. Medieval writers regularly express cosmology in encyclopedic catalogues— often on the plan of the six days of creation—which may be called hexamerons.[63] Alan of Lille and Bernard Sylvestris promulgated such catalogues in the later Middle Ages, and their work joins with *The Romance of the Rose* in influencing Chaucer.[64] The central idea of hexameral lists is the plenitude of nature. God sustains his creation in fullness, and abhors empty slots in the array of creatures.

Jean de Meun had already handled cosmological poetry in tones of mingled respect and humor. Jean's Nature, like Chaucer's Squire, in her enormous speech coursing over the things of the world, mentions that it is well to avoid prolixity.[65] Many of Chaucer's catalogues derive from the motive implicit in this encyclopedic tradition to say all, to imitate in plenitude of discourse the plenitude of nature. Further, a number of Chaucer's hexameral catalogues adopt Jean de Meun's witty attitude toward this fallacy of imitative form.[66] Of Chaucer's works the *Parliament* comes closest to a cosmological epic, and its movement from list-full garden to even more list-full hill of Nature resembles in little the movement from Guillaume's Deduit to Jean's stuffed places in the *Romance of the Rose*. But the *Parliament* brings the species into discord among themselves and brings the generative process of Nature to a halt—at least until the emergence of common sense and the resolving harmonies of a song. In the manner of Jean de Meun, but more lightly, Chaucer sets the list-making man of authority, represented by Aleyn, against mere humanity represented by the birds, who, unlike the trees, refuse to rest content as merely a list—a display in species of the genus "bird"—and thus disrupt the order of Nature.[67]

We are not far from satire, but before turning to it let us glance at a third tradition, medieval moral and homiletic literature. The most striking formal quality of a medieval treatise or sermon on vice is its use of ramification.[68] The Parson says Penitence "may be likned unto a tree" (112), and repeats the image of divisions of a topic as branches (388, 389, 728, 956). A ramified topic looks more orderly than a list, but only because the relation of genus to species is especially clear; in fact, the ramifications have that symmetry and intransitivity which characterizes disorder and lists. The branches have no order among themselves. So medieval sermons and treatises tend to ramble (to keep the vegetable metaphor) in spite of their specious formality. And why should they not? Even "Melibee", in spite of some literary offenses (its absurd "plot," its confused allegory), under a decently charitable reading accomplishes its parainetic intention.

The "Pardoner's Tale" exploits the listing tendency of a homiletic discourse and adds to it that zeal for energetic accumulation still heard in the hellfire sermon.[69] In his proem upon the tavern vices, the Pardoner repeatedly sneaks murder in among the lesser crimes of drinking, gambling, and swearing, as if the lists exfoliated out of control: a bad apple is grafted into the lemons. Yet the heaping up of vices is a necessary part of his art; their accumulation imitates the excesses of the sinners. The vicious terms spew out ("Thus spitte I out my venym" 421) in a process the reverse of the key tavern vice, gluttony. Monstrous listing of words tries to reverse the glut of food:

> Allas! the shorte throte, the tendre mouth,
> Maketh that est and west and north and south,
> In erthe, in eir, in water, men to swynke
> To gete a glotoun deyntee mete and drynke!
> (517–20)

That genre in which the gargantuan excesses of vice find their counterpart in a surfeited language of abused plenitude is satire.[70] As satire magnifies and deals in "disorderly profusion," it naturally uses lists.[71] When Juvenal names his work "farrago," he gives a list (quoted as this essay's epigraph). *Farrago* (from *far*, "spelt, meal") means "medley, hodgepodge, mixed grain, grab-bag" like *satura*, "mixed dish, medley." To these food-and-genre terms we add "farce" from *farcire*, "to stuff." Milton at his most rudely satiric describes the Paradise of Fools in lists: "Reliques, Beads, / Indulgences, Dispenses, Pardons, Bulls, / The Sport of Winds . . ." (*PL* 3.491–93), and Pope sums up the satiric spirit:

> A motley mixture! in long wigs, in bags,
> In silks, in crapes, in Garters, and in rags,
> From drawing rooms, from colleges, from garrets,
> On horse, on foot, in hacks, and gilded chariots. . . .[72]
> (Dunciad 2.21–24)

The motley mixture of satire revels in splenetic lists, whose function often, as in the one-liners cited before ("A theef, and eek a somnour, and a baude") is to level terms usually arranged hierarchically. Pope slyly levels Garters and rags, only hinting, if the capital letter is his, that this item is a metonymy (for members in the Order of the Garter) unlike the others. The cosmological poet emphasizes the gradations of things; the satirist says it's all the same thing. Technological madness, homiletic indignation, and encyclopedic abundance join *per saturam* in satiric lists.

The Pardoner's exhortation upon tavern vices and the Canon's Yeoman's account of alchemy are Chaucer's closest approaches to the satiric spirit outside of *The House of Fame*. This last, every niche stuffed with lists, itself a "ful confus matere" (*HF* 1517) like the babble of stories in the House, erratically jumping from topic to topic, jumbling epic tragedy with farce, distributing, like the goddess Fame, good and bad report by random chance, approaches the rabelaisian energy of high satire, lacking only spite. Geffrey cannot muster the Pardoner's venom.

Chaucer repeatedly deploys one formal device, a kind of list, with satiric intent. We have seen examples in the alliterative battle-scenes, in Jankyn's priamel, and in much of the rapid summary of the *Aeneid* in *The House of Fame*, namely rapid reviews of series of actions in which each action is given a single line.[73] On the level of the line, with emphasis on the verb, these "action lists" correspond to one-liners, which emphasize nouns on the level of the single word. If anything, action lists effect a sense of rushing even more than verse-filling asyndeton. They turn story into list and hasten by to return to the main narrative. Yet, as in these lines which perhaps only those experienced in the laboratory can fully appreciate, sometimes the rush of the lines can suggest in their relentless detail a disappointed retardation. The alchemists clean up their exploded trash ("mullok"):

> The mullok on an heep ysweped was,
> And on the floor ycast a canevas,
> And al this mullok in a syve ythrowe,
> And sifted, and ypiked many a throwe.
>   (CYT 938–41)

The verbs sink into a suffering passive; the Yeoman's *parade* of terms amounts to unsifted mullok.[74]

A happier and wilder list provides a fit end:

> . . . and after hym they ran,
> And eek with staves many another man.
> Ran Colle oure dogge, and Talbot and Gerland,
> And Malkyn, with a dystaf in hir hand;
> Ran cow and calf, end eek the verray hogges,

So fered for the berkyng of the dogges
And shoutyng of the men and wommen eeke,
They ronne so hem thoughte hir herte breeke.
They yolleden as feendes doon in helle;
The dokes cryden as men wolde hem quelle;
The gees for feere flowen over the trees;
Out of the hyve cam the swarm of bees.

. . . .

Of bras they broghten bemes, and of box,
Of horn, of boon, in whiche they blewe and powped,
And therwithal they skriked and they howped.
It semed as that hevene sholde falle.
(NPT 3381–401)

The whole farm gathers to chase the fox; all of *us* gather—
Colle is "oure" dog—in a typical Chaucerian community-
forming finale. The list of those who gather, who swarm like
the bees, hustles and bustles pell-mell, helter-skelter, hurry-
scurry, in a huggermugger hodgepodge higgledy-piggledy, a
topsy-turvy arsy-versy mishmash hurly-burly hoo-ha of
hitherandthithering.[75] As geese fly over trees, we hear
fiends yelling and heaven seems to fall, as it fell on Chicken
Licken. Here verbs carry the burden, especially the verb
"ran" which falls for a while into anaphora. This brief *cursus
mundi* focuses on the coursing. I suggested before that action
lists join the paradigmatic to the syntagmatic, because the
listing continues the narrative. That Malkyn has her distaff
in her hand symbolizes the paradigmatic—she is interrupted
in her work as a list interrupts a story—but this list hastens
the action (as she may after all use the distaff as a weapon, a
rural *Venus armata*). As it nears its end, the list turns into the
more common adjectival kind, naming the materials of the
horns, and it adopts alliteration, assimilating itself to the
alliterative battle-scene in the "Knight's Tale" and the
"Legend of Cleopatra." The scene is violent, told violently,
and would be satire (I omitted the political reference to Jack
Straw), except for the overriding fact that it is so good-
tempered and so funny: Chaucer makes in comedy.

Something about the dream-vision form encourages
lists. They derive from the European tradition of art poetry,
dominated by *The Romance of the Rose*, itself full of lists; their

dreamy logic avoids the syntax of the syntagmatic and lingers on the visible in the paradigmatic form of the *voie*; they are bookish and learned and display lore. They concentrate not on what happens—the hunt passing by— but on the presence of things, detail by detail. By multiplying instances of what seems unique—all these lovers met this fate, here is the fame of all these people—they stress the commonness of human experience, and make it comic. Each of them sets local and down-to-earth happenings against great universal paradigms, with affection but with humility. The Black Knight amplifies the lovely Lady White and her death by way of poetic amplification—lists—making her a metaphor for Beauty and Death, so that the principle of the lists, the lady herself, barely emerges (like the lady of *The Romance of the Rose*, whom we never see). But the tiny Chaucerian action of the dream, the dreamer's questioning, finally brings the knight from the woods of her qualities to the fact of her death, which may be as far as consolation can go without some greater healer.

Both *The Parliament of Fowls* and *The House of Fame* take us to the spheres, and lay out such great issues as erotic generation and human tradition in elaborate lists. The poems pit lists and stories against each other, and both neglect the cosmic paradigms against which the action evolves—the starry spheres, the garden of love—for the sake of love tidings. The birds in the *Parliament* represent the very principle of lists—speciation—but like the trees of the wood, which build, sail, complain, shoot, drink, divine, they are too human to remain slots in a paradigm. They bicker, and they put off for a year the arch-mating which would perpetuate the species. The poem has a kind of reconciliation in a song which, by repeating lines in a fixed pattern, opposes the essential open-enddedness of a list.

Great traditional structures seem to inform *The House of Fame*: the Scipio vision, or any high-flying vision (Chaucer lists the high-flyers: Ennok, Elye, Romulus, Ganymede, and Alixaundre, Scipio, Dedalus, Ykarus [588–89, 915–20]), the Dantesque *voie*, the story of Aeneas. Its abundant lists give it an air of encyclopedic comprehensiveness. Yet it veers waywardly with a conspicuous randomness. That we have an incomplete fragment seems to symbolize the fragmented state of its world. There are too many tidings of love to list, to set in order, to judge: humans do too many things, and Fortune operates too variously. Both poems exploit the sense lists give of plenitude and complete enumeration, and both poems are aware, with an essentially Chaucerian awareness, that the appearance of plenitude is specious, that abundance cannot substitute for perfection, that lists need imply no order or end, that it is hard to reconcile cosmic design with the buzzing confusion of human actions and human desires. Love is a craft hard to learn. Both poems leave us wondering what will happen next; at last they sacrifice lists, which cannot elicit suspense, for stories.

In the middle of *The Canterbury Tales* the pilgrim narrator tells his two tales, "Sir Thopas" and "Melibee." Both tales are full of lists: "Sir Thopas" lists the trappings which a crude minstrel would think proper to chivalric romance, and "Melibee" lists strings of wisdom, authorities, sentences, to further the proffered counsel by way of accumulation.[76] The tales neatly oppose each other, and between them—but not separately—they reveal the art of the complete story-teller. They seem to divide the world of fiction between them. "Sir Thopas" is all mindless action, *praxis,* insufficiently motivated, vapidly rapid, stupidly handled, with a veneer of rhetorical ornament in the form of those absurd lists; "Melibee" is all counsel, *dianoia,* whose plot is thin and confused, obviously a mere expediency. If one could conjoin the *aventure* of "Sir Thopas" with the *sens* of "Melibee," one might have a good piece of work, perhaps a "Knight's Tale." Chaucer's pilgrim *persona* knows what makes a good tale, but he lacks the craft to integrate his knowledge in a single effort. His lists are signs of his disability. In "Sir Thopas" he lists sets of objects out of a vague feeling for what is proper to the genre, hoping the listener will make sense of it, will smooth the excrescent lists into the whole consciousness of the action. But the lists dominate and degrade the action. In "Melibee" the lists, as they ramble on and on, point to the absurdity (in what I think is a serious piece of work) of varnishing with a story so much unvarnished truth. The essence of each tale aims to be the adornment of the other, but the proportions are wrong in both.

Let us glance for a final example at what we have of the opening and closing of *The Canterbury Tales.* The "Knight's Tale," an exemplar of the philosophical romance, perhaps the Middle Ages' most serious essay at a supreme fiction, may be taken as a balancing weight for the last group of tales—the "Second Nun's Tale" of St. Cecilie, the "Canon's Yeoman's Tale," the "Manciple's Tale" of Phebus and the crow, and the "Parson's Tale." As a group they seem to split apart what the "Knight's Tale" held together. The "Knight's Tale" treats its many and long lists subsumptively: the lists all serve clear purposes, and do not get out of hand; they are subsumed in a covering intelligence that parcels out narrative topics with firm control. The Knight can afford various whimsicalities and indignities because the main movements of the tale are so serenely sure. Even the bursting in of the infernal fury (2684) at the climax of the tale proves not so much a disruption as an evidence of the order of things. In one of the few places where we find self-consciousness about the rhetorical management of the tale, Theseus asks "What may I conclude of this longe serye" (3067). The series to which he refers—whether it is the series of sentences and exempla in his own speech on the stability of causes or the whole series of ups and downs in the tale—makes a show of the abundance of this world, both of its binary vicissitudes and of its multiply listed circumstances. But the Olympian control of so much matter under the sun finds an Olympian conclusion in the next lines: "But after wo I rede us to be merye, / And thanken Juppiter of al his grace."

The last four tales constitute an anthology of the use of lists. The "Second Nun's Tale" is unique in Chaucer for offering—except for a list of the "sapiences three" (338) which exemplify the Trinity (itself a unified three)—no lists. The life of the saint is unadorned narrative. In a saint's life nothing but action is needed, because the action itself, face to face with God, so abounds in meaning that any retardation would be superfluous if not blasphemous. The Second Nun, like Cecilie "swift and bisy evere in good werkynge" (116), need tell only the working. She lists only in her prologue.

It has often been noticed that the "Canon's Yeoman's Tale" answers in various ways the Second Nun's.[77] The alchemist's sweaty materialism issues in lists. In his study of the background of the tale, Joseph Grennen observes that "The 'unity' topic is the hallmark of all authors in the mainstream of alchemical literature, although, amazingly, it is blandly mouthed amidst the most confusing welter of terms and processes." Saint Cecilie knows only one order and ridicules the idol of stone. The "Knight's Tale" interfuses the orders of chivalry, of the pantheon, and of the prime forces of nature—love, change, death—and presents these orders in symmetrical lists. The Canon's Yeoman, immersed in the order of matter, drowns in things. D. W. Robertson, Jr. says the Yeoman's lists represent "false wisdom," a kind of parody of the "serye" of the "Knight's Tale."[78]

Another form of false wisdom appears in the lists of maxims and exhortations at the end of the "Manciple's Tale." Both Manciple and Yeoman present their tales as monitory exempla, and both conclude with lengthy warnings. But the Manciple's bouquet of maxims, we have noticed, misses the point. The Pardoner's inclusion of homicide in his lists of tavern vices proves true in the event; conversely the Manciple's omission of homicide after the event seems obtuse. If the Canon's Yeoman drowns in lists, the Manciple hides in them.

The Yeoman's and Manciple's lists precede and follow their stories. The "Second Nun's Tale" is all story (as "Sir Thopas" might have been if its barmy narrator had not heard minstrels listing), and the "Parson's Tale" (like "Melibee," if we omit its sorry plot) is all lists. The "Parson's Tale" seems to sum up, in a paradigmatic summation scheme, the long syntagm of the pilgrimage with its list of tales.[79] Every reader has noticed that the variety of human motive and conduct represented in the string of tales seems to recur, in another form, in the Parson's anatomy. On the one hand *The Canterbury Tales* resemble such works as the "Monk's Tale" and *The Legend of Good Women*, in which the separate stories by exemplifying a single theme become elements in a list; but on the other hand *The Canterbury Tales* resemble their "General Prologue," a series which suggests order but stands too close to the fullness of life—life human, divine, animal, demonic, saintly—to display the single principle that makes a list a list. To list is to attempt to comprehend, and Chaucer revels in and distrusts lists. The "Parson's Tale," may be the best a list can do by way of answering human needs, but although it concludes it does not complete.

Siegfried Wenzel

the Wisdom of the Fool

King Lear's fool—a minor character on Shakespeare's stage—continues to haunt the imagination of readers, audiences, actors, and critics alike. Much historical search and critical ingenuity have been spent in an effort to trace his ancestry, with the result that we are offered a welter of historical figures and literary types that may or may not lie behind Shakespeare's creation: classical mimes, medieval court fools and jesters, the Feast of Fools, French *sotties* and *sermons joyeux*, the Vice of morality plays and interludes, Sebastian Brant's *Ship of Fools*, Erasmus's *Praise of Folly*, Elizabethan jestbooks, Will Somers and Richard Tarlton, and the "fools in Christ" from St. Paul to the *devotio moderna*.[1] And yet, after working through this pot-pourri of possible backgrounds one is left with the impression that Lear's fool possesses a moral depth and earnestness and a personal solidity that differ profoundly from Erasmus's Folly or the dramatic fools in Shakespeare's contemporaries, or any of the other influences that have been suggested. In the following pages I wish to call attention to a literary character who in many ways resembles Shakespeare's great fools more closely but whose existence and possible influence have hardly been noticed at all. This is the domestic or court fool who teaches his master a moral lesson and thereby effects his conversion, a change of his ways to the better. This figure made his appearance in handbooks for preachers and in sermons from at least the beginning of the fourteenth century onward and continued in vogue well into Shakespeare's time.

Exempla about fools and their folly are of course quite frequent in medieval sermon literature. The story of one who, in order to protect his cheese from the mice, buys a cat, only to be rid of both mice and cheese, appears in several large *exempla* collections from France and England made in the thirteenth and fourteenth centuries.[2] Such lack of worldly knowledge and prudence appears also in the fool who burns his house in order to get rid of the flies,[3] or in his cousin who carries a lamb to market but lets go of it when he meets several people who (by previous arrangement among themselves) ask him why he is carrying a *dog* in his arms.[4] A disturbed perception of reality speaks from the story in which a fool is given a new pair of shoes which he carries off in his bosom because he does not want to damage them.[5] Such folly takes a more sinister turn with the fool on his way to the gallows who is admonished by a priest to make his last confession, but instead of listening, he complains that he lost his hood as he was taken from prison;[6] another who lies dying refuses to receive Holy Communion because his sister had taken Communion and then died![7] Excessive literal-mindedness or failure to perceive semantic multi-valence characterizes a fool who hears his master praise his favorite falcon, whereupon, in order to see for himself, he eats the bird and finds it exceedingly tough and unpraise-worthy;[8] similarly, another fool

heard his master command his servants and officers that in their judgments and punishments and other deeds they should never turn to the right or the left but always go straight. Then he tried to walk straight through houses and rocks and mountains and whatever lay before him, so that he would not go against his master's command.[9]

Such tales of folly were exceedingly common towards the end of the Middle Ages and accrued around popular figures like Till Eulenspiegel or the men of Gotham. But there is another kind of tale whose hero is not simply a foolish person but a domestic fool; his behavior is not a cause of laughter but rather elicits moral shock and reflection, especially in the audience within his own, fictional world. These are bitter fools who teach wisdom.

The only tale of this kind that has been known to Shakespeare students was printed by Furnivall in 1869.[10] Written in English, it fills one page of a miscellany (MS Harley 2252) in a hand of the very late fifteenth century. "The Sage Fool's Testament," as its editor named it, reports of "a great lord who had a 'sage fole' whom he loved marvelously well because of his entertainment." The fool loved his master equally well, and when the master died, the fool loved his son just as much. When the fool became ill a few years later, he made his testament, bequeathing his soul to the devil, his body to the churchyard, his hood to his master's steward, his bauble to the almoner, and all his money to his lord himself. In some astonishment the master asked him what he meant by these requests. The fool replied: "I have loved your father so well that I desire to be in his company above all else, for he loved me so well. And I know that he is in hell; therefore I want to be with him." In like fashion, his other belongings (including his bed, which went to his lord's wife) were willed to various members of the household as signs to call attention to their moral corruption. For instance, he gave his bauble to the almoner "because when he delivers your alms among the poor people, they press on him, and then he beats them with his staff that the blood runs about their ears; but my own bauble is softer." Similarly, his bed is to remind the lady of her soft, slothful life; his hood, the steward of his unfaithfulness in service; and his money, the lord of his own and his father's unamended wrongdoings.

"Touching" or even "quaint"[11] as this tale may be, it is by no means unique or chronologically the first of its kind. Its direct ancestor appeared nearly two centuries earlier in the Franciscan handbook for preachers, *Fasciculus morum*, written in England in the opening years of the fourteenth century.[12] In the long discussion of the sacrament of penance as one of the major remedies against sloth, the author illustrates the need for speedy confession with a story about "a certain fool (*fatuus*)" who loved his master dearly and, noticing his lord's unjust and sinful life, wanted to lead him to change his ways. He feigned sickness, made his testament in his master's presence, and bequeathed his bauble to the steward, his bowl to the butler, and his soul to hell. The shocked master then received an explanation much as in the preceding story; but in *Fasciculus morum* the master promises to change his life, whereupon the fool changes his testament. The text of the entire *exemplum* (which is not moralized) reads as follows:

[1] Vnde narratur de quodam fatuo qui multum dominum suum dilexerat. Considerans ergo illum iniuste viuere inuolutum peccatis multiplicibus, cupiens illum ad correcionem festinare, finxit se infirmum, et mittens pro domino rogauit si placeret quatinus condendo testamentum suum sibi assistere dignaretur. Quo annuente hec tria legauit: Primo pegma[13] siue babellum suum senescallo domini tanquam maximo fatuo quem vnquam vidisset, dicens: "Domine me, iste miser fatuus pauperes spoliat et multa mala committit vt te ditet et tibi placeat. Et certe ex hoc non tantum animam propriam dampnat, ymmo tuam, eo quod sic illum facere permittis. Dignus est ergo babello tanquam maximus fatuus. Ego enim dictus sum fatuus, et tamen nulli noceo. Secundo, magnum discum meum, Anglice *bolle*, lego pincerne tuo tanquam fortissimo potatori. Ipse enim nunquam cessat a mane vsque ad vesperam et pluries vsque ad mediam noctem cum intrantibus et exeuntibus ac eciam permanentibus ciphum leuare et nimium potare. Ego autem tercio lego animam meam ad infernum." Quod abhorrens dominus et seipsum signans quare sic legauit causam querens. At ille respondit: "Quia certus sum quod tu illuc ibis propter iniurias quas hic facis et facere permittis sine correccione; et quia semper hic tecum fui a natiuitate, nec ibi te derelinquam." Cui dominus: "Non sic, Willelme, non sic; quia pro certo me corrigam." Et fatuus: "Ergo," inquit, "tunc sanus sum et muto testamentum meum[14] et lego animam meam deo et omnibus sanctis." Et sic reduxit dominum ad confessionem et vite correccionem.[15]

Quite apart from the dates, comparison of the two stories suggests that the version in *Fasciculus morum* is the original and that of Harley 2252 a later expansion, making two masters out of one and increasing the number of possessions the fool bequeaths. The latter kind of narrative expansion, incidentally, can also be seen at work in one fifteenth-century manuscript of *Fasciculus morum* whose scribe increased the fool's legacy by adding marginally: "I further bequeath my fox-tail to your servants, that is, those who cover their faces with their hair, etc. And I bequeath my bells to the keepers of your horses who are so proud, etc."[16] Besides being more succinct, the original version of *Fasciculus morum* also creates a much greater narrative effect than that of Harley 2252 by keeping the shocking bequest of the fool's soul until the end of his will.[17]

I do not know of any earlier form of the story before the composition of *Fasciculus morum*.[18] The handbook incorporates a good deal of material that can be found in older *exempla* collections or sermons, but for many tales *Fasciculus morum* is our earliest witness. In any case, from about 1300 on the story remained popular. Apart from its preservation in all extant copies of *Fasciculus morum* that have the full text, and its derivative translation in Harley 2252, the story was also copied from *Fasciculus morum* by a monk at Canterbury in 1448,[19] and it was told in Anglo-Norman in a slightly different form by the Franciscan Nicole Bozon (after 1320):

I have heard that once there was a rich man who had brought up from childhood a servant whom he loved much. When this servant lay sick to death and was to make his testament, he willed his body to the churchyard and his soul to hell, and he would not change his statement for any of his companions. Then his master came and reproached him of his folly; and the servant responded that he would rather be with him in hell than live without him in heaven.[20]

It is worth noting that besides its greater brevity, Bozon's version makes the fool into a *sergeaunt* (*armiger* in the Latin translation) and consequently omits the belongings that are characteristic of a fool (bauble, bowl, etc.).

An echo of the same tale about "the fool's testament" can also be heard in the next two *exempla*. They—and others to follow—appear in the large alphabetical preacher's handbook, the *Summa praedicantium* by the Dominican John Bromyard, written in the 1330s and 1340s.[21] The first, from the section on "Predicacio," shares with *Fasciculus morum* the dying fool's desire to go to hell in order to be with his beloved master. Bromyard admonishes that one should not despise God's word even when it is spoken by ignorant or wicked preachers:

[2] Let them be held in honor so that God's truth in them may not be despised, because even though they are fools, yet, as Seneca says in a letter to Paul, "God sometimes speaks from the mouth of fools."[22] For the word of the fool can sometimes convert a sinner to the good, as is shown by what used to be reported by a trustworthy person [about a lord who frequently comforted his sick fool whenever he walked by him], saying "Hope in God, you'll go to heaven." But the fool always replied: "I don't want to go there." When his master asked him one day why he did not want to go there, he answered: "Because I want to go to hell."—"Why?" he asked.—"Because," he replied, "I love you, and as I have been with you in life, so I want to be with you in death and afterwards; and since you will go to hell, I want to do so too, in order to keep you company." Then the lord said: "How do you know that I'll go there?"—"Because," he answered, "the whole country says so, that you are a bad person and are going to hell." And in truth, he who before was a wicked man was stung in his conscience by the fool's words and emended his life afterwards.[23]

Like the previous story, this tale also gained some popularity. It was incorporated in English in the collection of *A Hundred Merry Tales*, printed in 1526;[24] and on the Continent it found its way into the large compendium of sermon *exempla* in German, made by the Alsatian Franciscan preacher Johannes Pauli (ca. 1450–1533).[25]

Bromyard includes another tale of similar tenor which is thematically related to the story from *Fasciculus morum*, but in contrast to the preceding story (No. 2) the common element here is not the desire to go to hell but the legacy of the fool's bauble.[26] This Latin tale also appears in a slightly abbreviated English translation in a vernacular sermon cycle of the fifteenth century, as part of a funeral sermon. The English version is in all essentials close to Bromyard's text:

[3] I fynde þere was a grete lorde vpon a tyme þat had a fool. The lord dyd make a babull and gafe it vnto þis fool and commaundid neuer to gefe his babull vnto he founde a more fool þan he was. So by þe visitacion of God þe lorde was passing sike vnto þe deþe. His meneall men seide oon to anoþer: "Mi lorde goeth, he may not abide." Þe fool herd þis. He toke his babull and went into þe chambre. He come to þe lorde and axed hym: "Whidir shall þou goo, lorde?" He answerd: "I wote not."—"Whan shall þou cum ayene?" Þe lorde seide: "I wote not."—"How longe shall þou abide þere?"—"I wote not."—"Now certes, I may wele say þou art a fole if þou go þou wote not whidir nor how shalt fare when þou

commyst þere, nore wotist not whan þou shall cum ageyn nor
how longe tyme þou shall abide þere. Whi [ne] sendist beforn þe
caryage with vitayll and such þinges as were necessari vnto þe
whan þu commyst þere? I holde þe a more fole þan I am. Have þou
now my babull." Þe lorde vnderstode þat wisdam was in his
wordis. So forthwith he gafe grete almous and gafe away with his
handis a grete parte of his goodis and disposid hym all to God-
ward and made an holy ende.[27]

It should be noted that the common element in this tale and
Fasciculus morum extends beyond the legacy of the bauble to
the motif of giving it to the greater fool.[28]

The just-quoted passage from Bromyard ends with the
sentence: "The same spirit spoke from his mouth that speaks
at D.i,13," a reference to the section on "Dampnacio" in the
Summa, which includes yet another tale involving a wise fool.

[4] There is a report of a nobleman who was led to deep remorse
of his sins by just such a word spoken before him by a fool. For as
someone said in the hearing of this fool, "If there were no hope,
the heart would break," the fool added: "How great will therefore
the pain be where there is no hope of liberation and the heart
cannot break!" When the lord heard this, he said with a sigh: "It
grieves me to hear this word from a fool." And nonetheless Seneca
witnesses in one of his letters to Paul: "God sometimes speaks out
of the mouth of fools."[29]

The proverb spoken in the fool's hearing is richly attested in
Middle English writings, from the *Ancrene Wisse* to works of
the late fifteenth century.[30] The fool applies it, quite naturally, to the common notion that hell's worst pain is the
eternity of suffering without hope of relief or end. As the
Anglo-Norman treatise *Les Peines de Purgatorie* puts it: "One
says in English, 'ʒif hope ne were, herte to-broste.' But
there, it will be that man's heart cannot break, for people
will live without end and will never have release from
suffering."[31]

In the stories we have so far seen, the fool's action or
words effected a change of heart in his master, but this is
not the case in the following two *exempla*. Bromyard reports a
case in which the fool conversely becomes an instrument of
punishment. Here, a magnate travels through his manorial
estates and has a written record made of all the tributes he
receives. His people think he does so in order to reward

them, but in fact he does it only so he can exact the same amount through his bailiffs in following years. The story continues:

[5] It happened that [the lord] lay sick with gout near the fireplace in his chamber. On one occasion, when a certain fool who used to provoke him to laughter was alone with him in the chamber, the straw caught fire, and he ordered the fool several times to extinguish it. But he did not want to and, playing with the fire, said, "It isn't hurting you yet." Finally, as the fire came nearer to his bed and the lord shouted at the fool in horror that he should extinguish the fire, the fool replied that he would not and, as his lord asked for his reason, replied: "Because you would only ask me to do the same again 'by custom,' as you do to other people." And thus he burned to death.[32]

Although this fool's behavior anticipates the stark and often extremely painful effects which some of the crude pranks played by later fools—as reported in Renaissance jestbooks—have on their victims, it is fortunately not characteristic of sermon *exempla*. Another story told by Bromyard, this one in his *Distincciones*, similarly fails to lead to conversion; it ends not in grisly death but only embarrassment. The tale appears in a sermon on the Conversion of St. Paul. In developing his theme, the preacher explains that anyone who begins his work late or badly like the Apostle must start over and then work hard, quickly, diligently, and perseveringly. Diligent work requires humility, and that is not shown by those people who behave as if they were not descended from Adam but from someone else made of gold or precious stones.

[6] These people put on such proud and vain clothes that they appear more like fools than like our first parents and are recognized as such. This is shown in a report that recently at a certain parliament a fool saw a knight marvelously dressed up and similar to himself, as it seemed to him. The fool said to him, in the presence of many magnates: "Whose household fool are you? I am the Abbot of Bury's fool and would love to make your acquaintance, for you are a pretty fool, to be sure." The knight blushed and did not know what to answer.[33]

My final story of a wise domestic fool comes once more from an unpublished sermon. The entire collection, in a fifteenth-century manuscript, follows upon a set of sermons or rather *Exortaciones* ascribed to "John Bromyard, O.P." I do not know if the later sermons can be related to Bromyard as well; in fact, the wording of this one suggests a fifteenth-century date of composition (see below).[34] The tale is part of a Latin Advent sermon on the theme "Behold, I come soon." In dealing with Christ's Second Coming, the preacher speaks of seven steps that are necessary to conducting a legal case, starting with the summons and leading to the judge's sentence. The fourth step is bringing the felon into court. Anagogically, at the Last Judgment, the preacher declares, the accused person will be completely naked:

[7] And thus the people who here are more concerned with physical clothes than with spiritual ones will then in their confusion stand naked before the whole world, naked in body and mind. Therefore, whatever happens to worldly goods, see to it that you have spiritual riches; because at the Judgment it will be just as it once happened in northern England. The Lord Neville had a natural fool, who on a feast day asked his master if he could distribute alms to the whole household. The master was much astonished by this, but he let him have his will. After dinner the lord came with his household into the hall to see how his fool would distribute the gifts. Now, as this fool got to the poor, when he saw one that was naked and had nothing, he gave him nothing. When he found one well clothed and with his lap full of bread, he gave him a lot. In this fashion he distributed the alms. His master and the others were much astounded by this, and the master asked why he gave to those who were not needy and left the needy with nothing. The fool replied: "Lord, in truth I do as you do, for if one of your clerics has a good church, you give him a prebend; if he has nothing, you give him nothing, just as to minstrels who know how to acquire much you give robes and money, and to the poor at your gate hardly anything or nothing at all." And this is today's custom.[35]

I believe these seven *exempla* furnish enough evidence to speak of a late-medieval English story type in which a domestic fool teaches his master wisdom. The lesson taught is not the general truth that all sinners are fools,[36] or that everybody is a fool,[37] but rather that one particular moral flaw puts the master's spiritual health and his salvation in jeopardy. In contrast to much other fool literature of the very late Middle Ages and the Renaissance, these tales do not so much expose sin and immorality as folly, but rather use a domestic fool as a catalyst to teach and to convert. And their emotional effect is not primarily to produce laughter (if they do that at all) but to shock and lead to earnest reflection. In these respects, tale No. 6 perhaps stands a little apart from the others, though it shares their main element, the figure of a bitter but wise fool.

Against my claiming that these tales form a conventional story type it might be objected that they appear instead to have been favorites of a single author, John Bromyard. It is true that he is responsible for giving us at least five of the seven. But their earliest representative made its appearance a generation before Bromyard's writings, and both it and Bromyard's own versions were copied and translated by later writers independently of his works. In addition, Bromyard poses as a mere transmitter who reports what he has heard or read elsewhere.[38] While he introduces several of these tales with a nondescript "notice the story" ("nota historiam," No. 3) or "it is reported" ("fertur," Nos. 4 and 6), in two cases he explicitly refers to a trustworthy source as if he had heard the stories from eyewitnesses ("quod a fidedigno narrari solebat," No. 2; "quod fidedignorum relacione narrari solet," No. 5). Though undeniably Bromyard had a strong personal taste for tales of this nature, they were just as clearly "in the air" when he wrote them down and—judging by their separate reappearance in later texts—must have fallen on receptive ears.

It is worth emphasizing that at least two tales seem to speak of historical characters and events: the fool of the "abbot of Bury," attending a recent parliament (No. 6), and the fool belonging to the Lord Neville in the north of England (No. 7). These references are tantalizing because so very little information about actual court fools in England is available. Apart from a few scattered references in household accounts,[39] the only English court fool from before the sixteenth century about whose person, life, and pranks any number of details have found their way into written records is John Scogan or Scogin. His life story is told in a book called *Scogin's Jests*, printed in 1626, and scholars have tentatively placed him in the reign of Edward IV (ca. 1480).[40] But in the words of Sidney Lee, "it is not unreasonable to suspect that the whole [i.e., *Scogin's Jests*] was a work of fiction, and that Scogan is a fictitious hero."[41] It is curious that the hero of

Scogin's Jests is reported to have had relations with both the abbot of Bury (St. Edmunds) and William de Neville— possibly the two figures we found in our sermon tales. Tale No. 7 (involving the Neville household) is likely to be of the fifteenth century; but tale No. 6 appears in a work (Bromyard's *Distincciones*) which seems to date from before 1354.⁴² *Scogin's Jests* may thus very well be a compilation of stories that circulated in the Middle Ages and early Renaissance and are found in a variety of sources;⁴³ but its fictitious hero may go back to a historic figure who lived much earlier than has hitherto been thought.

But whether the fools in our sermon tales were historical or not, they all are definitely members of noble households, personal attendants on some magnate, and tale No. 5 specifically says that its fool used to entertain his lord. The Latin stories I have presented are consistent in calling this character *fatuus*; though the broader term *stultus* may also be applied to these fools (Nos. 3, 4, 5, and 6), they all are consistently introduced as *fatui*. It is less clear whether they are indeed "cracked," mentally deficient or subject to temporary irrationality. Social, medical, and literary historians who have dealt with the medieval court fool regularly distinguish between the "natural" fool (a mentally deficient person kept as entertainer) and the "artificial" fool (a mentally normal person who pretends to be mad in order to be kept as entertainer). It appears that this distinction is recorded in English only from the early fifteenth century on.⁴⁴ Among our seven tales, only No. 7 calls its fool "naturaliter fatuus"; the authors of the other texts are unaware of such a verbal distinction. Yet several of these fools betray streaks of madness, by their unreasonable, inhuman acts, as in No. 5, or their literal understanding of a metaphor, as in No. 3. One should also recall that wishing to go to hell out of love for one's friend, while a heartwarming notion, is clearly sinful by the standards of medieval theology since such a desire places the love for a created being higher than the love of its Creator;⁴⁵ therefore, in the light of moral theology, the lovable fools of tales 1 and 2 are definitely and deeply foolish, and the reflection added by Bromyard that even out of their mouths some truth may come is more than rhetorical ornament. I suggest that the *fatuus* of our seven tales is the direct Latin ancestor of what would in English texts of a later date be called a *fol sage*. In both cases we deal with a person kept in a noble household "who is wiser than he seems,"[46] but our Latin tales give us a definite impression of a man whose mental resources, normally, are such as need the sympathetic protection of a wealthy patron. It is interesting that in a group of manuscripts of tale No. 1, a group which revises the text of *Fasciculus morum* throughout, the wording "de quodam fatuo" is changed to "de quodam fatuo *sagaci*."[47]

It must be emphasized that the *fatui* of our tales are not simple jesters. Historians of the fool have frequently mixed the two character types without discrimination, presumably on the ground that in medieval texts they are undistinguishable.[48] To be sure, our *fatui* live in or off noble households and entertain their patrons, like so many *histriones* or *joculatores*. But they do not travel from household to household; and more importantly, in the literature with which I am dealing a lexical distinction between the two types is clearly drawn and preserved. Bromyard, for instance, has a number of different stories about *mimi* and *joculatores*[49] who are not court fools, nor do they teach wisdom; and the same is true of *Fasciculus morum*.[50] The distinction is also neatly expressed in the *Summa virtutum de remediis anime* ("Postquam"), which Chaucer used in his "Parson's Tale." In praising the good effects of patience in suffering bodily harm, its author makes the following separate comparisons:

A juggler (*ioculator*) lets himself be heavily beaten for money or a small reward. Much more readily do patient men give their bodies over to torments for God's sake.... A truly patient man is also like a fool (*stulto*), who lets himself be beaten and treated with shame for the sake of food and drink. Such foolishness in Christ is the greatest wisdom.[51]

The difference between fools and minstrels is more than lexical in the *Elucidarium* by Honorius of Autun, written in the twelfth and popular through the following centuries, which declares that fools are saved, but for minstrels there is no hope.[52] This difference—tension, in fact—between the two even enters one of our sermon tales: No. 7 explicitly sets the *fatuus* who distributes alms in opposition to the *histriones* who receive greater gifts than the poor.

This differentiation notwithstanding, several of the

fools in our *exempla* do engage in play (in contrast to making only verbal comments), in acting out some form of make-believe, such as making their last wills in sickness (No. 1), or distributing their masters' alms (No. 7), or simply handing over their baubles as if this were a ceremonial act (Nos. 1, 3). But these forms of "playing" are immensely different from the entertainment expected of jesters (such as performing acrobatic jumps or juggling balls or doing a morris dance) because of their symbolic significance. It is hard to say whether that significance, the effect of their playing, is intended by the fools or not. The elaborate play-acting of Nos. 1 and 7 certainly is deliberate. But the actions reported in Nos. 2, 3, 5, and 6 could very well be genuine, unpretended "folly." While these *fatui*, then, as a group are court fools and not wandering jugglers, our texts do not give us any clear indication whether they are genuinely insane or merely pretend to be so. Perhaps such a distinction was of no concern to the storytellers.

Whatever their intellectual competence, these fools are clearly men of deep feeling. A strong bond of love attaches several to their masters (Nos. 1, 2, 3, and perhaps 7), and although I made a negative comment on this love earlier, the stories themselves carry no such condemnation but portray a deep and warm, human affection. There is, in addition, another feeling which runs through these *exempla* and radiates from the fools: a concern for the poor and for the plight of the lower classes. Failure to give alms to the needy is the theme of tales 1-3 and 7, while tale No. 5 focuses on the wicked customary right to extort yearly contributions. This connection between the wise fool and almsgiving or concern for the lower classes may be interpreted in several ways. It could simply reflect a very natural identification of the lowest of the low with his social equals: the poor are the fool's brethren. But these stories may also hint at a more abstract, philosophical concern of the period in which they appeared. In the Bible, foolishness means literally lack of prudence, shrewdness, worldly wisdom; when spiritually interpreted, the *stultus* becomes a *figura* of the sinner in general, of the enemy of God.[53] In the thought of St. Paul, however, the notion of foolishness is used metaphorically to characterize the absolute difference between faith in Christ and the beliefs and values of "the world": in Christ, "God has made foolish the wisdom of this world," and therefore, "if any man seems to be wise in this world, let him become a fool, so that he may be wise."[54] True folly, in other words, is to embrace the beliefs and values of "the world."

The notion of "the world," like so much else, became quite concrete in the later Middle Ages, almost painfully so. In the fourteenth and fifteenth centuries it is very specifically equated with the desire to possess, i.e., with greed. Suffice it to recall the scheme of the Three Enemies of Man and its connection with the seven deadly sins; in this period, the world is linked in this scheme to avarice.[55] This pattern is used dramatically in *The Castle of Perseverance*, where the greatest—and in the event successful—temptation comes from Avarice, who fights in the army of World, and World is associated with *Stultitia*.[56] Less schematically, the same notion runs through earlier sections of *Piers Plowman*, when the Dreamer learns that the search for Trewthe, which ultimately is wisdom and love, must begin with ordering one's attitude toward worldly goods.[57] I suggest that the same notion may underlie the *exempla* we have been studying. Here a literal fool is ironically set against men who are "wise" and powerful in the eyes of the world but spiritually foolish.[58] The court fool teaches true wisdom by reminding his audience to place God's love above false worldly values, which he does paradigmatically, and in fitting agreement with his social position as a pauper, by distributing the riches of the world to the poor and by not oppressing the lower classes.

The evangelical counsel to give one's possessions to the poor and follow Christ if one would be perfect is, of course, central to Christian teaching[59] and was never forgotten in the history of the Church. But in St. Francis and the mendicant orders the counsel not only found a peculiar response but also took on a new urgency, probably in light of the economic and social changes that affected Europe from the late twelfth century on.[60] It is not surprising that our *exempla* should, as they do, come from members of both mendicant orders. The author of *Fasciculus morum* was a Franciscan friar, Bromyard a Dominican, and both Nicole Bozon and Johannes Pauli, who repeated their tales, also Franciscans. That the wise fool who preaches almsgiving appeared regularly in the sermon stories of friars seems to

speak, not so much for the Franciscan ideal of friars as
ioculatores dei (as critics are perhaps too quick to say), but
rather for their authors' awareness of the breakup of a social
structure that had formerly been ruled and ordered by
aristocracy and higher clergy. Here, magnates are saved, not
through bishops and not even through itinerant preachers,
but through the babble of their fools.[61] I might add that the
very words of St. Francis underline this spiritual upgrading
of the domestic fool, as they also support the clear distinction noted earlier between fools and jesters. While the saint
called his followers *joculatores Domini*,[62] he reserved the name
of *pazzo*, "madman," for himself:

The Lord told me that he wished me to be a fool in the world, and
that he did not want to lead us by any other way than by that
wisdom; for by your learning and by your wisdom God will
confound you.[63]

Though court fools gifted with some form of wisdom
can be found here and there in the imaginative literature of
the Middle Ages,[64] the great poets of the fourteenth century
did not pick up this potentially very powerful figure and
utilize it. Langland, though he eventually arrived at a more
positive estimation of "Godes mynstrales," always held a
rather negative view of the "fol sage."[65] Chaucer devotes
one stanza to "the kynges fool" who teaches ladies that time
and their beauty will pass;[66] but the kind of spiritual wisdom
we find in the sermon *exempla* comes not from a fool but from
the mouth of a child, in the "Pardoner's Tale."[67] Gower and
Hoccleve each tell a story in which a court fool gives wise
counsel to his king and thereby surpasses the advice of the
official counsellors; but the advice given in both cases is
political rather than spiritual, although Gower's fool is much
closer to the sermon tales in this respect than Hoccleve's.[68]
Perhaps the most powerful medieval English poem that
deals with wisdom and the court fool is *Robert of Sicily*, in
which the king is converted to true humility by being forced
to become a court fool and painfully learns what he is. It is
just possible that this remarkable version of a common tale[69]
may have gained its unique form under the influence of such
exempla as I have been discussing. Yet for the fullest utiliza-
tion of the wise-fool figure in imaginative literature one has

to wait until Shakespeare's drama. And then it is surprising to notice how similar the Fool of *King Lear* is to the humble *fatuus* of the sermon tales. As a domestic fool he is closely attached to the lord he entertains; he is literal-minded, has an abnormal perception of language and reality, and play-acts; he loves his master, but more importantly, he teaches Lear wisdom by leading him to self-understanding, and a significant part of this wisdom lies in Lear's coming to "feel" the plight of the poor: "O! I have ta'en / Too little care of this."[70] When Lear has reached that point, the Fool disappears from the play, evidently because he is no longer needed for Lear's turn to sanity. Far-fetched as it may seem at first glance to suggest any connection between fourteenth-century preachers and Shakespeare, it is nonetheless a matter of historical record that some of the wise-fool stories were repeated in the jestbooks of Shakespeare's time.[71] Whether or not Shakespeare knew such tales, it is I hope evident that his wise fools had strikingly similar ancestors in a group of tales preserved and used by fourteenth-century English preachers.

George Hardin Brown

the Publications
of Morton W. Bloomfield:
1939–May, 1981

The more than two hundred items in this list of published works by Morton Bloomfield stand as a legacy to present and future students of language, medieval literature, and intellectual history. The catalogue below records the number and demonstrates the range of his investigations during the past forty-two years of continuous endeavor.

Professor Bloomfield himself provided a selection of his most significant articles and reviews in *Essays and Explorations* (no. 100). However, since its publication in 1970 he has added another hundred items to his bibliography, among which are major contributions in linguistics (no. 129), literary theory (nos. 103, 116, 120, 156, 182, 196), and critical analysis (nos. 144, 200), notably on Chaucer (nos. 104, 117, 119, 172, 190). Yet another dimension of his broad range of interests is reflected in his reports on Joachim of Fiore and Joachism (nos. 25, 36, 140, 199). Other articles have been reprinted in critical surveys that are widely available (nos. 14, 32, 56, 67).

Of his books, the encyclopedic *Seven Deadly Sins* (no. 19) has proved a mine of information; difficult to obtain for some years, it made a welcome reappearance in print in 1967 (no. 84). *Piers Plowman as a Fourteenth Century Apocalypse* (no. 54), his important critical study of that poem, appeared in 1962. Recently, the Medieval Academy of America published the monumental enterprise of many years' assiduity, *Incipits of Latin Works on the Virtues and Vices* (no. 183), for which he was the chief investigator and editor. He has also served as editor of various distinguished studies (nos. 103, 120, 138) and college texts (nos. 13, 63).

I have tried to provide here a complete, accurate list of Morton Bloomfield's publications to date. In such a large catalogue some mistakes or omissions are possible. I only hope that such errors are few indeed; for I wish to present this list of publications as a suitable gift to their own creator.

1. "Present State of *Piers Plowman* Studies." *Speculum* 14 (1939), 215–32.

2. Rev. of *Allegories of the Virtues and Vices in Medieval Art from Early Christian Times to the Thirteenth Century*, by Adolf Katzenellenbogen. *Speculum* 16 (1941), 494–96.

3. "The Origin of the Concept of the Seven Cardinal Sins." *Harvard Theological Review* 34 (1941), 121–28. Rpt. in no. 100 below, pp. 2–10.

4. "A Source of Prudentius' *Psychomachia*." *Speculum* 18 (1943), 87–90.

5. "Was William Langland a Benedictine Monk?" *MLQ* 4 (1943), 57–61.

6. Rev. of *The Pardon of Piers Plowman*, by Nevill Coghill. *Speculum* 22 (1947), 461–65. Rpt. in no. 100 below, pp. 283–88.

7. "Canadian English and Eighteenth Century American Speech." *JEGP* 47 (1948), 59–67. Rpt. in no. 100 below, pp. 218–31.

8. "'Doom is Dark and Deeper than any Sea-Dingle': W. H. Auden and *Sawles Warde*." *MLN* 58 (1948), 548–52.

9. Rev. of *A Commentary on the General Prologue to the Canterbury Tales*, by Muriel Bowden. *MLQ* 11 (1950), 105–06.

10. "Chaucer's Summoner and the Girls of the Diocese." *PQ* 28 (1949), 503–07.

11. "Trollope's Use of Canadian History in *Phineas Finn.*" *Nineteenth-Century Fiction* 5 (1950), 67–74.

12. Rev. of *Piers Plowman: The C-Text and Its Poet*, by E. Talbot Donaldson. *MLQ* 12 (1951), 230–31.

13. Ed., with R. C. Elliott. *Ten Plays: An Introduction to Drama.* New York: Rinehart, 1951 (see nos. 70, 146 below).

14. "*Beowulf* and Christian Allegory: An Interpretation of Unferth." *Traditio* 7 (1949–51), 410–15. Rpt. in *An Anthology of* Beowulf *Criticism.* Ed. Lewis E. Nicholson. Notre Dame: Univ. of Notre Dame Press, 1963, pp. 155–64. Also rpt. in *The Beowulf Poet: A Collection of Critical Essays.* Ed. Donald K. Fry. Englewood Cliffs, N. J.: Prentice-Hall, 1968, pp. 68–75.

15. Rev. of *Piers Plowman and Scriptural Tradition*, by D. W. Robertson and Bernard F. Huppé. *Speculum* 27 (1952), 245–49. Rpt. in no. 100 below, pp. 289–95.

16. "Chaucer's Sense of History." *JEGP* 51 (1952), 301–13. Rpt. in no. 100 below, pp. 12–26.

17. "The Source of Boccaccio's *Filostrato* III, 74–79 and its Bearing on the MS Tradition of Lucretius, *De Rerum Natura.*" *Classical Philology* 47 (1952), 437–43.

18. "Some Problems of Method in Linguistics," *Studium Generale* 5 (1952), 437–43.

19. *The Seven Deadly Sins: An Introduction to the History of a Religious Concept with Special Reference to Medieval English Literature.* E. Lansing: Michigan State College Press, 1952 (see no. 84 below).

20. Rev. of *Études sur Jean de Roquetaillade (Johannes de Rupescissa)*, by Jeanne Bignami-Odier. *Speculum* 27 (1952), 536–38.

21. Ed. with E. W. Robbins. *Form and Idea: Thirty Essays for College Study.* New York: Macmillan, 1953 (see no. 50 below).

22. "Final Root-Forming Morphemes in English." *American Speech* 28 (1953), 158–64. Rpt. in no. 100 below, pp. 232–40.

23. "The Problem of Fact and Value in the Teaching of English." *College English* 15 (1953), 33–37.

24. Rev. of *Daily Living in the Twelfth Century based on the Observations of Alexander Neckam on London and Paris*, by Urban Tigner Holmes. *The CEA Critic* 15, No. 4 (April, 1953), 5.

25. With Marjorie E. Reeves. "The Penetration of Joachism into Northern Europe." *Speculum* 29 (1954), 772–93.

26. "Research on *Piers Plowman*." *The Graduate School Record, The Ohio State University* 8 (December, 1954), 4–6.

27. Rev. of *Dictionary of Linguistics*, by Mario A. Pei and Frank Gaynor. *American Speech* 30 (1955), 125–26.

28. "The Magic of *In Principio*." *MLN* 70 (1955), 559–65.

29. "A Preliminary List of Incipits of Latin Works on the Virtues and Vices, Mainly of the Thirteenth, Fourteenth, and Fifteenth Centuries." *Traditio* 11 (1955), 259–379.

30. "The Pardons of Pamplona and the Pardoner of Rounceval: *Piers Plowman* B XVII 252 (C XX 218)." *PQ* 35 (1956), 60–68.

31. Rev. of *English Religious Drama of the Middle Ages*, by Hardin Craig. *MP* 54 (1956–57), 129–31.

32. "Distance and Predestination in *Troilus and Criseyde*." *PMLA* 72 (1957), 14–26. Rpt. in *Troilus and Criseyde & the Minor Poems*. Vol. II of *Chaucer Criticism*. Ed. Richard J. Schoeck and Jerome Taylor. Notre Dame: Univ. of Notre Dame Press, 1961, pp. 196–210. Also rpt. in no. 100 below, pp. 201–16, and in no. 197 below, pp. 75–89.

33. Rev. of *A Litil Tretys on the Seven Deadly Sins*, by Richard Lavynham. Ed. J. P. W. M. van Zutphen. *JEGP* 56 (1957), 472–73.

34. With B. A. Eilbott. "A Diachronic Approach to Lexical Number: Middle and Modern English." *American Speech* 32 (1957), 170–75.

35. "Some Reflections on the Medieval Idea of Perfection."

Franciscan Studies 17 (1957), 213–37. Rpt. in no. 100 below, pp. 28–55.

36. "Joachim of Flora, A Critical Survey of his Canon, Teachings, Sources, Biography and Influence." *Traditio* 13 (1957), 249–311.

37. Rev. of *The Ancrene Riwle* (*The Corpus MS: Ancrene Wisse*). Trans. M. B. Salu. *Speculum* 33 (1958), 128–30.

38. "The Eighth Sphere: A Note on Chaucer's *Troilus and Criseyde*, V, 1809." *MLR* 53 (1958), 408–10.

39. "*Piers Plowman* and the Three Grades of Chastity." *Anglia* 76 (1958), 227–53.

40. Rev. of *Early English*, by J. W. Clark. *American Speech* 33 (1958), 198–99.

41. "Symbolism in Medieval Literature." *MP* 56 (1958), 73–81. Rpt. in no. 100 below, pp. 82–95.

42. "Religion and the Teaching of Literature." *Religious Education* 53 (1958), 488–93.

43. Rev. of *A History of the English Language*, 2nd ed., by A. C. Baugh. *JEGP* 57 (1958), 796.

44. Rev. of *William Langlands "Piers Plowman"* (*Eine Interpretation des C-Textes*), by Willi Erzgräber. *Anglia* 76 (1958), 550–54.

45. Rev. of *The Summa contra Haereticos Ascribed to Praepositinus of Cremona*. Ed. Joseph N. Garvin and James A. Corbett. *Speculum* 34 (1959), 267–69.

46. Rev. of *Design in Chaucer's "Troilus,"* by Sanford B. Meech. *MLN* 75 (1959–60), 431–34. Rpt. in no. 100 below, pp. 297–301.

47. Rev. of *Piers Plowman: The A Version—Will's Visions of Piers Plowman and Do-Well*. Ed. George Kane. *Speculum* 36 (1961), 133–37.

48. Rev. of *A Deuout Treatyse called The Tree & XII. Frutes of the Holy Goost*. Ed. J. J. Vaissier. *MP* 58 (1960–61), 273–75.

49. "*Sir Gawain and the Green Knight*: An Appraisal." *PMLA* 76 (1961), 7–19. Rpt. in no. 100 below, pp. 130–57.

50. Ed. with E. W. Robbins. *Form and Idea: Thirty Essays for College Study.* 2nd ed. New York: Macmillan, 1961 (see no. 21 above).

51. "Joachim of Flora." *Encyclopedia Britannica,* 1961 ed.

52. "*Piers Plowman* as a Fourteenth-Century Apocalypse." *The Centennial Review* 5 (1961), 281–95. Rpt. in no. 100 below, pp. 158–72.

53. Rev. of Piers the Plowman: *Literary Relations of the A- and B-Texts,* by David C. Fowler. *Speculum* 37 (1962), 120–23.

54. *Piers Plowman as a Fourteenth-Century Apocalypse.* New Brunswick: Rutgers Univ. Press, 1962.

55. Rev. of *Studien zum kirchlichen Wortschatz des Mittelenglischen, 1100–1300,* by Hans Käsmann. *Archiv für das Studium der neueren Sprachen und Literaturen* 199 (1962), 49–51.

56. "Patristics and Old English Literature: Notes on Some Poems." *CL* 14 (1962), 36–43. Rpt. in *Studies in Old English Literature in Honor of Arthur G. Brodeur.* Ed. Stanley B. Greenfield. Eugene: Univ. of Oregon Press, 1963; rpt. New York, 1973, pp. 36–43. Rpt. partially in *An Anthology of Beowulf Criticism.* Ed. Lewis E. Nicholson. Notre Dame: Univ. of Notre Dame Press, 1963, pp. 367–72. Also rpt. in *Essential Articles for the Study of Old English Poetry.* Ed. Jess B. Bessinger, Jr., and Stanley J. Kahrl. Hamden, Conn.: Archon Books, 1968, pp. 63–73.

57. "Middle English *Gladly,* An Instance of Linguisticism." *NM* 63 (1962), 167–74.

58. "*The Many Implications.*" Rev. of *The Story of Jewish Philosophy,* by Joseph L. Blau, *The Jewish Mind,* by Gerald Abrahams, and *Portrait of a Jew,* by Albert Memmi. *Kenyon Review* 25 (1963), 178–83.

59. "A Grammatical Approach to Personification Allegory." *MP* 60 (1962–63), 161–71. Rpt. in no. 100 below, pp. 242–60.

60. Rev. of *Piers Plowman, An Essay in Criticism,* by John Lawlor. *Speculum* 38 (1963), 369–70.

61. Unsigned rev. of *Þe Liflade ant te Passiun of Seinte Iuliene.* Ed. S. R. T. O. d'Ardenne. *Speculum* 38 (1963), 342.

62. Rev. of *The Major Latin Works of John Gower*. Ed. and trans. Eric W. Stockton. *Speculum* 38 (1963), 506–07.

63. With Leonard Newmark. *A Linguistic Introduction to the History of English*. New York: Alfred A. Knopf, 1963. Rpt. Westport, Conn.: Greenwood Press, 1979 (see no. 81 below).

64. Rev. of *Classical and Christian Ideas of World Harmony: Prolegomena to an Interpretation of the Word 'Stimmung,'* by Leo Spitzer. Ed. Anna Granville Hatcher. *Speculum* 39 (1964), 337–39.

65. Rev. of *The Key of Remembrance: A Study of Chaucer's Poetics*, by Robert O. Payne. *CL* 16 (1964), 283–85.

66. Rev. of *The Meaning of Proper Names*, by Holger S. Sørensen. *Language* 40 (1964), 410–12.

67. "The Form of *Deor*." *PMLA* 79 (1964), 534–41. Rpt. in *Old English Literature: Twenty-Two Analytical Essays*. Eds. Martin Stevens and Jerome Mandel. Lincoln, Nebraska: Univ. of Nebraska Press, 1968, pp. 212–28.

68. "Authenticating Realism and the Realism of Chaucer." *Thought* 39 (1964), 335–58. Rpt. in no. 100 below, pp. 174–98.

69. Rev. of *Piers Plowman, An Introduction*, by Elizabeth Salter. *MP* 62 (1964–65), 62–64.

70. Ed. with R. C. Elliott. *Great Plays: Sophocles to Brecht*. 2nd ed. of *Ten Plays*. New York: Rinehart, 1965 (see nos. 13 and 146).

71. Rev. of *The Discarded Image*, by C. S. Lewis. *Speculum* 40 (1965), 354–56.

72. Rev. of *The Articulate Citizen and the English Renaissance*, by Arthur B. Ferguson. *Speculum* 41 (1966), 323–24.

73. Rev. of *A Critical History of Old English Literature*, by Stanley B. Greenfield. *Speculum* 41 (1966), 330–32.

74. Rev. of *The Structure of* Beowulf, by Kenneth Sisam. *Speculum* 41 (1966) 368–71. Rpt. in no. 100 below, pp. 277–81.

75. Rev. of *Alain de Lille: Textes Inédits*, by Marie-Thérèse d'Alverny. *Speculum* 41 (1966), 530–32.

76. Rev. of *A Manual of Old English Biblical Materials*, by Minnie Cate Morrell. *Speculum* 41 (1966), 561.

77. Rev. of *The Spiritual Basis of* Piers Plowman, by Edward Vasta. *Speculum* 42 (1967), 206–09.

78. Rev. of *Die englische Heiligenlegende des Mittelalters*, by Theodor Wolpers. *Archiv für das Studium der neueren Sprachen und Literaturen* 203 (1966–67), 464–65.

79. "Middle English" Section of "English Literature." *New Catholic Encyclopedia*, vol. 5, pp. 378–87.

80. Rev. of *Chaucer Life-Records*. Ed. Martin M. Crow and Clair C. Olson. *Speculum* 42 (1967), 365–66.

81. With Leonard Newmark. *A Linguistic Introduction to the History of English*. Trans. into Japanese. Tokyo, 1967 (see no. 63 above).

82. Rev. of *Supplement to the Index of Middle English Verse*, by Rossell Hope Robbins and John L. Cutler. *Speculum* 42 (1967), 548–50.

83. "The Syncategorematic in Poetry: From Semantics to Syntactics." In *To Honor Roman Jakobson, Essays on the Occasion of His Seventieth Birthday*. Vol. I. The Hague and Paris: Mouton, 1967, pp. 309–17. Rpt. in no. 100 below, pp. 262–74. Trans. into German, in *Literaturwissenschaft und Linguistik, Ergebnisse und Perspektiven*. Vol. 2 of Ars Poetica 8. Ed. Jens Ihwe. Frankfurt, 1971, pp. 62–74.

84. Rpt. with slight revisions, *The Seven Deadly Sins*. 1967 (see no. 19 above).

85. Rev. of *The Scale of Perfection and the English Mystical Tradition*, by Joseph E. Milosh. *MLQ* 27 (1967), 489–90.

86. Editor's Introduction to *An Introduction to the Language of Poetry*, by Seymour Chatman. Boston: Houghton Mifflin, 1968, pp. ix–x.

87. Rev. of *Books Known to the English, 597–1066*, by J. D. A. Ogilvy. *Speculum* 43 (1968), 529–30.

88. Rev. of *Word and Symbol: Studies in English Language*, by Charles L. Wrenn. *ELN* 6 (1968), 70–71.

89. Rev. of *Laments for the Dead in Medieval Narrative*, by Velma Bourgeois Richmond. *Speculum* 43 (1968), 535–37.

90. "Understanding Old English Poetry." *Annuale Mediaevale* 9 (1968), 5-25. Rpt. in no. 100 below, pp. 58-80.

91. Rev. of *A Manual of Writings in Middle English 1050-1500*, fascicule 1. Ed. J. Burke Severs. *Speculum* 43 (1968), 762.

92. "Some Notes on *Sir Gawain and the Green Knight* (lines 374, 546, 752, 1236) and *Pearl* (lines 1-12, 61, 775-776, 968). In *Studies in Language, Literature, and Culture of the Middle Ages and Later*. Ed. E. Bagby Atwood and Archibald A. Hill. Austin: The Univ. of Texas Press, 1969, pp. 300-02.

93. Rev. of *Old English Poetry, Fifteen Essays*. Ed. Robert P. Creed. *CL* 21 (1969), 285-86.

94. "A Brief History of the English Language." *The American Heritage Dictionary of the English Language*. Ed. William Morris. Boston: American Heritage and Houghton Mifflin, 1969, pp. XIV-XVIII.

95. "Il Racconto dell'*Uomo di legge*: La tragedia di una vittima e la commedia cristiana." *Strumenti critici* 9 (June, 1969), 195-207 (see no. 117 below).

96. "Beowulf, Byrhtnoth, and the Judgment of God: Trial by Combat in Anglo-Saxon England." *Speculum* 44 (1969), 545-59.

97. "Generative Grammar and the Theory of Literature." *Actes du Xᵉ Congrès International des Linguistes. Bucarest. 28 août-2 septembre 1967*. Ed. Alexandru Graur. Vol. 3, Bucharest: Ed. Acad. R. S. R., 1969-70, pp. 57-65. Trans. into German, in *Literaturwissenschaft und Linguistik, Ergebnisse und Perspektiven*. Vol. 2 of Ars Poetica 8. Ed. Jens Ihwe. Frankfurt, 1971, pp. 523-33.

98. "The Two Cognitive Dimensions of the Humanities." *Daedalus* 99 (1970), 256-67. Rpt. in no. 120 below, pp. 73-90.

99. "Episodic Motivation and Marvels in Epic and Romance." *Essays and Explorations: Studies in Ideas, Language, and Literature*. Cambridge: Harvard Univ. Press, 1970, pp. 96-128 (see no. 100 below).

100. *Essays and Explorations: Studies in Ideas, Language, and Literature*. Cambridge: Harvard Univ. Press, 1970. Includes a

preface and index, no. 99, and rpt. of nos. 3, 6, 7, 15, 16, 22, 32, 35, 41, 46, 49, 52, 59, 68, 74, 83, 90 above.

101. Rev. of *Chaucer und seine Zeit: Symposion für Walter F. Schirmer.* Ed. Arno Esch. *Archiv für das Studium der neueren Sprachen und Literaturen* 206 (1969-70), 376-77.

102. Rev. of *The Mirror of Language: A Study of the Medieval Theory of Knowledge,* by Marcia L. Colish. *Speculum* 45 (1970), 119-22.

103. *The Interpretation of Narrative: Theory and Practice.* Harvard English Studies, 1. Ed. with a preface by Morton W. Bloomfield. Cambridge: Harvard Univ. Press, 1970.

104. "The Miller's Tale—An Unboethian Interpretation." In *Medieval Literature and Folklore Studies: Essays in Honor of Francis Lee Utley.* Ed. Jerome Mandel and Bruce A. Rosenberg. New Brunswick: Rutgers Univ. Press, 1970, pp. 205-11.

105. "Do Literary Studies have an Ideology?" *PMLA* 86 (1971), 128-29.

106. Rev. of *Chaucer's Mind and Art,* by A. C. Cawley, and *Speaking of Chaucer,* by E. Talbot Donaldson. *Yale Review* 60 (1970-71), 438-40.

107. Rev. of *On Four Modern Humanists.* Ed. Arthur R. Evans, Jr. *Romance Philology* 24 (1970-71), 506-10.

108. "Jakobsonian Poetics and Evaluative Criticism." *University Review* 37 (1970-71), 165-73.

109. Rev. of *Music of the Spheres and the Dance of Death: Studies in Musical Iconology,* by Kathi Meyer-Baer. *Speculum* 46 (1971), 172-74.

110. Interview "The Apostrophe's Life Hasn't Been an Easy One," by B. D. Colen. *The Washington Post,* July 4, 1971, Section D, pp. 1, 8.

111. Rev. of *Medieval Literature and Civilization: Studies in Memory of G. N. Garmonsway.* Ed. Derek A. Pearsall and Ronald A. Waldron. *Anglia* 89 (1971), 377-78.

112. Unsigned rev. of *A Manual of Writings in Middle English*

1050-1500. Vol. 2, ed. J. Burke Severs. *Speculum* 46 (1971), 414.

113. Contribution to *Interdisciplinary Medieval Programs and the Training of Students: A Discussion.* Ed. John Leyerle and Thomas A. Ohlgren. Cambridge: The Medieval Academy of America, 1971, pp. 3–5.

114. "Judaism and the Study of Literature." *Tradition* 12, No. 2 (1971), 21–37.

115. "Subtleties of the Schlemiel." Rev. of *The Schlemiel as Modern Hero,* by Ruth R. Wisse. *Genesis* 2 (Thursday, January 20, 1972), 3.

116. "Allegory as Interpretation." *NLH* 3 (1971–72), 301–17 (see no. 147 below).

117. "The Man of Law's Tale: A Tragedy of Victimization and a Christian Comedy." *PMLA* 87 (1972), 384–90 (trans. and revised version of no. 95 above).

118. "Troilus' Paraclausithyron and its Setting: *Troilus and Criseyde* V. 519–602." *Studies Presented to Tauno E. Mustanoja on the Occasion of his Sixtieth Birthday. NM* 73 (1972), 15–24.

119. "The Gloomy Chaucer." *Veins of Humor.* Harvard English Studies, 3. Ed. Harry Levin. Cambridge: Harvard Univ. Press, 1972, pp. 57–68.

120. Ed. with preface. *In Search of Literary Theory.* Studies in the Humanities. Ithaca: Cornell Univ. Press, 1972 (see no. 98 above).

121. With Albert C. Baugh and Francis P. Magoun. Necrology of Kemp Malone. *Speculum* 47 (1972), 601–03.

122. With Harold Lee. "The Pierpont-Morgan Manuscript of *De Septem Sigillis." Recherches de théologie ancienne et médiévale* 38 (1971), 139–48.

123. Rev. of *The Epistle of Othea,* by Christine de Pisan. Trans. Stephen Scrope, ed. Curt F. Bühler. *Speculum* 47 (1972), 803–04.

124. Reply to Letter of K. J. Hughes entitled "The Man of Law's Tale" in Forum section of *PMLA* 88 (1973), 142.

125. Rev. of *The Divine Comedy*, vol. I: *Inferno*, by Dante Alighieri—1: *Italian Text and Translation*, 2: *Commentary*. Ed. and trans. Charles S. Singleton, and *Dante's* Inferno. Ed. and trans. Mark Musa. *Speculum* 48 (1973), 127–29.

126. Rev. of *A Manual of Writings in Middle English 1050–1500*. Vol. 3, ed. Albert E. Hartung. *Speculum* 48 (1973), 186.

127. Rev. of *The Friar as Critic: Literary Attitudes in the Later Middle Ages*, by Judson Boyce Allen. *Speculum* 48 (1973), 329–30.

128. Rev. of *Ricardian Poetry: Chaucer, Gower, Langland, and the Gawain Poet*, by J. A. Burrow. *Speculum* 48 (1973), 345–47.

129. "The Study of Language." *Daedalus* 102, No. 3 (Summer, 1973), 5–13. Rpt. in no. 138 below, pp. 5–13.

130. "Some Thoughts on the Future of English Studies." *Bulletin, International Association of University Professors of English* (Spring, 1973), pp. 1–8.

131. Rev. of *Structure in Medieval Narrative*, by William W. Ryding, and *The Rise of Romance*, by Eugène Vinaver. *Speculum* 48 (1973), 584–87.

132. "Chaucer and Reason." *Unisa English Studies, Journal of the Department of English, University of South Africa* 11 (1973), 1–3.

133. "Fourteenth-Century England: Realism and Rationalism in Wycliff and Chaucer." *English Studies in Africa: A Journal of the Humanities* 16 (1973), 59–70.

134. With Walter J. Ong. Introduction to *Why Talk? a Conversation about Language*, by Wayne Altree. The National Humanities Faculty Why Series. San Francisco: Chandler and Sharp, 1973.

135. Rev. of *Speculative Grammars of the Middle Ages: The Doctrine of "Partes orationis" of the Modistae*, by G. L. Bursill-Hall, and *Grammatica speculativa*, by Thomas of Erfurt. Ed. G. L. Bursill-Hall. *Speculum* 49 (1974), 102–05.

136. Rev. of *Essai de poétique médiévale*, by Paul Zumthor. *Speculum* 49 (1974) 388–90.

137. "Elitism in the Humanities." *Daedalus* 103, No. 4 (Fall, 1974), 128–37.

138. Ed. with Einar Haugen. *Language as a Human Problem.* Introd. Morton W. Bloomfield. New York: W. W. Norton, 1974 (see no. 129 above).

139. "National Humanities Center." *PMLA* 90 (1975), 136.

140. Rev. of *The "Figurae" of Joachim of Fiore*, by Marjorie Reeves and Beatrice Hirsch-Reich. *Speculum* 50 (1975), 147–49.

141. Rev. of *Chaucer and the Making of English Poetry.* Vol. 1, *Love Vision and Debate*, vol. 2, *The Art of Narrative*, by P. M. Kean. *MÆ* 43 (1974), 193–95.

142. "Interpretation, Fourfold Method." In *Princeton Encyclopedia of Poetry and Poetics.* Ed. Alex Preminger, Frank J. Warnke, and O. B. Hardison, Jr. Enlarged Edition. Princeton: Princeton Univ. Press, 1974, pp. 942–43.

143. Interview with Philip Nobile on American dialects, in the Rochester, N. Y., *Democrat and Chronicle*, May 25, 1975.

144. "The Problem of the Hero in the Later Medieval Period." In *Concepts of the Hero in the Middle Ages and Renaissance, Papers of the Fourth and Fifth Annual Conferences of the Center for Medieval and Early Renaissance Studies, SUNY Binghamton 2–3 May 1970, 1–2 May 1971.* Ed. Norman T. Burns and Christopher J. Reagan. Albany: SUNY Press, 1975, pp. 27–48.

145. With Paul O. Kristeller and Samuel E. Thorne. Necrology of Harry Austryn Wolfson. *Speculum* 50 (1975), 570–71.

146. *Great Plays: Sophocles to Albee.* 3rd ed. of *Ten Plays.* New York, Chicago: Holt, Rinehart and Winston, 1975 (see nos. 13 and 70 above).

147. "Alegoria jako interpretacja." *Pamiętnik Literacki* 66, No. 3 (1975), 217–35. Polish trans. of "Allegory as Interpretation" (see no. 116 above).

148. Rev. of *The Divine Comedy*, vol. II: *Purgatorio*, by Dante Alighieri—1: *Italian Text and Translation, 2: Commentary.* Ed. and trans. Charles S. Singleton. *Speculum* 51 (1976), 136-37.

149. Rev. of *A Manual of Writings in Middle English 1050-1500.* Vol. 4, ed. Albert E. Hartung. *Speculum* 51 (1976), 136-37.

150. Rev. of *Studies in Medieval and Jewish Philosophy*, by Israel Efros. *Speculum* 51 (1976), 162.

151. Rev. of *Chaucer and Middle English Studies in Honour of Rossell Hope Robbins.* Ed. Beryl Rowland. *Speculum* 51 (1976), 163-64.

152. Rev. of *A Check-List of Middle English Prose Writings of Spiritual Guidance*, by P. S. Jolliffe. *Speculum* 51 (1976), 371.

153. Rev. of *Essays in Honour of Anton Charles Pegis.* Ed. Reginald O'Donnell. *Speculum* 51 (1976), 374.

154. Rev. of *Classical and Medieval Literary Criticism: Translations and Interpretations.* Eds. Alex Preminger, O. B. Hardison, Jr., Kevin Kerrone. *Speculum* 51 (1976), 374-75.

155. "Leading Ladies." Rev. of *The Role of Woman in the Middle Ages.* Ed. P. Morewedge, and *Woman as Image in Medieval Literature*, by Joan Ferrante. *TLS* 9 April 1976, p. 426.

156. "Stylistics and the Theory of Literature." *NLH* 7 (1975-76), 271-311.

157. "A Valuable Commentary on *The Divine Comedy*." Rev. of *Guido da Pisa's* Expositiones et Glose super Comediam Dantis *or* Commentary on Dante's Inferno. Ed. Vincenzo Cioffari. *Boston University Journal* 24 (1976-77), 67-71.

158. "*Patience* and the *Mashal*." In *Medieval Studies in Honor of Lillian Herlands Hornstein.* Ed. Jess B. Bessinger, Jr., and Robert R. Raymo. New York: New York Univ. Press, 1976, pp. 41-49.

159. "Quoting and Alluding: Shakespeare in the English Language." *Shakespeare: Aspects of Influence*, Harvard

English Studies, 7. Ed. G. Blakemore Evans. Cambridge: Harvard Univ. Press, 1976, pp. 1-20.

160. Rev. of *The Commentary of Geoffrey of Vitry on Claudian "De Raptu Proserpinae."* Eds. A. K. Clarke and P. M. Giles. *Speculum* 51 (1976), 726-28.

161. Rev. of *Reden und Schweigen: Zur Tradition und Gestaltung eines mittelalterlichen Themas in der französischen Literatur*, by Volker Roloff. *Speculum* 51 (1976), 782-84.

162. Rev. of *After Babel: Aspects of Language and Translation*, by George Steiner. *CL* 28 (1976), 374-76.

163. Rev. of *The Divine Comedy*, vol. III: *Paradiso*, by Dante Alighieri—1: *Italian Text and Translation*, 2: *Commentary*. Ed. and trans. Charles S. Singleton. *Speculum* 52 (1977), 644-45.

164. Rev. of *Fabula: Explorations into the Uses of Myth in Medieval Platonism*, by Peter Dronke. *Speculum* 52 (1977), 654-57.

165. Rev. of *Langue, texte, énigme*, by Paul Zumthor. *Speculum* 52 (1977), 758-59.

166. Rev. of *The Owl and the Nightingale: The Poem and its Critics*, by Kathryn Hume. *Speculum* 52 (1977), 998-1000.

167. "The Maturation of America and Its Impact on American Culture" and discussion. In *The Idea of America: A Reassessment of the American Experiment*. Ed. E. M. Adams. Cambridge: Ballinger, 1977, pp. 75-91, 91-102.

168. Rev. of *The Merveilleux in Chrétien de Troyes's Romances*, by Lucienne Carasso-Bulow, and *Chrétien's Jewish Grail*, by Eugene J. Weinraub. *Speculum* 53 (1978), 130-33.

169. Rev. of *Die Zahlenallegorese im Mittelalter: Methode und Gebrauch*, by Heinz Meyer. *Speculum* 53 (1978), 170.

170. Rev. of *Tractatus de grammatica: Eine fälschlich Robert Grosseteste zugeschriebene spekulative Grammatik.* Ed. Karl Reichl. *Speculum* 53 (1978), 184-85.

171. Rev. of *Perspectives of Irony in Medieval French Literature*, by Vladimir R. Rossman. *Speculum* 53 (1978), 186-87.

172. *"The Merchant's Tale*: A Tragicomedy of the Neglect of

Counsel—The Limits of Art." *Medieval and Renaissance Studies: Proceedings of the Southeastern Institute of Medieval and Renaissance Studies, Summer 1975*, Medieval and Renaissance Series, 7. Ed. Siegfried Wenzel. Chapel Hill: Univ. of North Carolina Press, 1978.

173. Rev. of *The Persecution of Peter Olivi*, by David Burr. *Speculum* 53 (1978), 344–45.

174. Rev. of *Curiosity and Pilgrimage: The Literature of Discovery in Fourteenth-Century England*, by Christian K. Zacher. *Speculum* 53 (1978), 428–29.

175. Rev. of *Early Epic Scenery: Homer, Virgil and the Medieval Legacy*, by Theodore M. Andersson. *Speculum* 53 (1978), 559–60.

176. With Fritz Voigt. "The Wisdom Tradition." In *The Sixtieth Anniversary Memorial Lectures: Seijo Gakuen, Seijo University*. Tokyo: Seijo Gakuen, 1978, pp. 1–18.

177. Rev. of *Aquinas and the Problems of his Time*. Eds. G. Verbeke and D. Verhelst. *Speculum* 53 (1978), 869–70.

178. "What is Literary Theory." *Poetica* 8 (Autumn, 1977), 1–5.

179. Rev. of *Making Sense of Literature*, by John Reichert. *Western Humanities Review* 32 (1978), 361–63.

180. Rev. of *The Wars of the Lord, Treatise Three: On God's Knowledge*, by Gersonides. Trans. and commentary, Norbert Max Samuelson. *Speculum* 54 (1979), 136–37.

181. Rev. of *Jewish Philosophical Polemics against Christianity in the Middle Ages*, by Daniel J. Lasker. *Speculum* 54 (1979), 167–69.

182. "Continuities and Discontinuities." In "Medieval Literature and Contemporary Theory," special issue of *NLH* 10, No. 2 (1978–79), 409–16.

183. With B. G. Guyot, O. P., Donald R. Howard, and Thyra B. Kabealo. *Incipits of Latin Works on the Virtues and Vices, 1100–1500, Including a Section of Incipits of Works on the Pater Noster*. Introd. Morton W. Bloomfield. Cambridge: Medieval Academy of America, 1979.

184. Rev. of *Yeats' "Sorrow of Love" Through the Years*, by Roman Jakobson and Stephen Rudy. *Poetics Today* 1 (1979-80), 409-10.

185. Rev. of *Selections from English Wycliffite Writings.* Ed. Anne Hudson. *Speculum* 54 (1979), 588-89.

186. Rev. of *Bible et Civilisation anglais*, by M. M. Larès. *Revue Belge de Philologie et d'Histoire* 77 (1979), 95-97.

187. Rev. of *Théorie de la prophétie et philosophie de la connaissance aux environs de 1230: La Contribution d'Hugues de Saint-Cher (Ms. Douai 434, Question 481)*, by Jean-Pierre Torrell, O. P. *Speculum* 54 (1979), 865-67.

188. Rev. of *Essays in Medieval Jewish and Islamic Philosophy: Studies from the Publications of the American Academy for Jewish Research.* Ed. Arthur Hyman. *Speculum* 54 (1979), 883.

189. Rev. of *Disenchanted Images: A Literary Iconology*, by Theodore Ziolkowski. *The Humanities Association Review* 29 (1978), 294-96.

190. "The Wisdom of the Nun's Priest's Tale." in *Chaucerian Problems and Perspectives: Essays Presented to Paul E. Beichner, C. S. C.* Eds. Edward Vasta and Zacharias P. Thundy. Notre Dame: Notre Dame Univ. Press, 1979, pp. 70-82.

191. Rev. of *Linguistics and the Novel*, by Roger Fowler. *Ars Semeiotica* 2 (1979), 237-41.

192. Rev. of *Dante's "Paradiso" and the Limitations of Modern Criticism: A Study of Style and Poetic Theory*, by Robin Kirkpatrick. *Speculum* 55 (1980), 136-37.

193. Rev. of *By Things Seen: Reference and Recognition in Medieval Thought.* Ed. David L. Jeffrey. *Speculum* 55 (1980), 408.

194. Rev. of *A Book of Showings to the Anchoress Julian of Norwich.* Eds. Edmund Colledge, O. S. A., and James Walsh, S. J. *Speculum* 55 (1980), 548-49.

195. Rev. of *The Bible and Medieval Culture.* Eds. W. Lourdaux and D. Verhelst. *Speculum* 55 (1980), 628-29.

196. "Episodic Juxtaposition or the Syntax of Episodes in Narration." In *Studies in English Linguistics for Randolph*

Quirk. Eds. Sidney Greenbaum, Geoffrey Leech, and Jan Svartvik. London: Longman, 1980, pp. 210–20.

197. Rpt. of "Distance and Predestination in *Troilus and Criseyde*," with Afterword. In *Chaucer's* Troilus: *Essays in Criticism*. Ed. Stephen A. Barney. Archon Books. Hamden, Conn.: The Shoe String Press, 1980, pp. 75–89, 89–90 (see no. 32 above).

198. "Some Traps in Literary Theorizing." *Hebrew University Studies in Literature* 8 (1980), 183–94.

199. "Recent Scholarship on Joachim of Fiore and his Influence." In *Prophecy and Millenarianism: Essays in Honour of Marjorie Reeves*. Ed. Ann Williams. Harlow, Essex: Longman, 1980, pp. 21–52.

200. "Personification Metaphors." In *Directions in Medieval Literary Criticism: Eleven Essays in Honour of Robert Worth Frank, Jr.* Eds. Michael A. Stugrin and Eric D. Brown. *ChauR* 14 (1979–80), 287–97.

201. With Barbara Nolan. "*Bēotword, Gilpcwidas*, and the *Gilphlæden* Scop of *Beowulf*." *JEGP* 79 (1980), 499–516.

202. Rev. of *Classical Rhetoric and Its Christian and Secular Tradition from Ancient to Modern Times*, by George A. Kennedy. *Speculum* 56 (1981), 218.

203. Rev. of *Preachers, Florilegia, and Sermons: Studies on the "Manipulus florum" of Thomas of Ireland*, by Richard H. and Mary A. Rouse. *Speculum* 56 (1981), 220.

Abbreviations Used in Notes

AnBol	Analecta Bollandiana
AnM	Annuale Mediaevale
ArL	Archivum Linguisticum
ASE	Anglo-Saxon England
CC	Corpus Christianorum (Turnhout: Brepols)
CCM	Cahiers de Civilisation Médiévale
CCrit	Comparative Criticism
ChauR	Chaucer Review
CL	Comparative Literature
C&M	Classica et Mediaevalia
CSEL	Corpus Scriptorum Ecclesiasticorum Latinorum (Vienna: F. Tempsky)
DAEM	Deutsches Archiv für Erforschung des Mittelalters
EETS	Early English Text Society
ELH	Journal of English Literary History
ES	English Studies: A Journal of English Language and Literature
EStn	Englische Studien
JAAR	Journal of the American Academy of Religion
JbÄAK	Jahrbuch für Ästhetik und allgemeine Kunstwissenschaft
JCS	Journal of Celtic Studies
JEGP	Journal of English and Germanic Philology
JWCI	Journal of the Warburg and Courtald Institute
MÆ	Medium Aevum
MED	Middle English Dictionary
M&H	Medievalia et Humanistica
MHRA	Modern Humanities Research Association
MichA	Michigan Academician
MLN	Modern Language Notes
MLQ	Modern Language Quarterly
MLR	Modern Language Review
MP	Modern Philology
MRS	Medieval and Renaissance Studies
MS	Medieval Studies
MSE	Massachusetts Studies in English

Neophil.	Neophilologus
NLH	New Literary History
NM	Neuphilologische Mitteilungen
OED	The Oxford English Dictionary
PBA	Proceedings of the British Academy
PCP	Pacific Coast Philology
PL	J.-P. Migne, Patrologiae Cursus Completus. Series Latina (Paris, 1844 ff.)
PMLA	Publications of the Modern Language Association of America
RES	Review of English Studies
SAC	Studies in the Age of Chaucer
SATF	Société des Anciens Textes Francais
SBVS	Saga Book: Viking Society of Northern Research
SC	Sources Chrétiennes
SP	Studies in Philology
TCAAS	Transactions of the Connecticut Academy of Arts and Sciences
TRHS	Transactions of the Royal Historical Society
TRSC	Transactions of the Royal Society of Canada
TSLL	Texas Studies in Language and Literature
TZ	Theologische Zeitschrift

Fred C. Robinson

¹Line 10a. The full context is quoted below, p. 8, from *The Anglo-Saxon Minor Poems*, ed. Elliott Van Kirk Dobbie, The Anglo-Saxon Poetic Records, 6 (New York, 1942), pp. 55–56, but I restore the manuscript reading *swicolost* both here and there.

²Henry Sweet, *An Anglo-Saxon Reader in Prose and Verse* (Oxford, 1876), p. 183; Walter J. Sedgefield, *An Anglo-Saxon Verse-Book* (Manchester, 1922), p. 104; A. J. Wyatt, *The Threshold of Anglo-Saxon* (Cambridge, 1926), p. 34; *Sweet's Anglo-Saxon Reader*, rev. throughout by Dorothy Whitelock (Oxford, 1967), p. 174; Richard Hamer, *A Choice of Anglo-Saxon Verse* (London, 1970), p. 110. John Earle was troubled by the maxim because it "has a strange Machiavellian look" (*Two of the Saxon Chronicles Parallel* [Oxford, 1865], p. xxxv).

³Blanche Colton Williams, *Gnomic Poetry in Anglo-Saxon* (New York, 1914), p. 148; Dobbie, p. 175; Frederic G. Cassidy and Richard N. Ringler, eds., *Bright's Old English Grammar and Reader* (New York, 1971), p. 374; Stanley B. Greenfield and Richard Evert, "*Maxims II*: Gnome and Poem" in *Anglo-Saxon Poetry: Essays in Appreciation for John C. McGalliard*, ed. Lewis E. Nicholson and Dolores Warwick Frese (Notre Dame, 1975), p. 341.

⁴Alois Brandl, *Vom kosmologischen Denken des heidnisch-christlichen Germanentums; der frühangelsächsische Schicksalsspruch der Handschrift Tiberius B. I und seine Verwandheit mit Boethius* (Berlin, 1937), pp. 8–9; Ludwig Ettmüller, *Engla and Seaxna Scôpas and Bôceras* (Quedlinburg, 1850), p. 283; Christian W. M. Grein, *Bibliothek der angelsächsischen Poesie* (Göttingen, 1857), 1:346; Friedrich Kluge, *Angelsächsisches Lesebuch* (Halle, 1915), p. 141; Richard Paul Wülcker, *Bibliothek der angelsächsischen Poesie neu bearbeitet* (Kassel, 1883), 1:339.

⁵J. K. Bollard of Leeds, in a very good edition and discussion of the poem, preserves *swicolost*, like the German editors, because "we should not reject the MS. reading merely because we cannot immediately comprehend its full significance. . . . I have chosen to retain the MS. reading rather than run the risk of eliminating what could well be an insight into a very elusive subject"; see his article "The Cotton Maxims," *Neophil* 57 (1973), 185. The American James R. Hulbert, on the other hand, adopts Sweet's *swutolost* rather than Williams' *switolost* in his revision of *Bright's Anglo-Saxon Reader* (New York, 1935), p. 177. Walther Fischer, in a review in *Anglia Beiblatt* 48 (1937), 364, takes issue with Brandl's spirited defense of the manuscript reading *swicolost*.

[6]Morton W. Bloomfield, "Understanding Old English Poetry," *AnM* 9 (1968), 18; rpt. in Bloomfield's *Essays and Explorations: Studies in Ideas, Language, and Literature* (Cambridge, Mass., 1970), p.73.

[7]Hans Walther, *Proverbia Sententiaeque Latinitatis Medii Aevi* (Göttingen, 1967), vol. 5, no. 33157.

[8]See the recent edition by Olof Arngart, "The Durham Proverbs," *Speculum* 56 (1981), 288–300, esp. p. 293. See also Bartlett Jere Whiting and Helen Wescott Whiting, *Proverbs, Sentences, and Proverbial Phrases From English Writings Mainly Before 1500* (Cambridge, Mass., 1968), p. 533. Whiting cites this maxim (as Arngart notes) and lists ten subsequent variations on the phrase in English writings from Chaucer to Horman's *Vulgaria*. He does not notice the occurrence of the maxim in *Blickling Homily XV*.

[9]*The Blickling Homilies of the Tenth Century*, ed. Richard Morris, EETS, 58, 63, 73 (London, 1874–80), p. 187.

[10]Williams, p. 148.

[11]Cassidy and Ringler, p. 374.

[12]*A Microfiche Concordance to Old English* compiled by Antonette di Paolo Healey and Richard L. Venezky and published by the Dictionary of Old English Project, Centre for Medieval Studies, University of Toronto (Toronto, 1980). For the figures cited here I have used the "Word and Frequency Lists" at the end of the microfiche concordance, but for other data in this essay I have drawn on the concordance proper.

[13]*The Pastoral Care*, ed. from British Library MS Cotton Otho B.ii by Ingvar Carlson, completed by Lars-G. Hallander *et al.* (Stockholm, 1978), Pt. 2, p. 89, n. to line 6.

[14]Alistair Campbell, *Enlarged Addenda and Corrigenda* (Oxford, 1972) to T. Northcote Toller's supplement to *An Anglo-Saxon Dictionary* by Joseph Bosworth and T. Northcote Toller, s.v. *oferswicol*. Another spelling of *swicol* is recorded by Campbell in his *Old English Grammar* (Oxford, 1959), p. 92. par. 218, where he records *swiocol* as a frequent form in Old English. Since I could not find one documentation of this spelling in the microfiche concordance, I have taken no account of it in my calculations.

[15]*Die angelsächsischen Prosabearbeitungen der Benediktinerregel*, ed. Arnold Schröer, zweite Auflage mit einem Anhang von Helmut Gneuss (Darmstadt, 1964), p. 30, n. to lines 5–6.

[16]Joseph Bosworth, *An Anglo-Saxon Dictionary*, ed. and enlarged by T. Northcote Toller (London, 1898), s.v. *swicol*, II.

[17]Whiting, pp. 532–33. The sentiment is common in various languages and in various forms: "Veritas odium parit," "Il n'y a que la vérité qui offense," "Non c'è niente che offenda come la verità,"

"Wahrheit bringt Hass," "Quien dice las verdades, pierde las amistades," etc.

[18]Pierre Daniel Chantepie de la Saussaye, *The Religion of the Teutons*, trans. Bert J. Vos (Boston, 1902), pp. 409–10. Williams refers to this book on p. 148 of her edition.

[19]*Edda: die Lieder des Codex Regius nebst verwandten Denkmälern*, ed. Gustav Neckel, 4th rev. ed. Hans Kuhn (Heidelberg, 1962), p. 23.

[20]Quoted by Chantepie de Saussaye, p. 409.

[21]*The Oxford Dictionary of English Proverbs*, 3rd ed., rev. by F. P. Wilson (Oxford, 1970), p. 844. Cf. Karl Friedrich Wilhelm Wander, *Deutsches Sprichwörter-Lexikon* (Leipzig, 1876), 4:1756, no. 257.

[22]Blaise Pascal, *Pensées*, Librairie Générale Française (Paris, 1972), p. 142.

[23]Thomasin von Ziclaria, *Der Welsche Gast*, ed. H. Rückert (Berlin, 1965).

[24]"Was nennt ihr Wahrheit? Die Täuschung, die Jahrhunderte alt geworden. Was Täuschung? Die Wahrheit, die nur eine Minute gelebt." Quoted in Martin Hürlimann, *Stimmen der Völker im Sprichwort* (Zurich, 1945), p. 167.

[25]Contrasting with this formulation of Ventura Ruiz Aguilar's, and yet leading to a similar conclusion, is the observation of the Frenchman Louis Aragon quoted recently in *The New York Review of Books*, March 19, 1981, p. 43: "Surely it must be realized that the face of error and the face of truth cannot fail to have identical features."

[26]*Wulfstan: Sammlung der ihm zugeschriebenen Homilien*, ed. Arthur Napier, rpt. with a bibliographical supplement by Klaus Ostheeren (Weidmann, 1967), p. 268. Cf. p. 128, lines 7–10. These two texts are compilations of phrases from other works by Wulfstan rather than independent compositions by him.

[27]*The Homilies of Wulfstan*, ed. Dorothy Bethurum (Oxford, 1957), p. 190, lines 133–35; cf. p. 277, lines 23–25 for a similar formulation.

[28]Bethurum, p. 186, lines 42–44. Cf. Napier, pp. 57, line 20–58, line 2.

[29]*Early English Homilies from the Twelfth-Century MS. Vespasian D.XIV*, ed. R. D.-N. Warner, EETS, 152 (1917), p. 91, line 1.

[30]*King Alfred's Version of St. Augustine's Soliloquies*, ed. Thomas A. Carnicelli (Cambridge, Mass., 1969), pp. 81–82.

[31]See, for example, P. L. Henry, *The Early English and Celtic Lyric* (London, 1966), p. 97, and R. MacGregor Dawson, "The Structure of the Old English Gnomic Poems," *JEGP* 61 (1962), 14–22.

³²*Die Hirtenbriefe Ælfrics*, ed. Bernhard Fehr, rpt. with a supplement by Peter Clemoes (Darmstadt, 1966), p. 202, lines 6–9.

³³*Homilies of Ælfric: A Supplementary Collection*, ed. John C. Pope, EETS, 260 (London, 1968), 2:501.

³⁴*Ælfric's Catholic Homilies: The Second Series*, ed. Malcolm Godden, EETS, s.s. 5 (London, 1979), p. 139, lines 58–60.

³⁵Ibid.

³⁶*Ælfric's Lives of Saints*, ed. Walter W. Skeat, EETS, 82 (London, 1885), p. 430, lines 233–38.

³⁷*The Old English Version of the Heptateuch*, ed. S. J. Crawford, EETS, 160 (London, 1922), p. 353.

³⁸R. S. Cox, "The Old English Dicts of Cato," *Anglia* 90 (1972), 16.

³⁹Skeat, p. 430, lines 241–43. For yet another version, see note 41 below.

⁴⁰*Die Gesetze der Angelsachsen*, ed. Felix Liebermann (Halle, 1903), 1:476.

⁴¹Liebermann, p. 474.

⁴²Roland Torkar, "Eine altenglische Übersetzung von Alcuins 'De virtutibus et vitiis, Kap. 20'" (Ph.D. diss., Göttingen, 1976). I am grateful to Dr. Torkar for kindly sending me Xerox copies of relevant pages of his dissertation.

⁴³PL 101:628–29.

⁴⁴*Beowulf and the Fight at Finnsburg*, ed. Frederick Klaeber, 3rd ed. (Boston, 1950), lines 2765–67.

⁴⁵See Klaeber's n. to lines 2764b–66, p. 220.

⁴⁶*The Exeter Book*, Part 2, ed. W. S. Mackie, EETS, 194 (London, 1934), p. 59.

⁴⁷Alexandra Olsen, "The Heroic World: Icelandic Sagas and the Old English *Riming Poem*," PCP 14 (1979), 54. Olsen sees the possibility of a second meaning as well: "treasure was made with skill."

⁴⁸*Juan Ruiz, Libro de Buen Amor*, ed. Joan Corominas (Madrid, 1967), p. 227.

 R. E. Kaske

¹"*Sapientia et Fortitudo* as the Controlling Theme of *Beowulf*," SP 55 (1958), 423–56. This interpretation has been extended in various ways in my articles "The Sigemund-Heremod and Hama-Hygelac Passages in *Beowulf*," *PMLA* 74 (1959), 489–94;

"Weohstan's Sword," *MLN* 75 (1960), 465–68; "'Hygelac' and 'Hygd'," in *Studies in Old English Literature in Honor of Arthur G. Brodeur,* ed. Stanley B. Greenfield (Eugene, Ore., 1963), pp. 200–06 (with an important modification by Fred C. Robinson, "The Significance of Names in Old English Literature," *Anglia* 86 [1968], 52–57); "The *Eotenas* in *Beowulf*," in *Old English Poetry: Fifteen Essays,* ed. Robert P. Creed (Providence, R.I., 1967), pp. 285–310; and "*Beowulf,*" in *Critical Approaches to Six Major English Works: Beowulf through Paradise Lost,* ed. Robert M. Lumiansky and Herschel Baker (Philadelphia, 1968), pp. 3–40.

²I.xxxix.9, ed. W. M. Lindsay (Oxford, 1911); note also VIII.xi.98, and X.2. For examples elsewhere, see "*Sapientia et Fortitudo* as Controlling Theme," pp. 423–25.

³It can, of course, be objected that Old English poets habitually surround characters with a good many adjectives and descriptive nouns, that they seem particularly fond of epithets connected with wisdom and boldness, and that it is therefore no great marvel if a hero happens to be described as wise and brave (often along with other qualities) within a fairly brief passage. The very frequency of these attributions of wisdom and/or boldness, however, together with the great popularity of the ideal *sapientia et fortitudo* itself and the thematic pattern it apparently produces in poems like *Beowulf* and *Judith* (below), seems to me ultimately to speak against this objection.

⁴Note also "halig cempa, / ðeawum geþancul . . . / eadig oreta" (461–63); "wis hæleð" (919); "eorl ellenheard . . . searoþancum beseted" (1254–55); "mihtig ond modrof . . . wis, wundrum gleaw" (1496–97); and "cene collenferð . . . gleawmod" (1578–79). None of these expressions is paralleled in the Greek and Latin legends accepted as approximate sources for *Andreas,* ed. respectively by Maximilian Bonnet, *Acta Andreae et Matthiae,* in *Acta Apostolorum Apocrypha,* ed. Konstantin von Tischendorf, rev. R. A. Lipsius and M. Bonnet (Leipzig, 1898), II.i.65–116, and Franz Blatt, *Die lateinischen Bearbeitungen der Acta Andreae et Matthiae apud anthropophagos,* Beihefte zur Zeitschrift für die neutestamentliche Wissenschaft, 12 (Giessen, 1930). All references to Old English poems are from *The Anglo-Saxon Poetic Records,* ed. George Philip Krapp and Elliott Van Kirk Dobbie, 6 vols. (New York, 1931–53), by line numbers.

⁵*Moralia in Iob,* XI.viii.11, on Job 12:13 (PL 75:958). See my article "*Beowulf,*" pp. 31–32.

⁶None of these expressions in *Guð lac A* and *B* is paralleled in the *Vita Sancti Guthlaci,* ed. Bertram Colgrave, *Felix's Life of Saint Guthlac* (Cambridge, 1956), or the Old English translation of it,

ed. Paul Gonser, *Das angelsächsische Prosa-Leben des hl. Guthlac,* Anglistische Forschungen, 27 (Heidelberg, 1909); for the passage in *Guð lac B,* see *Vita,* 50 (p. 154), *Prosa-Leben,* 20 (p. 163).

[7]Ernst Otto presents a useful summary based on the figure of the queen, concluding, "Die Eigenschaften des Königs als Volksbeschützer und Richter sind bei [der Königin] passend in einen Zug übergegangen: friedenstiftende Milde . . ." (*Typische Motive in dem weltlichen Epos der Angelsachsen* [Berlin, 1902], pp. 8–10). See also the survey by Elaine Tuttle Hanson, "Women in Old English Poetry Reconsidered," *Mich A* 9 (1976), 109-17.

[8]For this interpretation of Hygd and "þryð," see "*Sapientia et Fortitudo* as Controlling Theme," pp. 440-41; "'Hygelac' and 'Hygd'," pp. 200-02; and "*Beowulf,*" pp. 20-21. The stories of Hildeburh in the Finn Episode and of Freawaru as predicted by Beowulf (2024 ff.), though they make no mention of woman's wisdom, dramatize at least incidentally her lack of the prowess necessary to deal successfully with violence.

[9]*Germania,* VIII.2. Other examples are cited by E. Mogk, "Weise Frauen," *Reallexikon der germanischen Altertumskunde,* ed. Johannes Hoops (Strassburg, 1911-19), 4:504-05.

[10]In line 550 I follow William Strunk, ed., Belles-Lettres Series (Boston, 1904), p. 125, and C. W. M. Grein, *Sprachschatz der angelsächsischen Dichter,* rev. J. J. Köhler (Heidelberg, 1912), p. 733; they understand *pweorhtimbran* as "perverse," which fits my interpretation perfectly: Juliana's unwomanly boldness is "perverse" from the demon's viewpoint. Rosemary Woolf, in her edition, explains *pweorhtimbran* as "resolutely made" (Methuen's Old English Library [London, 1955], p. 47). None of the expressions of the heroic ideal in *Juliana* is paralleled in the *Acta auctore anonymo,* I–II, in *Acta Sanctorum,* Feb., II.875-76 (Feb. 16th).

[11]None of these expressions is paralleled in the *Acta apocrypha* of St. Quiriacus (Cyriacus), I.7 and 11, in *Acta Sanctorum,* May, I.451-52 (May 4th), or in the version edited by Alfred Holder, *Inventio Sanctae Crucis* (Leipzig, 1889).

[12]See especially Thomas D. Hill, "Sapiential Structure and Figural Narrative in the Old English 'Elene'," *Traditio* 27 (1971), 159-77; for other such interpretations, see Jackson J. Campbell, "Cynewulf's Multiple Revelations," *M&H,* n.s. 3 (1972), 257-77, and Catharine A. Regan, "Evangelicalism as the Informing Principle of Cynewulf's 'Elene'," *Traditio* 29 (1973), 27-52.

[13]R. E. Woolf, "The Lost Opening of the 'Judith'," *MLR* 50 (1955), 168-72. The controversy to date is conveniently surveyed by David Chamberlain, "*Judith*: A Fragmentary and Political Poem" in *Anglo-Saxon Poetry: Essays in Appreciation for John C. McGalliard,* ed.

Lewis E. Nicholson and Dolores Warwick Frese (Notre Dame, 1975), pp. 135 ff.

¹⁴See esp. James F. Doubleday, "The Principle of Contrast in *Judith*," NM 72 (1971), 436–41; for a more elaborate though much less successful analysis, see Bernard F. Huppé, *The Web of Words: Structural Analyses of the Old English Poems Vainglory, The Wonder of Creation, The Dream of the Rood, and Judith* (Albany, N.Y., 1970), pp. 148–89.

¹⁵*Bibliorum Sacrorum Latinæ versiones antiquæ, seu Vetus Italica*, ed. Pierre Sabbathier (Paris, 1751), I.ii.765–77. Fulgentius (quoting 8:7), *Epistola 2 ad Gallam viduam*, 29, ed. J. Fraipont, *Opera*, CC, 91 (Turnhout, 1968), p. 207.

¹⁶*Apologia adversus libros Rufini*, 18 (PL 23:412).

¹⁷Ps.-Augustinian sermon 48 (PL 39:1839).

¹⁸PL 109:540.

¹⁹Hom. 9, lines 242–43, ed. Bruno Assmann, *Angelsächsische Homilien und Heiligenleben*, Bibliothek der angelsächsischen Prosa, 3 (Kassel, 1889), p. 109; note also lines 210 (p. 108) and 264–65 (p. 110).

²⁰Lines 1157–58, 1175, and 1215, ed. Hiltgunt Monecke, *Die jüngere Judith aus der Vorauer Handschrift*, Altdeutsche Textbibliothek, 61 (Tübingen, 1964), pp. 37–39; note also the expansion of Judith 11:18–19 in lines 1315–20 (p. 42). Judith's wisdom receives no emphasis in the fifth-century summary of her story by Dracontius, *De laudibus Dei*, III.480–95, ed. Friedrich Vollmer, MGH, Auctores antiquissimi, 14 (Berlin, 1905), p. 105; in Aldhelm's prose *De virginitate*, LVII, or verse *De virginitate*, 2560–70, both ed. Rudolf Ehwald, *Aldhelmi opera*, MGH, Auctores antiquissimi, 15 (Berlin, 1919), pp. 316–17 and 457; in the ninth-century summary by Milo of St. Amand, *De sobrietate*, I.xvi.331–93, ed. Ludwig Traube, MGH, Poetae Latini aevi Carolini, 3 (Berlin, 1896), pp. 625–27; in the ninth-century *Versus de Iudit et Olofernum*, ed. Karl Strecker, *Rhythmi aevi Merovingici et Carolini*, MGH, Poetae Latini aevi Carolini, 4:2 (Berlin, 1923), pp. 459–62; or in the probably eleventh-century *Ältere Judith*, ed. Albert Waag, *Kleinere deutsche Gedichte des 11. und 12. Jahrhunderts*, rev. Werner Schröder, Altdeutsche Textbibliothek, 71–72 (Tübingen, 1972), pp. 63–67.

²¹Jane Mushabac remarks, "When she has completed [the killing of Holofernes] and set out for home with her trophy, she is described for the first time in the extant poem with the double epithet, 'the maiden of wisdom, the woman of valour,' as if by her deed she has achieved the twin ideal to her wisdom" ("*Judith* and the Theme of *Sapientia et Fortitudo*," MSE 4 [1973], 6). Professor Mushabac's study, which otherwise does not touch on the pattern

proposed here, appeared after the present interpretation had been developed.

²²See for example Prov. 2:6, Eccles. 2:26, Dan. 2:21–23, and James 1:15; Augustine, *De libero arbitrio*, III.xxiv.72, ed. William C. Green, CC, 29 (Turnhout, 1970), p. 318, and *De gratia et libero arbitrio*, xxiv.46 (PL 44:912); and Jerome, *Epistola C*, 3 (PL 22:815).

²³Ed., *Judith*, Methuen's Old English Library (London, 1952), p. 49.

²⁴*In Psalmum CXVIII expositio*, IV.27 (PL 15:1249). See also Augustine on Ps. 4:2, "in tribulatione dilatasti mihi," *Enarrationes in Psalmos*, ed. E. Dekkers and J. Fraipont, CC, 38 (Turnhout, 1956), 1:14–15; and Cassiodorus on Ps. 118:32, *Expositio Psalmorum*, ed. M. Adriaen, CC, 98 (Turnhout, 1958), 2:1073.

²⁵See note 14 above.

²⁶"*Sapientia et Fortitudo* as Controlling Theme," pp. 432–34.

²⁷On the difference between wise and unwise *tristitia*, see "*Sapientia et Fortitudo* as Controlling Theme," p. 445 and n. 66.

²⁸In the Book of Judith, see particularly the speech of Achior in 5:5–25, and that of Judith in 9:2–19.

²⁹Lines 62, 64–65, ed. Maurice P. Cunningham, *Aurelii Prudentii Clementis carmina*, CC, 126 (Turnhout, 1966), p. 153. See also Clement of Rome, *Epistle to the Corinthians*, LV.3.5, ed. Annie Jaubert, SC, 167 (Paris, 1971), p. 188; Ambrose, *De viduis*, VII (PL 16:246–47), and *De officiis ministrorum*, III.13 (PL 16:169); and ps.-Augustinian sermon 49, *De Judith* (PL 39:1840).

³⁰It is perhaps worth pointing out that if this interpretation has been reasonably convincing, the two Old English poems in which *sapientia et fortitudo* produces the clearest, most extended, and most symmetrical patterns—*Beowulf* and *Judith*—are precisely the two which are found in MS BL Cotton Vitellius A xv.

 William Alfred

¹T. M. Raysor, ed., *Coleridge's Shakespearean Criticism* (Cambridge, Mass., 1930), 2:352.

²See T. P. Dunning and A. J. Bliss, eds., *The Wanderer* (London, 1969), pp. 79–80. I agree with them that the poet intervenes at lines 6–7, 88–91 and 111. See also R. M. Lumiansky, "The Dramatic Structure of the Old English *Wanderer*," *Neophil* 34 (1950), 104–12, and of course S. B. Greenfield, "*The Wanderer*: A Reconsideration of Theme and Structure," *JEGP* 50 (1951), 451–65; J. E. Cross, "On the Genre of *The Wanderer*," *Neophil* 45 (1961), 63–72; J. C. Pope, "Second Thoughts on the Interpretation of *The Seafarer*,"

ASE 3 (1974), 75–86; and the unbrokenly fascinating and illuminating book by P. L. Henry, *The Early English and Celtic Lyric* (London, 1966).

[3]T. A. Shippey, *Old English Verse* (London, 1972), p. 56.

[4]Shippey, p. 67: "The stress on insight and decision has been seen in Anglo-Saxon military heroes; the idea that the mind changes reality by changing itself is the structure of *The Wanderer*." Cf. T. C. Rumble, "From *Eardstapa* to *Snottor on Mode*: The Structural Principle of *The Wanderer*," *MLQ* 19 (1958), 225–30.

[5]Quotations from *The Wanderer* are from the edition by Dunning and Bliss. The most cursory reading of my translation will establish my deep indebtedness to their sure learning. I am also indebted to R. F. Leslie, ed., *The Wanderer* (Manchester, 1966). But I must remind my readers that translators are not only traitors, they are also surreptitious editors.

[6]I emend *eft* in line 45 to *oft* and translate accordingly. The scribe miscopies *eft* as *oft* in 53.

[7]I adopt Dunning and Bliss's emendation of *worian* to *wonian*, *The Wanderer*, pp. 118–19.

[8]*The Wanderer*, p. 118.

[9]With *gehealdeþ* (112) as with *gebīdeð* (1) I have invoked the option of rendering finite verbs prefixed with *ge-* as conveying an action seen through to completion. Cf. the last lines of the elegy given the title "Alcuin's Cell" and ascribed to Alcuin's English pupil and successor at Tours, Fredegis (d. 834) in E. L. Duemmler, ed., *Poetae Latini aevi Carolini* (Berlin, 1881–1922), 1:23 (more readily available in Helen Waddell, *Mediaeval Latin Lyrics* [New York, 1938], pp. 96–99):

> nil manet aeternum, nihil immutabile vere est.
>   obscurat sacrum nox tenebrosa diem,
> decutit et flores subito hiems frigida pulcros,
>   perturbat placidum et tristior aura mare.
> quae campis cervos agitabat sacra iuventus
>   incumbit fessus nunc baculo senior.
> nos miseri, cur te fugitivum, mundus, amamus?
>   tu fugis a nobis semper ubique ruens.
> tu fugiens fugias, Christum nos semper amemus.
>   semper amor teneat pectora nostra dei.
> ille pius famulos diro defendat ab hoste
>   ad caelum rapiens pectora nostra, suos.
> pectore quem pariter toto laudemus, amemus.
>   nostra est ille pius gloria, vita, salus.

This essay is in no way intended to take issue with the ascription of the poem to the genre of the consolation. For me, the poem is still the interior debate making use of the elegiac mode for sapiential ends, cognate, if only by assimilation, with such less intimate debates as Boethius's *De Consolatione Philosophiae* and Isidore of Seville's *Synonyma de Lamentatione Animae Peccatricis* (PL 83:826–68), which Lumiansky and Cross and others have so well argued it to be.

✿ Stanley B. Greenfield

[1] Lines from *Beowulf* are quoted from Fr. Klaeber, ed., 3rd ed. (Boston, 1950).

[2] T. A. Shippey, *Beowulf* (London, 1978), p. 13. These opinions are, respectively, W. S. Mackie's, in *MLR* 34 (1939), 517; Klaeber's, in his edition, p. 139; James Smith's, in *English* 25 (1976), 227; and M. Pepperdene's, in *ES* 47 (1966), 409–19.

[3] Shippey, p. 12.

[4] Constance B. Hieatt, *Beowulf and Other Old English Poems* (New York, 1967), p. 29.

[5] R. E. Kaske, "*Sapientia et Fortitudo* as the Controlling Theme of *Beowulf*," *SP* 55 (1958), 423–56; rpt. in *An Anthology of Beowulf Criticism*, ed. Lewis E. Nicholson (Notre Dame, 1963), pp. 269–310.

[6] Kaske, in Nicholson, p. 277.

[7] Shippey, pp. 12–13.

[8] Shippey, p. 14.

[9] I quote from MS CCCC 41, as printed in the variant readings in *The Old English Version of Bede's Ecclesiastical History of the English People*, ed. Thomas Miller, EETS 95, 96, 110, 111 (London, 1890–98). Miller uses the Tanner MS for his principal text; there the reading is *pis gescead* (95:100, line 31)—the CCCC 41 variant is in vol. 110, p. 87. Toller, in his *Supplement* to the Bosworth-Toller *Dictionary*, lists these variant translations under different definitions; I do not think his discrimination between meanings holds up, given the context of the passage.

[10] *Scyldwiga* is a hapax legomenon. Either Beowulf or the coastguard could be a legitimate referent.

[11] David Wright, *Beowulf* (Baltimore, 1957), p. 33.

[12] Pepperdene sees the maxim as saying that the coastguard must tell the Geats, "but more importantly himself, that he cannot be fooled by smooth talking" (p. 416). She does not argue her case.

[13] As Klaeber's note indicates, some earlier critics placed the maxim in parentheses, as a reflection of the poet's (pp. 139–40); but Klaeber's argument against this procedure is convincing.

Roberta Frank

[1]Peter Burke, *The Renaissance Sense of the Past* (London, 1969), pp. 1–6; Michael Hunter, "Germanic and Roman Antiquity and the Sense of the Past in Anglo-Saxon England," *ASE* 3 (1974), 45–48.

[2]"Chaucer's Sense of History," *JEGP* 51 (1952), 301–13; rpt. in Morton Bloomfield, *Essays and Explorations: Studies in Ideas, Language, and Literature* (Cambridge, Mass., 1970), pp. 13–26.

[3]In assuming that literate composition indicates authorship by a cleric, I am following, among others, C. P. Wormald, "The Uses of Literacy in Anglo-Saxon England and its Neighbours," *TRHS*, 5th ser., 27 (1977), 95–114.

[4]On the use of *Beowulf* as a historical document, see J. R. R. Tolkien, "*Beowulf*: The Monsters and the Critics," *PBA* 22 (1936), 245–51; sep. rpt. (London, 1937, 1958, 1960), pp. 1–6; Robert T. Farrell, "*Beowulf*, Swedes and Geats," *SBVS* 18 (1972), 225–86. Kemp Malone found the most remarkable feature of *Beowulf* to be its "high standard of historical accuracy": the anachronisms "that one would expect in a poem of the eighth century" are missing ("Beowulf," *ES* 29 [1948], 161–72, esp. 164). But the *Beowulf* poet occasionally nodded; see Walter Goffart, "Hetware and Hugas: Datable Anachronisms in *Beowulf*" in *The Dating of Beowulf*, ed. Colin Chase, Toronto Old English Series, 6 (1981), pp. 83–100.

[5]Larry D. Benson, "The Pagan Coloring of *Beowulf*" in *Old English Poetry: Fifteen Essays*, ed. Robert P. Creed (Providence, 1967), p. 194.

[6]The same line is used to place Grendel's downfall in the distant past (806). Citations of *Beowulf* refer to Frederick Klaeber, ed., *Beowulf and The Fight at Finnsburg*, 3rd ed. (Boston, 1950).

[7]Morton W. Bloomfield observes that Chaucer employs "as was tho the gyse" to qualify pagan funeral customs (line 993), sacrificial rites (line 2279), and cremations (line 2911) (*Essays and Explorations*, p. 21). Citations from *The Legend of Good Women* are to lines 586 and 1813 in the second edition of F. N. Robinson (Boston, 1957).

[8]Hans Kuhn relates Ongentheow's threat (*getan* = *gautian*) to a boast by the pagan tenth-century skald Helgi trausti Ólafsson: "I paid to the gallows-prince [Odin] Gautr's [Odin's] sacrifice" ("Gaut," *Festschrift für Jost Trier zu seinem 60. Geburtstag*, ed. Benno von Wiese and Karl Heinz Borck [Meisenheim, 1954], pp. 417–33).

[9]Ursula Dronke points out that *Beowulf* contains human analogues for two additional mythological incidents recorded in

Norse poetry ("*Beowulf* and Ragnarǫk," *SBVS* 17 [1969], 322-25). On Scandinavian heroes' faith in their own *megin* (OE *mægen*), see Peter Foote and David M. Wilson, *The Viking Achievement* (London, 1970), p. 404. A raven, "oath-brother of the eagle," converses again in a section of the tenth-century pagan Norse *Hrafnsmál* (or *Haraldskvæði*) attributed to the skald Þórbjǫrn Hornklofi.

[10]Noted by E. G. Stanley, "The Narrative Art of *Beowulf*," in *Medieval Narrative: A Symposium*, ed. Hans Bekker-Nielsen et al. (Odense, 1979), pp. 59-60.

[11]See Ursula and Peter Dronke, "The Prologue of the Prose *Edda*: Explorations of a Latin Background" in *Sjötíu ritgerðir helgaðar Jakobi Benediktssyni* (Reykjavík, 1977), pp. 169-70.

[12]See H. M. and N. K. Chadwick, *The Growth of Literature* (Cambridge, Eng., 1932-40), 1:556-57; Patrick Wormald, "Bede, *Beowulf*, and the Conversion of the Anglo-Saxon Aristocracy" in *Bede and Anglo-Saxon England*, ed. Robert T. Farrell, British Archaeological Reports, 46 (1978), pp. 42-49.

[13]Chaucer, *The Book of the Duchess*, line 56 (*The Works of Geoffrey Chaucer*, ed. F. N. Robinson, 2nd ed. [Boston, 1957]).

[14]Kenneth Sisam long ago interpreted the Scyld Scefing preamble to *Beowulf* as a contemporary allusion to the West Saxon dynasty; but since he took *Beowulf* as a whole to be seventh or eighth century, the opening episode had to be a late, post-Alfredian addition: better a composite poem than a Viking one. See Sisam, "Anglo-Saxon Royal Genealogies," *PBA* 39 (1953), 287-346, esp. 339. The Offa digression of *Beowulf*—a probable allusion to the great ancestor of the Mercian house—would have flattered not only Offa of Mercia but also the descendants of Alfred who had succeeded to the rule of Mercia and who were themselves descendants of the Mercian royal line. But commentators, reluctant to look outside the age of Bede, either reject the Mercian associations of this digression or declare it, too, a later interpolation. See the important article by Nicolas Jacobs, "Anglo-Danish Relations, Poetic Archaism and the Date of *Beowulf*: A Reconsideration of the Evidence," *Poetica* (Tokyo) 8 (1977) [1978], 23-43. Jacobs demonstrates that no linguistic or historical fact compels us to anchor *Beowulf* before the tenth century.

[15]*Speculum* 41 (1966), 368-71.

[16]*The Structure of Beowulf* (New York and Oxford, 1965), p. 77.

[17]"Patristics and Old English Literature: Notes on Some Poems," *CL* 14 (Winter 1962), 36-43; rpt. twice in its entirety, and partially in *An Anthology of Beowulf Criticism*, ed. Lewis E. Nicholson (Notre Dame, 1963), p. 370.

[18]"Beowulf, Byrhtnoth, and the Judgment of God: Trial by Combat in Anglo-Saxon England," *Speculum* 44 (1969), 545–59.

[19]*The Mode and Meaning of 'Beowulf'* (London, 1970).

[20]*Alcuini Epistolae*, 124, ed. Ernest Dümmler, MGH, *Epistolae* IV.2 (Berlin, 1895), p. 183.

[21]*Alcuin and Beowulf: An Eighth-Century View* (New Brunswick, N. J., 1978), esp. pp. 152–54, 165–70.

[22]"*Beowulf*, Ireland, and the Natural Good," *Traditio* 7 (1949–51), 263–77; "*Beowulf* and Christian Tradition: A Reconsideration from a Celtic Stance," *Traditio* 21 (1965), 55–116.

[23]"*Beowulf*, Ireland, and the Natural Good," p. 277.

[24]"Bede, *Beowulf*, and the Conversion of the Anglo-Saxon Aristocracy," esp. pp. 49–58.

[25]According to Wormald, "the aristocratic climate of early English Christianity is, if anything, more apparent in the age of Offa than in the age of Bede" ("Bede, *Beowulf*, and the Conversion of the Anglo-Saxon Aristocracy," p. 94). Royal and monastic interests seem even more closely integrated in the age of Athelstan. Accompanying that king on his military expedition to Scotland in 934 were the two archbishops, fourteen bishops, seven ealdormen, six jarls with Norse names, three Welsh kings, and twenty-four others including eleven royal thegns. One of Athelstan's laws commanded that every Friday at every monastery all monks were to sing fifty psalms "for the king and those who want what he wants. . . ." See P. H. Sawyer, *From Roman Britain to Norman England* (New York, 1978), pp. 126, 192, 243. For a glimpse of aristocratic climates in tenth-century Saxony, see K. J. Leyser, *Rule and Conflict in an Early Medieval Society: Ottonian Saxony* (London, 1979).

[26]"Bede, *Beowulf*, and the Conversion of the Anglo-Saxon Aristocracy," p. 36.

[27]See Dorothy Whitelock, "The Prose of Alfred's Reign" in *Continuations and Beginnings: Studies in Old English Literature*, ed. E. G. Stanley (London, 1966), p. 91. For the Old English text, see *The Old English Orosius*, ed. Janet Bately, EETS, s. s. 6 (Oxford, 1980), p. xcix; for the Latin, *Pauli Orosii Presbyteri Hispani adversum Paganos Historiarum Libri Septem*, ed. Karl Zangemeister, CSEL, 5 (Vienna, 1882).

[28]See J. M. Wallace-Hadrill, *Early Germanic Kingship in England and on the Continent* (Oxford, 1971), pp. 145–46.

[29]Kurt Otten surveys attempts from Schepss (1881) to Courcelle (1937) to locate the Remigian commentaries available to

Alfred (*König Alfreds Boethius*, Studien zur englischen Philologie, N. F. 3 [Tübingen, 1964], pp. 4-9). See also Brian Donaghey, "The Sources of King Alfred's Translation of Boethius' *De Consolatione Philosophiae*," *Anglia* 82 (1964), 23-57. Pierre Courcelle favors a ninth-century commentary by an anonymous monk of St. Gall (*La Consolation de Philosophie dans la tradition littéraire: antécédents et postérité de Boèce* [Paris, 1967]). But even if Alfred (d. 899) did not have access to Remigius' work in its final Parisian form (c. 902-908), he could have followed a version modelled on Remigius' earlier teaching at Auxerre and Rheims. See Diane Bolton, "Remigian Commentaries on the *Consolation of Philosophy* and their Sources," *Traditio* 33 (1977), 381-94, and "The Study of the *Consolation of Philosophy* in Anglo-Saxon England," *Archives d'histoire doctrinale et littéraire du Moyen Âge* 44 (1977), [1978], 33-78.

[30]Bolton, *Alcuin and Beowulf*, pp. 139, 177.

[31]*Anicii Manlii Severini Boethii Philosophiae Consolatio*, ed. L. Bieler, CC, 94 (Turnhout, 1957), III, m. 12, lines 52-58; *King Alfred's Old English Version of Boethius' De Consolatione Philosophiae*, ed. W. J. Sedgefield (Oxford, 1900), p. 103, lines 14-16. Otten, *König Alfreds Boethius*, p. 133.

[32]*De Consolatione Philosophiae*, III, pr. 12, lines 64-65; *King Alfred's Old English Version*, p. 99, lines 4-20. Otten, *König Alfreds Boethius*, pp. 129-32.

[33]*De Consolatione Philosophiae*, IV, m. 7; *King Alfred's Old English Version*, p. 139, lines 5-18. Otten, *König Alfreds Boethius*, p. 38.

[34]*King Alfred's Old English Version*, p. 116, lines 2-34.

[35]*De Consolatione Philosophiae*, II, m. 7; *King Alfred's Old English Version*, p. 46, lines 16-17.

[36]See n. 20. The Council of Clovesho (746/7) specified that priests were not to chatter in church like secular poets (*Councils and Ecclesiastical Documents Relating to Great Britain and Ireland*, ed. A. W. Haddan and W. Stubbs [Oxford, 1869-78], 3:366); for additional examples, including one from the early eleventh century, see Wormald, "Bede, *Beowulf*, and the Conversion of the Anglo-Saxon Aristocracy," pp. 51-52.

[37]The reference is to Eormenric of heroic legend and *Beowulf* (1201). Flodoard, *Historia Remensis Ecclesiae*, IV.5, ed. J. Heller and G. Waitz, MGH, Scriptores Rerum Germanicarum (in folio), 13 (Hanover, 1881), pp. 564, 574.

[38]Carl Erdmann, *Studien zur Briefliteratur Deutschlands im elften Jahrhundert*, Schriften des Reichsinstituts für ältere deutsche Geschichtskunde (=MGH), 1 (Leipzig, 1938), p. 102; K. Leyser, "The German Aristocracy from the Ninth to the Early Twelfth

Centuries: A Social and Cultural Survey," *Past and Present* 41 (1968), 25–53.

[39]On the poet's featuring of pagan elements, see Benson, "Pagan Coloring," pp. 193–213.

[40]Rudolf of Fulda, *Translatio Sancti Alexandri*, ed. B. Krusch, *Nachrichten von der Gesellschaft der Wissenschaften zu Göttingen*, Phil.-Hist. Klasse, 1933, pp. 405–36.

[41]See Wormald, "Bede, *Beowulf*, and the Conversion of the Anglo-Saxon Aristocracy," pp. 58–63.

[42]Larry D. Benson, "The Originality of *Beowulf*" in *The Interpretation of Narrative: Theory and Practice*, Harvard English Studies, 1 (Cambridge, Mass., 1970), pp. 1–43.

[43]*Widukindi Monachi Corbeiensis Rerum Gestarum Saxonicarum Libri Tres*, ed. H.-E. Lohmann and P. Hirsch, 5th ed., MGH, Scriptores Rerum Germanicarum in usum scholarum (Hanover, 1935), Bk. I, chs. 1–15. On Widukind, see especially Helmut Beumann, *Widukind von Korvei* (Weimar, 1950), and "Historiographische Konzeption und politische Ziele Widukinds von Korvei," *Settimane di studio del Centro Italiano di Studi sull'alto medioevo* 17 (Spoleto, 1970), 857–94.

[44]*The Old English Orosius*, 49.1–3; 103.27–29.

[45]*Scriptores Rerum Mythicarum Latini Tres*, ed. G. H. Bode (Cellis, 1834), 1:74. See Ursula and Peter Dronke, "The Prologue of the Prose *Edda*," p. 166.

[46]John Scotus Eriugena, whose teaching is reflected in the school of Auxerre, wrote commentaries on all three authors. On his life, see E. Jeauneau, *Jean Scot, Homélie sur le Prologue de Jean*, SC, 151 (Paris, 1969), pp. 9–50, and *Jean Scot, Commentaire sur l'Évangile de Jean*, SC, 180 (Paris, 1972), pp. 11–21.

[47]Otten, *König Alfreds Boethius*, pp. 99–118.

[48]See especially Levin L. Schücking, "Das Königsideal im Beowulf" in *MHRA Bulletin* 3 (1929), 143–54; rpt. *EStn* 67 (1932), 1–14. English trans. as "The Ideal of Kingship in *Beowulf*" in *An Anthology of Beowulf Criticism*, ed. Nicholson, pp. 35–49. Robert E. Kaske, "*Sapientia et Fortitudo* as the Controlling Theme of *Beowulf*," *SP* 55 (1958), 423–56; rpt. in *An Anthology of Beowulf Criticism*, pp. 269–310.

[49]*Felix's Life of Saint Guthlac*, ed. and trans. Bertram Colgrave (Cambridge, Eng., 1956), pp. 81–83. See E. G. Stanley, "Hæthenra Hyht in *Beowulf*" in *Studies in Old English Literature in Honor of Arthur G. Brodeur*, ed. Stanley B. Greenfield (Eugene, Ore., 1963), pp. 136–51, and Colin Chase, "Saints' Lives, Royal Lives, and the Date of *Beowulf*" in *The Dating of Beowulf*, pp. 161–71.

⁵⁰Odo, *Vita S. Geraldi Aureliacensis Comitis,* PL 133:639–703. See Carl Erdmann (*Die Entstehung des Kreuzzugsgedankens* [Stuttgart, 1935]), trans. M. W. Baldwin and W. Goffart, *The Origin of the Idea of Crusade* (Princeton, 1977), pp. 87–89. Odo was among Remigius' students at Paris (*Vita Odonis Abbatis Cluniacensis,* ch. 19, in J. Mabillon and L. d'Achery, *Acta Sanctorum Ordinis S. Benedicti* [Paris, 1668–1701], VII.124).

⁵¹Leyser, passim.

⁵²*Hrotsvithae Opera,* ed. P. Winterfeld, MGH, Scriptores Rerum Germanicarum in usum scholarum (Berlin, 1902), pp. 35–51; *Ruotgeri Vita Brunonis Archiepiscopi Coloniensis,* ed. Irene Schmale-Ott, MGH, Scriptores Rerum Germanicarum, n. s. 10 (Weimar, 1951), p. 19.

⁵³See Rosemary Woolf, "The Ideal of Men Dying with their Lord in the *Germania* and in *The Battle of Maldon,*" ASE 5 (1976), 63–81.

⁵⁴E.g., Wayland in Leeds Parish Church, Thor in Gosforth Church, and Sigemund at Winchester Old Minster. See Richard N. Bailey, *Viking Age Sculpture in Northern England* (London, 1980).

⁵⁵"Skaldic Verse and the Date of *Beowulf*" in *The Dating of Beowulf,* pp. 123–39 and Alexander Murray, "*Beowulf,* the Danish Invasions, and Royal Genealogy," pp. 101–11 in the same volume.

⁵⁶See discussion in Horst Zettel, *Das Bild der Normannen und der Normanneneinfälle in westfränkischen, ostfränkischen und angelsächsischen Quellen des 8. bis 11. Jahrhunderts* (Munich, 1977), pp. 69–84. On West Saxon hegemonial tendencies during the first half of the tenth century, see E. E. Stengel, "Imperator und Imperium bei den Angelsachsen," DAEM 16 (1960), 15–72; J. L. Nelson, "Inauguration Rituals" in *Early Medieval Kingship,* ed. P. H. Sawyer and I. N. Wood (Leeds, 1977), pp. 68–70.

⁵⁷See Robert W. Hanning, *The Vision of History in Early Britain* (New York, 1966), p. 19. Tom Burns Haber makes one of several attempts to list verbal echoes and narrative parallels between the two poems (*A Comparative Study of the 'Beowulf' and the 'Aeneid'* [Princeton, 1931]). Recent publications demonstrating Virgilian influence on the narrative structure and perspective of *Beowulf* include Theodore M. Andersson, *Early Epic Scenery: Homer, Virgil, and the Medieval Legacy* (Ithaca, N. Y., 1976), pp. 145–59, and Alistair Campbell, "The Use in *Beowulf* of Earlier Heroic Verse" in *England before the Conquest: Studies in Primary Sources Presented to Dorothy Whitelock,* ed. Peter Clemoes and Kathleen Hughes (Cambridge, Eng., 1971), pp. 283–92.

⁵⁸R. H. C. Davis, *The Normans and their Myth* (London, 1976), pp. 27, 54.

[59]Oda, bishop of Ramsbury under Athelstan and archbishop of Canterbury from 940–958, was the son of a Dane who came to England with the first settlers. Oskytel, kinsman of Oda, was the archbishop of York. Oda's nephew was St. Oswald, prominent founder and renovator of monasteries. See J. Armitage Robinson, *St. Oswald and the Church of Worcester*, British Academy Supplemental Papers, 5 (London, 1919), pp. 38–51. The Danes appear to have been widely accepted in English society from at least 927 onwards; see Jacobs, p. 40, and R. I. Page, "The Audience of *Beowulf* and the Vikings" in *The Dating of Beowulf*, pp. 113–22.

[60]Bloomfield, "Chaucer's Sense of History" in *Essays and Explorations*, p. 25.

[61]Max Horkeimer and Theodor Adorno, *Dialectic of Enlightenment*, tr. John Cumming (New York, 1972), p. xv.

[62]*King Alfred's Old English Version of Boethius*, p. 44, lines 1–4.

[63]*Speculum* 41 (1966), 369.

 # E. Talbot Donaldson

[1]*ELH* 17 (1950), 163–90.

[2]References to the B-text are to George Kane and E. T. Donaldson, eds., *Piers Plowman: The B Version* (London, 1975); to the A-text, George Kane, ed., *Piers Plowman: The A Version* (London, 1960); and to the C-Text, W. W. Skeat, ed., *The Vision of William Concerning Piers the Plowman . . . Text C*, EETS, 54 (London, 1873).

[3]Skeat refers to an explanation of *vix* given by Wycliffe, who reads it as V + I + X, signifying the five wounds of Jesus Christ: V = 5, I = J(esus), X = Ch(rist). "And so þis resoun seiþ þat þe just man shal be saved by þe V woundis of Iesus Crist oure Lord" (*Vision*, Pt. IV, EETS, 67 [London, 1877], p. 300, n. to C 16.23). But whether or not Langland had this in mind, his joke remains; Skeat's explanation no more replaces Langland's text than exegesis replaces the Bible's.

[4]See Mikhail Bakhtin, *Rabelais and His World*, tr. Helene Iswolksky (Cambridge, Mass., 1968), pp. 413–15.

[6]The quotation is repeated in a more obviously fitting context after B 11.279 in MSS OC², but is probably a scribal addition: see *B Version*, p. 221.

[7]The sentence occurs in Book iii, ch. 18, of Innocent's *Of the Wretchedness of the Human Condition*.

[8]"MSS R and F in the B-Tradition of *Piers Plowman*," *TCAAS* 39 (1955), 199, n. 47.

⁹Langland quotes this sentence after 9.100, changing the subjunctive of the verb to the indicative.

¹⁰In the A-text (11.253–54) the wordplay is even more licentious: "For he seiþ it hymself in his ten hestis; / *Ne mecaberis,* ne sle nouȝt, is þe kynde englissh," unless, as Kane suggests, the English and Latin verbs are in a parallel construction governed by *Ne . . . ne* (p. 456).

¹¹John A. Alford, "The Role of the Quotations in *Piers Plowman,*" *Speculum* 52 (1977), 80–99.

¹²A. V. C. Schmidt, ed., *The Vision of Piers Plowman* (New York & London, 1978), p. 352, n. to line 396a. Schmidt observes that the C-text "certainly makes explicit the (implied) distinction between pagans/pre-Christians and Christians," but he believes the C-text represents revision (p. 298, n. to line 394). Without the reading *haluebreperen,* however, B seems to make inadequate sense.

¹³See M. E. Marcett, *Uhtred de Boldon, Friar William Jordan, and Piers Plowman* (New York, 1938); David Knowles, "Two Treatises of Uhtred of Boldon on the Monastic Life," *Studies in Medieval History Presented to F. M. Powicke,* ed. R. W. Hunt, W. A. Pantin, and R. W. Southern (Oxford, 1948), pp. 368 ff.; and Knowles, "The Censured Opinions of Uhtred of Boldon," *PBA* 37 (1951), 305ff.

¹⁴G. H. Russell, "The Salvation of the Heathen: The Exploration of a Theme in *Piers Plowman,*" *JWCI* 29 (1966), 101–16.

¹⁵Russell, p. 116.

¹⁶*Speculum* 14 (1939), 215–32.

 # George Kane

¹Compare Gordon Leff, *Heresy in the Later Middle Ages* (Manchester, 1967) 1:330, 2:411.

²Lines 127–29. My *Piers* quotations are from Kane (London, 1960) for A, from Kane-Donaldson (London, 1975) for B, and from Skeat (Oxford, 1886) for C.

³F. R. H. Du Boulay, *An Age of Ambition* (London, 1970), pp. 66, 67. Compare *Piers Plowman* C 6.70 ff.

⁴Quoted by G. R. Owst, *Literature and Pulpit in Medieval England* (Cambridge, 1933), p. 558.

⁵Owst, pp. 291–93.

⁶F. N. Robinson, ed., *The Works of Geoffrey Chaucer,* 2nd ed. (Boston, 1957), p. 252.

⁷B 10.305, 306. See Morton Bloomfield, *Piers Plowman as a Fourteenth-century Apocalypse* (Brunswick, N. J., 1961), pp. 68–73.

[8] A Prologue 63, 64; B Prologue 66, 67; C 1.64, 65. In C the expression in the first of these lines is made more violent: "But holy churche & charite choppe adoun swich shryuers."

[9] Bloomfield, pp. 78 ff.

[10] W. H. Pantin, *The English Church in the Fourteenth Century* (Cambridge, 1955), pp. 159, 160.

[11] Bloomfield, p. 80.

[12] Lines 18 ff. The passage recalls Chaucer's representation of a similar attitude in the "Summoner's Tale" (1919-28).

[13] See Kane, *The Liberating Truth: the Concept of Integrity in Chaucer's Writings* (London, 1980), pp. 9 and 24, n. 15.

[14] *De officio regis,* cited by Leff, 2:543. There is a scribal error in Leff's footnote: the text actually reads "Nec est fingendum ministerium huius differencie verborum nisi quod rex gerit ymaginem deitatis Cristi, sicut episcopus ymaginem sue humanitatis."

[15] "This World Fares as a Fantasy," lines 97-100, in Carleton Brown, *Religious Lyrics of the XIVth Century* (Oxford, 1924), p. 163.

[16] If Langland was, as seems likely, acquainted with Innocent's tirade against the intellect, *De studio sapientum* (Robert E. Lewis, ed., *De Miseria Condicionis Humane* [Athens, Georgia, 1978], pp. 109, 110), then the pathos of the Dreamer's ambition is deepened by the quotation of Prov. 25:27 at 15.55, with which Innocent makes play.

[17] An example is B 14.60, 61:
  if þow lyue after his loore, þe shorter lif þe bettre:
  Si quis amat christum mundum non diligit istum.

[18] This is a handy moment to write of Morton Bloomfield's *Piers Plowman as a Fourteenth-century Apocalypse* that it taught me more about *Piers Plowman* than any other single book. Detail after detail of his scholarship continues to fit into place. Here one might notice his intriguing information about the dates forecast for Antichrist's arrival (pp. 92, 93).

[19] Leff, 1:138.

[20] Compare Elizabeth Kirk, *The Dream Thought of Piers Plowman* (New Haven, 1972), pp. 118, 119.

[21] See Ceslaus Spicq, *Saint Paul: Les épîtres pastorales* (Paris, 1947), pp. 57, 58: "qui omnes homines vult saluos fieri et ad agnitionem veritatis venire"; "qui dedit redemptionem semetipsum pro omnibus." Origen came to the belief by another route. See Jean Daniélou, *Origen,* trans. W. Mitchell (New York, 1955), pp. 287–89.

[22] For an early fifteenth-century instance see Leff, 1:397, 398.

[23] Quoted by Spicq, *Saint Paul,* p. 57: "omnia quaecumque voluit fecit: ergo omnes salvat."

[24]"Rectitudo est quod vult et rationale est omnino quod fiat sibi." Adam of Woodham, quoted by Leff, 1:298.

[25]Used as an argument by Truth in the debate of the Four Daughters of God at 18.149.

 # Anne Middleton

[1]Pierre Macherey, *A Theory of Literary Production*, tr. Geoffrey Wall (London, 1978), p. 92.

[2]Macherey, p. 94.

[3]Macherey, p. 72.

[4]See Morton Bloomfield, "Episodic Juxtaposition or the Syntax of Episodes in Narration," in *Studies in English Linguistics for Randolph Quirk*, ed. Sidney Greenbaum, Geoffrey Leech, and Jan Svartvik (London, 1980), pp. 210–20.

[5]I am indebted to my colleague Ann Banfield, whose forthcoming book *Unspeakable Sentences* deals with the narrative grammar of free indirect discourse.

[6]John Alford, "The Role of the Quotations in *Piers Plowman*," *Speculum* 52 (1977), 80–99.

[7]C 19.163–83. Citations of the C text are to the edition of W. W. Skeat, *The Vision of William Concerning Piers the Plowman . . . in Three Parallel Texts* (London, 1886). Those of the B text are to *Piers Plowman: The B Version*, ed. George Kane and E. T. Donaldson (London, 1975); and of the A text to the Athlone edition by George Kane (London, 1960).

[8]Cf. David Mills, "The Role of the Dreamer in *Piers Plowman*" in *Piers Plowman: Critical Approaches*, ed. S. S. Hussey (London, 1969), p. 196: "Langland has created a situation in which the reader must question the arguments advanced by the abstractions at every point."

[9]William Birnes has explicated in detail the governing legal metaphors of this episode, and the contemporary legal practices and political theories to which they refer ("Patterns of Legality in *Piers Plowman*" [Ph.D. diss., New York University, 1974], chs. 3 and 4, pp. 66–122).

[10]Denise Baker, "Dialectic Form in *Pearl* and *Piers Plowman*," paper presented at the meeting of the Middle English Division of the Modern Language Association, December, 1980.

[11]Priscilla Martin, *Piers Plowman: The Field and the Tower* (New York, 1979), p. 56.

¹²See Elizabeth Kirk, *The Dream Thought of Piers Plowman* (New Haven, 1972), pp. 33–40; she presents a valuable brief discussion of these and their correlatives in the philosophy and systematic theology of the fourteenth century.

¹³See G. A. Borgese, "The Wrath of Dante," *Speculum* 13 (1938), 183–93; rpt. in *Essays on Dante*, ed. Mark Musa (Bloomington, Ind., 1964), pp. 94–109.

¹⁴On "horizontal motivation," see Morton Bloomfield, "Episodic Motivation and Marvels in Epic and Romance" in *Essays and Explorations: Studies in Ideas, Language, and Literature* (Cambridge, Mass., 1970), pp. 97–128.

¹⁵The distinction is that of Erich Auerbach, and crucial to the description of the situation of high literacy in this period. See "The Western Public and Its Language" in *Literary Language and Its Public in Late Latin Antiquity and in the Middle Ages*, tr. Ralph Manheim (New York, 1965), pp. 237–338, esp. 318–19, 296–98.

¹⁶On the "treatise" versus the "poetical text" in *Piers*, see Herbert Engels, *Piers Plowman: Eine Untersuchung der Textstruktur mit einer Einleitung zur mittelalterlichen Allegorie* (Ph.D. diss., Köln, 1968).

¹⁷See Lester K. Little, *Religious Poverty and the Profit Economy in Medieval Europe* (Ithaca, N. Y., 1978), pp. 114–16, and M.-D. Chenu, *Nature, Man and Society in the Twelfth Century*, tr. Jerome Taylor and Lester K. Little (Chicago, 1968), pp. 260–61.

¹⁸For a discussion of genre as the action-rules and use-rules of a text, and a very valuable account of the "rules" of early modern autobiography, with a good deal of bearing on what I am claiming about *Piers*, see Elizabeth Bruss, *Autobiographical Acts: The Changing Situation of a Literary Genre* (Baltimore, 1976), pp. 4–6.

¹⁹See Mable Day, "The Revisions of *Piers Plowman*," *MLR* 23 (1928), 2, and E. Talbot Donaldson, *Piers Plowman: The C-Text and Its Poet*, Yale Studies in English, 113 (New Haven, 1949); rpt. Hamden, Conn., 1966), p. 26. Donaldson and Kane have cautioned about the precariousness of dating or determining the exact sequence of any addition to the poem, but some guesses are possible on external evidence. While several other passages unique to C are echoed in the *Testament of Love* of Thomas Usk, who was executed early in 1388, I believe this passage—from which he draws no material— was composed between late 1388 and 1390. It seems to allude in some detail to the Second Statute of Laborers, an act of the Cambridge Parliament of September 1388, and is composed as an imaginary inquiry before the Justices empowered to enforce it. If this is correct, then it offers some corroboration of Day's and Donaldson's opinion that this passage—along with two hundred

lines or so added to Truth's message to Piers in C 10, and, like this one, bearing on the question of legitimate labor—is among the very last additions to the poem.

[20]See Morton Bloomfield, *Piers Plowman as a Fourteenth-century Apocalypse* (New Brunswick, N. J., 1962), App. 3, pp. 170–74 and notes, pp. 230–31.

[21]In what follows I describe the B version of the dialogue. The C text cancels the passage containing the challenge to Will's "makynges"; its function is taken over by the new "autobiographical" addition, which is built up from this dialogue, together with suggestions from the passus immediately preceding the insertion, and some from the passus preceding Ymaginatif's entry (B 11.130–32 and 295).

[22]B 11.91–107, 376–404. See Martin for a valuable discussion of the morality of satire as it figures in the explicit poetics of *Piers* (pp. 66–70).

[23]For a similar claim that the man of letters has a discipline analogous to that of the cleric, a "rule" to which he is committed in his practice as a writer, see my essay, "The Clerk and His Tale: Some Literary Contexts," *SAC* 2 (1980), p. 132.

[24]R. W. Chambers, "Robert or William Longland?," *London Medieval Studies* 1 (1948, for 1939), 430–62; George Kane, *Piers Plowman: The Evidence for Authorship* (London, 1965), pp. 52–70. Kane's Chambers Memorial Lecture also deals with these matters in literary history (*The Autobiographical Fallacy in Chaucer and Langland Studies* [London, 1965]).

[25]See Kane, *Authorship*, p. 65.

[26]Frank Kermode, *The Sense of an Ending: Studies in the Theory of Fiction* (London, 1966), p. 39.

[27]Cf. Mills, p. 191: "[It is the Dreamer's] function within his own dream . . . to assert the primacy of the present and of the individual against the denial which the dream-experience proposes of any such primacy. It is this assertion which destroys the unity of the vision but which also makes the vision uniquely the Dreamer's."

[28]Kermode, p. 56.

[29]On the self-presentation of court and curial writers of the fourteenth century, see Daniel Poirion, *Le Poete et le Prince* (Paris, 1965; rpt. Geneva, 1978), pp. 145–235.

[30]Roland Barthes, *Writing Degree Zero*, tr. Annette Lavers and Colin Smith (New York, 1968), pp. 14–16.

[31]See Bertha Haven Putnam, ed., *Proceedings before the Justices of the Peace in the Fourteenth and Fifteenth Centuries* (London, 1938), p. cxxv;

Alan Harding, "Plaints and Bills in the History of English Law" in *Legal History Studies, 1972,* ed. Dafydd Jenkins (Cardiff, 1975), p. 70.

❧ Larry D. Benson

[1]F. N. Robinson, ed., *The Works of Geoffrey Chaucer,* 2nd ed. (Cambridge, Mass., 1957), p. 309. All quotations from Chaucer in this essay are from Robinson's edition.

[2]John Koch, "The Date and Personages of the *Parlement of Foules,*" in *Essays on Chaucer,* Chaucer Soc, 2nd ser., 18 (London, 1878), pp. 400-09; Samuel Moore, "A Further Note on the Suitors in the *Parlement of Foules,*" *MLN* 26 (1911), 8-12; O. F. Emerson, "The Suitors in the *Parlement of Foules,*" *MP* 8 (1910), 45-62 and "What is the *Parlement of Foules?*" *JEGP* 13 (1914), 566-82, both rpt. in *Chaucer Essays and Studies* (Cleveland, Ohio, 1929), pp. 58-89, 98-122; John M. Manly, "What is the *Parlement of Foules?*" *Festchrift für Lorenz Morsbach,* ed. F. Holthausen and H. Spies, Studien zur englischen Philologie, 50 (Halle, 1913), pp. 259-90; Edith Rickert, "Geoffrey Chaucer: A New Interpretation of the *Parlement of Foules,*" *MP* 18 (1920), 1-29.

[3]Manly, p. 280. Koch himself later came to date the poem in 1382, seeing no objection to placing the poem after the marriage and thinking that in 1380 "the enterprise was too doubtful to found a complimentary poem upon." See *The Chronology of Chaucer's Writings,* Chaucer Soc, 2nd ser., 27 (London, 1890), p. 38. Manly's point, however, seems valid to me.

[4]Rickert and Haldeen Braddy, "*The Parlement of Foules:* A New Proposal," *PMLA* 46 (1931), 1007-19; rpt. with revisions in Russell Kraus, Haldeen Braddy, C. Robert Case, *Three Chaucer Studies* (New York, 1932). Only Braddy's date has received much serious consideration as an alternative to Manly's 1382 or 1380, which a number of scholars accept. John H. Fisher regards the Richard-Marie theory as most probable and suggests, cautiously, 1377-78 for the *Parliament,* 1380 for the *House of Fame* (*The Complete Poetry and Prose of Geoffrey Chaucer* [New York, 1977], p. 564). There are considerable problems with this order of composition; see, for example, R. A. Pratt, "Chaucer Borrowing from Himself," *MLQ* 7 (1946), 262-69, and M. H. Shackford, "The Date of Chaucer's *House of Fame,*" *MLN* 31 (1916), 507-08.

[5]*The Parlement of Foules: An Interpretation* (Oxford, 1957), p. 2.

[6]For a helpful review of criticism see Donald C. Baker, "*The Parliament of Fowls,*" in Beryl Rowland, ed., *Companion to Chaucer Studies,* rev. ed. (Toronto, 1979), pp. 428-44.

[7]See, for example, M. R. Kelley, "Antithesis as the Principle of Design in the *Parlement of Foules*," *ChauR* 14 (1979), 61: "The major obstacle facing those who would seek to identify the source of unity in the poem is that its three clearly distinct sections have little in common with one another in meaning, characterization, or stylistic technique."

[8]See, for example, Dorothy Bethurum, "The Center of the *Parlement of Foules*," in *Essays in Honor of Walter Clyde Curry*, Vanderbilt Studies in the Humanities, 2 (Nashville, 1955), pp. 39–50.

[9]Charles Muscatine, *Chaucer and the French Tradition* (Berkeley and Los Angeles, 1957), p. 116.

[10]R. K. Root, *The Poetry of Chaucer*, 2nd ed. (Boston, 1922), p. 66.

[11]Wolfgang Clemen, *Chaucer's Early Poetry*, tr. C. A. M. Sym (London, 1963), p. 134.

[12]Derek S. Brewer, ed., *The Parlement of Foulys* (London, 1960), p. 18.

[13]"The Gloomy Chaucer" in *Veins of Humor*, ed. Harry Levin, Harvard English Studies, 3 (Cambridge, Mass., 1972), pp. 57–68.

[14]*Macrobius: Commentary on the Dream of Scipio*, tr. W. H. Stahl, Columbia Records of Civilization, 48 (New York, 1952).

[15]Shackford, pp. 507–08; see also Brewer, p. 3. The references appear in *Rom* 10, *BD* 284–86, and *HF* 916. In *The Book of the Duchess* Macrobius is said to be the author of the dream, an error repeated in the "Nun's Priest's Tale" (3123–24).

[16]It seems likely that Chaucer read Macrobius, though he gives no clear indication of this; see E. P. Anderson, "Some Notes on Chaucer's Treatment of the *Somnium Scipionis*," *Proc. Amer. Phil. Assoc.* 33 (1902), xcviii–xcix.

[17]I use the translation provided in Brewer's edition, to which the page numbers refer.

[18]See the n. on line 65 in Brewer, p. 102, and Robinson, p. 903.

[19]Benign but heretical; see George Kane's discussion of Langland's Passus XVIII in this volume (p. 88).

[20]See Brewer's note on line 47, p. 102; cf. *Bo.* 1, pr. 4.86, *CT* 4.431, 1194, and 10.773; on the importance of the idea to Chaucer's friend John Gower, see Russell A. Peck, *Kingship and Common Profit in Gower's Confessio Amantis* (Carbondale and Edwardsville, Ill., 1978).

[21]See esp. Macrobius' chs. 7 and 8.

[22]Cf. *CT* 5.722 and 7.1164ff. The *Somnium Scipionis* is apparently the only work by Cicero that he actually read; see Bruce Harbert, "Chaucer and the Latin Classics," in *Geoffrey Chaucer*, ed. Derek S. Brewer (London, 1974); the reference to Cicero as a

rhetorician probably refers to the *Rhetorica ad Herennium*, now attributed to Cornificius, and the quotations in the Melibee are taken over from the source that Chaucer is translating.

23See Mary E. Reid, "The Historical Interpretation of the *Parlement of Foules*," Studies by Members of the English Department, No. 3 (Madison, Wis., 1923), pp. 60–70.

24Bennett, p. 145.

25Thomas Rymer, ed., *Foedera, conventiones, litterae*, etc., rev. J. Caley and F. Holbrooke (London, 1869), 4:118.

26*Ibid.*, 120.

27See, for example, Charles O. McDonald, "An Interpretation of Chaucer's *Parlement of Foules*," *Speculum* 30 (1955), 444–57.

28This is well illustrated in the analogous story in *Il Paradiso degli Alberti* adduced by W. E. Farnham ("The Sources of Chaucer's *Parlement of Foules*," *PMLA* 32 [1917], 492–518). Farnham summarizes the tale (pp. 476–500) from the edition of Alessandro Wesselkofsky ([Bologna, 1867] 2:98–117). The cases of four equally eligible suitors are presented in detail; the heroine, who begins as a bird but is restored to human shape before the courtship begins, makes her choice and marries one of her four suitors. The audience, however, is not told which she chooses. That is left for debate, though in the framing narrative Guido, the teller, discusses only the heroine's relation to various place names in Prato, while the others comment, in terms reminiscent of Boccaccio's *Genealogia*, on the theme of transformation.

29See Richard F. Green, *Poets and Princepleasers: Literature and the English Court in the Late Middle Ages* (Toronto, 1980), p. 109, and Gervase Mathew, *The Court of Richard II* (London, 1968), p. 22. Mathew speculates on the possibility that Richard himself was a poet.

30See W. E. Farnham, "The Contending Lovers," *PMLA* 35 (1920), 247–323.

31The following is based principally on Édouard Perroy, *L'Angleterre et le Grand Schisme d'Occident* (Paris, 1933), pp. 136–46.

32*Chronicles*, tr. Thomas Johnes (London, 1868), 1:592. Froissart seems to be telescoping the talk about Anne with the interest during the previous year in the projected marriage with Caterina Visconti of Milan, since he says this was about the time of the death of the Emperor Charles, who died in November of 1378.

33*Foedera* 4:113; for a typical chronicler's comment see *Polychronicon Ranulphi Higden*, ed. Joseph R. Lumby, Rolls Series (London, 1866), 9:12.

34Rickert, pp. 6–7.

[35]Rickert refers to Franz M. Pelzel [Pelçel], *Lebensgeschichte des König Wenzel* (Prague, 1788); in his earlier *Kaiser Karl der Vierte* (Prague, 1780) Pelzel tells of Anne's betrothal to Friedrich and adds "Es wurde aber her nach aus dieser Heyrat nichts und die Prinzessin ward nach des Kaisers Tode an den König Eduard von England, vermählet," p. 862, which gets the English king's name wrong but seems to echo the chroniclers cited below.

[36](Leipzig, 1733), p. 81.

[37]Horn, p. 84, referring to Io. B. Menckenius [Mencke], *Scriptores rerum Germanicarum, praecipue Saxonicarum* etc. (Leipzig, 1728–30), 2, cols. 443–44 (the Chronicon Vetero-Cellense Minus, s.a. MCCCLXXI): "obiit gloriosissimus Princeps & Domnus Domnus Fredericus Marchio Misnensis . . . Idem Princeps fuit multum familiaris Domno Karolo quatro Imperatori, qui Imperator desponsavit filiam suam filio Domni Marchionis. sed post mortem Imperatoris Wenceslaus & Sigismundis filii ejus immutarent & dederunt eam Regi Anglie." The chronicle is also printed in Jo. Georgius Eccardus [Eckhart], *Historia genealogica principum Saxoniae* etc. (Leipzig, 1722), col. 102.

[38]Horn, p. 83, quotes from Johannis Tylich, *Chronicon Missnense*, in Johannis Frederici Schannat, *Vindemiae Literariae* etc., Collectio Secunda (Fulda and Leipzig 1724). Since the work is not easily available, I quote the full account, a part of which is translated in the text:

> Hic inclytus princeps adeo amabilis Imperatori Karolo IV. Bohemiae Regi fuit, ut filiam suam parvulam Friderico ejus filio tunc adhuc impuberi desponsaverit, poena apposita pecuniaria si hujusmodi dispositioni contra venirent, datis desuper ab Imperatore & Friderico Marchione litteris sigillatis & certis civitatibus pro pignore in dictis litteris expressis hinc inde, quarum litterarum tenores ex post in consilio Friderici Marchionis moderni ego Johannes Tylich Decretorum Doctor minimus, Praepositus Canonicorum Regularium Monasterii S. Mauritii extra muros Nuembergenses & in studio Lipsiensi Lector ordinarius audivi anno MCCCCXIII [sic; for MCCCLXXIII?]. Sed mortuo Karolo Imperatore Anno MCCCLXXVIII. & post etiam Friderico Marchione patre Friderici praesentis, Wenceslaus Romanorum & Bohemiae Rex, Sigismundus Hungariae Rex & Johannes Dux Poloniae fratres & filii Imperatoris Karoli defuncti sororem suam, filio Friderici Marchionis desponsatam, Regi Angliae in matrimonium dederunt, promissiones & litteras Imperatoris temere violando, quae postmodum fuerunt causa ruinarum, depraeda-

tionum & multorum malorum inter Regem Bo-
hemiae & Marchionem Missnensem.

[39]*Vitae paparum Avenionensium*, ed. Stephanus Baluzius; rev. ed.
G. Mollat (Paris, 1922), 4, esp. p. 211.

[40]Perroy, p. 144. Froissart reports that even on his deathbed
later that same year the "wily Valois" had hopes that the marriage
would occur (tr. Johnes, 1:616).

[41]*Works of Geoffrey Chaucer*, p. 391.

[42]*Three Chaucer Studies*, p. 58. More recently J. D. North has
calculated the date of the dream as 1392, but this is on the
assumption that Chaucer wrote the poem on Valentine's Day,
which the text does not support ("Kalenderes Enlumyned Ben
They: Some Astronomical Themes in Chaucer," *RES* 20 [1969],
270–74). Braddy's dates remain an important influence on thought
about the date of the poem; see, for example, Fisher, *The Complete
Poetry and Prose*, n. to line 117.

[43]*Chapters on Chaucer* (Baltimore, 1951), pp. 78–79; B. H.
Bronson also suggests this is a terrestial compass direction and
speculates that it is intended to indicate John of Gaunt's residence
("*The Parlement of Foules* Revisited," *ELH* 15 [1948], 247–60).

[44]Brewer, p. 104.

[45]B. H. Bronson, "In Appreciation of Chaucer's *Parlement of
Foules*," Univ. of Calif. Publ. in English, 3 (Berkeley and Los
Angeles, 1935), esp. pp. 204–08. This was first suggested by
Manly. A metaphorical meaning seems unlikely for a technical
term that, if *north-north-west* is the correct reading, is (according to
the *OED*) used here for the first time.

[46]H. M. Smyser, "Chaucer's View of Astronomy," *Speculum* 45
(1970), 364.

[47]"Chaucer and Science" in Derek S. Brewer, ed., *Geoffrey
Chaucer* (London, 1974), p. 234.

[48]H. Lange, "Hat Chaucer den Kompass gekannt und
benutzt?" *Anglia* 58 (1934), 333–44; H. Lange and H. Nippolt, "Die
Deklination am 20.Mai 1380 in London," *Quellen und Studien der
Naturwissenschaft und der Medizin* 5 (1936), 518–36. G. K. Brown
observes that the deviation suggested by Lange and Nippolt
assumes a theory of secular cycles of variation now rejected by
geophysicists ("English Compass Points," *MÆ* 47 [1978]).

[49]Brown, p. 246.

[50]For example, Bennett suggests Venus must be a morning
star (p. 60); apparently he adopts the reading "north nor west" (for
"north-north-west") and interprets that as "neither north nor
west; i.e., southeast," since Venus as a morning star appears in the
southern skies.

[51]"Chaucer's View of Astronomy," p. 364.

[52]Robinson thought it earlier than 1382; he put it among the poems of 1380–86 and remarked "possibly a little earlier" (p. xxix). 1382 seems a bit late, since by that time Chaucer was probably working on his translation of *Boece*, and one would expect to find more traces of that work in a poem written contemporaneously with its translation.

[53]Perroy, pp. 142, 145.

 # Donald R. Howard

[1]*PMLA* 72 (1957), 14–26. The essay was reprinted in *Chaucer Criticism*, ed. Richard J. Schoeck and Jerome Taylor (Notre Dame, 1961), 2:196–210; in Morton W. Bloomfield, *Essays and Explorations: Studies in Ideas, Language, and Literature* (Cambridge, Mass., 1970), pp. 200–216; and in *Chaucer's Troilus: Essays in Criticism*, ed. Stephen A. Barney (Hamden, Conn., 1980), pp. 75–90. I quote from the first appearance.

[2]*Chaucer: The Critical Heritage*, ed. Derek S. Brewer (London, 1978), 1:246.

[3]*Fall of Princes*, lines 283–87, quoted in Brewer, 1:53. See W. W. Skeat, *Complete Works* (Oxford, 1894–1900), 2:liv–lvi and Eleanor Prescott Hammond, *Chaucer: A Bibliographical Manual* (New York, 1908), p. 98.

[4]Alfons Kissner, *Chaucer in seinen Beziehungen zur italienischen Litteratur* (Ph.D. diss., Marburg, 1867), and W. M. Rossetti, ed., *Chaucer's Troylus and Cryseyde compared with Boccaccio's Filostrato*, Chaucer Soc, 1st ser., 44 (London, 1873). See Hammond, pp. 398–99.

[5]Skeat, 2:xlix; the italics are his.

[6]George Lyman Kittredge, *Chaucer and His Poetry* (Cambridge, Mass., 1915), p. 122.

[7]Hubertis M. Cummings, *The Indebtedness of Chaucer's Works to the Italian Works of Boccaccio* (1916; rpt. New York, 1967).

[8]*Essays and Studies* 17 (1932), 56–75.

[9]John S. P. Tatlock, "The Epilog of Chaucer's *Troilus*," *MP* 18 (1921), 625–59; Walter Clyde Curry, *Chaucer and the Mediaeval Sciences* (1926; rpt. New York, 1960), pp. 241–98; C. S. Lewis, *The Allegory of Love* (Oxford, 1936), pp. 43, 176–97.

[10]Of other religious interpretations, the principal ones would be that the story is an ironic allegory opposing cupidity (see D. W. Robertson, Jr., "Chaucerian Tragedy," *ELH* 19 [1952], 1–37); or that courtly love was itself a heresy accepted by a doctrine of "double truth" (see Alexander J. Denomy, "The Two Moralities of

Chaucer's *Troilus and Criseyde*," *TRSC* 44, ser. 3, sec. 2 [June 1950], 35–46); or that the love story is a Platonistic representation of divine love (see Donald W. Rowe, *O Love, O Charite! Contraries Harmonized in Chaucer's Troilus* [Carbondale, Ill., 1976]).

[11]"Troilus on Determinism," *Speculum* 6 (1929), 225–43. A much earlier effort of this kind was Bernard L. Jefferson, *Chaucer and the Consolation of Philosophy of Boethius* (1917; rpt. New York, 1968), pp. 120–32.

[12]For a summary of these, though it somewhat confounds religion and philosophy, see Alice R. Kaminsky, *Chaucer's "Troilus and Criseyde" and the Critics* (Athens, O., 1980), pp. 41–71.

[13]"Distance and Predestination," pp. 22–23.

[14]*Chaucer's Troilus*, p. 89.

[15]"Distance and Predestination," p. 23. It seems to me that recent studies of the philosophical background of Chaucer's time support this insight; for example, see Russell A. Peck, "Chaucer and the Nominalist Questions," *Speculum* 53 (1978), 745–60.

[16]"Distance and Predestination," pp. 24–26.

[17]This is apart from direct influence. To give just one example, E. Talbot Donaldson's 1963 essay "The Ending of 'Troilus'" proceeded from the givens of Donaldson's previous writings on the narrator and presented a new aspect of the ending: the narrator's faltering tone and seeming panic before he turns to what "can alone resolve paradox" (rpt. in *Speaking of Chaucer* [New York, 1970], pp. 84–101). But this is implicit in the concept of the narrator's distance at the end, and it would seem the less significant but for the association of that distance with predestination.

[18]This was the basis of my view, then radical, that the narrator *is* Chaucer; see *The Three Temptations: Medieval Man in Search of the World* (Princeton, N.J., 1966), pp. 143–49 and "Chaucer the Man," *PMLA* 80 (1965), 337–43.

[19]"Distance and Predestination," p. 19; see *The Three Temptations*, pp. 114–18.

[20]See *The Three Temptations*, pp. 135–38; the notion is developed some in the introduction to *Troilus and Criseyde and Selected Short Poems* (New York, 1976) edited by me and James Dean, from which incidentally I quote the poem in the present essay.

[21]Godwin wrote in 1803 that Pandarus "comes elevated and refined from the pen of Chaucer: his occupation loses its grossness, in the disinterestedness of his motive, and the sincerity of his friendship"; see Brewer, 1:242. C. S. Lewis said he is "a friend according to the old, high code of friendship, and a man of sentiment" (p. 191). Eugene E. Slaughter argued that Chaucer meant his role "to be ideal, and wholly commendable; Pandarus

acts always within the limits set by the classical ideal of friendship" ("Chaucer's Pandarus: Virtuous Uncle and Friend," *JEGP* 48 [1949], 186–95).

22Kittredge, pp. 136–37.

23The argument was made by Willard Farnham in *The Medieval Heritage of Elizabethan Tragedy* (1936; rpt. Oxford, 1956), pp. 14–29.

24See John Frankis, "Paganism and Pagan Love in *Troilus and Criseyde*," in *Essays on Troilus and Criseyde*, ed. Mary Salu (Cambridge, Eng., 1979), pp. 57–72.

25E.g., Kaminsky, p. 44 and passim. Edmund Reiss argues against the *contemptus mundi* idea but still treats it as a philosophical concept ("Troilus and the Failure of Understanding," *MLQ* 29 [1968], 131–44).

26*Christianisme et Valeurs Humaines: La Doctrine du Mépris du Monde, en Occident, de S. Ambroise à Innocent III* (Louvain, 1963–   ), projected in 6 tomes, of which to my knowledge only the two volumes of tome 4 appeared.

27In fact the bibliographical part of it, the works I found and the locations of the manuscripts, was published in *Incipits of Latin Works on the Virtues and Vices, 1100–1500 A.D.* (Cambridge, Mass., 1979). This was a work begun many years before by Morton Bloomfield, and I am deeply in his debt for inviting me to become one of the coeditors, thus making of my material the rare instance of an abandoned project that appears in print. Bibliography aside, I had my say about *contemptus mundi* in *The Three Temptations* and in various introductions and articles.

28*New Catholic Encyclopedia* (New York, 1967–74), 14:109.

29See John H. Fisher, *John Gower: Moral Philosopher and Friend of Chaucer* (New York, 1964), esp. pp. 225–35, and my article "Fiction and Religion in Boccaccio and Chaucer," *JAAR* 47, Supplement (1979), 307–28.

30See Tatlock, esp. pp. 631–35 and 656, n. 2.

❧ Robert Worth Frank, Jr.

1F. N. Robinson, ed., *The Works of Geoffrey Chaucer*, 2nd ed. (Boston, 1957).

2There is a review of scholarship and criticism on this point in the indispensable study by Florence H. Ridley, *The Prioress and the Critics*, Univ. of California English Studies, no. 30 (Berkeley and Los Angeles, 1965), esp. pp. 1–4.

3*The Middle English Miracles of the Virgin* (San Marino, Calif., 1964), p. 10.

⁴"Juden and Jüdisches in christlichen Wundererzählungen," *TS* 10 (1954), 417–46. Reprinted as item IX in Bernhard Blumenkranz, *Juifs et Chrétiens Patristique et Moyen Age* (London, 1977).

⁵Eugen Wolter, *Der Judenknabe*, Bibliotheca normannica, 2 (Halle, 1879).

⁶"The English Origins of the 'Miracles of the Virgin,'" *MRS* 4 (1958), 178.

⁷The injunction to read such collections is, unfortunately, not easy to heed. Not many are in print, and there are few modern editions. Evelyn Faye Wilson provides a useful list of Latin, Anglo-Norman, French, Provençal, Spanish, Italian, English, German, Norse, and Ethiopian "collections of legends" in her edition of *The "Stella Maris" of John of Garland* (Mediaeval Academy of America, Publication no. 45 [Cambridge, Mass., 1946], pp. v–ix); but not all the items are collections limited to miracles of the Virgin. Her edition of the *Stella Maris* is valuable, not least because it provides just such a collection, and one popular in England (see p. 69). Another recent edition of a collection is José M. Canal, ed., *El Libro "De Laudibus et Miraculis Sanctae Mariae" de Guillermo de Malmesbury*, OBS (†c 1143), 2nd ed. (Rome, 1968). There is an excellent edition of Gautier de Coinci, *Les Miracles de Nostre Dame*, ed. V. Frederick Koenig (Geneva, 1966–70). Gautier de Coinci gives the form splendid literary treatment, but his own anti-Semitism is scarifying. I shall be trying here to limit my discussion to collections of English provenience, and so I shall ignore Gautier.

Beverly Boyd's *Middle English Miracles of the Virgin* is useful in many ways, but it gathers Middle English miracles from a variety of sources and, while representative of the collections, is not an edition of any one collection. Her notes, however, give lists of the miracles in the manuscripts she draws on, as well as much other helpful information. We do have two edited Middle English collections: one in the Vernon MS, originally, according to the Index in the MS, consisting of forty-two miracles, though only the first nine survive (see Carl Horstmann, ed., *The Minor Poems of the Vernon MS.*, Part 1, EETS, 98 [London, 1892], pp. 138–67) and an edition of British Library Add. MS 39996 (Ruth Wilson Tryon, "Miracles of Our Lady in Middle English Verse," *PMLA* 38 [1923], 308–88).

The great majority of collections are in Latin and are still in manuscript. There is no reason to believe that all such collections have been identified. The magisterial study by Adolf Mussafia contains considerable information about manuscript collections ("Studien zu den mittelalterlichen Marienlegenden," *Sitzungsberichte der kaiserlichen Akademie der Wissenschaften in Wien* 113 [1886], 917–94; 115 [1887], 5–93; 119 [1889], fasc. ix, 1–66; 123 [1890], fasc. viii, 1–85; 139 [1898], fasc. viii, 1–74). Mussafia was primarily concerned with the form of early collections, and I shall not refer to him here. I have found useful the list of incipits for individual miracles in Latin compiled by A. Poncelet, "Miraculorum B. V. Mariae quae saec. VI–XV latine conscripta sunt index, postea perficiendus," *AnBol* 21 (1902), 241–360. I shall also make reference to two unpublished Latin manuscript collections of English provenience. One, Sidney Sussex Cambridge MS 95, is the largest known surviving Latin collection and dates from the early fifteenth century (1409). The other, Magdalene College Cambridge Pepys Library MS 2359, is an early fifteenth-century collection of ninety-three miracles; it seems to have gone unused and unnoticed, although M. R. James identified and indexed it in his *Bibliotheca Pepysiana* (London, 1914), pp. 94–103.

The quickest and easiest way to get a sense of the composition of these collections is to read the section on Miracles of the Virgin in H. L. D. Ward, *Catalogue of Romances in the Department of Manuscripts in the British Museum* (London, 1903), 2:586–740. Ward indexes each manuscript and provides useful comment. It is still a basic work in this area. C. C. Swinton Bland's *Miracles of the Blessed Virgin Mary,* with preface, notes, and introduction by Eileen Power (London, 1928), is a translation of an early fifteenth-century collection of one hundred miracles, that of Johannes Herolt, called Discipulus, *Promptuarium Discipuli de Miraculis Beatae Mariae Virginis,* the best known collection of the sixteenth century.

[8]Of twenty-seven manuscript collections listed in Ward (pp. 586–740), Latin, French, Anglo-Norman, and English, only three have no anti-Semitic tales. The collections contain from five to ninety-three items; of the total, 9 percent of the tales are anti-Semitic. Evelyn Faye Wilson indexes a total of 146 individual legends, including the ten anti-Semitic miracles that occur most frequently and an eleventh ("Beirut") only slightly less popular. This gives us 7½ percent as a rough figure.

[9]Cecil Roth, *A History of the Jews* (New York, 1961), pp. 165–68.

[10]Roth, *History,* pp. 192–97; Henri Pirenne, *Economic and Social History of Western Europe* (New York, 1937), pp. 11–12.

[11]Roth, pp. 192–97; Pirenne, pp. 133–35. Dr. Lea Dasberö links the rise of anti-Semitism to the Investiture controversy: *Untersuchungen über die Entwertung des Judenstatus im 11. Jh.,* École pratique des hautes études, Sorbonne, VIᵉ section: Sciences economiques et sociales, Études Juives, 11 (Paris, 1965). She discounts the economic factor. There is a useful summary in Alexander Murray, *Reason and Society in the Middle Ages* (Oxford, 1978), pp. 68–69. Murray's own analysis (pp. 68–71) supports the economic factor.

[12]Bernhard Blumenkranz, *Le Juif médiéval au miroir de l'art chrétien* (Paris, 1966), p. 19.

[13]J. B. Russell, *Dissent and Reform in the Early Middle Ages* (Berkeley, 1965), pp. 48–53. For the First Crusade and the Jews see Steven Runciman, *A History of the Crusades*, vol. 1, *The First Crusade and the Foundation of the Kingdom of Jerusalem* (Cambridge, Eng., 1951), pp. 134–41; for the Second Crusade, vol. 2, *The Kingdom of Jerusalem and the Frankish East: 1100–1187* (Cambridge, Eng., 1952), pp. 254–55.

[14]Roth, pp. 197–98.

[15]*The Jew in the Medieval World: A Source Book, 315–1791* (New York, 1972), p. 137. Marcus provides a translation of the four legislative actions, pp. 137–41.

[16]Roth, pp. 214–15, 212.

[17]"St. Anselm" in *Medieval Humanism and Other Studies* (Oxford, 1970), p. 11.

[18]*Saint Anselm and his Biographers: A Study of Monastic Life and Thought, 1059–c. 1130* (Cambridge, Eng., 1963), p. 89.

[19]Southern, *Saint Anselm*, p. 90; Blumenkranz, *Le Juif médiéval*, p. 47. For miniatures showing controversies between Jews and Christians, see plates 47–49 (pp. 48–49) and 50–58 (pp. 50–57). See also Margaret Schlauch, "The Allegory of Church and Synagogue," *Speculum* 14 (1939), 448–64; J. de Ghellinck, *L'Essor de la littérature latine au XIIᵉ siècle* (Brussels, 1946), 1:158, n. 9, 161–68; and R. W. Hunt, "The Disputation of Peter of Cornwall against Symon the Jew" in *Studies in Medieval History Presented to Frederick Maurice Powicke*, ed. R. W. Hunt, W. A. Pantin, and R. W. Southern (Oxford, 1948), pp. 143–56.

[20]Blumenkranz, *Le Juif médiéval*, pp. 28–33; see plates 17–18 (France), 19 (Germany), 20–21 (Spain), and 23–26 (England). Blumenkranz notes that even after the expulsion of the Jews from England the hooked nose caricature appears in England in many encyclopedias of canon law and theology (plates 25, 26).

[21]Blumenkranz, *Le Juif médiéval*, pp. 42–45. For heretics represented pictorially as Jews see plates 38–41; for Vices, plates 42–43.

[22]Blumenkranz, *Le Juif médiéval*, pp. 53–62 and plates 54–58, 61–72; and pp. 105–15.

[23]Blumenkranz, *Le Juif médiéval*, pp. 79–104 and plates 84–117. See also Henry Kraus, "Anti-Semitism in Medieval Art" in *The Living Theatre of Medieval Art* (London, 1967), pp. 139–62.

[24]Hilda Graef, *Mary: A History of Doctrine and Devotion*, vol. 1, *From the Beginnings to the Eve of the Reformation* (London, 1963), p. 134.

[25]*Vita Beate Virginis Marie et Salvatoris Rhythmica*, ed. A. Vögtlin,

Bibliothek des Litterarischen Vereins in Stuttgart, clxxx (Tübingen, 1888), lines 7328–413.

[26]*The Blickling Homilies*, ed. R. Morris, EETS, 58 (London, 1880), p. 151; *Assumption of Our Lady* in *King Horn, Floriz and Blauncheflur, &c*, ed. J. R. Lumby (London, 1866), re-ed. G. H. McKnight, EETS, 14 (London, 1962), p. 128; *Cursor Mundi*, ed. R. Morris, EETS, 57, 62, 66, 68, 99, 101 (London, 1874–92), p. 1186 (MS Cotton); *South English Legendary*, Corpus Christi Cambridge MS 145, f. 137b. I owe these references to Anna J. Mill, "The York Plays of the Dying, Assumption, and Coronation of the Virgin," *PMLA* 65 (1950), 867–68.

[27]For example, in Sidney Sussex Cambridge MS 95, Liber I, cap. 79; and in Vincent de Beauvais, *Speculum Historiale*, Liber VII, cap. 77 (the miracles follow in capp. 81–120).

[28]*Ludus Coventriae or the Plaie Called Corpus Christi*, ed. K. S. Block, EETS, e.s. 120 (London, 1922 for 1917), pp. 367–71, lines 343–445. Chester and Wakefield once included a dramatization of the Assumption, as did Lincoln Cathedral in the fifteenth century; see Rosemary Woolf, *The English Mystery Plays* (London, 1972), pp. 286–88. The York Assumption omits the burial of Mary and the scene at the bier, but that was once part of the play; see Mill, pp. 866–76. According to the York records Mill cites (pp. 868–69), the play aroused laughter in this form and sometimes led to blows.

[29]*Saint Anselm: Basic Writings*, trans. S. N. Deane, 2nd ed. (La Salle, Ill., 1962), p. 182.

[30]"In quodam vos valde ridemus et insanos judicamus. Dicitis enim Deum, in maternis visceribus obceno [sic] carcere fetidi ventris clausum, novem mensibus pati, et tandem pudendo exitu (qui intuitum sine confusione non admittit), decimo mense progredi, inferentes Deo tantum . . . " PL 160:1110.

[31]In Group A of the chorister miracle the boy sings the "Gaude Maria" of the responsorium: See Carleton Brown, "The Prioress's Tale" in *Sources and Analogues of Chaucer's Canterbury Tales*, ed. W. F. Bryan and Germaine Dempster (New York, 1958), p. 448 and n. 1 (for the text of the "Gaude Maria").

[32]The standard work on this is Joshua Trachtenberg, *The Devil and the Jews: The Medieval Conception of the Jew and its Relation to Modern Anti-Semitism* (New Haven, 1943).

[33]". . . Quidam nefandissimus hebreus . . . omni gen*e*re maleficiorum imbutus, qui iam multos infidelitatis uiros in baratru*m* p*e*rdicionis immerserat" (III.30). For further information about this miracle and bibliographic references see Wilson, pp. 208–09 and Boyd, pp. 68–87 (a Middle English version, Bodleian Library

Rawlinson Poetry MS 225) and 127–29. There is a version in Magdalene College Cambridge Pepys Library MS 2359, II.30.

For each miracle cited, I will refer the reader to a source where examples of the miracle can be found, together with comments and further references in most instances. When the miracle appears in John of Garland's *Stella Maris*, I will refer the reader to Wilson's notes, which supply valuable information and bibliography.

34See Ward, 2:629 (British Library Add. MS 15,723, no. 19, and a variant, no. 20, in which the intermediary is not a Jew); Ward, 2:654 (Royal 5 A.viii, no. 22: "quidam iudeus"); Vincent de Beauvais, *Speculum Historiale*, VII.105 (not a Jew).

35Wilson, pp. 185–86; Sidney Sussex Cambridge MS 95, II.49.

36"Contigit ipsum forte ingredi plateas Judaismi, vbi gens dure ceruicis & domus exasperans habitabat, que Mariae virginis fecunditati contradicens dei filium incarnatum in virginis vtero diffitetur" (*Sources and Analogues*, p. 481, from Trinity College Cambridge MS O.9.38).

37Sidney Sussex Cambridge MS 95, IV.99 (the only example of this I have seen).

38Ibid., I.15 (again, the only example I have seen).

39Wilson, pp. 189–90.

40Ward, 2:631 (British Library Add. MS 15,723, no. 25) and p. 690 (Harley MS 2250, the last of five "Church Tales"); Sidney Sussex Cambridge MS 95, V.56 (missing); Vincent de Beauvais, *Speculum Historiale*, VII.111. There is a version in *Mirk's Festial*, ed. Theodore Erbe, EETS, e.s. 95 (London, 1905), pp. 248–49 (not a collection); see Boyd, p. 140.

41The only example of this I have seen is in *Mirk's Festial*, pp. 108–09; see Boyd, p. 140.

42Vincent de Beauvais, *Speculum Historiale*, XIX.6; Sidney Sussex Cambridge MS 95, V.50.

43"... quantum in cognatae gentis conuersione laboret industria Mariae": William of Malmesbury, *De Laudibus et Miraculis Sanctae Mariae*, ed. Canal, p. 136. Canal says the comment is omitted from the Salisbury MS, "Más bien parece una nota provisoria" (n.37). In the *Fortalicium fidei contra Iudeos, Saracenos aliosque Christiane fidei inimicos* (Basel, 1475), written in 1459, Alphonsus à Spina relates a group of miracles, some of them miracles of the Virgin, wrought he says by God to convert the Jews. They include the false conversion, the Jew of Bourges, and what appear to be three versions of the Christ image wounded (ccxx–ccxxiii).

44William of Malmesbury, II.5 (pp. 74–76); Sidney Sussex Cambridge MS 95, V.51; *Fortalicium fidei,* ccxx.

45Wilson, pp. 172–73. The language describing the defilement is unusually explicit in Magdalene College Cambridge Pepys Library MS 2359, III.5.

46The miracle is known by the catchword "Lydda," sometimes mistakenly rendered "Libia," and is also sometimes known as "Diopolis." See Wilson, p. 172; Sidney Sussex Cambridge MS 95, II.20; Magdalene College Cambridge Pepys Library MS 2359, III.8.

47Wilson, pp. 202–04; Sidney Sussex Cambridge MS 95, II.16; Magdalene College Cambridge Pepys Library MS 2359, III.17.

48Wilson, p. 166; Vincent de Beauvais, *Speculum Historiale,* VII.81; Sidney Sussex Cambridge MS 95, II.17; Magdalene College Cambridge Pepys Library MS 2359, II.21.

49Wilson, pp. 177–78; Magdalene College Cambridge Pepys Library MS 2359, III.18.

50Wilson, pp. 194–95; *Sources and Analogues,* pp. 447–85; Boyd, pp. 33–37 (Vernon MS) and 116–17.

51Wilson, pp. 173–75; William of Malmesbury, III.32 (pp. 132–36); Vincent de Beauvais, *Speculum Historiale,* VII.82; Boyd, pp. 44–49 (Vernon MS) and 118–19; Sidney Sussex Cambridge MS 95, II.31; Magdalene College Cambridge Pepys Library MS 2359, II.23.

52Wolter, passim; Wilson, pp. 157–59; William of Malmesbury, III.33 (pp. 137–38); Vincent de Beauvais, *Speculum Historiale,* XXI.78; Boyd, pp. 38–43 (Vernon MS) and 117–18; Sidney Sussex Cambridge MS 95, II.31; Magdalene College Cambridge Pepys Library MS 2359, III.6.

53"O virosa iudaice preuaricacionis obstinacio! Nomen *christi* blasphemant & *cum* in *christu*m non possunt in *christi* membra deseuiunt. Nec eos emollit, sed magis obstinatos reddit, quod *prophet*arum vaticinia in aduentu *christi* & ceremoniarum suarum abolicionem vident euiden*ter* expleta. Non enim *spiritu*m viuificantem sed solam attendunt littere sup*er*ficiem occidentem. O soli diabolo priuilegiate persone! Culpam exaggerat in contrarium versa crudelitas & fomes obstinacio fiet, a patrib*us* in filios deriuatus error diffidencie. Nec mouet eos quod vbiq*ue* terrarum se vident esse obprobrium hominum & plebis abieccionem." Sidney Sussex Cambridge MS 95, II.83. The text of this version was printed by Carleton Brown in his *A Study of the Miracle of Our Lady Told by Chaucer's Prioress,* Chaucer Soc., 2nd Ser., 45 (London, 1910), pp. 12–16.

54For an acknowledgment of Chaucer's interest in the pathetic, see Morton W. Bloomfield, "The Man of Law's Tale: A

Tragedy of Victimization and a Christian Comedy," *PMLA* 87 (1972), 384–90.

⁵⁵A helpful view is provided by Gavin Langmuir, "The Jews and the Archives of Angevin England: Reflections on Medieval Anti-Semitism," *Traditio* 19 (1963), 189–93.

⁵⁶Though I would not wish to appear to be invoking Professor Bloomfield's name to support an argument he may not find persuasive, I have been attempting here to be faithful to his suggestion in "Continuities and Discontinuities," *New Literary History* 10 (1979), 416, n. 2: "We should approach the Western Middle Ages as we might approach a different culture in Africa or Australia so that we can see and learn how a society can operate differently from ours and yet have obvious links to modern times." It is advice I believe all medievalists should heed.

Stephen A. Barney

¹*Poetry and Prose of Alexander Pope*, ed. Aubrey Williams (Boston, 1969), pp. 404, 405.

²"The Canterbury Tales: Style of the Man and Style of the Work" in *Chaucer and Chaucerians*, ed. Derek S. Brewer (University, Ala., 1966), pp. 88–113, esp. pp. 94–95.

³These *praeteritiones* and other hastening remarks are examined by W. Nelson Francis, "Chaucer Shortens a Tale," *PMLA* 68 (1953), 1126–41, and Robert W. Frank, Jr., "The Legend of the *Legend of Good Women*," *ChauR* 1 (1966), 110–33.

⁴J. B. Greenough, G. L. Kittredge, et al., eds., *Allen and Greenough's New Latin Grammar* (Boston, 1888, 1931), sect. 341.

⁵For "undo" see *BD* 898, where it parallels "discryven": the Black Knight cannot "undo" the Lady White's "visage." F. N. Robinson, ed., *The Works of Geoffrey Chaucer*, 2nd ed. (Boston, 1957) is the edition cited. Chaucer (and Middle English: the 15th-century citation in the *MED* is dubious) did not use "list" in the the sense of this essay—nor "catalogue" nor "index." He could use "registre" or "table." For such observations I rely on John S. P. Tatlock and Arthur G. Kennedy, *A Concordance to the Complete Works of Geoffrey Chaucer* (Washington, 1927) and the *MED*.

⁶See Paul G. Kuntz, Introduction, *The Concept of Order* (Seattle, 1968), and his article "Order" in the *New Catholic Encyclopedia*.

⁷A side-argument would distinguish lists from nearly any other discourse on these same grounds of symmetry and intransitivity. Socrates, for example, finds an epitaph or an oration defective if not orderly (*Phaedrus* 264D–E).

⁸The term and its witty example are from Richard A. Lanham, *A Handlist of Rhetorical Terms* (Berkeley and Los Angeles, 1968).

⁹*The Rape of the Lock*, 1.138 and 100.

¹⁰Roman Jakobson, "Two Aspects of Language and Two Types of Aphasic Disturbance," in Jakobson and Morris Halle, *Fundamentals of Language* (The Hague, 1956).

¹¹The indeterminate number of elements in a list associates it with the sophism *sorites*, the "fallacy of the heap," which asks "how many straws are needed to make a heap?" The question leaves me helpless. I assume for convenience that a minimum list has three elements: two would yield a doublet or an antithesis, one lacks aliorelativity.

¹²C. S. Lewis, *The Discarded Image* (Cambridge, Eng., 1964), pp. 198-99, 206.

¹³The Greek *pinax*, like the Latin *tabellum*, developed in sense from "board" to "writing surface," especially for the inscription of lists of names, as for military or tax rolls.

¹⁴I am glad to have this public opportunity to thank Professor Bloomfield for his generosity toward me, and for his scrupulous attention to the onera of thesis-advising and other magisterial duties. He is a fitting student of wisdom.

¹⁵I include the use of exempla under the rubric "wisdom" for convenience. The Greek for exemplum is *paradeigma*: wisdom and the paradigmatic sort together. Special studies of Chaucer's forms of wisdom include Bartlett Jere Whiting and Helen Wescott Whiting, *Proverbs, Sentences, and Proverbial Phrases from English Writings Mainly before 1500* (Cambridge, Mass., 1968); B. J. Whiting, *Chaucer's Use of Proverbs*, Harvard Studies in Comparative Literature, 11 (Cambridge, Mass., 1934); Robert M. Lumiansky, "The Function of Proverbial Monitory Elements in Chaucer's *Troilus and Criseyde*," *Tulane Studies in English* 2 (1950), 5-48; Morton W. Bloomfield, "The Wisdom of the Nun's Priest's Tale" in *Chaucerian Problems and Perspectives: Essays Presented to Paul E. Beichner, C.S.C.*, ed. Edward Vasta and Zacharias P. Thundy (Notre Dame, 1979); exempla and sentences compiled in Traugott Naunin, *Der Einfluss der mittelalterlichen Rhetorik auf Chaucers Dichtung* (Ph.D. diss., Bonn, 1929), pp. 32-35; Donald MacDonald, "Proverbs, *Sententiae*, and *Exempla* in Chaucer's Comic Tales: The Function of Comic Mis-application," *Speculum* 41 (1966), 453-65; D. W. Robertson, Jr., *A Preface to Chaucer* (Princeton, 1962), pp. 273-75; Stewart Justman, "Medieval Monism and the Abuse of Authority in Chaucer," *ChauR* 11 (1976), 95-111; two recent essays, Barbara Newman, "'Feynede Loves,' Feigned Lore, and Faith in Trouthe," and Karla

Taylor, "Proverbs and the Authentication of Convention in *Troilus and Criseyde*" in *Chaucer's Troilus: Essays in Criticism*, ed. Stephen A. Barney (Hamden, 1980), pp. 257–75 and 277–96.

[16]To B. J. Whiting's brief survey of early English proverb collections ("A Collection of Proverbs in BM MS. 37075," in *Franciplegius*, ed. Jess B. Bessinger, Jr., and Robert P. Creed [New York, 1965], pp. 274–89) can be added Elaine Tuttle Hansen, *"Precepts*: An Old English Instruction," *Speculum* 56 (1981), 1–16, and Olof Arngart's revised edition of one of the earliest (11th c.) English proverb collections, "The Durham Proverbs," *Speculum* 56 (1981), 288–300. Still useful surveys of medieval wisdom collections are Joseph A. Mosher, *The Exemplum in the Early Religious and Didactic Literature of England* (New York, 1911); Jean Thiébault Welter, *L'Exemplum dans la littérature religieuse et didactique du moyen âge* (Paris, 1927); Ernst Robert Curtius, *European Literature and the Latin Middle Ages*, trans. Willard R. Trask (Bern, 1948; New York, 1953), pp. 58–60. Curtius's influence on this whole essay will be obvious. The work of Walter J. Ong, S.J. has also influenced my thinking about lists; see "Media Transformation: The Talked Book" in his *Interfaces of the Word: Studies in the Evolution of Consciousness and Culture* (Ithaca, 1977); "Oral Residue in Tudor Prose Style" in his *Rhetoric, Romance and Technology* (Ithaca, 1971), and *The Presence of the Word* (New Haven, 1967).

[17]On these forms, and especially on the priamel (on which more below), see the comprehensive study by Karl Euling, *Das Priamel bis Hans Rosenplüt: Studien zur Volkspoesie*, Germanistische Abhandlungen, 25 (Breslau, 1905); also Walter Kröhling, *Die Priamel (Beispielreihung) als Stilmittel in der griechisch-römischen Dichtung*, Greifswalder Beiträge, 10 (Greifswald, 1935). Job 28 is a great priamel; *Mel* 1107 is I think Chaucer's only example of a chain speech.

[18]*MancT* 316–62. On the "my son" form in preceptive wisdom see Hansen and William McKane, *Proverbs: A New Approach* (London and Philadelphia, 1970).

[19]John M. Manly and Edith Rickert, *The Text of the Canterbury Tales* (Chicago, 1940), 2:315. James Sledd surveys other cases of loosely appropriate exempla in Chaucer ("Dorigen's Complaint," *MP* 45 [1947–48], 36–45). For a detailed study of the compilation of Dorigen's list from its source in Jerome's *Adversus Jovinianum*, see Germaine Dempster, "Chaucer at Work on the Complaint in the Franklin's Tale," *MLN* 52 (1937), 16–23. MacDonald's "Proverbs, *Sententiae*, and *Exempla*" represents recent opinion about Chaucer's wisdom.

[20]*TC* 1.756, 760, *WBProl* 773–74, *MerchT* 1567. See also *WBProl*

659-60: "I sette noght an hawe / Of his proverbes n'of his olde sawe." Curtius quotes Ovid: "Quid moror exemplis quorum me turba fatigat" ("Mittelalterlicher und barocker Dichtungsstil," *MP* 38 [1941], 325-33).

[21]See for instance *LGW Prol* F 249-69, *FrankT* 1367-1456, *Mel* 1098-1101, *MerchT* 1362-74, *WBProl* 715-71, and the threatened list, *MerchT* 2240. Quintilian observed that too many *sententiae* could get in each other's way: "Densitas earum obstat invicem" (*Inst*.8.5.26).

[22]Curtius gives many examples (pp. 510-14). He quotes Usener on Sophistic discourses: "Early systematics would naturally compensate for inexperience in thinking by strict regularities of structure" (p. 510). This idea may be false, but it corresponds to Chaucer's substitution of easy wisdom for hard thought. I cite Scripture in the Douay version. Prov. 30 has five numerical apophthegms; see McKane.

[23]*RvProl* 3383-84; *Mel* 1086. The latter is varied in *WBProl* 278-80 and *ParsT* 631, in neither case with the number mentioned. The apophthegm was widespread; see Robinson's note on the *Mel* passage. The numerical apophthegm can be found in English as early as *The Seafarer* 67-71.

[24]*WBProl* 401-02. Robinson's note to the line quotes a Latin source: "Fallere, flere, nere, dedit deus in muliere." See Hans Walther, *Proverbia Sententiaeque latinitatis medii aevi* (Göttingen, 1963 ff.), No. 8751.

[25]MacDonald rightly associates the Wife of Bath, Dame Prudence, and Pertelote as keepers of wisdom. The first two often say the same thing.

[26]On priamels see note 17 above and Curtius on the "summation scheme" (pp. 289-91). The term is from the Latin *praeambulum*. Euling observes that the four-line priamel, listing three phenomena and then drawing the conclusion, is the "primitive" or essential scheme (ch. 5). Although Robinson says Jankyn's priamel is proverbial, Whiting lists no example before Chaucer (*Proverbs*, p. 299). That the other example Whiting quotes (ca. 1417) uses the same rhymes but somewhat differs in wording elsewhere reinforces the notion that the priamel is a mnemonic device.

[27]The study of Chaucer's tree-lists (here and in *KnT* 2921-23) is likewise a venerable tradition, founded by Skeat (*Works*, 2nd ed. [Oxford, 1899], 1:511-12); recent additions are Curtius, pp. 194-95; Piero Boitani, "Chaucer and Lists of Trees," *Reading Medieval Studies* (Univ. of Reading) 2 (1976), 28-44; and Ernst Th. Sehrt, "Der Wald des Irrtums: Zur allegorischen Funktion von Spensers *FQ* I. [i.] 7-9," *Anglia* 86 (1968), 463-91. Virgil's short list

(*Aen.* 6.179–82), like the Knight's, names trees used in a funeral pyre. Keats's list appears in *The Fall of Hyperion* 1.19–21.

28My colleagues at Wesleyan University, Khachig Tololyan, writing on catalogues in the "cosmographic novel" after Rabelais, and Harris Friedberg, writing on oral poetics, linguistics, and poetry, have graciously shared with me ideas especially relevant to this section, particularly with regard to the "mobilization" of paradigmatic catalogues. My thanks also to Lawrence Manley, Fred C. Robinson, and Allen Shoaf of Yale for their help.

29Eric A. Havelock, *Preface to Plato* (Cambridge, Mass., 1963), esp. chs. 3–6.

30Ibid., p. 66.

31*HF* 523–27, based (as Robinson noted) on addresses to the "mente" in Dante, *Inf.* 2.7–9 and *Par.* 1.10–11; the latter passage has "nella mia mente . . . tesoro."

32Ecclesiasticus repeatedly speaks of the "thesauri sapientiae" (1:26, etc.).

33For important studies on copiousness, see Terence Cave, *The Cornucopian Text: Problems of Writing in the French Renaissance* (Oxford, 1979) and his "Copia and Cornucopia" in *French Renaissance Studies 1540–70: Humanism and the Encyclopedia*, ed. Peter Sharratt (Edinburgh, 1976), pp. 52–69.

34Havelock, p. 180, and in general ch. 10, "The Content and Quality of the Poetised Statement." Compare Donald R. Howard's summary of "the habits of 'artificial' memory—order, association, and visualization" (*The Idea of the Canterbury Tales* [Berkeley and Los Angeles, 1976], p. 148; see pp. 146–48). Francis A. Yates surveys the rhetorical and post-classical tradition of mnemonics, with emphasis on the theory of "places" (*The Art of Memory* [Chicago, 1966]).

35Professor Bloomfield observes that personifications, ably handled by such a poet as Pope, often *do* things: the verbs associated with the nouns give them their energy ("A Grammatical Approach to Personification Allegory," *MP* 40 [1963], 161–71). One could add that personifications in narrative often come in bunches, practically in list form, and hence constitute a "happening" catalogue.

36*LGW* 635–39; and see *KnT* 2602–16.

37Besides material in Ong and Havelock, the neglected work by Marcel Jousse has material on rhythm and memory (*Le Style oral rythmique et mnemotechnique chez les Verbo-moteurs*, Archives de Philos., vol. 2, cahier 4 [Paris, 1925]). Consult also Albert B. Lord, *The Singer of Tales* (Cambridge, Mass., 1960). The remarkable feats of memory accomplished by musicians seem related to a similar interaction of the horizontal or syntagmatic (melody, rhythm, functional harmony) and the vertical or paradigmatic (chord structures or the concurrence of tones in polyphony). Chaucer often lists musical instruments (*PardT* 466, *MancT* 268, *NPT* 3398-99, *HF* 1217-26, 1240, and the surprisingly beautiful line in Sir Thopas: "With harpe and pipe and symphonye" 815), perhaps reflecting the association of lists, memory, and music. Laura Hibbard Loomis prints music lists in her section, "The Catalogue Lists," of analogues to Sir Thopas (*Sources and Analogues of Chaucer's Canterbury Tales*, ed. W. F. Bryan and Germaine Dempster [New York, 1941, 1958], p. 555).

[38]Havelock, pp. 180, 183-85: "the memorized record consists of a vast plurality of acts and events, not integrated into chained groups of cause and effect . . . an opposition between . . . paratactic . . . and . . . periodic. . . ." "Abstract" thinking, in our terms the dominance of the principle over the elements of a list, is post-Homeric (p. 188).

[39]*KnT* 2516-19, *SqT* 202. For similar examples see ("some") *Mars* 203-07, *KnT* 3031-32, *WBT* 925-48, *MillT* 3381-82, *WBProl* 766-71, *FrT* 1483-1503, *CYT* 912-15, *HF* 5-6, 29-35, 1538-40; ("divers") *RvProl* 3857, *MLT* 211, *WBProl* 44c-d, *FrT* 1486, *MerchT* 1469. Alfred L. Kellogg has traced the "some" distribution back to the Old English *Wanderer*, lines 80-84, and forward to *King Richard II*, 3.2.157-60 (*Chaucer, Langland, Arthur: Essays in Middle English Literature* [New Brunswick, 1972], p. 178). The footnote to the lines in *The Wanderer* has full references to other OE examples (T. P. Dunning and A. J. Bliss, eds. [London, 1969]). The OE and the Shakespeare passages show that the things distributed were usually fates or kinds of death, as in *KnT* 3031-32. The base *cata-* of "catalogue" can signify distribution as well as downwardness: two ways of looking at a list. Traugott Lawler writes suggestively on these passages in Chaucer in his book on Chaucer's *polla* (*The One and the Many in the Canterbury Tales* [Hamden, 1980], pp. 11-15).

[40]The term "summation scheme" is from Curtius, pp. 287-91.

[41]"Epideictic" often means "encomiastic, praising" among the rhetoricians, but its "showing" sense remains, as they Latinize the term "demonstrative," which along with the judicial and deliberative make up the three parts of rhetoric.

[42]Cave notes that *enargeia* (distinctness, vividness) and *energeia* (activity, vigor) were happily confused in the Renaissance. The dictionaries indicate that the words were confused by Latin writers even in the classical period. Medieval writers (e.g. Isidore, *Etym.* II.20.4) probably knew no distinction, and used *energia* alone.

⁴³A brillant essay on inscription poetry, with full bibliography of studies of early epigrams, is Geoffrey H. Hartman, "Wordsworth, Inscriptions, and Romantic Nature Poetry" in his *Beyond Formalism* (New Haven and London, 1970), pp. 206–30; see p. 209 on "votive epigrams" of the sort left on a hearse. Siegfried Wenzel kindly draws my attention to the treatment of inscription poetry (*tituli*) in Douglas Gray, *Themes and Images in the Medieval English Religious Lyric* (London, 1972), pp. 45–55, 200–07, with references to other studies of medieval epigrams and epitaphs.

⁴⁴Saturn has no oratory, and as if to make up for this deficiency he defines himself in a powerful anaphora: "Myn is the drenching in the see so wan; / Myn is. . . .Myn is. . . ." (*KnT* 2456–69).

⁴⁵See note 34 above.

⁴⁶D. D. R. Owen has a full bibliography; see *The Vision of Hell: Infernal Journeys in Medieval French Literature* (Edinburgh, 1970), esp. ch. 6. Casting a wider net is Francis Bar, *Les Routes de l'autre monde* (Paris, 1946). For the French tradition and the *voies* see Hans Robert Jauss and Uda Ebel in *La Littérature didactique, allégorique, et satirique*, Grundriss der romanischen Literaturen des Mittelalters, vol. 6, tome 1 (Heidelberg, 1968), and for bibliography tome 2 (1970). On related literary forms see Morton W. Bloomfield, *Piers Plowman as a Fourteenth Century Apocalypse* (New Brunswick, 1961), ch. 1.

⁴⁷Havelock compares the movement of oral epic with a man's passing through a great house, lingering over its furniture (p. 87): epic as *voie*.

⁴⁸Howard treats the "General Prologue" in terms of mnemonic theory, and refers to earlier attempts to find order in the arrangement of portraits (pp. 149–58). Muscatine observes that the Prologue is one of Chaucer's catalogues.

⁴⁹Chaucer here (*TC* 5.583, 585) and several times elsewhere rhymes "storie" amd memorie." Professor Bloomfield has written on the context of Troilus's complaint before the palace: "Troilus' Paraclausithyron and Its Setting: *Troilus and Criseyde* V. 519–602," *NM* 73 (1972), 15–24.

⁵⁰Its sharpest reader is E. Talbot Donaldson, whose brief essay in *Chaucer's Poetry: An Anthology for the Modern Reader* has fine remarks on the function of rhetoric and Chaucer's attitude towards it (2nd ed. [New York, 1975], pp. 1104–08). Important treatments of Chaucerian rhetoric are Robert O. Payne, *The Key of Remembrance* (New Haven and London, 1963), and Richard A. Lanham, *The Motives of Eloquence: Literary Rhetoric in the Renaissance* (New Haven, 1976). Lanham notes rhetoric's "fondness for overschematized

cataloging" (p. 28). I have made some general remarks about rhetoric in *Allegories of History, Allegories of Love* (Hamden, 1979), pp. 182–94.

[51] The notion of "professionalism" in Chaucer is from Lawler, ch. 2: "Professionalism: The Poem as Fabliau." Other batches of professional terms in Chaucer tell the symptoms of Arcite's "maladye / Of Hereos" (*KnT* 1361–76), his mortal wound (2743–56), and the names and causes of dreams (*HF* 7–52). The eagle disclaims hard terms (*HF* 854–63).

[52] By "the rhetoricians" I mean the composite sense we have of the art as surveyed by James J. Murphy, *Rhetoric in the Middle Ages* (Berkeley and Los Angeles, 1974), with his *Medieval Rhetoric: A Select Bibliography* (Toronto, 1971). The lists made in *occupatio*, or more properly *praeteritio* (*paraleipsis*), in which the speaker makes as if not to say something while he says it abundantly (*KnT* 2919–66, Arcite's funeral, is the longest example) have been studied by Francis and Frank.

[53] Final summary lists in a legal argument are not the same as the occasional final lists of deserts or comeuppances in *The Canterbury Tales* (*KnT* 3101–06, *MillT* 3850–53, *RvT* 4313–17, *PhysT* 269–76), but both types of *frequentatio* rise from a natural sense that a work should close with a reckoning. Of *enumeratio* (*anacephalaiosis*) Quintilian says "turba valet" (*Inst.* 6.1.1).

[54] For extended analysis of this "reson" see Ralph Baldwin, *The Unity of the Canterbury Tales*, Anglistica, 5 (Copenhagen, 1955). On catalogues in the *GP* see Eugene Green, "The Voices of the Pilgrims in the *General Prologue* to the Canterbury Tales," *Style* 9 (1975), 55–81. On Chaucer's variations upon the rhetorical conventions of description see Kevin S. Kiernan, "The Art of the Descending Catalogue, and a Fresh Look at Alisoun," *ChauR* 10 (1975), 1–16. Leo Spitzer remarks on the assimilation in the Middle Ages of perfection with completion and on enumerative descriptions, in his analysis of "Blow, northerne wynd" in *"Explication de Texte* Applied to Three Great Middle English Poems," *ArL* 3 (1951), 1–22, 157–65.

[55] The phrase is J. V. Cunningham's; he places the portrait series in its rhetorical context ("Convention as Structure: The *Prologue* to the *Canterbury Tales*," *MP* 49 [1952], 172–81; rpt. in John Burrow, ed., *Geoffrey Chaucer*, Penguin Critical Anthologies [Baltimore, 1969], pp. 218–32). When Chaucer chose to make conventional descriptions (the rhetorician's terms are *effictiones, ecphrases,* blazons, devices), he could, as in the descriptions of Lygurge and Emetrius (*KnT* 2129–78).

[56] Ed. George A. Panton, EETS, 39, 56 (London, 1869, 1874), 11.1584–98. The lines may derive, like some passages in *Piers*

Plowman, from the Pauline topics of the division of graces and the stability of vocation. The Wife's critique of the friars' multiplication (quoted below) also recalls *Piers*. The list of what the archdeacon punished (*FrT* 1304-10) looks like pure, perhaps confused, respect for office.

⁵⁷I am putting in spatial terms an idea that Loy D. Martin puts temporally: he sees catalogues as intrusions of the timeless into time, and sees the catalogue of pilgrims as a society entering a new time ("History and Form in the General Prologue to the *Canterbury Tales*," *ELH* 45 [1978], 1-17).

⁵⁸The Squire, as often, exemplifies the excess: he lists some twenty virtues of Cambyuskan (12-27). Virginia's virtues provoke another long list, appropriate to the abstract moralizing (to the point of inhumanity) of the "Physician's Tale" (39-57). The royal tersel lists the vices he promises not to be (*PF* 428-30). A recurrent type of virtues list sums up what "thynges six" (or three) women want in a man (*ShipT* 173-77, *NPT* 2914-15, *WBT* 1259): see Roland M. Smith, "The Six Gifts," *JCS* 1 (1949), 98-104.

⁵⁹*To the Palace of Wisdom* (Carbondale and Edwardsville, 1964), pp. 28-32.

⁶⁰*Vers rapportés* (versus rapportati) link sets in grammatical parallel: The A,B,C of my A1, B1, C1 will A2, B2, C2 your A3, B3, C3." See Curtius, pp. 286-87, and Bruno Berger, *Vers rapportés: Ein Beitrag zur Stilgeschichte der französischen Renaissance-Dichtung*, Diss. Freiburg i. Br. (Karlsruhe i. B., 1930). The "Miller's Tale" lines more vigorously collapse the sets: Who A's and A's with B,C,D,E,F.

⁶¹On this and such lines see my "An Evaluation of the *Pardoner's Tale*" in Dewey R. Faulkner, ed., *Twentieth Century Interpretations of the Pardoner's Tale* (Englewood Cliffs, N.J., 1973), pp. 88-89. I treat related questions of narrative pace in Chaucer in an essay forthcoming in *ChauR* (perhaps 1982), "Suddenness and Process in Chaucer."

⁶²Muscatine suggests that it may instead be Christian; he says of the *CYT*, "This chaos of matter, refuse, excrement, represents the universe of technology," which he finds unchristian rather than unscientific (*Chaucer and the French Tradition* [Berkeley and Los Angeles, 1957], pp. 213-21).

⁶³See my *Allegories*, pp. 191-94, and to the bibliography (pp. 213-14) add Peter W. Hurst, "The Encyclopedic Tradition, the Cosmological Epic, and the Validation of Medieval Romance," *CCrit* 1 (1979), 53-71.

⁶⁴Chaucer names "Aleyn" in *PF* 316, and he uses Bernard's *Cosmographia* in *MLT* 197-202 (see Skeat's note for the passage, *Works*, 3:147).

[65]*Roman*, ed. Langlois, line 18298, "Bon fait prolixité foïr"; *SqT* 401–05.

[66]That the tradition comes to Chaucer through the French is obvious. William J. Farrell notes that *BD*, a deeply French poem, has as many catalogues (eighteen) as either *Troilus* or *The House of Fame*, and observes that the "catalogue itself is an object of parody" ("Chaucer's Use of the Catalogue," *TSLL* 5[1963], 64–78). I have not touched on Chaucer's catalogues of poets and of his own works, which have classical precedents. See Curtius, pp. 260–64, and Franz Skutsch, *Aus Vergils Frühzeit* (Leipzig, 1901), ch. 3, "Kataloggedichte."

[67]Nowhere in Chaucer has a hexameral catalogue the invocative sublimity of Dan. 3:57–83. Curtius's treatment of this topic quotes Jotsald's lament, in which he "mobilizes" the things of the world, "cuncta movebo," like a muster-list (pp. 92–94). Chaucer's "The Former Age" is a kind of anti-hexameron in the primitivist tradition, as it lists the pleasures of nature before the advent of technology; it is like the tree-list of *PF* with emphasis on the human uses of the trees.

[68]The principle of ramification was thoroughly formalized by the time of the Renaissance, as Father Ong's work has shown. Ong notices the coincidence of the name of the great ramifier, Peter Ramus, with the art itself. I treat the principle as it appears in the medieval genre *distinctiones* in "Visible Allegory: The *Distinctiones Abel* of Peter the Chanter" forthcoming in *Harvard English Studies* 9 (1982).

[69]See note 61 above and Susan Gallick, "A Look at Chaucer and His Preachers," *Speculum* 50 (1975), 456–76.

[70]Juvenal made the same turn, from the definition of his "farrago"—the epigraph of this essay—to vice, avarice, hazard, in terms of their abundance: "et quando uberior vitiorum copia? quando / maior avaritiae patuit sinus? alea quando / hos animos?" (*Sat.* 1.87–88). On satire among homilists a start is made by Jean Leclercq, "Aspects littéraires de l'œuvre de saint Bernard, I," *CCM* 1 (1958), 425–50.

[71]Note the special feature of satire, that it can be opened at random, because like a list its form is not syntagmatic. Michael Seidel speaks of satire's "untoward, unrestrained, and encroaching characteristics," terms that might be applied to lists (*Satiric Inheritance: Rabelais to Sterne* [Princeton, 1979], p. 9). Seidel associates, by etymology, satire with farce. See also Heinrich Schneegans, *Geschichte der grotesken Satire* (Strasbourg, 1894), ch. 3, "Der Stil Rabelais," on accumulative lists. Seidel, Schneegans, and Cave all make the rabelaisian connection betwen satire and gluttony.

[72]Compare also Curtius's remark that Horace uses verse-filling asyndeton "when he wants to dispose scornfully of an entire class of things," citing *Ep.* 2.2.180-81 (p. 285).

[73]Some of these lists fall into Claes Schaar's category "summary narrative," treated in Chapter 2 of *Some Types of Narrative in Chaucer's Poetry* (Lund, 1954). Some action lists: *KnT* 875-84 (in an *occupatio*), 2599-618, *MillT* 3373-80, 3850-53, *RvT* 4313-17, *MLT* 599-602, *SqT* 81-85, 661-70, *ShipT* 250-54, *MkT* 2098-110, *BD* 848-52, *HF* 157-238, 433-60.

[74]Muscatine (pp. 219, 270) adduces the term *parade*, the list of medicinal or other wares and—in satiric use—a mountebank's tumultuous patter (see *Volpone* 2.1 for a great example), and he refers to P. Abraham, "The Mercator-Scenes in Medieval French Passion-Plays," *MÆ* 3 (1934), 112-23. The Pardoner, the Canon's Yeoman, Pertelote, in a way the Wife of Bath, deliver *parades*.

[75]The mixture of animals, people, and fiends, of heaven and earth, vaguely recalls the topic of the "impossibles" (Curtius, pp. 94-98); the pooped "bemes" (trumpets), rising tumult, and falling sky suggest a comic Doomsday. I am grateful to Marie Borroff for suggesting some of these imitative iteratives; she finds "hither-andthithering" in *Finnegans Wake*, on what page *nescio, Deus scit.*

[76]Loomis gives an excellent survey of the *Thopas* lists and analogues in the English romances. She refers to William E. Mead, ed., *The Squyr of Lowe Degre: A Middle English Metrical Romance* (Boston, 1904), pp. liv–lxv.

[77]See Paul Taylor, "The Canon's Yeoman's Breath: Emanations of a Metaphor," *ES* 60 (1979), 380-88, and the earlier work cited there. I found especially helpful on the background of alchemical treatises the essay by Joseph E. Grennen, "Chaucer and the Commonplaces of Alchemy," *C&M* 26 (1965), 306-33.

[78]*A Preface to Chaucer* (Princeton, 1962), p. 259.

[79]On summation schemes, Curtius, pp. 287-91. Frederick Tupper's idea that the tales exemplify the seven deadly sins, summed up at the end, is incorrect but symptomatic ("Chaucer and the Seven Deadly Sins," *PMLA* 29 [1914], 93-128). See the summary of such efforts by Charles A. Owen, Jr., "The Design of the Canterbury Tales" in *Companion to Chaucer Studies*, ed. Beryl Rowland (Toronto, 1968), pp. 192-207.

 Siegfried Wenzel

[1]Basic modern studies of the medieval fool are Enid Welsford, *The Fool. His Social and Literary History* (London, 1935) and Barbara

Swain, *Fools and Folly during the Middle Ages and the Renaissance* (New York, 1932). More directly concerned with Shakespeare or English Renaissance drama but also analyzing the medieval background are Olive M. Busby, *Studies in the Development of the Fool in Elizabethan Drama* (Oxford, 1923); Walter Gaedick, *Der Weise Narr in der englischen Literatur von Erasmus bis Shakespeare* (Weimar and Leipzig, 1928); Robert H. Goldsmith, *Wise Fools in Shakespeare* (East Lansing, Michigan, 1955); and Annemarie Schöne, "Shakespeares weise Narren und ihre Vorfahren," *JbÄAK* 5 (1960), 202–45. The following studies deal with the fool in the European Renaissance and summarize his medieval backgrounds: Heinz Wyss, *Der Narr im schweizerischen Drama des 16. Jahrhunderts* (Bern, 1959); Walter Kaiser, *Praisers of Folly* (Cambridge, Mass., 1963), on Erasmus, Rabelais, and Shakespeare's Falstaff; Barbara Könneker, *Wesen und Wandlung der Narrenidee im Zeitalter des Humanismus: Brant—Murner—Erasmus* (Wiesbaden, 1966); Joel Lefèbvre, *Les Fols et la folie* (Paris, 1968), dealing with the German Renaissance. Bernard Chaput surveys the legal standing of medieval fools and the medical care they received ("La condition juridique et sociale de l'aliéné mental" in *Aspects de la marginalité au moyen âge*, ed. Guy H. Allard et al. [Montreal, 1975], pp. 38–47); and Robert Klein classifies Renaissance fools and their ancestors ("Le thème du fou et l'ironie humaniste" in *La forme et l'intelligible. Écrits sur la Renaissance et l'art moderne* [Paris, 1970], pp. 433–50).

[2]Frederic C. Tubach, *Index exemplorum* (Helsinki, 1969), No. 886; recorded by Étienne de Bourbon, Jacques de Vitry, Vincent de Beauvais, the *Speculum morale*, and others, including Bromyard, *Summa praedicantium*, "Prelatus," P.xiii.36 (fol. 490rb). In quoting Bromyard I refer to British Library MS Royal 7.E.iv.

[3]*The Exempla of Jacques de Vitry*, ed. Thomas F. Crane (London, 1890), No. 306.

[4]Tubach, No. 2975. Bromyard calls this fool a simpleton, "cuius simplicitas non multum distabat a stulticia" (*Summa praedicantium*, "Sequi," S.vii.9 [fol. 550va]; printed by Thomas Wright, ed., *A Selection of Latin Stories from Manuscripts of the Thirteenth and Fourteenth Centuries*, Percy Society, 8 [London, 1842], No. 27).

[5]Tubach, No. 4351.

[6]Bromyard, *Summa praedicantium*, "Superbia," S.xiv.7 (fol. 569r–v).

[7]Ibid., "Servire," S.viii.4 (fol. 551va).

[8]Tubach, No. 1968.

[9]Bromyard, *Summa praedicantium*, "Iusticia," I.xiii.31 (fol. 279va); printed by Wright, *Selection*, No. 130.

[10]F. J. Furnivall (ed.), *A Booke of Precedence* . . . , EETS, e.s. 8

(London, 1869), pp. 77-78. It is reproduced by Swain, p. 64; partially by Welsford, pp. 122-23; and by Goldsmith, p. 26.

[11]The terms are Welsford's and Goldsmith's, respectively.

[12]For this work, see S. Wenzel, *Verses in Sermons. "Fasciculus Morum" and Its Middle English Poems* (Cambridge, Mass., 1978), ch. 1.

[13]This curious word appears in only five of the twenty-five manuscripts that contain the story, albeit the "better" texts. A fifteenth-century Latin-English dictionary (Cambridge, Trinity College MS 1285) defines *pegma* as "baculus cum massa plumbi in summitate pendente" and glosses it as "a babul"; Thomas Wright, *Anglo-Saxon and Old English Vocabularies*, 2nd ed., ed. and collated by R. P. Wülcker (London, 1884; rpt. Darmstadt, 1968), 1:601. The source of the definition is the *Catholicon* of Joannes Balbus (Mainz, 1460; rpt. Farnborough, Hants., 1971), unpaginated.

[14]The words "muto testamentum meum et" are omitted in many manuscripts.

[15]The text is taken from Bodleian Library MS Rawlinson C.670 (S.C. 12514), fol. 101r; abbreviations are silently expanded, and modern capitalization and punctuation have been introduced. A complete translation can be found in Wenzel, "Chaucer and the Language of Contemporary Preaching," *SP* 73 (1976), 149.

[16]"Item lego caudam wlpis seruitoribus tuis, scilicet hiis qui tegunt faciem suam crinibus suis, etc. Item lego nolas meas custodibus equorum tuorum qui sunt tam superbi, etc." Durham, Univ. Library MS Cosin V.iv.2, fol. 52r. Written in 1477 by Thomas Olyphant, chaplain.

[17]The order of bequests in Harley 2252 (soul-body-goods) follows the standard formula observed in actual wills.

[18]Tubach (No. 2782) refers to a tale by Étienne de Bourbon, which has hardly anything in common with the story under discussion. Tubach's reference to "a jester," borrowed from Herbert, is equally misleading.

[19]William Chartham; see *Verses in Sermons*, pp. 42-43.

[20]The text can be found in *Les Contes moralisés de Nicole Bozon, Frère Mineur*, ed. L. T. Smith and P. Meyer, SATF (Paris, 1889), No. 5, pp. 12-13. For Bozon see M. Dominica Legge, *Anglo-Norman Literature and Its Background* (Oxford, 1963), pp. 229-32.

[21]My translations of Bromyard's texts are based on British Library MS Royal 7.E.iv, and identified by folio as well as by section number and paragraph. The Summa was printed several times between 1484 and (at least) 1614, and the section numbering in the printed editions is the same as in the Royal manuscript. I have checked all passages against the edition of Venice, 1586.

[22] Epistola vii.12 in *Epistolae Senecae ad Paulum et Pauli ad Senecam quae vocantur*, ed. Claude W. Barrow (Rome, 1938), p. 129. Notice that the original has "ore innocentium," not "ore fatuorum."

[23] Bromyard, *Summa praedicantium*, "Predicacio," P.xii.38 (fol. 481v,a-b). In the Latin original the bracketed words are missing in MS Royal 7.E.iv—clearly a case of omission by homoteleuton; they have been supplied here from the edition of Venice, 1586.

[24] Tale No. 46. *A Hundred Merry Tales* was reprinted by H. Oesterley as *Shakespeare's Jest-Book* (London, 1866; rpt. Gainesville, Florida, 1970) and more recently by Paul M. Zall, *A Hundred Merry Tales and Other English Jestbooks of the Fifteenth and Sixteenth Centuries* (Lincoln, Nebraska, 1963).

[25] *Schimpf und Ernst*, ed. Johannes Bolte (Berlin, 1924), No. 46.

[26] Bromyard, *Summa praedicantium*, "Elemosina," E.iii.23 (fol. 148va).

[27] British Library MS Harley 2247, fol. 213v. These sermons were edited by Lillian L. Steckman in "A Fifteenth Century Festival Book," (Ph.D. diss., Yale Univ., 1934). They are being edited again by Susan Powell in a University of London dissertation.

[28] Notice that in tale No. 1, in the sentence where the fool bequeaths his bauble to the steward, the phrase "tanquam maximo fatuo" appears as "tanquam maiori fatuo" in a large number of manuscripts. This may well indicate a very close genetic relation between tales 1 and 3.

[29] Bromyard, *Summa praedicantium*, "Dampnacio," D.i.13 (fol. 116rb). The passage closes with a cross-reference to E.iii.23, i.e., our tale No. 3.

[30] Bartlett Jere Whiting and Helen Wescott Whiting, *Proverbs, Sentences, and Proverbial Phrases from English Writings Mainly before 1500* (Cambridge, Mass., 1968), H.475; see also G. R. Owst, *Literature and Pulpit in Medieval England*, second revised edition (Oxford, 1961), p. 43 and n. 4.

[31] "L'en dit en engleis 3*if hope ne were, herte to broste*. Mes la serra ke queor de homme crever ne porra, ke saunz nul fin vivront e jammes relees de peyne n'averont" (Robert J. Relihan, Jr., "A Critical Edition of the Anglo-Norman and Latin Versions of *Les Peines de Purgatorie*," [Ph.D. diss., Univ. of Iowa, 1978], pp. 209–10). I owe a copy of the dissertation to Dr. Relihan's generosity.

[32] Bromyard, *Summa praedicantium*, "Consuetudo," C.viii.37 (fol. 95ra). The passage closes by quoting Seneca's letter to Paul again with the moral that "he was tortured by the same things through which he sinned," i.e., *malae consuetudines*, wicked acts made into customary rights.

33"Isti vero tam superbe et tam vane induunt se quod plus assimulantur stultis quam primis parentibus et pro talibus cognoscuntur. Sicut patet per hoc quod fertur quod nuper in quodam parliamento quidam fatuus videns vnum militem mirabiliter vestitum et sibi similem ut sibi videbatur dixit ad eum coram multis magnatibus: 'Consors cuius stultus es tu? Ego sum stultus abbatis de Bury et libenter vellem habere noticiam persone tue, quia certe tu es pulcher fatuus.' Miles erubescens ignorauit quid ei responderet." Bodleian Library MS Bodley 859, fol. 166v.

34Cambridge Univ. Library MS Kk.iv.24, "Exortaciones fratris Iohannis de Bromiard de ordine fratrum predicatorum" (fol. 1ra), ending on fol. 114va and followed by a list of sermon themes and an alphabetical table of subjects. A new series of sermons begins on fol. 121r.

35"Et ideo qui sunt soliciti plus hic pro inducione corporali quam spirituali, tunc confusibiliter coram toto mundo stabunt nudi et corporaliter et spiritualiter. Et ideo qualitercumque fuerit de bonis temporalibus, videatis quod habeatis divicias spirituales, quia ita erit ibi pro toto mundo sicut accidit semel in partibus borialibus. Dominus de Neuyle habuit quemdam naturaliter fatuum. Iste fatuus quodam solemni die petivit a domino suo to dele þe relefe totius aule. Dominus de isto multum mirabatur, tamen concessit sibi. Post prandium dominus cum tota familia inerunt ad videndum qualiter divideret. / Iste fatuus quando venit ad pauperes, si invenit ibi unum quasi nudum et nihil habentem, nihil sibi dedit; si unum bene indutum cum gremio pleno pane, multum sibi contulit; et isto modo divisit elemosinas. De isto facto dominus cum aliis multum admiratur et quesivit ab eo quare dedit non indigentibus et indigentes dimisit vacuos. Cui ille: 'Domine, vere, domine, ego facio sicut tu facis, quia si unus de clericis tuis habuit unam bonam ecclesiam, das sibi prebendam; si nihil habeat, nihil sibi das; sicut histrionibus, quia sciunt multa adquirere, largiris robas et pecuniam, et pauperibus in porta vix aliquid vel nihil.' Et ista est modo consuetudo." Cambridge Univ. Library MS Kk.iv.24, fols. 236vb–237ra.

36This generalization underlies medieval treatments of the chief vices in which the proud, the angry, the envious, etc., are very frequently called fools. It likewise is the conceptual basis for the catalogue of the many sins and forms of misbehavior assembled in *The Ship of Fools* and similar works.

37Such is, in brief, the moral of *The Praise of Folly* by Erasmus.

38Notice, however, that on occasion Bromyard does report his own observations, as in the description he gives in his *Distincciones* of a discourteous (*incurialis*) sparrow he used to feed at his study window. Greedy people, he says, are like "parue auicule quam aliquando paui in fenestra studii mei" (MS Bodley 859, fol. 164r).

39See Welsford, pp. 115–16.

40The fullest account is still S[idney] L[ee], "Scogan," in *Dictionary of National Biography*, 17:940–41. Modern edition of "Scogin's Jests" in W. Carew Hazlitt, ed., *Shakespeare Jest-Books* (London, 1864; rpt. New York, n. d.), 2:46–161. See also Welsford, pp. 41–42, and Paul M. Zall, *A Nest of Ninnies and Other English Jestbooks of the Sixteenth Century* (Lincoln, Nebraska, 1970), p. 105.

41S[idney] L[ee], p. 940.

42For the date of *Distincciones* see A. B. Emden, *A Biographical Register of the University of Oxford to A. D. 1500* (Oxford, 1957), 1:278. Emden's opinion is based on the unpublished work by G. Mifsud. I have added some further proof in *NM* 77 (1976), 87–88.

43Some of Scogin's jests are common medieval tales: the trick practiced on the man driving sheep to market (Hazlitt, pp. 56–58) is a variant of Tubach, No. 2975 (see also above, n. 4); the tale of the king who whispers into the fool's ear (Hazlitt, pp. 118–19) is Tubach, Nos. 4091 and 2132; and the tale about how to make three eggs out of two by sophistry, etc. (Hazlitt, pp. 62–63), goes back at least as far as Giraldus Cambrensis, *Gemma ecclesiastica*, in his *Opera*, ed. J. S. Brewer (London, 1862), 2:350, and has a variant in *A Hundred Merry Tales*, pp. 118–20.

44The *Middle English Dictionary* records the phrase from ca. 1450 on (s.v. "natural" [p. 852]); *Dives and Pauper*, which was written between 1405 and 1410, gives a story in which a *fole sage* and a *naturel fole* are opposed (IX,xi); see Priscilla H. Barnum, ed., *Dives and Pauper*, EETS, 275 (London, 1976), p. xi (date), and 280 (London, 1980), p. 278 (the story).

45"Soothly, whan man loveth any creature moore than Jhesu Crist oure Creatour, thanne is it deedly synne" (Chaucer, "Parson's Tale," 358. Chaucer references are to *The Works of Geoffrey Chaucer*, ed. F. N. Robinson, 2nd ed. [Boston, 1957]).

46*Middle English Dictionary*, s.v. "fol," p. 673.

47This is the manuscript group Co.Li.C; see *Verses in Sermons*, pp. 32–33 and 110. The earliest manuscript, Co, dates from the end of the fourteenth century.

48See E. K. Chambers' remark made in 1903: "Much of this [secondary] literature fails to distinguish between the stultus and the ioculator regis" (*The Mediaeval Stage* [Oxford, 1903], 1:372). Welsford heeds the warning (p. 114), even though she pays a good deal of attention to court jesters.

49Stories about a *mimus* appear at C.xi.34; O.vi.20; R.i.16; V.i.9–10; about a *ioculator* at A.xxvii.60 (two different tales); T.iv.17.

[50]See my paper "Vices, Virtues, and Popular Preaching," in *Medieval and Renaissance Studies. Proceedings of the Southeastern Institute of Medieval and Renaissance Studies, Summer 1974*, ed. Dale B. J. Randall (Durham, N. C., 1976), pp. 43 and 47.

[51]A critical edition of the *Summa* is to appear soon in the Chaucer Library series.

[52]Yves Lefèvre (ed.), *L'Elucidarium et les lucidaires* (Paris, 1954), pp. 428-29 (II.58 and 60); also in PL 172:1148-49 (II.18).

[53]Thus primarily in the exegesis of Ps. 13:1 and 52:1.

[54]1 Cor. 1:20 (commenting on Isa. 29:14) and ff.; 3:18 ff. See Gerhard Kittel, *Theological Dictionary of the New Testament*, trans. G. W. Bromiley (Grand Rapids, Mich., 1967), 4:845-47 (*mōros*). See also the entry on *phrēn* (including *aphrōn*), in Kittel, *Theologisches Wörterbuch zum Neuen Testament* (Stuttgart, 1969), 9:216-31. Both articles are by Bertram.

[55]Cf. Morton W. Bloomfield, *The Seven Deadly Sins* (East Lansing, 1952), passim; and Wenzel, "The Three Enemies of Man," *MS* 29 (1967), 62. A good discussion of the late medieval concern with the World has been given by Donald R. Howard, *The Three Temptations* (Princeton, 1966), esp. ch. 6.

[56]*The Castle of Perseverance*, ed. David Bevington, *Medieval Drama* (Boston, 1975), lines 504 ff. The successful attack of World and Avarice, after the other chief vices have been beaten back, begins with line 2413.

[57]Passus II-IV are concerned with the proper evaluation and use of *Mede*, who ultimately stands for *bona temporalia*; the problem of properly ordering temporal duties and values in man's spiritual pilgrimage occupies the Dreamer from Passus VI on.

[58]Notice the explicit contrast between (foolish) steward and (wise) fool in tale No. 1 from *Fasciculus morum*: "Iste miser fatuus [the lord's steward] pauperes spoliat. . . . Ego autem dictus sum fatuus, et tamen nulli noceo." The same tension between the World and a fool also seems to underlie the setting of Robert Armin's *Foole upon Foole* (1600 and later), in which the World is entertained and taught true understanding by a philosopher (at least he seems to attempt to do that); the latter is named Sotto (from French *sot*, "fool"?).

[59]Matt. 19:21 and parallels, and Luke 12:33.

[60]For a recent discussion of these changes and the role of the mendicants, see Lester K. Little, *Religious Poverty and the Profit Economy in Medieval Europe* (Ithaca, N.Y., 1978).

[61]From this point of view, too, tale No. 6 stands somewhat apart. Since the setting of the story is a *parliamentum*, the *miles* would be a member of the commons. Because of his foolishly sumptuous clothes he is embarrassed by the fool of a peer, and the

tale is not so much an instrument of moral disapproval as of social comedy.

⁶²See Brother Leo, *Speculum perfectionis,* ed. Paul Sabatier (Paris, 1898), pp. 197–98.

⁶³See John Moorman, *A History of the Franciscan Order from Its Origins to the Year 1517* (Oxford, 1968), p. 55 and n. 1. The original text may be found in H. Boehmer, ed., *Analekten zur Geschichte des Franciscus von Assisi* (Tübingen and Leipzig, 1904), p. 86.

⁶⁴The best known and earliest case is the *sot* or *fols* who prophesies, in Chrétien's *Perceval,* ed. William Roach, 2nd ed. (Geneva, 1960), lines 1054 ff. and 1252 ff. No convincing source for this literary figure seems to be known.

⁶⁵See the discussion by E. T. Donaldson, *Piers Plowman. The C-Text and Its Poet* (New Haven, 1949), pp. 136–55.

⁶⁶Chaucer, *Troilus and Criseyde,* 2.400–06.

⁶⁷*Canterbury Tales,* VI (C),670–91. There is, of course, a close connection between children and fools. The saying quoted several times by Bromyard, "Deus quandoque ex ore fatuorum effatur," is strongly reminiscent of the biblical "ex ore infantium . . . perfecisti laudem" (Ps. 8:3 and Matt. 21:16). The passage of the *Elucidarium* quoted above says that fools "inter pueros deputantur." The connection of children and fools in proverbs (for instance, "Children and fools cannot lie," Whiting, C.229) seems to occur only after 1500.

⁶⁸*Confessio Amantis,* VII.3945–4010; ed. G. C. Macaulay, EETS e.s. 82 (London, 1901), 2:346–47; no source for the tale has been identified. Hoccleve, *Regement of Princes,* lines 3123–64; ed. F. J. Furnivall, EETS, e.s. 72 (London, 1897), p. 114. I owe the Hoccleve reference to my former student Judith Shaw. Another good piece of political advice coming from a fool (*quidam stultus*) appears in Petrarch, *Epistolae seniles,* XIII.17, in *Opera* (Basel, 1554), 2:1029.

⁶⁹See the perceptive article by Lillian H. Hornstein, "King Robert of Sicily: Analogues and Origins," *PMLA* 79 (1964), 13–21. The tale has been retold by Longfellow.

⁷⁰*King Lear,*ed. K. Muir (London, 1972), 3.4.32–33.

⁷¹Notably our tale No. 2, retold in *A Hundred Merry Tales,* which was published in 1526 (apparently twice) and again in 1548.